Anglo-Saxon Studies 47

LAW, LITERATURE, AND SOCIAL REGULATION IN EARLY MEDIEVAL ENGLAND

Anglo-Saxon Studies

ISSN 1475-2468

'Anglo-Saxon Studies' aims to provide a forum for the best scholarship on the Anglo-Saxon peoples in the period from the end of Roman Britain to the Norman Conquest, including comparative studies involving adjacent populations and periods; both new research and major re-assessments of central topics are welcomed.

Books in the series may be based in any one of the principal disciplines of archaeology, art history, history, language and literature, and inter- or multi-disciplinary studies are encouraged.

Proposals or enquiries may be sent directly to the editors or the publisher at the addresses given below; all submissions will receive prompt and informed consideration.

Professor Emeritus John Hines, School of History, Archaeology and Religion, Cardiff University, John Percival Building, Colum Drive, Cardiff, Wales, CF10 3EU, UK

Professor Catherine Cubitt, School of History, Faculty of Arts and Humanities, University of East Anglia, Norwich, England, NR4 7TJ, UK

Boydell & Brewer, PO Box 9, Woodbridge, Suffolk, England, IP12 3DF, UK

Recently published volumes in the series are listed at the back of this book

LAW, LITERATURE, AND SOCIAL REGULATION IN EARLY MEDIEVAL ENGLAND

Edited by
Anya Adair and Andrew Rabin

THE BOYDELL PRESS

First published 2023
The Boydell Press, Woodbridge

ISBN 978-1-78327-760-5

The Boydell Press is an imprint of Boydell & Brewer Ltd
PO Box 9, Woodbridge, Suffolk IP12 3DF, UK
and of Boydell & Brewer Inc.
668 Mt Hope Avenue, Rochester, NY 14620–2731, USA
website: www.boydellandbrewer.com

A CIP catalogue record for this book is available
from the British Library

This publication is printed on acid-free paper

Contents

Acknowledgments

By its very nature, an edited collection is a project defined by collaboration, and with collaboration comes gratitude. We have been fortunate to have a group of contributors dedicated to this collection and the ideas that animate it. Like much scholarship produced over the past few years, this volume encountered unexpected delays and unanticipated challenges on its way to publication, so we are especially grateful to them for their efforts and their patience. Thanks are due also to Sarah Cheng at the University of Hong Kong for her assistance in the formatting of the manuscript.

At Boydell, we are grateful to Caroline Palmer for her guidance and generosity in shepherding the collection all the way from proposal to print. Many thanks also to series editors Catherine Cubitt and John Hines, as well as to the anonymous reviewer, for their generosity and recommendations.

Contributors

Sherif Abdelkarim	Assistant Professor, Grinnell College, Iowa
Anya Adair	Assistant Professor of Law and Humanities, University of Hong Kong
Mary Elizabeth Blanchard	Assistant Professor of History, Ave Maria University, Florida
Kristen Carella	Professor of English, Assumption University, Worcester, Massachusetts
Jay Paul Gates	Associate Professor of English, John Jay College of Criminal Justice in The City University of New York
Stefan Jurasinski	Professor of English, State University of New York, Brockport
Arendse Lund	University College London
Nicole Marafioti	Professor of History, Trinity University, San Antonio, Texas
Andrew Rabin	Professor of English, University of Louisville, Kentucky
Chelsea Shields-Más	Assistant Professor of History, State University of New York, Old Westbury
Scott T. Smith	Associate Professor of English and Comparative Literature, Pennsylvania State University

Abbreviations

AS Charters	A. J. Robertson, ed. and trans., *Anglo-Saxon Charters*, 2nd ed. (Cambridge: Cambridge University Press, 1956)
BL	The British Library, London
Bodl.	The Bodleian Library, University of Oxford
Bosworth-Toller	Joseph Bosworth, *An Anglo-Saxon Dictionary Online*, ed. Thomas Northcote Toller, Sean Christ, and Ondřej Tichý (Prague: Charles University, 2014). The dictionary can be accessed online at <https://bosworthtoller.com>
DOE	Angus Cameron, Ashley Crandell Amos, Antonette diPaolo Healey et al., eds., *Dictionary of Old English: A to I Online.* (Dictionary of Old English Project, 2016). <https://www.doe.utoronto.ca>
EETS	Early English Text Society
EHD	Dorothy Whitelock, ed. and trans., *English Historical Documents. Volume I: c.500–1042*, 2nd ed. (London: Oxford University Press, 1979)
Gesetze	Felix Liebermann, ed., *Die Gesetze der Angelsachsen*, 3 vols. (Halle: Max Niemeyer, 1903–16)
JEGP	*Journal of English and Germanic Philology*
Klaeber 4	R. D. Fulk, Robert E. Bjork, and John D. Niles, eds., *Klaeber's Beowulf and the Fight at Finnsburg*, 4th ed. (Toronto: University of Toronto Press, 2008)
L	Liebermann's edition (where an alternative citation is first given); see *Gesetze*
LE	Janet Fairweather, trans., *Liber Eliensis: A History of the Isle of Ely from the Seventh Century to the Twelfth* (Woodbridge: Boydell, 2005)

MGH Epp. IV	Monumenta Germaniae Historica, Epistolae. (Alcuin, *Epistolae*, ed. E. Dümmler, MGH Epp. 4 (Berlin: Weidmann, 1895))
MS	Manuscript
n.s.	New Series
Napier	Homilies cited according to their number in Arthur S. Napier, ed., *Wulfstan: Sammlung der ihm zugeschrieben Homilien nebst Untersuchungen über ihre Echtheit* (Berlin: Weidmann, 1883)
OE	Old English
OED	*Oxford English Dictionary Online,* https://www.oed.com/
OLD	P. G. W. Glare, ed., *Oxford Latin Dictionary* (Oxford: Clarendon, 1982)
o.s.	Original Series
PL	J.-P. Migne, ed. *Patrologia Latina* (1844–55 and 1862–65). See the online database at < http://pld.chadwyck.co.uk/>
S	Charters cited according to their number in P. H. Sawyer, *Anglo-Saxon Charters: An Annotated List and Bibliography* (London: Royal Historical Society, 1968). A revised and updated version of Sawyer is available at https://esawyer.lib.cam.ac.uk/
s.s.	Supplementary Series
TRHS	*Transactions of the Royal Historical Society*
Wormald, *Legal Culture*	Patrick Wormald, *Legal Culture in the Early Medieval West: Law as Text, Image, and Experience* (London: Hambledon, 1999)
Wormald, *Making of English Law*	Patrick Wormald, *The Making of English Law: King Alfred to the Twelfth Century* (Malden: Blackwell, 1999)
Writs	Florence E. Harmer, ed. *Anglo-Saxon Writs*, 2nd ed. (Stamford: Paul Watkins, 1989)

Introduction: Law as Literature/Literature as Law

Andrew Rabin and Anya Adair

> Our law hath, as some say, certaine lawfull fictions, on which it groundeth the truth of justice.
>
> Montaigne, *Essays* II.12 (*Apology for Raymond Sebond*)

A passage in the so-called *Fonthill Letter*, the record of a late ninth-century legal dispute, recounts that a judicial panel found in favor of one of the litigants because his testimony convinced its members that he was "nearer the oath" (*aðe ðæs ðe near*) than any of the other parties.[1] This striking phrase is not unique to this text – a Latin analogue occurs in the record of a tenth-century dispute preserved in the *Liber Eliensis*[2] – suggesting that, if not necessarily common, it was nonetheless a recognizable legal formula. The panel reached its judgment after each litigant "gave his account" (*reahta heora ægðer his spell*) and the defendant was permitted to present (*geagnigean*) the charters that validated his ownership. Underlying this passage is a complex interplay of narratives: the oral testimonies delivered by the litigants, the written histories recorded in the charters, and

[1] The *Fonthill Letter* has been edited most recently in S 1445, in Nicholas P. Brooks and S. E. Kelly, eds., *Charters of Christ Church, Canterbury*, 2 vols. (Oxford: Oxford University Press, 2013), 2:852–56 (no. 104). On the text, see Simon Keynes, "The Fonthill Letter," in *Words, Texts, and Manuscripts: Studies in Anglo-Saxon Culture Presented to Helmut Gneuss on the Occasion of his Sixty-Fifth Birthday*, ed. Michael Korhammer (Cambridge: D. S. Brewer, 1992), 53–97; Wormald, *Making of English Law*, 144–48; Carole A. Hough, "Cattle-Tracking in the Fonthill Letter," *English Historical Review* 115 (2000): 864–92; Scott T. Smith, "Of Kings and Cattle Thieves: The Rhetorical Work of the Fonthill Letter," *JEGP* 106 (2007): 447–67; Nicholas P. Brooks, "The Fonthill Letter, Ealdorman Ordlaf, and Anglo-Saxon Law in Practice," in *Early Medieval Studies in Memory of Patrick Wormald*, ed. Stephen Baxter et al. (Farnham: Ashgate, 2009), 301–18; Andrew Rabin, "Testimony and Authority in Old English Law: Writing the Subject in the 'Fonthill Letter,'" in *Law and Sovereignty in the Middle Ages and the Renaissance*, ed. Robert Sturges (Tempe: Arizona Center for Medieval and Renaissance Studies, 2011), 147–71; Nicole Marafioti, "Seeking Alfred's Body: Royal Tomb as Political Object in the Reign of Edward the Elder," *Early Medieval Europe* 23 (2015): 202–28. Unless otherwise indicated, all translations are our own.

[2] E. O. Blake, ed., *Liber Eliensis* (London: The Royal Historical Society, 1962), 99 (cap. 25).

the panel's judgment concerning whose narrative would be authorized as "true" via legal ritual – that is, which narrative brought the litigant "nearer the oath."[3] The phrase is a potent one, evoking a courtroom setting where the stories presented are judged according to their proximity to the central oaths taken by the participants: the oaths themselves become palpable players in the drama.

This small detail from the *Fonthill Letter* provides just one illustration of the close relationship between the legal and the literary in pre-Conquest texts, though its recognition of the symbiotic connection between these two modes of discourse was hardly a new one. Plato's critique of the literary in the *Republic* represents an implicit acknowledgment of the normative power of narrative, while the discussion of the cathartic importance of tragedy in Aristotle's *Poetics* is founded on the belief that narrative release was essential to the maintenance of a civil society. The courtroom speeches of Demosthenes and, later, of Cicero demonstrate a nuanced understanding of the place of narrative and literary style in legal advocacy (and invective). Perhaps most influentially, the *Novellae constitutiones*, the fourth component of the *Corpus juris civilis*, incorporate narrative as precedent to justify additions to the laws of Justinian. Given this pedigree, there can be little surprise that similar connections between law and literature can be found in texts produced in England prior to the Norman Conquest of 1066. Although the *Fonthill Letter* is unusual in its rich level of detail, the narrative conventions it follows are found in other early dispute narratives: the portrayal of the losing party as fickle or opportunistic; the erasure of any evidence that might undermine the claims of the victorious litigant; the emphasis on the authorization of the resolution by a higher legal authority; and the characterization of the record's narrative content as an extension of the evidentiary narrative proffered by the victorious litigant. Through these conventions, narrative becomes law.

The centrality of literary discourse to juridical texts and vice versa is by no means limited to dispute records. The metrical preface to the laws of Hlothere and Eadric, the portrayal of Saint Guthlac's conflict with devils over his retreat as a legal dispute, the critique of civil law in Ælfric's *Eugenia*, and the blurring of the line between homily and law in the works of Archbishop Wulfstan of York all testify to the interweaving of legal and literary discourse in the textual world of pre-Conquest England. The many connections between early English law and other genres of text have not gone unnoticed. Owing to the work of scholars such as Patrick Wormald and Lisi Oliver – as well as that of several contributors to this volume – pre-Conquest English legislation has come to be recognized as

[3] On the interplay of text and testimony in the *Fonthill Letter*, see Rabin, "Testimony and Authority," 169–71.

among the most sophisticated in medieval Europe and as exerting a major influence on the development of the Common Law.[4] This revitalization of Old English legal studies has had a profound impact on other areas of scholarship, including linguistics, literature, and cultural studies. It is all the more surprising therefore that the relationship between early English law and literature has received so little scholarly attention. Nonetheless, although medievalists are – as Emily Steiner has observed – "enviably placed to make new inroads into the subject of law and literature," scholarship that approaches pre-Conquest legal culture from this perspective is, if not absent, at least sorely lacking.[5] It has yet to be the subject of a full-scale monograph or, prior to this volume, an edited collection. Indeed, it is telling that the recently published *Cambridge Companion to Medieval English Law and Literature* contains only one chapter devoted to the pre-Conquest period (by a contributor to this collection).[6] The lack of scholarship on the relationship between early medieval literature and law thus represents an unusually large gap in our understanding of early medieval England. The purpose of this collection is to address that gap.

4 The body of scholarship on this topic is far too great to be included here, but see especially Wormald, *Legal Culture*; Wormald, *Making of English Law*; Lisi Oliver, *The Body Legal in Barbarian Law* (Toronto: University of Toronto Press, 2011); Stefan Jurasinski, *The Old English Penitentials and Anglo-Saxon Law* (Cambridge: Cambridge University Press, 2015); Andrew Rabin, *Crime and Punishment in Anglo-Saxon England* (Cambridge: Cambridge University Press, 2020); Andrew Rabin, ed. and trans., *The Political Writings of Archbishop Wulfstan of York* (Manchester: Manchester University Press, 2015); Stefan Jurasinski, Lisi Oliver, and Andrew Rabin, eds. *English Law Before Magna Carta: Felix Liebermann and Die Gesetze der Angelsachsen* (Leiden: Brill, 2010); Nicole Marafioti and Jay Paul Gates, eds. *Capital and Corporal Punishment in Anglo-Saxon England* (Woodbridge: Boydell, 2014); Scott T. Smith, *Land and Book: Literature and Land Tenure in Anglo-Saxon England* (Toronto: University of Toronto Press, 2012); Stefan Jurasinski and Andrew Rabin, eds. *Languages of the Law in Early Medieval England: Essays in Memory of Lisi Oliver* (Leuven: Peeters, 2019); Tom Lambert, *Law and Order in Anglo-Saxon England* (Oxford: Oxford University Press, 2017); Levi Roach, *Kingship and Consent in Anglo-Saxon England, 871–978: Assemblies and the State in the Early Middle Ages* (Cambridge: Cambridge University Press, 2013); John Hudson, *The Oxford History of the Laws of England, Volume II: 871–1216* (Oxford: Oxford University Press, 2012); Katherine O'Brien O'Keeffe, "Body and Law in Late Anglo-Saxon England," *Anglo-Saxon England* 27 (1998).

5 Emily Steiner and Candace Barrington, eds., *The Letter of the Law: Legal Practice and Literary Production in Medieval England* (Ithaca: Cornell University Press, 2002), 2.

6 Stefan Jurasinski, "English Law Before the Conquest," in *The Cambridge Companion to Medieval English Law and Literature*, ed. Candace Barrington and Sebastian Sobecki (Cambridge: Cambridge University Press, 2019), 3–16.

Defining the Genres

When dealing with categories as amorphous as law and literature some attempt must be made to define the boundaries of each genre, if for no other reason than to prevent the full – and reductive – identification of one with the other. We may begin with law, yet immediately we encounter a difficulty: it is not possible to identify a single coherent or explicit definition of the law in the surviving legal record. Early English legislation may set out the reasons for the promulgation of a particular law code, but little evidence survives of a comprehensive legal philosophy.[7] This lack of jurisprudential reflection is further complicated by the practice in other types of legal documents such as charters, writs, and wills, which clearly state their immediate purpose, but which cite neither specific acts of legislation nor any overarching principle of law to contextualize or justify their execution.[8] Some help may be found, however, in the *Etymologiae* of Isidore of Seville, which circulated widely in pre-Conquest England. In Book II, *De rhetorica et dialecta* ("On rhetoric and reason"), Isidore characterizes law as "established" (*sancierunt*) by humans, "those who are of nobler birth and the commons" (*maiores natu cum plebibus*) which either "allows something" (*permittit*) or "forbids it" (*vetat*).[9] For Isidore, "human life is regulated by the reward or punishment of law" (*Legis enim praemio aut poena vita moderatur humana*).[10] These rewards and punishments are not merely a matter of the application of external force, however: "Indeed, laws are enacted in order to control human audacity through the fear they arouse, and so that innocent people may be safe in the midst of reprobates, and so that even among the impious the power of doing harm may be restrained by a dreaded punishment" (*Factae sunt autem leges, ut earum metu humana coherceatur audacia, tutaque sit inter inprobos innocentia, et in*

[7] On this point, see George T. Dempsey, "Legal Terminology in Anglo-Saxon England: The Trinoda Necessitas Charter," *Speculum* 57 (1982): 843–49; Mary P. Richards, "The Dictionary of Old English and Old English Legal Terminology," in *The Dictionary of Old English: Retrospects and Prospects*, ed. M. J. Toswell (Kalamazoo, MI: Medieval Institute Publications, 1998), 57–61; Rabin, *Crime and Punishment*, 2–4.

[8] Patrick Wormald, "*Lex scripta* and *verbum regis*: Legislation and Germanic Kingship, from Euric to Cnut," in Wormald, *Legal Culture*, 22–24. A recent critique of Wormald's position can be found in Alice Taylor, "*Lex Scripta* and the Problem of Enforcement: Anglo-Saxon, Welsh, and Scottish Law Compared," in *Legalism: Community and Justice*, ed. Fernanda Pirie and Judith Scheele (Oxford: Oxford University Press, 2014), 47–75.

[9] W. M. Lindsay, ed., *Isidori hispalensis episcopi: Etymologarium sive originum, libri xx*, vol. 1 (Oxford: Clarendon, 1911), II.x.4.

[10] Ibid., II.x.5.

ipsis inprobis formidato supplicio refrenetur nocendi facultas).[11] For Isidore, the force of law thus rests on the governance of the external by governance of the internal. In other words, instilling fear through the promise of punishment curbs man's natural "audacity," thus constituting him as a legal subject. And the illegal acts of subjects so constituted are also acts of impiety, as the condition of the soul is a pertinent legal consideration in a deeply Christian society.

This broad view of law will remain remarkably stable throughout the early Middle Ages. In the late ninth-century legislation of Alfred the Great, the opening clause decrees that each of his subjects "carefully adhere to his oath and pledge" (*his að 7 his wed wærlice healde*) while the early eleventh-century laws drafted by Archbishop Wulfstan of York link the order of society to the properly ordered internal self of the subject.[12] As in the *Etymologiae*, law's efficacy rests, not merely on the application of external force, but also on the internal consent – conscious or unconscious – of the subject. But how this consent is to be obtained is the subject of ongoing appeals, tensions, negotiations, and renovations, many of which take place in arenas as much literary as legal. What exactly the law is – how it is understood and the extent of its boundaries – remains implicit and in flux.

An understanding of what is meant by literature in this context is, if anything, more complicated, not least because the Latin *litterae* ("letters," "epistles," or "written texts") bore a somewhat different range of meaning than does its modern descendant. Moreover, the range of genres evidenced by the texts that are grouped by modern scholars under the umbrella of 'literature' is not only diverse, but also has not found a terminology that

11 Ibid.

12 Alfred 1. All quotations from the laws of Alfred and Ine are taken from Stefan Jurasinski and Lisi Oliver, *Laws of Alfred: The Domboc and the Making of Anglo-Saxon Law* (Cambridge: Cambridge University Press, 2021). On Alfred's injunction, see Matthias Ammon, "'Ge mid wedde ge mid aðe': The Functions of Oath and Pledge in Anglo-Saxon Legal Culture," *Historical Research* 86 (2013): 518–19; David Pratt, *The Political Thought of King Alfred the Great* (Cambridge: Cambridge University Press, 2007), 233–38. On Wulfstan, see Andrew Rabin, "The Wolf's Testimony to the English: Law and the Witness in the *Sermo Lupi ad Anglos*," *JEGP* 105 (2006): 388–414; Rabin, *Political Writings*, 43–44; Pratt, *Political Thought*, 58–85; Jay Paul Gates, "Preaching, Politics and Episcopal Reform in Wulfstan's Early Writings," *Early Medieval Europe* 23 (2015): 93–116; Patrick Wormald, "Archbishop Wulfstan and the Holiness of Society," in Wormald, *Legal Culture*, 225–52; Patrick Wormald, "Archbishop Wulfstan: Eleventh-Century Statebuilder," in *Wulfstan, Archbishop of York: The Proceedings of the Second Alcuin Conference*, ed. Matthew Townend (Turnhout: Brepols, 2004), 9–27; Joyce M. Hill, "Archbishop Wulfstan: Reformer?" in *Wulfstan, Archbishop of York: The Proceedings of the Second Alcuin Conference*, ed. Matthew Townend (Turnhout: Brepols, 2004), 309–24.

would both reflect that diversity and mark the line between that which is 'literary' and that which is not. This border is particularly porous when it comes to distinguishing between didactic literature and prescriptive legislation, both of which draw on many of the same stylistic, generic, and rhetorical features. Indeed, the multifarious nature of pre-Conquest literary production makes any attempt to comprehensibly categorize early English literature so as to differentiate it from early English law a bit of a fool's errand. As a result, we are left with something akin to Supreme Court Justice Potter Stewart's description of pornography: we may not be able to define it, but we know it when we see it.[13]

Yet although the boundaries defining the literary – particularly in relationship to the legal – may be blurred, instances in which pre-Conquest authors explicitly work to distinguish between prose genres, for example, suggest that a distinction between the two was recognized. The clearest example of a differentiation of this sort can be found in the works of Archbishop Wulfstan. In response to the landing of a Danish army led by Thorkell the Tall in 1009, Wulfstan drafted a set of laws to be issued in the name of King Æthelred prescribing, among other things, a period of kingdom-wide penance. The law code, dubbed *VII Æthelred* by modern editors, was most likely issued in Latin, with the most accurate version surviving in the twelfth-century compilation *Quadripartitus*. Yet three other versions of *VII Æthelred* also survive, all in manuscripts closely associated with Wulfstan himself: an Old English rendering, preserved solely in Cambridge, Corpus Christi College 201; a homiletic adaptation entitled *On Various Misfortunes* (Napier 35), preserved in Cambridge, Corpus Christi College 201 and Oxford, Bodleian Library, Hatton 113; and a much less faithful homiletic adaptation (Napier 36), preserved in London, British Library, Cotton Tiberius A.iii. Of these, only the Old English translation (designated *VIIa Æthelred*) and the homily *On Various Misfortunes* can be securely attributed to Wulfstan.[14] The second homiletic version may derive from *On Various Misfortunes*, but its numerous digressions, errors, and paraphrases make it seem not so much a deliberate revision as the frantic scribbling of an eager notetaker, an Old English version of a Shakespearean 'Bad Quarto.'[15] However, a comparison of the other

13 *Jacobellis v. Ohio*, 378 U.S. 184 (1964).

14 *VII* and *VIIa Æthelred* have been edited in Felix Liebermann, ed., *Die Gesetze der Angelsachsen*, 3 vols. (Halle: Max Niemeyer, 1903–16), 260–63, and in Andrew Rabin, ed. and trans., *Wulfstan: Old English Legal Writings* (Cambridge, MA: Harvard University Press, 2020), 180–89. *On Various Misfortunes* has been edited in Arthur S. Napier, ed., *Wulfstan: Sammlung der ihm zugeschrieben Homilien nebst Untersuchungen über ihre Echtheit* (Berlin: Weidmann, 1883), 169–72 (XXXV). All three texts are included in Rabin, *Political Writings*, 130–32, 184–91.

15 Napier, *Wulfstan*, 172–75 (XXXVI).

three versions is instructive: the clauses of *VII Æthelred* are clear, specific, and enforceable, while their analogues in *VIIa Æthelred* and *On Various Misfortunes* gradually become less specific and less tied to the specific circumstances that led to the code's initial issuance in 1009. For reasons of length, a single example will have to suffice. The table below contains the opening sections of each text.

Table 0.1. *VII Æthelred* and Adaptations.

VII Æthelred	*VIIa Æthelred*	*On Various Misfortunes*
[Prologue] King Æthelred and his councilors decreed this at Bath: [1] First, that the one God is to be praised and honored above all, and that all should obey their king according to the best customs of their ancestors, and together with him defend his kingdom.	*This was decreed when the great army came to this land:* [Prologue] We all must strive diligently so that we may receive God's mercy and compassion and, with his help, withstand our enemies.	If it so happens that a great misfortune befalls the realm because of the people's deeds – war or hunger, fire or bloodshed, crop failure or bad weather, the death of men or cattle from a sudden plague – then amends always is to be made to God himself.

As the law code evolves into a homily, the king's name, his subjects' obligations, and the place of promulgation all drop away. Likewise, the circumstances of *VII Æthelred*'s issuance are first generalized (there had been no shortage of "great armies" invading England during Æthelred's reign and before) and then omitted altogether in an opening that bears no similarity to its source whatsoever. The revisions to *VII Æthelred* thus provide an illustration of how legal composition might be differentiated from 'literary' – or, at least, non-legal – composition. Where *VII Æthelred* is an explicit legal enactment by the king and issued at a named meeting of the royal council, *VIIa Æthelred* and *On Various Misfortunes* gradually divest themselves of any markers of historical specificity, converting a royal decree to a moral admonition. For Wulfstan, law represents a contingent response to a specific set of historical circumstances, while the homiletic mode requires a movement from the specific to the general, from the narrowly legal to the broadly applicable, and from the authority of the king to the greater authority of God. This is not to suggest that Wulfstan's practice here can be extended to encompass the whole of Old English – or even just early eleventh-century – composition. Rather, it demonstrates one way in which the legal might be distinguished from the literary and what some characteristics of the latter might be. Wulfstan's process of composition suggests his understanding of an intellectual and artistic space within which lie generically distinct modes of delivering his desired message. In other words, while the inhabitants of pre-Conquest England may not have articulated an explicit, exclusive, and comprehensive definition of literature, they certainly knew it when they saw it.

Law and Literature: Normative Alliances

Yet if legal texts were understood to be more narrowly applicable than literary or non-legal prescriptive texts, the genres were nonetheless closely related. Perhaps the most immediately visible point of connection is the shared prioritization of narrative. Although law's coercive power could be backed by force of arms, its authority derived from the narrative of its origin. In the case of legislation, this narrative resided in the fiction that written law was an extension of the king's own voice. Accordingly, in hearing the law the subject was also "hearing" the voice of the king and – metaphorically, at least – standing in his presence.[16] The narrative of the king meeting with his council, speaking the law, and then disseminating the law through his kingdom enabled the document to assert the king's authority, and at the same time enabled the fiction of his immediacy to substitute for his physical presence. At times, the textual manifestation of this fiction was minimal – in many cases, little more than an *Ic beod* or, as in *I Edmund*, a record of the assembly at which the law was issued. But elsewhere, such as the preface to the code of Ine, the sequence is explicitly narrated:

> Ic, Ine, mid Godes gife Wesseaxna kyning, mid geðeahte 7 mid lare Cenredes mines fæder 7 Heddes mines biscepes 7 Eorcenwoldes mines biscepes, mid eallum minum ealdormonnum 7 þæm ieldstan witum minre ðeode 7 eac micelre gesomnunge Godes ðeowa, wæs smeagende be ðære hælo urra sawla 7 be ðam staþole ures rices, þætte ryht æw 7 ryhte cynedomas ðurh ure folc gefæstnode 7 getrymede wæron, þætte næning ealdormonna ne us undergeðeodedra æfter þam wære awendende ðas ure domas.[17]

> I, Ine, by God's gift king of the West Saxons, with the counsel and with the teaching of Cenred my father and Hædde my bishop and

[16] Andrew Rabin, "Witnessing Kingship: Royal Power and the Legal Subject in the Old English Laws," in *Kingship, Legislation and Power in Anglo-Saxon England*, ed. Gale R. Owen-Crocker and Brian Schneider (Woodbridge: Boydell, 2013), 223.

[17] Jurasinski and Oliver, *Laws of Alfred*, 370–71.

> Eorcenwold my bishop, with all my ealdormen and the senior counselors of my people and also a great gathering of God's servants, have been considering the health of our souls and the foundation of our kingdom, so that just law and just royal decrees should be fixed and arranged throughout our people, so that after this time no ealdorman nor any other subject to us should pervert these our judgments.

Ine and his counselors have met for the purpose of considering (*smeagende*) the need for law. The participle "smeagende" situates this consideration both *in* time – that is, within the specific temporal boundaries of the assembly – and *out* of time – that is, as an ongoing political concern neither originating with this meeting of the royal council nor fully resolved at its close. The clause that immediately follows is spoken as if by the collective political entity of king and council: "First we command" (*Ærest we bebodað*).[18] But this polyphony of authority builds upon the strong sense of Ine's personal presence created in the opening lines. The first person address carefully crafts his royal authority: dutiful son of Cenred and the Church, respectful of advice from the wise and holy, pondering deeply upon the welfare of his people. The preface stresses the close connection of God, king and law, and the alliterative and parallel phrases – *ðære hælo urra sawla 7 be ðam staþole ures rices* – artfully balance the health of the soul with the stability of the kingdom. The narrative here serves deliberate jurisprudential, religious, and ideological ends, and the fiction of the king's presence lies at its center. In elaborate instances like Ine's prologue, and the purposive specificity of certain later codes (such as IV Edgar's promulgation in response to a plague) the urgency of the narrative frame enhances both the authority of the document and the demand for the subject's loyalty.

The link between narrative authority and juridical legitimacy was no less important in other types of legal text. An explicit, though far from the only, acknowledgment of this importance occurs in a charter from 1016 × 1035: following the resolution of a property dispute, one of the beneficiaries by the name of Thorkell "rode then to Saint Æthelberht's minster, with everyone's consent and awareness, and had it recorded in a gospel book" (*rad ða to sancte Æþelberhtes mynstre be ealles þæs folces leafe 7 gewitnesse 7 let settan on ane Cristes boc*).[19] In effect, the true subject

[18] Ibid., 371 and see note 13.

[19] S 1462, ed. in A. J. Robertson, ed. and trans., *Anglo-Saxon Charters,* 2nd ed. (Cambridge: Cambridge University Press, 1956), 150–53 (no. 78). On this text, see Andrew Rabin, "'Sharper than a Serpent's Tooth': Parent-Child Litigation in Anglo-Saxon England," in *Childhood and Adolescence in Anglo-Saxon Literary Culture,* ed. Susan Irvine and Winfried Rudolph (Toronto: University of Toronto Press, 2018), 284–90.

of the text is its own origin. Put differently, the account of the dispute – significant enough to be preserved in the Hereford Gospels – here serves as the frame narrative from which the text derives its authority, not just as a legal record but also as a form of preventive legal exemplum intended to discourage future lawsuits.[20] Although lacking the oral markers of royal legislation, the account of Thorkell's performative ride to Hereford and public sponsorship of the record creates its own fiction of presence: if readers cannot 'hear' Thorkell's voice, they can nonetheless be assured of reading his words.

However, and as Thorkell's addition to the *Cristes boc* suggests, if the law's authority derives from its origin, it is necessary that the narrative of that origin characterize the law as something transcending the ephemeral nature of worldly governance.[21] Human law was, by its very nature, transient: rulers and the dynasties from which they descended might rise and fall to finally disappear, so any claim regarding the law's essential rightfulness demanded that its foundation withstand the vagaries of worldly politics and human mortality. Limited beings can only make limited laws. Accordingly, investing the law's origin with divine attributes made possible the characterization of legal authority as absolute and objective, unaffected by time, challenge, or change in government.[22] This impulse

20 Paul R. Hyams, "The Charter as a Source for the Early Common Law," *The Journal of Legal History* 12 (1991): 173–74. Warren Brown, "Charters as Weapons: On the Role Played by Early Medieval Dispute Records in the Disputes they Record," *Journal of Medieval History* 28 (2002): 230. Sarah Foot, "Reading Anglo-Saxon Charters: Memory, Record, or Story?" in *Narrative and History in the Early Medieval West*, ed. Elizabeth M. Tyler and Ross Balzaretti (Turnhout: Brepols, 2006), 40–41.

21 Fritz Kern, *Kingship and Law in the Middle Ages*, trans. S. B. Chrimes (Oxford: Basil Blackwell, 1948), esp. 27–34; Ernst H. Kantorowicz, *The King's Two Bodies: A Study in Medieval Political Theology* (Princeton: Princeton University Press, 1957), 42–86; Wormald, *Making of English Law*, 416–65, 481–82; Anthony Musson, *Medieval Law in Context: The Growth of Legal Consciousness from Magna Carta to the Peasants' Revolt* (New York: Manchester University Press, 2001), 18–28; Rabin, "Witnessing Kingship."

22 Peter Goodrich, *Law in the Courts of Love: Literature and Other Minor Jurisprudences* (London: Routledge, 1996), 138–59; Alex Woolf, "Community, Identity and Kingship in Early England," in *Social Identity in Early Medieval Britain*, ed. William O. Frazer and Andrew Tyrrell (London: Bloomsbury, 2000), 91–94; Musson, *Medieval Law*, 217–40; Jonathan Burnside, *God, Justice and Society: Aspects of Law and Legality in the Bible* (Oxford: Oxford University Press, 2011), 45–50; Rabin, "Parent-Child Litigation," 270–73. Mary P. Richards has noted that the laws reinforce this connection to an authoritative origin through linguistic and textual features: see "Elements of a Written Standard in the Old English Laws," in *Standardizing English: Essays in the History of Language Change*, ed. Joseph B. Trahern (Knoxville: University of Tennessee Press, 1989),

underlies the most influential of pre-Conquest law codes – that of Alfred the Great, the lengthy preface of which arranges biblical citations in order to frame the laws of Wessex as an extension of the laws of Moses.[23] Indeed, so successful was Alfred that for the next century the laws of his successors were understood primarily as additions to the Alfredian text. Alfred's successors were in large part enabled to adopt the originary narrative of his laws as their own.

Alfred's preface may be the most famous example of this sort of mythologization, but it was hardly the first. Indeed, examples can be found as far back as the laws of Æthelberht. In his obituary for the king, Bede famously (and perplexingly) writes that Æthelberht's laws were made "following the examples of the Romans" (*iuxta exempla Romanorum*).[24] It has long been recognized that there is little, if any, evidence of Roman influence on Æthelberht's laws – much as there is little, if any, evidence of the influence of Æthelberht's laws on Alfred's legislation, despite the latter in his prologue naming his Kentish predecessor as one of his principal sources. Although the specifics of the "examples" (*exempla*) mentioned by Bede still resist identification by modern scholars, his emphasis that they were Roman is itself significant. Not only does Rome provide an imperial model for the ambitious king – whose marriage to the Merovingian princess Bertha suggests a desire to ally himself with more powerful continental dynasties – it also links Æthelberht's laws to Bede's account of the Roman origin of the Kentish conversion.[25] The presence of a Christian queen and her attendant priests at Æthelberht's court suggests that Christianity was not new to Æthelberht when Bishop Augustine arrived as an emissary from Pope Gregory I, yet Bede is eager to emphasize the Kentish king's

1–22, and "Anglo-Saxonism in the Old English Laws," in *Anglo-Saxonism and the Construction of Social Identity*, ed. Allen J. Frantzen and John D. Niles (Gainesville: The University Press of Florida, 1997), 40–59. A similar point, albeit in a broader context, can be found in Michael Clanchy, "Literacy, Law, and the Power of the State," in *Culture et idéologie dans la genèse de l'État moderne* (Rome: École Française de Rome, 1985), 25–34.

23 Felix Liebermann, "King Alfred and Mosaic Law," *Transactions of the Jewish Historical Society of England* 6 (1908): 21–31; Wormald, *Making of English Law*, 216–21; Michael Treschow, "The Prologue to Alfred's Law Code: Instruction in the Spirit of Mercy," *Florilegium* 13 (1994): 80–107.

24 Bede, *Historia ecclesiastica gens Anglorum*, II.5, in Bertram Colgrave and R. A. B. Mynors, eds., *Bede's Ecclesiastical History of the English People*, corr. repr. ed. (Oxford: Clarendon, 1991), 150.

25 J. M. Wallace-Hadrill, *Bede's Ecclesiastical History of the English People: A Historical Commentary* (London: Oxford University Press, 1988), 60; Nicholas P. Brooks, "The Laws of King Æthelberht of Kent: Preservation, Content, and Composition," in *Textus Roffensis: Law, Language, and Libraries in Early Medieval England*, ed. Bruce O'Brien and Barbara Bombi (Turnhout: Brepols, 2015).

ignorance and even mistrust of the new religion.[26] In doing so, he effectively erases Christianity's initial arrival as a "feminine" import, brought to the kingdom by the queen. This reading of events was inconvenient for Bede's purpose not least because while Bertha provided Æthelberht with a powerful ally, her presence also served as a constant reminder of the king's subservient status. Instead, in Bede's narrative, Æthelberht's laws come to be associated with Augustine's Roman mission, itself inspired by Gregory's apocryphal encounter with Anglian slave boys.[27] This encounter appears only in insular texts, suggesting that it filled a similar function as an originary myth intended to bolster the self-perception of the early English as a "chosen people."[28] The inclusion of this narrative in his obituary of Gregory rather than his account of the conversion suggests that Bede may have felt a degree of skepticism about its veracity. Even so, the narrative allows Bede to frame the conversion as essentially masculine: God, by means of the slave boys, inspires Gregory, who then sends Augustine to convert Æthelberht, a sequence of events that erases Bertha's role by substituting a masculine genealogy for a feminine one. The issuance of Æthelberht's laws serves as the culmination of this narrative by following – as did the conversion itself – the examples of the Romans. If the myth of origins surrounding Æthelberht's legislation is less explicitly narrated than that of Alfred's *domboc*, it is nonetheless powerful. The laws derive their authority, not only as utterances of the king, but as the extension of a quasi-mythic progression that began with Gregory's revelation in the slave market. As was the case with the laws of Alfred, the legislation of Æthelberht exists within a manufactured history that presents them not merely as human enactments, but as the fulfillment of a plan whose author was God and whose divine agents were pope, missionary, and king.

An emphasis on the mythic or divine origins of legal authority extended beyond the framing of royal legislation.[29] The elaborate curses found at the end of many early English charters perform a similar func-

26 Brooks, "Laws of King Æthelberht," 130.

27 Patrick Wormald, "Bede, the *Bretwaldas* and the Origins of the *Gens Anglorum*," in *The Times of Bede: Studies in Early English Christian Society and its Historian* (Malden: Blackwell, 2006), 106–34. On the history of Bede's narrative, see Stephen J. Harris, "Bede and Gregory's Allusive Angles," *Criticism* 44 (2002): 271–89.

28 Nicholas Howe, *Migration and Mythmaking in Anglo-Saxon England* (Notre Dame: University of Notre Dame Press, 2001), 49–71.

29 On this point, see especially Herwig Wolfram, "Political Theory and Narrative in Charters," *Viator* 26 (1995): 39–51; Rolf H. Bremmer, "The Final Countdown: Apocalyptic Expectations in Anglo-Saxon Charters," in *Time and Eternity: The Medieval Discourse*, ed. Gerhard Jaritz and Gerson Moreno-Riano (Turnhout: Brepols, 2003), 506–14.

tion. Thus, a charter of 949 recording a grant of property by King Eadred to the archdiocese of Canterbury concludes its dispositive clause with the warning that,

> Si quis autem quod absit tirannica fretus potestate regalis, episcopalis, siue homo alicuius dignitatis, hoc decretum a Deo [...] conlatum infringere temptauerit siue huiusce donationis a prefata ecclesia uel passum pedis segregauerit, ni prius hoc inorme scelus poenitendo deterserit; se sacrilegii culpam incurrisse et a Domino Iesu Christo in perpetuum sine ullo subtractionis refocilatu damnaturum persentiat.[30]

> If, however, anyone who relies on the tyrannical power of royal, episcopal, or anyone of rank should attempt (God forbid!) to destroy this decision granted by God [...] or should alienate even a foot of this gift from the aforementioned church, unless that person first expunges this enormous crime by penance, may he know that he has incurred blame for his sacrilege and will be damned by the Lord Jesus Christ forever without any consolation of a mitigation.

In this instance, and in other texts of this type, the threat of divine punishment itself is less interesting than the fact that there is no secular counterpart. Although the grant may have been given by the king – in formal terms, at least – its violation is a sacrilege (*sacrilegus*) not a crime (*delictus* or *crimen*). In effect, the king here operates only as an agent, so a violation of the grant's terms is a violation of divine, not merely royal, prerogative. The legal authority that permits the king to transfer ownership of these lands does not have its origin in earthly law, nor does royal authority itself reside in the earthly ruler. The grant may have been an act of man, but it took place under the authority of God. The utterance of the curse in Latin here gives it an appropriate *ex cathedra* linguistic authority; its threat is in the lexicon of the Church and directed at the soul. Similar narratives in the vernacular are no less effective. The wills of the wealthy landholders Ælfgar and Ælfhelm, as well as that of Bishop Ælfsige, to mention but a few, contain similar or still more forceful execrations – and all without mention of secular penalty.[31] Bishop Ælfsige wishes to prevent any alteration to his will, and so ends it with the declaration "If anyone do

[30] S 546, ed. in Brooks and Kelly, *Charters of Christ Church, Canterbury*, 2:934–36 (no. 120). On curses in charters more generally, see Brenda Danet and Bryna Bogoch, "'Whoever Alters This, May God Turn His Face from Him on the Day of Judgement': Curses in Anglo-Saxon Legal Documents," *Journal of American Folklore* 105 (1992).

[31] Dorothy Whitelock, *Anglo-Saxon Wills*, Cambridge Studies in English Legal History (Cambridge: University Press, 1930), 6–10 (no. ii), 16 (no. iv), 30–34 (no. xiii).

so, may God destroy him both soul and body, both here and in the future, unless I myself change it" (*Gif hit þonne hwa do God hine fordo ge mid sawle ge mid lichoman ge her ge on þan to feondan [=toweardan] buton Io[=ic] hit self on oþer wænde*).[32] The threat of eternal punishment, conventional in such documents, is raised here to oratorical heights by alliterative phrase and rhythmic balance: legal formula is charged with rhetorical power.

The foregoing suggests that stylistic strategies drawn from texts conventionally categorized as literary by modern scholars were neither simple adornments nor ancillary to the composition, imposition, and enforcement of pre-Conquest law. Insofar as law functioned as something more than just a set of rules – that is, as more than a relatively ineffective set of statutes comparable, in the words of Pollock and Maitland, to those "in the less settled parts of the western American states"[33] – literary rhetoric provided the moral and normative architecture needed to translate external decrees into an internal acceptance of legal authority. In this sense, the literary becomes the foundation of what Anthony Musson calls legal consciousness: "an active element shaping people's values, beliefs and aspirations and also as a passive agent providing a reserve of knowledge, memory and reflective thought, influencing not simply the development of the law and legal system, but also political attitudes."[34] In other words, the literary makes it possible for the subject to obey the law, not out of compulsion, but out of a sense of moral and ethical obligation. Just as literary techniques enabled the law to enhance its authority as an instrument of political power, the incorporation of recognizably legal language into works of literature gave it the cultural force necessary to establish the norms and traditions that shaped early English notions of community and identity. Indeed, the influence of literature on law was no less great – and no less important – than the influence of law on literature.

Literature and Law: Normative Renewals

At their core, law and literature are genres rooted in a complex interplay of prescription and imagination.[35] Law is grounded in a vision of social order achievable through authoritative dicta; literature, subject to its own

32 Whitelock, *Anglo-Saxon Wills*, 16.

33 Frederick Pollock and Frederic William Maitland, *The History of English Law before the Time of Edward I*, 2nd ed., 2 vols. (Cambridge: Cambridge University Press, 1911), 1:56.

34 Musson, *Medieval Law*, 1–2.

35 On the role of imagination in the making of early medieval law (Wales, in particular), see Robin Chapman Stacey, *Law and the Imagination in Medieval Wales* (Philadelphia: University of Pennsylvania Press, 2018).

linguistic and aesthetic mandates, constructs imagined worlds – plausible, fictional, aspirational, didactic, or admonitory – through its reliance upon, and reinforcement of, the norms of the community in which it was produced. Its representation of communal norms grants the literary text a legitimacy that enables both its acceptance by its readers and its influence over them. The deployment of norms in this way is not limited to narrative: a range of text-types frequently categorized as 'literary' by modern scholars – including homilies, riddles, elegies, maxims, and charms – generate their own imagined worlds that rely on the evocation of normative beliefs and practices to move their audiences.[36] A particularly vivid example of this process can be found in the contrasting aims and approaches of the previously-discussed *VII Æthelred* and its associated homily *On Various Misfortunes*. The shift from law to homily is marked, not only by the transition from legal dictate to moral admonition, but also by the movement from the historical into the hypothetical. The rubric and opening clauses of *VII* and *VIIa Æthelred* frame their decrees as retrospective, that is, as juridical responses to a specific historical event. On the other hand, the opening phrases of *On Various Misfortunes* – "If it so happens that a great misfortune befalls the realm because of the people's deeds [...] then amends always is to be made to God himself" – characterize the text as a hypothetical response to imagined crises: "war or hunger, fire or bloodshed, crop failure or bad weather, the death of men or cattle from a sudden plague." The text then replaces the sense of exigency evoked in the law codes by the arrival of the Viking "great army" (*se micele here*) with allusions to the prayers of King David (somewhat anachronistically directed

[36] See, for instance, Rebecca V. Colman, "Reason and Unreason in Early Medieval Law," *The Journal of Interdisciplinary History* 4 (1974): 571–91; Leonore McGaffey Abraham, "Cynewulf's *Juliana*: A Case at Law," *Allegorica* 3 (1978): 172–89; M. K. Lawson, "Archbishop Wulfstan and the Homiletic Element in the Laws of Æthelred II and Cnut," *English Historical Review* 107 (1992): 565–86; Rolf H. Bremmer, "Grendel's Arm and the Law," in *Doubt Wisely: Papers in Honour of E. G. Stanley*, ed. M. J. Toswell and E. M. Tyler (London: Routledge, 1996), 121–32; Stefan Jurasinski, *Ancient Privileges: Beowulf, Law, and the Making of Germanic Antiquity* (Morgantown: West Virginia University Press, 2006); Andrew Rabin, "Ritual Magic or Legal Performance? Reconsidering An Old English Charm Against Theft," in *English Law Before Magna Carta: Felix Liebermann and Die Gesetze der Angelsachsen*, ed. Stefan Jurasinski, Lisi Oliver, and Andrew Rabin (Leiden: Brill, 2010), 177–95; Rolf H. Bremmer, "Proverbs in the Anglo-Saxon Laws," in *Languages of the Law in Early Medieval England: Essays in Memory of Lisi Oliver*, ed. Stefan Jurasinski and Andrew Rabin (Leuven: Peeters, 2019), 179–92; Benjamin A. Saltzman, *Bonds of Secrecy: Law, Spirituality, and the Literature of Concealment in Early Medieval England* (Philadelphia: University of Pennsylvania Press, 2019), 161–243.

toward Christ) and the penance of the Ninevites.[37] In so doing, the homily contextualizes its call for repentance, not in the immediacy of invasion, but in the trans-historical typology of biblical narrative. This reimagining and repurposing of the legal extends into the body of the homily itself: even in those passages drawn directly from Æthelred's legislation, the text substitutes moral norms for royal decrees. Thus, the repeated royal plurals of *VII Æthelred* – *prohibemus*, *praecipimus*, and *instituimus* – frame injunctions such as that against laboring on a fast day as a royal command and their violation an offense against the king.[38] In contrast, the homily omits the royal plurals and attributes violations of penitential practice to such failures as sin (*unriht*) or greed (*fræc*) that contravene not just divine authority but also the necessary means by which communities may come together in all times of crisis. But *On Various Misfortunes* does not erase its legal source material: references are made to legal institutions, including the king's council (*witan*) and the shire court (*scire witan*). The homily opens with the contingent "if/then" syntax typical of pre-Conquest royal legislation, a structure which even in law implies and exploits narratives of imagined events. This legal frame is extended by the early appearance of *ærest* (first), a word common at the outset of law codes from Ine to II Cnut; with Wulfstan, its enumerative function is transmuted into the broader sense of preeminent principle: "foremost among all things" (*ealra þinga ærest*).[39] These structural devices and linguistic echoes provide an explicit reminder of the link between law and homily. The moral authority of the text derives from the manner in which it combines its pastoral tone of address with familiar legal tropes, appeals to communal norms, and invocations of divine power. The homily thus evokes an imagined world grounded in shared communal anxieties yet one capable of realizing the consolations of spiritual renewal in the real world.

The continual renewal of communal norms marks a crucial point of convergence between the legal and the literary, yet each prioritizes its use in different, even opposing, ways. The law's need to mythologize its origin requires its literary aspects to remain largely unmarked. For the law to acknowledge its appropriation of the literary would be to risk undermining its authority by reframing what ought to be an extension of divine governance as merely a product of human artifice. The paradox of Montaigne's "lawfull fiction" is at the heart of this tension. On the one hand, the law's self-presentation through text militates against its association with the interpretive instabilities of fiction; on the other hand, it is often through fiction – of a shared norm or unifying authority, for

37 Napier 35, ed. in Napier, *Wulfstan*, 170; Rabin, *Political Writings*, 131. This passage is discussed in more detail in Rabin, *Political Writings*, 42–43.

38 See VII Æthelred Pr., 2, 3, 4, 5, 6.

39 Napier 35, ed. in Napier, *Wulfstan*, 170; Rabin, *Political Writings*, 131.

example – that the law is made to function. In contrast, literature often calls attention to its deployments of the legal. That is, insofar as literature is, by its nature, a work of artifice, the adoption of legal language and concepts enriches the reality of the experience in question, and places the text in a familiar (and often dramatic) cultural context. In the poem *Guthlac A*, for example, the anonymous poet portrays the saint's attempt to claim his chosen retreat – a barrow (*beorg*) then occupied by devils – as a formal property dispute, and so employs both terms and procedures drawn from pre-Conquest law.[40] The conflict rests on the nature of legitimate ownership: insofar as the whole of the earth belongs to God, should the devils' occupancy of the barrow be treated as full possession or simply as a temporary tenancy? Unsurprisingly, the "dispute" is resolved in Guthlac's favor, but the legal conceit is telling. Not only does the poem employ the just exercise of worldly authority as a metaphor for the absolute authority of the divine, but – and perhaps more importantly for its author – the legitimacy of Guthlac's claim also serves as an argument for the inalienability of Church land. Highlighting God's authority as a divine landowner frames secular (especially royal and aristocratic) property ownership as a leasehold to which the Church had ultimate claim and whose right to it can no more be withheld than could the barrow by its devilish squatters. The efficacy of the conceit lies in its symmetry: the perfect alignment of Guthlac's arguments with the law's protection of tenurial rights appropriates the forms of secular legal authority in support of Church claims concerning landholding and property ownership. To challenge those claims is to act as unruly tenants denying the legal rights of their landlords, fallen angels rebelling against the law of God.

Guthlac A is unusual, however, in its complementary arrangement of earthly and divine law. In the early English context, those texts in which the portrayal of secular law is used to reveal its fundamental inadequacy when compared with the perfection of the divine are more common. This may be the result of selection bias: the majority of Old English literary texts survive from the late tenth or early eleventh centuries, a period characterized by a tense relationship between king and Church. The Church experienced a period of disenchantment with secular political authorities in the years following the death of King Edgar in 975.[41] The

[40] See Jane Roberts, ed., *The Guthlac Poems of the Exeter Book* (Oxford: Oxford University Press, 1979), 50–51; Stephanie Clark, "A More Permanent Homeland: Land Tenure in *Guthlac A*," *Anglo-Saxon England* 40 (2012): 75–102; Catherine A. M. Clarke, *Writing Power in Anglo-Saxon England: Texts, Hierarchies, Economies* (Cambridge: D. S. Brewer, 2012), 21–26; Smith, *Land and Book*, 198–205; Andrew Rabin, "The Oldest English Lawyer Joke? *Guthlac A*, l.265a and *Christ II*, l.733a," *Notes and Queries* 28 (2021): 156–57.

[41] Malcolm R. Godden, "Ælfric and Anglo-Saxon Kingship," *English Historical*

reigns of Edgar's sons Edward and Ælthelred witnessed a new hostility toward the Church hierarchy – sometimes referred to (albeit not entirely accurately) as the "anti-monastic reaction" – that resulted in the cooling of the alliance between *rex* and *ecclesia* that had made possible the monastic reforms of a generation before. In many of the texts produced in this period – particularly those authored by Ælfric, abbot of Eynsham – earthly law is characterized as a corrupt institution overseen by feckless, fraudulent kings. For Ælfric and many of his contemporaries, the failure of Edward and Ælthelred to defend ecclesiastical prerogatives exemplified the dangers that could result from overmuch involvement by the Church in secular affairs.

Ælfric's life of *Saint Eugenia* provides a useful example of the ways in which this suspicion of secular legal authority was expressed in literary narrative.[42] Much like the anonymous author of *Guthlac A*, Ælfric highlights the jurisprudential perspective of his narrative through his frequent recourse to recognizable Old English legal terminology and court processes, in many cases adding legal content absent from his Latin source.[43] At the narrative's climax, Eugenia – hitherto disguised as a male under the name of Eugenius – is dragged into court on a false charge of sexual assault. The judge – Eugenia's father, though he fails to recognize his daughter – commands Eugenia, her female accuser, and the servants whose testimony could exonerate her to "testify to this matter if they had heard it" (*cyðan be ðison gif hi ðis gehyrdon*), phrasing reminiscent of that in the Old English formulary *Swerian* requiring witnesses to swear "as their [...] ears heard" (*swa heo* [...] *earum oferhyrdon*).[44] However, the servants perjure themselves, as Ælfric specifies, "with an oath" (*mid aþe*), leaving

Review 102 (1987): 913; Christopher A. Jones, "Ælfric and the Limits of 'Benedictine Reform,'" in *A Companion to Ælfric*, ed. Hugh Magennis and Mary Swan (Leiden: Brill, 2009), 67–108; Christopher A. Jones, *Ælfric's Letter to the Monks of Eynsham* (Cambridge: Cambridge University Press, 1998), 47, 49; Robert K. Upchurch, "A Big Dog Barks: Ælfric of Eynsham's Indictment of the English Pastorate and Witan," *Speculum* 85 (2010): 505–33; Andrew Rabin, "The Reception of Kentish Law in the Eleventh Century: Archbishop Wulfstan as Legal Historian," in *Languages of the Law in Early Medieval England*, ed. Stefan Jurasinski and Andrew Rabin (Leuven: Peeters, 2019), 225–40; Andrew Rabin, "Holy Bodies, Legal Matters: Reaction and Reform in Ælfric's *Eugenia* and the Ely Privilege," *Studies in Philology* 110 (2013): 220–65.

42 Ælfric's life of Eugenia has been edited most recently in Mary Clayton and Juliet Mullins, *Ælfric: Old English Lives of the Saints*, 3 vols. (Cambridge, MA: Harvard University Press, 2019), 1:43–74.

43 Rabin, "Holy Bodies, Legal Matters," 243–49.

44 Eugenia's trial is recounted in Clayton and Mullins, *Ælfric: Old English Lives of the Saints*, 1:58–60, lines 210–57. The text for *Swerian* can be found in Liebermann, *Gesetze*, 1:396–400.

Eugenia with no recourse but to expose her breasts to the shocked court. Eugenia's unrecognizing father, the perjured servants, and the fraudulence of the charge itself illustrate Ælfric's view of secular law as blind, corrupt, and incapable of meting out justice.[45] The extent to which these failures troubled Ælfric is reflected in Eugenia's forced uncovering of her breasts, an act both shamefully immodest (especially to the conservative abbot of Eynsham) and imitative of the uncovering of the female body necessary for the legal confirmation of sexual assault – the very crime of which Eugenia is accused.[46] Yet Ælfric's highly alliterative prose reaches its climax without any clerical shrinking from its more sensational details: "After these words she tore apart her clothes and revealed her breasts to the illustrious Philip and said to him: 'You are my father...'" (*Æfter þysum wordum heo totær hyre gewædu / and ætæwde hyre breost þam breman Phillipe / and cwæþ him to: "Þu eart min fæder..."*).[47] The strong alliteration and internal rhyme foreground the shock of the disrobement. The (literary) hagiographer in Ælfric recognized the power of the scene to achieve his complex of ends: Eugenia is legal victim and triumphant martyr; she is saved from execution, yet suffers a public moral death; she is naked, but clothed in God's innocence – it is the clothed who are seen to be naked in their pagan sin. The series of paradoxes dramatized at the trial's climax prefigures the glorious and final paradox of martyrdom: Eugenia lives as a saint the moment she dies under the executioner's axe. And as was the case in *Guthlac A*, Ælfric's critique of secular law depends upon his explicit incorporation the legal language and customs of early eleventh-century England; he frames the trial in *Eugenia* as an easily recognizable comparandum for contemporary legal practice. This particularly dense weaving of the legal and the literary exploits the potential for drama inherent in contexts of legal disruption, whose dynamics enable their reimagining as narratives of heroic conflict and inspired victory against the forces of evil. Ælfric mounts his critique of secular law by dramatizing its flaws; in the final judgment, its earthly inadequacies are exposed by the eternal truths of Christianity.

The widely-differing uses to which the legal elements in *Guthlac A* and *Eugenia* are put illustrate the perennial dichotomy in the Church's attitude to worldly matters which sees it on the one hand strive to build its power in the secular world while on the other decrying that same worldliness as dangerously inimical to the Christian life – particularly

45 Rabin, "Holy Bodies, Legal Matters," 251–54.

46 Mary P. Richards, "The Body as Text in Early Anglo-Saxon Law," in *Naked Before God: Uncovering the Body in Anglo-Saxon England*, ed. Benjamin C. Withers and Jonathan Wilcox (Morgantown: West Virginia University Press, 2003): 107–08; Rabin, "Holy Bodies, Legal Matters," 258.

47 Clayton and Mullins, *Ælfric*, 1:58, lines 234–36.

if that life is lived by an ecclesiastic. This clash of secular and spiritual priorities, and the literary and legal attempts to clarify and rectify them, underpin much of the work of Ælfric and of his more publicly-prominent contemporary Wulfstan. In his Old English life of the sainted King Edmund, Ælfric cites approvingly the warning of Abbo of Fleury that ecclesiastics should heed "the injunction of the apostle, in which he says, 'If then you have judgments relating to secular matters, appoint those to judge who are least esteemed in the church,' by that meaning laymen" (*Apostoli etiam praeceptum, quo dicit, "Saecularia negotia si habueritis, contemptibiles qui sunt in ecclesia," id est, viros saeculares, "constituite ad judicandum"*).[48] Glossing this passage, Ælfric argues that, regarding the enforcement of secular law,

> þa halgan canones gehadodum forbeodaþ,
> ge bisceopum ge preostum to beonne embe þeofas,
> forþan þe hit ne gebyraþ þam þe beoþ gecorene
> Gode to þegnigenne [...] gif hi beoþ Drihtnes þenas.

> The holy canons forbade those in orders, both bishops and priests, from being concerned with thieves, for it is not fitting for those chosen for God's service [...] if they are servants of the Lord.[49]

Ælfric attempts to achieve his own set of normative practices through means that are both intensely dramatic and at the same time reliant on the structures and models of the law. Ælfric returns to this theme frequently in his work, not merely in saints' lives such as those of Saints Edmund, Eugenia, and Julian and Basilissa, but also in homilies and his many admonitory letters. And as his *Saint Eugenia* demonstrates, Ælfric works to achieve his own set of normative practices through means that are intensely dramatic, and at the same time reliant on the structures and models of canon and secular law. His letters to Archbishop Wulfstan of York, whose political involvement met with the abbot's stern censure,[50]

[48] Ælfric's life of Edmund can be found in Michael Winterbottom, *Three Lives of English Saints* (Toronto: Pontifical Institute of Mediaeval Studies, 1972), 65–88. The quoted passage occurs on p. 84 (15.37–45).

[49] Ælfric's life of Edmund can be found in Clayton and Mullins, *Ælfric*, 3:185–206. The quoted passage occurs on p. 200, lines 207–13.

[50] See, for instance, Bernard Fehr, ed., *Die Hirtenbriefe Ælfrics in altenglischer und lateinischer Fassung* (Hamburg: H. Grand, 1914), 140: "We must not be implicated in a man's death. Even if he has committed manslaughter or murder or he is a great thief, nonetheless we must not pronounce death for him [...] But let laymen sentence him to life or death" (*We ne moton beon ymbe mannes deaðe. Þeah he manslaga beo oþþe morð gefremede oððe mycel þeofman, swa-þeah we ne scylan him deað getæcean. [...] Ac tæcean þa læwedan men him lif oþþe deað*). On this passage see Nicole Marafioti, "Punishing Bodies and Saving Souls: Capital

point up the (perceived) theological dangers of such involvement, and were in part responsible for the defense of his position put forward by the archbishop.

The tensions inherent in the competing demands of Church and state are clearly to be seen in the work of Archbishop Wulfstan, the diversity of whose corpus often resists attempts by modern scholars to place individual texts within the neatness of defined genre. Indeed, the centrality of Wulfstan's writings to discussions of the relationship between pre-Conquest law and literature is reflected by the prominence accorded his work in this collection. Wulfstan's status as archbishop of York and preeminence as a legislator at the courts of Ælthelred and Cnut enabled him to serve as both the voice of the government and its principal critic. In his law codes and homilies, he embraced these twin and somewhat contradictory roles in order to advance his political vision of a "Holy Society," a model community only achievable through the establishment of a properly ordered Christian polity.[51] Wulfstan set forth the architecture of this vision most explicitly in cross-genre texts such as the *Sermo lupi ad Anglos* (1016), the *Institutes of Polity* (*c.* 1018 × 1020), and the law code I–II Cnut (*c.* 1018 × 1020). Even if – as *VII Æthelred* indicated – Wulfstan did recognize a division between legal and literary composition, he was not bound by it. Accordingly, chapters of *Institutes of Polity* are written in a rhythmic prose closely approximating Old English alliterative verse; the *Sermo lupi* incorporates, unrevised, clauses from the laws of Æthelred; and lengthy passages from I–II Cnut are taken from his homilies, making them wholly unenforceable as prescriptive law.[52] This generic cross-pollination is used as a deliberate rhetorical strategy intended to harness multiple genres and text-types in support of a vision of politico-social reform that fully comprehends all aspects of his pre-Conquest culture. The breadth of Wulfstan's vision is expressed most explicitly in a passage repeated virtually word for word at the conclusion of both *Institutes of Polity* and the *Sermo lupi* and reiterated with variation in nearly all of the legislation he drafted for Æthelred and Cnut:

> utan word and weorc rihtlice fadian, and ure ingeðanc clænsian georne and að and wedd werlice healdan and gelome understandan þone mycclan dom, þe we ealle to scylon; and beorgan us georne wið

and Corporal Punishment in Anglo-Saxon England," *Haskins Society Journal* 20 (2008): 44–45; Andrew Rabin, "The Mound, the Altar, and the Tomb: Sanctuary, Jurisdiction, and Punishment in Early Medieval Hagiography," *Studies in Philology* 117 (2020): 453–54.

51 Wormald, "Archbishop Wulfstan and the Holiness of Society," 244–46.

52 Rabin, *Political Writings*, 31–35.

> þone weallendan bryne hellewites, and geearnian us ða mærða and ða myrhða, ðe God hæfð gegearwod þam ðe his willan on worulde gewyrcað.[53]

> let us order our words and deeds rightly, fervently cleanse our inmost thoughts, truly keep our oath and pledge, and frequently reflect on the great judgment to which we all must go; and zealously shield ourselves against the surging flame of hellish torments, and earn for ourselves the glories and happiness which God has prepared for those who work his will in the world.

Wulfstan here highlights his view of the inter-connectiveness at the core of his "Holy Society": political order should not only echo the ordered nature of creation as a whole, but also provide a model for the ordering of the Christian soul. The properly ordered self interiorizes both the divine logic underlying the ordering of the cosmos and the political logic underlying the ordering of the kingdom. In the passage quoted above, the strength of its plea is carried forward by stylistic means much favored by its composer: the exploitation of the emotional impact of adverbs, abundant alliterations and rhythmic symmetry. The *að and wedd* of Alfred sits at the center of Wulfstan's implied jurisprudence just as it sits at the heart of his loyalty to God and his Church. It is in Wulfstan that we perhaps most clearly see the significance of the interactions and alliances of law and literature – and the normative renewals (and transformations) that their intersection makes possible. In terms of genre, it is not so much that Wulfstan's habitual authorial practice works to resist generic definition as it is the case that the moral and rhetorical force of his claims cannot be separated from their legal relevance. Put differently, Wulfstan does not (merely) blend genres in his interweaving of the conventions of legislation, homily, celebratory verse, administrative treatise and socio-political essay; rather, he strives to transcend them.

Interactions and Transformations

The chapters of this collection share this spirit of transcendence in their various explorations of the collaboration, overlap, and mutual influence of the legal and the literary across England's pre-Conquest period. Richard Firth Green has categorized the standard scholarly approaches to medieval law and literature as involving either "the formal question of legal writing as a species of literature, or the thematic question of the law as it

[53] Wulfstan's *Institutes of Polity* can be found in Rabin, *Wulfstan: Old English Legal Writings*, 60–99. The quoted passage occurs on p. 98, lines 33–41.

has been represented in literature":[54] that is, law *as* literature, and law *in* literature. The productivity of both approaches is well represented among the essays in this collection; but as Green himself notes, this dichotomy is not a complete picture of the interaction of the genres – nor of the range of critical approaches they invite. The discussion above has surveyed a pre-Conquest textual world in which the relationship of the legal and the literary is multi-layered and multi-directional, and in which the line that separates the genres is frequently blurred. The alliance of law and literature revealed itself in (among other things) the mutual privileging of narrative – fictions of origin and legitimation that ground the authority of law. Equally, the alliance of literature and law is seen to facilitate an ongoing creative process of renewal through which communal norms are mobilized, reinforced, and redeveloped. In the complex of political and ideological tensions that characterizes the early English negotiation of Church versus state authority, writers set the allied forces of law and literature to reinforce old-established norms – and to win hearts and minds to new visions of society. The tactical and artistic alliances evidenced in pre-Conquest legal and literary text are precisely the focus of this collection. The chapters that follow are grouped under broad rubrics: "Law and Literature: Normative Alliances" and "Literature and Law: Normative Renewals," categories meant to disrupt tendencies to examine genre per se, and to bring together the perspectives and techniques of a variety of scholarly fields. The two sections, as will be seen, are in close conversation with one another: alliance generates innovation; renewal reinforces ancient collaboration. The perspectives of legal history and of literary and textual criticism which the contributors bring to their subjects make possible a range of approaches, and together attest to the value of the critical union of law and literature.

What might be said to unite the chapters of the first part is their shared recognition of the collusion of the legal and literary in creating the kind of foundational fictions and mutually-accepted normative models that have been explored above. In Chapter 1, Jay Paul Gates reads the Alfredian Prose Psalms and the *domboc* of Alfred together, situating both as part of a larger political effort. Psalms and legal preface together enact the project of scriptural translation that was central to Alfred's educational program. Suggestive structural similarities between the texts reveal a common logic in their narrative of law's origins; the carefully-limited vocabulary of law in the Psalms – seen especially in the use of the term *dom* – aligns their translation closely with the legal culture of the *domboc*. The shared project

[54] Richard Firth Green, "Medieval Literature and Law," in *The Cambridge History of Middle English Literature*, ed. David Wallace (Cambridge: Cambridge University Press, 1998), 407.

of psalm translation and law code introduction is to offer the English the foundation for a shared national identity via the return to a united kingdom ruled by wise kings and judges. The resonances of language choice – and its power to influence and educate an audience – are at the center of the analysis here. Chapter 2 similarly finds its entry into early English legal and textual culture via a recognition of the significance of language choice. Arendse Lund proposes that the term *cynescipe* ("royal dignity") be added to the list of Winchester vocabulary favored by Æthelwold and his circle. The spread of this term, itself revealing of medieval ideas of kingship, is traced from legal to non-legal texts in tenth- and eleventh-century England, and is shown to be tied to the influence of scribal communities and the role of monastic centers in the tenth century. Æthelwold is the decisive force here: argued to be involved in the production of the legislative texts under Edgar in which *cynescipe* makes its earliest appearances, he is also implicated in the development of the term beyond its legal role. In the hands of Ælfric (educated in Æthelwold's school), the term links kingship and divine will – a sense that was later to be exploited by Wulfstan. The short life of *cynescipe* shows the composers of codes and narratives working to establish and fix a foundational definition of royal authority. The authoritative connotations of the term, and its divine underpinnings, are developed and reinforced in literary text via aesthetic means: stylistic choices buttress the authority of the language. But the authorizing power of such literary device is also to be found in legal text. In Chapter 3, the rhetorical properties of the charter reveal the role of aesthetic factors in the legitimation of legal documents, while also helping the critic to uncover the detail of their compositional history. Scott T. Smith's close examination of the literary and rhetorical display of Sawyer 404 shows the charter to be a multivocal text, the product of several diplomatic traditions. His analysis reveals the richly rhetorical nature of charter composition, enables the reconstruction of a complex history of composition, and offers insight into the process by which charters could be constructed to assert through their language an artistic and documentary legitimacy. Artful prose rhythms and prominent alliteration (among many other devices) imbue the charter with literary showmanship even as they shape its meaning; this dense but deliberate ornamentation emphatically asserts its association with diplomatic tradition, and thereby proclaims its legal legitimacy.

Legal procedure is at the heart of the shared discourses of law and literature explored in the final chapters in this first group. In Chapter 4, Anya Adair examines early English legal texts for the procedural application of reasoning based on what would in modern law be classified as circumstantial evidence. Laws that interest themselves in corpse-hiding, cattle tracking, late-night traveling and the fattening of pigs disclose a consistent legal interest in the process of interpreting physical evidence.

This same process is found in *Beowulf*, where Grendel's depredations give rise to a similar application of reasoning, logic, and imagination to material evidence. Across the Old English corpus, bodies, blood, tracks, and texts are read for what they might reveal of things not seen: an application as productive of drama in poetry as it is determinative of legal action at law. The interpretation of signs is also at the heart of a more visible probative procedure in early English law: the ordeal. In Chapter 5, Andrew Rabin examines the ordeal through the narrative offered by Lantfred's late tenth-century hagiography, *Miracula s. Swithuni*. Ordeals, and the literary narratives that recorded their application, are shown to reaffirm communal norms through the interplay of their ritual performativity and interpretive flexibility. Legal narrative emerges as an important factor in shaping readers' memories of legal events, their views of the legitimacy of the legal authority that sanctioned them, and the communal legal norms that underpin the whole. Lantfred's narrative dramatizes an unfair example of the ordeal of hot iron: the potential for multiple interpretations of the resulting wound is at the heart of the miraculous intervention that follows. In recounting a violation of legal norms followed by their (divine) reinstatement, the narrative offers a strong confirmation of the legitimacy of the ordeal: divine intervention agrees with the norms of the community's legal customs. In this miracle narrative, as in the texts of the foregoing chapters, legal authority and legal legitimacy emerge from a normative alliance of law and literature.

In the second part of the volume, contributors touch more conspicuously on the dynamics of cultural change and renovation to demonstrate some of the ways in which literary and legal imperatives may be ordered or reconciled. Textual innovation and legal aspiration produce normative renewals as law and literature come together in new ways to reinforce old precepts, as new political hopes are presented through a rhetoric of tradition, and as ritual and rhetorical invention work to establish a new normal. In Chapter 6, Kristen Carella examines the textual detail and compositional strategies of the *Legatine Capitulary* of 786. Placing this legal text in its literary and cultural context reveals the degree to which it incorporates the language and techniques of preaching. Alcuin (identified as author or influencer of the text) is seen here to reimagine the genre of the capitulary – a transformation that was to influence the broader capitulary tradition and help to articulate the sweeping cultural reforms of the Carolingian *Renovatio*. The *Legatine Capitulary* is shown to stand both as a Northumbrian legislative production with a local English legal focus, and as an early test for the mode of writing and process of legislating that Alcuin was to develop on the continent. The modification of generic convention is also a focus in Chapter 7: Nicole Marafioti shows how tenth-century royal coronation rites were reconstructed to claim a certain kind of legal force. The obligations their performance seeks to impose upon kings codify essentially legal precepts in liturgical form. The new version of the coronation *ordo* that emerged in the late ninth or early tenth century is argued here to be a liturgical expression of political ideology, articulated by churchmen who were closely involved with royal governance: Christian rhetoric deployed in support of royal political goals exemplifies the (claimed) ideological alignment between the new king and his ecclesiastical advisors.

Following the human figures who are active players in the legal system can offer new insight into legal culture and textual production. Examining royal officials as legal entities and as narrative subjects in codes, charters, and the writings of Wulfstan reveals that in a changing legal and political landscape, the role of such officials is at once pivotal and contested. In Chapter 8, Mary Elizabeth Blanchard traces the figure of the ealdorman through both law codes and the narratives that emerge from "dispute charters"; the two text-types – ostensibly representing the same legal system – reveal contradictory pictures of this important figure. As legal texts, dispute charters stand between the formality of legislation and the license of literary narrative, and their (often partisan) chronicling of legal reality emerges as crucial to a fuller understanding of the early English legal landscape. From a critical perspective, the comparison of code and charter shows that the at times one-dimensional ideal of legal culture depicted in the law codes is usefully augmented by the more dynamic picture that emerges from the land disputes of the charters. In Chapter 9, Chelsea Shields-Más demonstrates that Wulfstan's vision of reform paid particular attention to the work of royal officials. In the centralization of these officials (and especially of the secular figure of the reeve) can be seen not only the archbishop's recognition of the importance of secular figures to the support of the Church within a "Holy Society," but the varied legal and literary means by which Wulfstan sought to realize his vision. The new niche Wulfstan carves for the reeve in his mission to create and uphold the Christian kingdom he envisaged for the English is articulated via persuasions, exhortations, and regulations that make full use of legal and literary modes.

Literary expressions of legal precepts and prohibitions are at the center of narratives and admonitions respecting validity and veracity in the final two chapters of the volume. Here, the texts themselves can prove untrustworthy witnesses: the errors of the holy are hidden by narrative art, and denunciations of human dishonesty reach for a rhetorical and authorial artifice that itself strays close to practical deception. In Chapter 10, Stefan Jurasinski finds a literary response to rebaptism (a practice that ecclesiastical authorities of the early eighth century were concerned to forbid) in a narrative episode in *Felix's Life of Saint Guthlac*. Read in the light of their legal and spiritual setting, Felix's linguistic and narrative choices suggest a conscious effort to camouflage Guthlac's apparent contraventions of ecclesiastical law. In his departure from the traditions of his genre we catch a glimpse of the tensions between secular and regular clergy manifest in the conciliar legislation of the period. Literary narrative here reveals an ability to lend the appearance of lawfulness to certain acts that legislation expressly forbids – or at least to articulate them in such a way as to obscure their departure from accepted communal norms. And finally, in Chapter 11 Sherif Abdelkarim opens many avenues of interpretation and analysis in his examination of hypocrisy across the homiletic, legal, and hagiographic traditions in early English. Here again, both narrative and normative texts work to influence behavior in public life. The treatment of hypocrisy in the writing of Ælfric and Wulfstan reveals some of the means by which these authors attempted to imagine into existence a society that fulfilled God's work through the rule of law, and how they strove to indoctrinate and reform that society. These spiritual legislators, it would seem, find the literary mode as amenable as the legal to this work of reform. At the same time, examining hypocrisy (particularly in the homilies) reveals nuanced and not always positive attitudes to the uses and abuses of law. Hypocrisy offers a site of interpretive and critical openings, rather than closure. Anxieties about the truth and its right expression arise here with particular and pointed emphasis at the intersection of the spiritual and the secular, individual ethics and collective norms, and the legal and the literary.

Implicit in the arguments of the chapters in this volume, and in the details of the preceding discussion of the prose of the early laws, of Wulfstan, Bede, and Ælfric, of the poet of *Guthlac* and the anonymous composers of wills and charters, is the use made by both legal and literary authors of their common medium: a flexible, responsive, and variously rhetorical language. In the line from Montaigne's *Apology* that opens this introduction, the author writes (rather dismissively, in his own context) of "certaine lawfull fictions" upon which the law "groundeth the truth" of its justice. The verb is apposite – the mythic foundation of law's authority is born of a collusion of law and literature; and in the fictions and artifices of their ongoing interaction, law's legitimacy is constantly renewed. The lawful and literary facts and fictions explored here speak to the normative forces they set in motion, and to the productivity of a perspective that examines legal text through the eyes of the literary critic, and literary text from the perspective of the legal historian. Indeed, as so many of the chapters reveal, neither perspective alone can fully account for the form and development of either genre: a view from the bridges that unite them often provides the best prospect. Ultimately, what is most productively shared in the relationship between law and literature is perhaps a certain attitude toward language, an awareness of its potency to reflect and transform experience, and an appreciation of the role of the writer in guiding the interpretation of the legal: as normative, as legitimate, as authoritative.

PART I

LAW AND LITERATURE: NORMATIVE ALLIANCES

1

The Alfredian Prose Psalms and a Legal English Identity[1]

Jay Paul Gates

The Old English prose translation of the first fifty Psalms survives only in the manuscript Paris, Bibliothèque nationale de France, MS fonds latin 8824,[2] known as the Paris Psalter. The text has been attributed to the translation project that appears to have been foundational to King Alfred's larger educational agenda to ensure that the nobility were able to read English, that clergy knew Latin, and that civil and ecclesiastical office-holders considered themselves to be doing divine service in upholding law and suppressing sin.[3] However, the prose Psalms have received limited scholarly attention, often being eclipsed by the poetic translation of the Psalms.[4] What scholarship exists has been focused largely on issues of vocabulary and translation, on manuscript studies, or on the relationship of the Psalms in English to the larger place of the Psalms and the liturgy in early England.[5] Yet the prose Psalms deserve attention for how they

1 The author would like to thank Drs Nicole Marafioti, Brian O'Camb, Adrian Papahagi, Andrew Rabin, and Anya Adair for their feedback on earlier drafts of this paper.

2 A digital facsimile of the manuscript is available at https://gallica.bnf.fr/ark:/12148/btv1b8451636f.image. Throughout this paper, all references to the Romanum version of the Psalms, from which the Old English translation works, will be to the Latin text of the manuscript.

3 David Pratt, *The Political Thought of King Alfred the Great* (Cambridge: Cambridge University Press, 2007), 115 and 133–35. Asser concludes his Life of King Alfred with a commentary on the king's insistence that his judges be informed and make wise and just judgments, as Alfred himself would. If a judge were to be found wanting and refused to learn what was just, Alfred would remove him from his office. William Henry Stevenson, ed., *Asser's Life of King Alfred* (Oxford: Clarendon, 1959), c. 106.

4 E.g. Evert Wiesenekker, *Word be worde, andgit of andgite: Translation Performance in the Old English Interlinear Glosses of the Vespasian, Regius and Lambeth Psalters* (Huizen: Drukkerij J. Bout & Zn., 1991); Elisa Miller Mangina, "Selfhood and the Psalms: The First-Person Voice in Old English Poetry" (PhD diss., Cornell University, 2002). The major exception to this is M. J. Toswell, *The Anglo-Saxon Psalter* (Turnhout: Brepols, 2014).

5 John D. Tinkler, *Vocabulary and Syntax of the Old English Version in the Paris*

work with Alfred's laws to participate in establishing a vocabulary that connects English law in the reign of Alfred to Scripture, and for how they offer a model ideology of Christian English kingship.

Bringing together the only two Alfredian texts that directly translate Scripture and that are roughly contemporary, I argue that the prose Psalms and the prologue to Alfred's laws are key texts in Alfred's educational project. These two texts merit discussion together not only because they both make use of biblical translation, but also because reading them in tandem sheds light on Alfred's educational agenda. I explore the ways that they use Old Testament kings as models of kingship and textual authority, the common structural logic of the introductions to the Psalms and the prologue to the laws, and similarities of vocabulary choice in the two texts' translations from Latin to English. On this basis, I demonstrate their shared concerns with law, judges, identification with the king, and a sense of belonging to a common people. Moreover, the two texts would have functioned as guides for English nobles who would have been the beneficiaries of Alfred's educational agenda in how to think about their own roles as leaders in the face of foreign invasion and as judges under West Saxon hegemony.

Alfred's preface to the Old English translation of Gregory the Great's *Pastoral Care* has commonly been read as a statement of the guiding concerns and principles of Alfred's educational program and it offers a framework for the consideration of Alfredian texts. In the preface, Alfred invokes a past in which his predecessors were learned and moral, and the nation prospered:

> þæt me com suiðe oft on gemynd, hwelce wutan gio wæron geond Angelkynn, ægðer ge godcundra hadas age woruldcundra; 7 hu gesæliglica a tida þa wæron geond Angelcynn; 7 hu þa kyningas þe ðone anwald hæfdon ðæs folces Gode 7 his ærendwrecum hirsumedon; 7 hu hi ægðer ge hiora sibbe ge hiora sido ge hiora anwald innanbordes gehioldon, 7 eac ut hiora oeðel rymdon; 7 hu him ða speow ægðer ge mid wige ge mid wisdome; 7 eac ða godcundan hadas hu georne hie wæron ægðer ge ymb lare ge ymb leornunga, 7 ymb ealle þa ðeowutdomas þe hie Gode don sceoldon; 7 hu mon utanbordes wisdom 7 lare hider on lond sohte, 7 hu we hi nu sceoldon ute begietan gif we hie habban sceoldon.[6]

Psalter: A Critical Commentary (The Hague: Mouton, 1971); Frank-Günter Berghaus, *Die Verwandtschaftsverhältnisse der altenglischen Interlinearversionen des Psalters und der Cantica* (Göttingen: Vandenhoeck & Ruprecht, 1979); George H. Brown, "The Psalms as the Foundation of Anglo-Saxon Learning," in *The Place of the Psalms in the Intellectual Culture of the Middle Ages*, ed. Nancy Van Deusen (Albany: State University Press of New York, 1999), 1–24; Toswell, *The Anglo-Saxon Psalter*.

6 Henry Sweet, ed., *King Alfred's West-Saxon Version of Gregory's Pastoral Care*,

> It has often come to my mind what wise men there were formerly throughout the English people, both in sacred and in secular orders; and how the kings who had rule over the people in those days were obedient to God and his messengers, and both maintained their peace and their morality and their authority at home, and also enlarged their territory abroad; and how they prospered both in warfare and in wisdom; and also how zealous the sacred orders were both about teaching and about learning and all the services which they had to perform for God; and how men from abroad came here to this land in search of knowledge and instruction.[7]

It is noteworthy that Alfred's remarks, addressed to his bishops, focus not on the English people but on their religious and secular leaders, and on the kings who ruled them. The phrasing in this passage is both subtle and apparently intentionally vague in certain respects that advance the argument. The presumably disparate peoples are unified under a single term (*Angelkynn*), and whether the text refers to the multiple English kingdoms or imposes the English kingdom under West Saxon hegemony backwards, it provides the impression of a kingdom by referring merely to the rule of kings within and without their borders (*innanbordes/utanbordes*). Since the leaders and kings were learned and moral, the people prospered and the kingdom expanded, the clergy were eager to learn and to teach, and those desiring wisdom were drawn to England. The model presented is one of people unified within a single kingdom, inspired by wise, moral, and, therefore, effective kings. This corresponds with Susan Reynolds's description of the early medieval understanding of a world "as divided into 'peoples' (*gentes, nationes, populi*) of common biological descent and culture who normally and naturally formed separate political units." Likewise, Sarah Foot suggests that "King Alfred might be credited with the invention of the English as a political community."[8] The preface gives the common name *Angelkynn* to the people he is discussing, but it also describes that people as politically unified and successful because of their leaders' wisdom and adherence to God. Alfred continues in a later passage:

> Ða gemunde ic hu sio æ wæs ærest on Ebreisc geðiode funden, 7 eft, þa þa hie Crecas geleornodon, þa wendon hi hie on hiora ægen geðiode ealle, 7 eac oðre bec. And eft Lædenware swa same, siððan hi hie geleornodon, hi hie wendon ealla ðurh wise wealhstodas on hiroa agen

---

Part I, EETS, o.s. 45 (London: Oxford University Press, 1871), 1–6.

7 Michael Swanton, trans., "Preface to Gregory's *Pastoral Care*," in *Anglo-Saxon Prose* (London: Dent, 1975), 30–32.

8 Susan Reynolds, "What Do We Mean by 'Anglo-Saxon' and 'Anglo-Saxons'?" *Journal of British Studies* 4 (1985): 399; Sarah Foot, "The Making of *Angelcynn*: English Identity before the Norman Conquest," *TRHS*, 6th series, 6 (1995): 25.

geðeode. 7 eac ealla oðra Cristena ðioda sumne dæl hiora on hiora agen geðiode wendon. Forðy me ðyncð betre, gif iow swa ðyncð, þæt we eac suma bec, ða þe niedbeðyrfesta sien eallum monnum to witanne, þæt we þa on ðæt geðeode wenden þe we ealle gecnawan mægen, 7 ge don swa we swiðe eaðe magon mid Godes fultume, gif we þa stilnesse habbað, ðætte eal sio gioguð þe nu is on Angel kynne friora monna, þara þe þa speda hæbben þæt hie ðæm befeolan mægen, sien to leornunga oðfæste, þa hwile þe hi to nanre oðerre note ne mægen, oð ðone first þe hie wel cunnen Englisc gewrit arædan: lære mon siððan furður on Lædengeðeode þa þe mon furðor læran wille 7 to hierran hade don wille.

Then I remembered how the law was first found in the Hebrew language, and afterwards, when the Greeks learned it, they translated it all into their own language, and all the other books as well. And afterwards in the same way the Romans, when they had learned them, they translated them all into their own language through learned interpreters. And all other Christian nations also translated some part of them into their own language. Therefore it seems better to me, if it seems so to you, that we also should translate certain books which are most necessary for all men to know, into the language that we can all understand, and also arrange it, as with God's help we very easily can if we have peace, so that all the youth of free men now among the English people, who have the means to be able to devote themselves to it, may be set to study for as long as they are of no other use, until the time they are able to read English writing well; afterwards one may teach further in the Latin language those whom one wishes to teach further and wishes to promote to holy orders.

In this, Alfred presents himself as a king who wishes to return to the model of his good predecessors and, in so doing, establishes an English cultural model rooted in textual authority. Martin Irvine observes that Alfred was not the first to do this. The Carolingians had advanced an ideological framework for Christian kingship, "guaranteeing the cultural work performed by *grammatica* and its related institutions was understood to be the responsibility of Christian rulers who authorized the written products of that culture as images of *imperium* and *auctoritas*."[9] Yet, Irvine reads Alfred as building on the Carolingian model and contributing something new: national identity came to encompass "learning, literacy, language, and literature," and without troubling either Irvine's argument or his alliteration, we may justly add "law."[10] Indeed, Stefan Jurasinski and Lisi Oliver make clear that, in its "unapologetic

[9] Martin Irvine, *The Making of Textual Culture: "Grammatica" and Literary Theory, 350–1100* (Cambridge: Cambridge University Press, 1994), 415–16.

[10] Irvine, *Making of Textual Culture*, 416. Cf. Pratt, *Political Thought*, esp. Chapter 8;

treatment of laws *as texts* and its deliberate arrangement of them into a historical framework" Alfred's *domboc* "is the first English legislative statement to present law as primarily something to be learned from books and to suggest that it may not be adequately grasped without some depth of historical knowledge."[11] Further, Kathleen Davis has discussed the passage from the *Preface* as presenting the translation of Christian texts as bound to the "emergence of Christian peoples," and the development of a vernacular literature as evidence for a national identity.[12] "Alfred was king only of the West Saxons, yet throughout the *Preface* he presupposes a nation in which many political kingdoms become *Angelcynn*, and all its inhabitants speak *Englisc*."[13] And as Sarah Foot has observed, it is the very naming of the common political community that provides the people with a way to think about themselves as unified.[14] The preface thus ties together the peoples of the English kingdoms under the unifying name *Angelkynn*, provides a narrative of a common Christian identity, and suggests a foundation for a national identity in the translation of Latin texts into a vernacular canon. Or, as Davis puts it, "it is in the communication between the real and the ideal that the perception of the nation emerges."[15]

The extant texts that comprise the Alfredian corpus have frequently been divided by scholars into two groups, although reading such a firm split between them obscures the Alfredian innovation that Irvine argues for. The first group is a series of translations that have traditionally been taken as supporting Alfred's educational agenda: the *Pastoral Care* and *Dialogues* of Gregory the Great, Boethius' *Consolation of Philosophy*, the *Soliloquies* of Augustine, the *Orosius*, and the prose Psalms. The second group is comprised of Alfred's laws and the "common stock" of the Anglo-Saxon Chronicle, which have been read as oriented toward practical rule, legitimation, and nation-building.[16] Although the translations

---

Todd Preston, *King Alfred's Book of Laws: A Study of the Domboc and its Influence on English Identity, with a Complete Translation* (Jefferson, NC: McFarland, 2012), 18–33.

11 Stefan Jurasinski and Lisi Oliver, eds., *The Laws of Alfred: The Domboc and the Making of Anglo-Saxon Law* (Cambridge: Cambridge University Press, 2021), 7–8.

12 Kathleen Davis, "National Writing in the Ninth Century: A Reminder for Postcolonial Thinking about the Nation," *Journal of Medieval and Early Modern Studies* 28 (1998): 615.

13 Ibid., 617.

14 Foot, "The Making of *Angelcynn*," 25–26.

15 Davis, "National Writing in the Ninth Century," 619.

16 Thomas A. Bredehoft, *Textual Histories: Readings in the Anglo-Saxon Chronicle* (Toronto: University of Toronto Press, 2001), 1–13 and 30–60; Barbara Yorke, "The Representation of Early West Saxon History in the Anglo-Saxon Chronicle," *Reading the Anglo-Saxon Chronicle: Language, Literature, History*, ed.

were almost certainly not the work of Alfred himself, we can reasonably associate them with a common Alfredian project since they present Alfred as a guiding force and a learned figure to emulate in pursuit of wisdom.[17] Yet, however much these texts make Alfred a central figure to be emulated, Daniel Anlezark has argued that the texts that we refer to as Alfredian can hardly be taken as what the preface to the *Pastoral Care* calls "books which are most necessary for all men to know."[18] He suggests that we have misread Alfred's meaning because we have tended to attribute to his educational project the texts that are extant in his name. Rather, Anlezark argues persuasively that what Alfred must have been referring to were the books of Scripture rather than the seemingly random collection of texts that have come down to us.[19] However, Anlezark does not consider the place of Alfred's law code in this project of scriptural translation, though, as Matthew Gillis has observed, the prologue makes extensive use of Scripture, translating and adapting significant selections from the Old Testament book of

---

Alice Jorgensen (Turnhout: Brepols, 2010), 141–59; Kenneth Sisam, "The West Saxon Royal Genealogies," *Proceedings of the British Academy* 39 (1953): 287–348.

17 Pratt, *Political Thought*, 116. Patrick Wormald points out that peculiarities of language indicate that the *Pastoral Care, Consolation, Soliloquies,* and Psalms were "products of the same mind," and all but the Psalms declare Alfred as their author: Wormald, *Making of English Law*, 273. As such, I refer to Alfred and his agency as stated or implied in the texts throughout this chapter as a shorthand for the more complicated relationship of Alfred to the texts. On which texts are Alfred's or Alfredian there continues to be much dispute. Malcolm Godden considers Alfred's role in these texts to have been very limited."Did King Alfred Write Anything?" *Medium Ævum* 76 (2007): 18. Janet Bately maintains that "there was one mind at work (though probably never entirely on its own)" guiding the *Pastoral Care, Consolation, Soliloquies,* and *Psalms,* and that it was Alfred's. "Alfred as Author and Translator," *A Companion to Alfred the Great,* ed. Nicole G. Discenza and Paul E. Szarmach (Leiden: Brill, 2015), 111–42. Susan Irvine holds more to the middle ground, focusing on the rhetorical effects of first-person pronouns in her examination of the prefaces and epilogues of the Alfredian texts: "Uncertain Beginnings: The Prefatory Tradition in Old English," *H.M. Chadwick Memorial Lectures* 27 (2017): 17–18.

18 Daniel Anlezark, "Which Books are 'Most Necessary' to Know? The Old English *Pastoral Care* Preface and King Alfred's Educational Reform," *English Studies* 98 (2017): 760.

19 There is no question that Gregory the Great was of primary importance to Alfred and that he was a model for the pursuit of wisdom and for good rulership. Pratt has discussed at length the importance of Gregory as a model for Alfred and one he wished both his clergy and his nobles to follow: *Political Thought,* 134–50 and 193–213. That the prose Psalms and the *Pastoral Care* appear to have been written by the same person offers reasonable grounds for considering them, based on the preface to the *Pastoral Care,* as among "those texts most necessary for men to know."

Exodus, as well as from the Gospel of Matthew and the Acts of the Apostles.[20] Although the scriptural source material of the laws has long been recognized, the particular value of Gillis's point is to draw the laws into Anlezark's discussion of the texts Alfred intended to include in his educational project.[21] Indeed, the prologue follows much the same narrative of translation of the law that was advanced in his preface to the Old English *Pastoral Care*. Therefore, working from Anlezark's conclusion that the texts Alfred intended were books of Scripture, I take the prose Psalms and the prologue to Alfred's laws as representations of the Alfredian educational program. They are written in different genres but should be read as two sides of the same coin. Moreover, recognizing their common project, we may more firmly unify the unnecessarily divided Alfredian canon.

The prose Psalms and Alfred's laws are roughly contemporary. They were likely produced in the 890s, the final decade of Alfred's reign, although the translation of the Psalms was probably produced first. However, the extant copies are both somewhat removed from Alfred. The prose Psalms appear in the Paris Psalter, a manuscript dating to the mid eleventh century. The laws are recorded in some form in ten manuscripts, produced between the second quarter of the tenth century and the second quarter of the twelfth.[22] Since the earliest extant versions of the prose Psalms and the laws were copied at least a quarter of a century after Alfred's reign, we are limited in what we can say about the texts based on their manuscript presentation, and must focus instead on the texts themselves and the features they seem to share.

Although the Psalms and the laws have been read as both participating in the promotion of biblical wisdom, they have not received sustained comparison.[23] It has been widely observed that Alfred looked to Old

[20] Matthew Gillis, "Legal Traditions, Manuscripts of Law, and Influences on King Alfred's *Domboc*," (presentation at the Books of Law in the Very Long Tenth Century conference, Vienna, Austria, September 5, 2019), to be published in *Books of Law in the Long Tenth Century*, ed. Thom Gobbitt (Binghamton: Gracchi Books).

[21] Milton Haight Turk, *The Legal Code of Ælfred the Great* (Halle: Max Niemeyer, 1893), 30–40; Wormald, *Making of English Law*, 277–85; Preston, *King Alfred's Book of Laws*, 18–30. For a full discussion of the likely sources for Alfred's laws, see Jurasinski and Oliver, *The Laws of Alfred*, 41–77.

[22] Wormald, *Making of English Law*, 265. For a full discussion of the manuscript witnesses and the subsequent reception of Alfred's laws, see Jurasinski and Oliver, *Laws of Alfred*, 113–74.

[23] Pratt groups the prose Psalms and Alfred's laws as participating in a Solomonic language and their sources, the Psalter and Exodus, as participating in biblical associations between wisdom and law, but his interests are largely in how Alfredian thought was influenced by early medieval commentary on kingship. *Political Thought*, 157–65.

Testament kings as models of wisdom, and that the texts of his reign associate him with these kings, particularly with Solomon, David, and, although not properly a king, Moses.[24] The common invocation of Old Testament models to create a textual authority for Alfred's rule aligns the king with those moral and effective royal predecessors he refers to in the preface to the *Pastoral Care*, but it also offers a model for moral instruction for an audience that shows them their relationship to their king and the divine role of his office. Moreover, Sarah Foot clearly describes the rhetorical thrust of Alfred's use of the Old Testament in his preface to define a common English people:[25]

> He was showing the Anglo-Saxons how similar their laws were to those of Ancient Israel and also inviting them to remodel themselves as a new Chosen People. Bede had conceived of the *gens Anglorum* as the new Israel, but Alfred went further: he purported to restore a state that had formerly existed, equivalent to the state of Israel restored after the Babylonian captivity, not to create a new unitary structure of diverse peoples brought together under one Christian law.

Foot's reading of the preface in relation to Israel after the Babylonian captivity is also suggestive, then, of why we should read it in relation to the Psalms.

Both the prose Psalms and Alfred's laws have prefatory material that frames the texts in relation to Old Testament figures and Christian history. Moreover, both texts seem to show evidence of Irish influence that may indicate a common intellectual milieu. As Kristen Carella has argued concerning Alfred's use of Irish source material to shape his thought in the prose Psalms and the prologue to his laws, "Alfred not only understood the ideas he found in Hiberno-Latin texts, but was willing to adapt and apply them to English texts in order to facilitate his own agenda."[26] The

[24] Paul J. E. Kershaw, *Peaceful Kings: Peace, Power, and the Early Medieval Political Imagination* (Oxford: Oxford University Press, 2011), 260; Pratt, *Political Thought*, 214 and 242; Toswell, *Anglo-Saxon Psalter*, 66; Preston, *King Alfred's Book of Laws*, 18.

[25] Although the text of the prose Psalms never names Alfred as their translator, and although the earliest association of Alfred with the prose Psalms that we have comes from William of Malmesbury, there is sufficient evidence in the common approaches across the prose Psalms and the other Alfredian texts that their original audience would have understood them as emanating from Alfred's court. Patrick P. O'Neill, *King Alfred's Old English Prose Translation of the First Fifty Psalms* (Cambridge, MA: Medieval Academy of America, 2001), 73–96.

[26] Bryan Carella [who now publishes as Kristen Carella], "Evidence for Hiberno-Latin Thought in the Prologue to the Laws of Alfred," *Studies in Philology* 108 (2011): 19. See also Carella, "The Source of the Prologue to the Laws of Alfred," *Peritia* 19 (2005): 91–118.

Paris Psalter presents Psalms 2–50 with unusual introductions that put the Psalm into David's mouth and explain how that Psalm was and will be relevant to subsequent audiences.[27] While the Psalms were frequently accompanied by commentary, the Alfredian prose Psalms are introduced by a model of interpretation influenced especially by Cassiodorus and Theodore of Mopsuestia's commentaries.[28] Although Theodore's work had been declared heretical long before the Old English prose Psalms were produced, it was still in common use in Ireland. This model emphasized literal and historical interpretations over allegorical and the prose Psalms largely adhere to it. "Fifteen have a three-fold scheme and four others have only one interpretation," though, as Patrick O'Neill observes, "these are not exceptions but accommodations of the composer to reconcile the four-fold scheme with his main source."[29] Every introduction begins with a Davidic reading: "David sang this Psalm…" Thirty-two interpret the Psalm according to a later biblical historical event, the vast majority (thirty) focusing on Hezekiah, the Babylonian captivity, or Maccabees, which the historical figure experiences or is prophesied by David to experience in the way that David did when he sang the Psalm. Forty-three offer an interpretation or prophecy of how everyone or *ælc rihtwis*, "every just/righteous" person or *ælc cristen*, "every Christian" will sing the Psalm when having a comparable experience to David's when he sang it. Forty-two relate the Psalm to how Christ sang the Psalm when persecuted by the Jews.[30]

On their own, the Latin Psalms already held expansive significance in Anglo-Saxon England. M. J. Toswell explains:

> Oblates learned the psalter for two reasons: it taught the basic rules and methods of devotion to God, and also provided the rudiments of Latin grammar and syntax. As prophecy, the psalter was first of all a prefiguration in the Old Testament of Christ's coming, and thereby an allegorical text of the greatest significance, the greatest guide for correct living. Moreover, as the reported work of David—the prophet king, psalmist, and direct ancestor of Christ—the psalms had great cumulative authority, even regnal authority, as words of praise and prophecy. In Anglo-Saxon England, this cumulative authority appears to have been especially significant, for the royal genealogies by the time of King Alfred include David (and his descendant Christ by implication) as a direct ancestor to the present king. The words Christ spoke to God were

27 Presumably, Psalm 1 originally had an introduction that has since been lost.

28 O'Neill, *Alfred's Old English Translation*, 23–44, esp. 34–40 for a full list of commentary sources.

29 Ibid., 24.

30 Two examples diverge slightly from this pattern, putting the Psalm into the mouths of the Apostles about Christ: Psalms 19 and 22.

> therefore the words of his own ancestor, the psalmist and king, David, whose image very commonly appears at the beginning of Anglo-Saxon psalter manuscripts.[31]

The value of fourfold interpretation added as introductions to the Old English prose Psalms lay in making the direct connection between the Psalm's meaning for contemporaries and original Davidic circumstances. Emily Butler states that "it seems likely that the Old English introductions were designed to encourage empathy and even identification with the Old Testament-era Israelites, as well as with Christ himself."[32] As Pratt makes clear, Alfred's authority came from his presence; the texts were a direct extension of his person and acted as a kind of performance of the royal presence beyond the court.[33] If we assume the prose Psalms are a product of the Alfredian court, they may be taken as a royal performance. As such, they tie the person of Alfred to biblical kings for readers through their historically inflected frames, which invite English audiences to read their own present experiences in relation to the biblical contexts provided by the introductions.[34] In the case of a late ninth-century English audience, it would not be difficult to compare their experience of Scandinavian invasion (and in the case of Mercia, conquest) with the enemies David faced or with the Babylonian captivity, and would, in fact, be an easy point of entry into the kind of reading the prose Psalms invite. By introducing the experience first of David, with whom Alfred associated himself, and then of Hezekiah (or another biblical king), before invoking the individual Christian, the audience is invited to imagine themselves as historical subjects of two biblical kings and, consequently, to invest themselves in their own king. Never do the prose Psalms explicitly compare David and Alfred; never do they draw an overt connection between a specific contemporary event and biblical history; never is the audience addressed directly. Rather, the translation builds on the Psalms as a foundational Christian text, as the primary educational text for a religious audience,[35] as a guide for correct living,[36] and as an expression of collective identity.[37] Translated into English and provided with a (generally) fourfold historical introduction, the prose

31 Toswell, *Anglo-Saxon Psalter*, 8.

32 Emily Butler, "The Role of the Compiler in the Paris Psalter," *English Studies* 98 (2017): 30.

33 Pratt, *Political Thought*, 171.

34 Ibid., 251.

35 Brown, "Psalms as the Foundation"; Susan Gillingham, *Psalms Through the Centuries: Volume One* (Malden: Wiley-Blackwell, 2012), 53.

36 Toswell, *Anglo-Saxon Psalter*, 8.

37 Helen Appleton and Francis Leneghan, "The Psalms in Anglo-Saxon and Anglo-Norman England," *English Studies* 98 (2017): 1.

Psalms exploit the audience's familiarity with them and their authoritative status to nudge them toward identification with a collective English identity and acceptance of (presumably) Alfred's kingship. As such, the prose Psalms are integral to the Alfredian educational program: the audience must read to understand, interpret, and expand knowledge and faith in order to prosper as a nation.[38]

In the pages that follow, I focus on the first of the prose Psalms with an introduction: Psalm 2. This psalm is exemplary of the prose Psalms project because it acts as the introduction to the text. The introduction to Psalm 2 is tripartite and reads:

> Ðæs æfteran sealmes capitul is gecweden "Psalmus Dauid," þæt ys on Englisc, "Dauides sealm," for þæm he is hys sealm gecweden for þi he seofode on þæm sealme and mænde to Drihtne be his feondum, ægðder ge inlendum ge utlendum, and be eallum his earfoðum; and swa deð ælc þæra þe þysne sealm sincgð be his sylfes feondum; and swa dyde Crist be Iudeum.[39]

> The second Psalm's heading is entitled "Psalmus Dauid," that is in English, "David's Psalm," and it is called his Psalm because he lamented in the Psalm and complained to God about his enemies, domestic and foreign, and about all his difficulties; and everyone who recites this Psalm does likewise about his own enemies; and so did Christ about the Jews.[40]

Although the introduction here is only threefold, omitting a biblical historical king corresponding to David, it sets forth a clear theme according to which the Psalms will proceed and how they should be read: that is, the reader should focus on David as a historical king with enemies from

38 Susan Irvine has studied the prefaces and epilogues to the texts of the Alfredian corpus, arguing that they "exploit in a variety of ways the potential of the frame structure to justify and authorize the works themselves." "The Alfredian Prefaces and Epilogues," *A Companion to Alfred the Great*, ed. Nicole G. Discenza and Paul E. Szarmach (Leiden: Brill, 2015), 147. Cf. Susan Irvine, "Uncertain Beginnings." However, in her studies, Irvine omits discussion of the introductions to the prose Psalms. Drawing these introductions into the discussion enhances our understanding not only of how Scripture and scriptural commentary were used in the framing of the Alfredian texts and authorizing the Alfredian educational agenda, but of how the Psalms as the most fundamental of educational texts was provided with a guide that we can see carry across other texts, not least the prologue to Alfred's laws.

39 O'Neill, *Alfred's Old English Translation*, 100–01. All quotations of the prose Psalms are taken from this edition.

40 Translations of the prose Psalms are taken from Patrick P. O'Neill, ed. and trans., *The Old English Psalms* (Cambridge, MA: Harvard University Press, 2016).

within the kingdom and without; on how every subsequent singer of the Psalm follows David's example, albeit concerning his own enemies; and how Christ himself sang it when facing the Jews as enemies. In this, we can see the logical connections that M. J. Toswell identified. David is associated with Christ, and every singer of the Psalm is invited into the experience of the Psalm. Moreover, we can see the logic of Alfred's preface to the *Pastoral Care* playing out in the introduction to Psalm 2. In the preface, Alfred looks to his wise and learned predecessors as models for establishing peace and prosperity among the English, and he establishes a model of textual authority for the English people. In the introduction to Psalm 2, he looks to models of David as a wise king in a time of strife and invites his audience to view their own tribulations in light of David's, Christ's, and Alfred's. As such, Alfred provides biblical and English textual authority in support of a unified English identity.[41]

Similarly, the prologue to Alfred's laws follows a structure that is familiar from the preface to the Old English *Pastoral Care* and the introductions to the prose Psalms, but associates him with the Old Testament lawgiver, Moses. Opening with the statement *DRYHTEN WÆS SPRECENde ðas word to Moyse* ("The Lord was speaking these words to Moses"), it translates Exodus 20 23:13, with a few omissions and additions.[42] The prologue then shifts to

[41] Irvine, *Making of Textual Culture*, 416. Cf. Pratt, *Political Thought*, esp. Chapter 8; cf. Preston, *King Alfred's Book of Laws*, 18–33.

[42] Mosaic Prologue 1–48. All references to Alfred's and Ine's laws are taken from Jurasinski and Oliver, *The Laws of Alfred*. All references to the laws of Hlothere and Eadric and to those of Wihtred are taken from Lisi Oliver, *The Beginnings of English Law* (Toronto: University of Toronto Press, 2002). Where clausal numbering varies between these and that in Felix Liebermann, ed., *Die Gesetze der Angelsachsen*, 3 vols. (Halle: Max Niemeyer, 1903–16), Liebermann's numbering is included in brackets. All translations of the prologue are taken from Jay Paul Gates, "Prologue to the Laws of King Alfred: An Edition and Translation for Students," *The Heroic Age* 18 (2018) https://www.heroicage.org/issues/18/gates.php. Omissions include Exodus 20:4–6, 20:18–22, 23:5, 23:10–12. MP 39, which translates that flesh that wild beasts leave should be left for the dogs omits Exodus 22:31 *Viri sancti eritis mihi* ("You shall be holy men to me"). Additions or clarifications appear in the following clauses: MP 24 adds concerning one who steals an ox, *Gif he næbbe hwæt he selle, sie he self beboht wið ðam fio* ("If he does not have what he must give, he himself must be sold for the price"). MP 28 on entrusting property to a friend that is stolen, adds *Gif hit ðone cucu feoh wære, and he secgge, þæt hit here name oððe hit self acwæle ⁊ gewitnesse hæbbe, ne þearf he þæt geldan. Gif he ðonne gewitnesse næbbe, ⁊ he him ne getriewe swerige he þonne* ("However, if it was live cattle, and he says that an army took it or it died on its own, and he has a witness, he need not pay for that. But if he does not have a witness and he does not believe him, then let him swear"). MP 30 states *ða fæmnan þe gewuniað onfon gealdorcræftigan ⁊ scinlæcan ⁊ wiccan ne læt þu ða libban* ("Maidens who associate with or entertain enchanters and magicians and

the New Testament, with Christ asserting that he did not come to destroy the law but to fulfill it.[43] The prologue to the laws, however, adds a message of mercy: *7 mildheortnesse 7 eaðmodnesse he lærde* ("and he taught mild-heartedness and humbleness of spirit").[44] The transition from Old Testament law to Christ's commentary on his relationship to the law in Matthew 5:17 follows the logic both of the preface to the Old English *Pastoral Care,* in which law moved from the Hebrew language into the languages of Christian nations, and of the introductions to the prose Psalms, where David originally sang them but they became relevant to later Old Testament figures and then to Christians. The prologue follows Acts 15:23–29 in narrating the apostles' conversion of heathen peoples, their teaching of Christ's law, and the tempering of the strictures of Jewish law. It then provides a negative Golden Rule, which it declares the foundation of all judgments:

> and þæt ge willen, þæt oðre men eow ne don, ne doð ge ðæt oþrum monnum. Of ðissum anum dome mon mæg geðencean, þæt he æghwelcne on ryht gedemeð; ne ðearf he nanra domboca oþerra. Geðence he, þæt he nanum men ne deme þæt he nolde ðæt he him demde, gif he ðone dom ofer hine sohte.

> And what you wish other men not do to you, do not do that to other men. From this one law can one be mindful that he judge each justly. Nor does he need any other lawbooks. Let him remember that he should judge no man as he would not want himself to be judged by him if he sought judgement over him.[45]

Again, following the logic of both the preface to the Old English *Pastoral Care* and the introductions to the prose Psalms, the prologue to the laws narrates the teaching of the laws and Christ's mercy in Christian synods and their adoption by various nations, including the English.[46]

Finally, the prologue to the laws turns to Alfred gathering the laws of previous English kings, whether those of "Ine, my kinsman" or "Offa,

---

witches, do not let them live"). However, Exodus 22:18 merely states *Maleficos non patieris vivere* ("Wizards thou shalt not suffer to live"). MP 43 adds significant clarification to Exodus 23:6 *Non declinabis in iudicio pauperis* ("Thou shalt not go aside in the poor man's judgement"): *dem ðu swiðe emne. Ne dem ðu oðerne dom þam welegan oðerne ðam earman; ne oðerne þam liofran 7 oðerne þam laþran ne dem ðu* ("Judge very equally. Do not give one judgment for the rich and another for the poor, nor for one you love and one you loathe").

43 Matthew 5:17.

44 MP 49. On Alfred's introduction of a spirit of mercy into his laws, see Michael Treschow, "The Prologue to Alfred's Law Code: Instruction in the Spirit of Mercy," *Florilegium* 13 (1994), 79–110.

45 MP 49.5–6. This passage translates Matthew 7:1–2 and 12.

46 MP 49.7–8.

king of the Mercians," or "Æthelberht, who first among the English accepted baptism,"[47] and closes on Alfred's counselors approving the laws. Through this narrative, the prologue presents the movement of law and lawgiving from God to Moses, then to the Hebrew people, then to Christ and the Apostles, who spread the law, to the synods, and then to the English kingdoms. This is a tidy framing of a unified English legal history grounded in textual authority.

Therefore, there is a common logic guiding three texts associated with Alfred, two explicitly in his voice: the introduction to the Old English prose Psalms, the preface to the Old English *Pastoral Care*, and the prologue to the laws. The preface to the *Pastoral Care* grounds the law in its Old Testament Hebrew origins while the prose Psalms place the Psalms' origins in David's voice, and the prologue to the laws has the Lord speaking the laws to Moses. All three texts also demonstrate the translation and relevance of the texts to later contexts, particularly to Christian and English audiences.

Alfred's preface to the *Pastoral Care* invokes issues of law and translation, that law (æ) began in Hebrew and then was translated into Greek and subsequently into Latin. As such, he provides a place to begin thinking about legal vocabulary and how Alfredian texts draw together biblical and civil law.[48] The language of the prose Psalms is indicative of legal concerns as well. Although the biblical Psalms themselves use legalistic vocabulary, the translation choices very much align the prose Psalms with early English legal culture, especially Alfred's laws.

Prose Psalm 2 is presented alongside the *Romanum* text of the Psalm in the Paris Psalter:

47 Alfred Prol. 49.9. On Æthelberht's significance and Alfred's manipulation of historical narrative, see Jurasinski and Oliver, *King Alfred's Laws*, 3–40. Cf. Preston, *King Alfred's Book of Laws*, 29–31.

48 Nicole Marafioti argues that the laws proper, as distinct from the prologue, do not structurally pair divine and civil law in practice. "Crime and Sin in the Laws of Alfred," *Languages of the Law in Early Medieval England: Essays in Memory of Lisi Oliver*, ed. Stefan Jurasinski and Andrew Rabin (Leuven: Peeters, 2019), 59–84. However, the prologue's narrative of law-giving authority extending from God, the grounding of all legal judgment in the Golden Rule, and the sole requirement in the laws that the man imprisoned in the king's house complete forty nights and do the penance given him by the bishop give an overall impression that the audience should understand the two as operating in common.

Table 1.1. Psalm 2.

[1] Hwy ryð ælc folc, and hwi smeagað hi unnytt?	[1] Why does every nation rage, and why do they make futile plans?	[1] Quare fremuerun[t] gentes et populi meditati sunt inania?	[1] Why have the Gentiles raged, and the people devised vain things?
[2] And hwy arisað eorðcynincgas, and ealdormenn cumað tosomne wið Gode and wið þam þe he to hlaforde geceas and gesmyrede? Hi cweðað:	[2] And why do earth's kings rise up, and princes band together against God and him whom he chose and anointed as ruler? They declare:	[2] Adstiterunt reges terre et principes conven-erunt in unum adversus Dominum et adversus chris-tum eius:	[2] The kings of the earth stood up, and the princes met together, against the Lord and against his Christ.
[3] "Utan tobrecan heora bendas and aweorpan heora geocu of us."	[3] "Let us break asunder their fetters and cast off from us their yoke."	[3] "Disrumpamus vincula eorum et proiciamus a nobis iugum ipsorum."	[3] "Let us break their bonds asunder, and let us cast away their yoke from us."
[4] Hwæt forstent heora spræc (cwæð se witega) þeah hi swa cweðen, for þam se God þe on heofonum ys hig gehyspð, and Drihten hyg gescent;	[4] What use (said the prophet) is their declaration, delivered like this, since God in heaven will mock them, and the Lord will confound them;	[4] Qui habitat in celis inridebit eos et Dominus subsannabit eos.	[4] He that dwelleth in heaven shall laugh at them, and the Lord shall deride them.
[5] and he clypað to him on his yrre and gedrefð heora geþeaht.	[5] and he will shout at them in his anger, and upset their plans.	[5] Tunc loquetur ad eos in ira sua et in furore suo conturba[b]it[49] eos;	[5] Then shall he speak to them in his anger and trouble them in his rage.

[49] The MS here has *conturbauit*.

6 And ic eam, þeah, cincg geset fram Gode ofer his ðone halgan munt Syon to þam þæt ic lære his willan and his æ.	6 But I, however, am appointed by God king over Zion, that holy mountain of his, to teach his will and his law.	6 ego autem constitutus sum rex ab eo super Sion montem sanctum eius predicans preceptum Domini.	6 But I am appointed king by him over Zion, his holy mountain, preaching the Lord's commandment.
7 For þan cwæð Drihten to me: "Þu eart min sunu; nu todæg ic ðe acende.	7 Therefore the Lord said to me: "You are my son; see! today I have begotten you.	7 Dominus dixit ad me "filius meus es tu ego hodie genui te.	7 The Lord hath said to me, "Thou art my son. This day have I begotten thee.
8 Bide me, and ic þe sylle þeoda to agnum yrfe, and þinne anwald ic gebræde ofer ðeoda gemæro.	8 Ask me, and I will give you nations as your own inheritance, extending your dominion throughout the boundaries of the nations.	8 Postula a me et dabo tibi gentes hereditatem tuam et possessionem tuam terminos terre,	8 Ask of me, and I will give thee the Gentiles for thy inheritance and the utmost parts of the earth for thy possession.
9 And ic gedo þæt þu heora wylst mid isernre gyrde, and hi miht swa eaðe abrecan swa se croccwyrhta mæg ænne croccan."	9 And causing you to rule them with an iron rod and have the power to smash them into pieces as easily as a potter smashes a pitcher."	9 reges eos in virga ferrea et tamquam uas figuli confringes eos."	9 Thou shalt rule them with a rod of iron and shalt break them in pieces like a potter's vessel."
10 Ongytað nu, kyningas, and leorniað ge domeras þe ofer eorðan demað.	10 Kings, and you judges who judge throughout the earth, understand now, be instructed.	10 Et nunc reges intellegite erudimini omnes qui iudicatis terram:	10 And now, O ye kings, understand. Receive instruction, you that judge the earth.
11 Þeowiað Drihtne and ondrædað hine, blissiað on Gode, and ðeah mid ege.	11 Serve the Lord and fear him, rejoice in God, and yet do so in trepidation.	11 servite Domino in timore et exultate ei cum tremore;	11 Serve ye the Lord with fear, and rejoice unto him with trembling.

12 Onfoð lare þy læs eow God yrre weorðe, and þy læs ge wendon of rihtum wege,	12 Accept discipline lest God become angry with you, and lest you turn from the right way,	12 adprehendite disciplinam nequando irascatur Dominus et pereatis de uia iusta,	12 Embrace discipline lest at any time the Lord be angry and you perish from the just way.
13 for þæm þonne yrre byð onæled, þonne beoð eadige þa þe nu on hine getrywað.	13 because whenever his anger is kindled, then they who now trust in him will be blessed.[50]	13 cum exarserit in breui ira eius beati omnes qui confidunt in eum.	13 When his wrath shall be kindled in a short time, blessed are all they that trust in him.[51]

Several features of this translation stand out that will guide the reading of the subsequent Psalms, both in comparison with the Latin and as a frame for reading the Psalms that will follow. First, there are more questions posed in the Old English than in the Latin. The Latin opens with a single question and moves on to statements. The Old English poses three questions, in verses 1, 2, and 4. The emphasis is placed on questions, particularly concerning the peoples of the earth, kings turning from their duties to the God that made them kings, and the uselessness of resisting God. This emphatic questioning then sets up David's statement that God has appointed him as king in order that he "lære his willan and his æ." And those David instructs in verse 10 are kings (*kyningas*) and judges (*domeras*).[52]

However, this translation is selective. The Latin does not necessarily say that David teaches, but uses the verb *predicans*, which implies more proclamation or preaching than teaching.[53] And he preaches *preceptum*, a word that can variously mean "order," "lesson," "teaching," or "rule."[54] The Old English is much more specific, narrowing the possible meaning of the passage to state that David *teaches* God's will and His law.

Finally, in the Old English, David addresses kings and judges, telling them to learn, whereas in the Latin he only addresses kings.[55] The addition

50 Translation from O'Neill, *Old English Psalms*, 4–7.

51 The translation follows the Douay-Rheims, with silent adjustments for the *Romanum* text. Swift Edgar and Angela M. Kinney, eds., *The Vulgate Bible, Volume III: The Poetical Books* (Cambridge, MA: Harvard University Press, 2011), 153.

52 Psalms 2:6.

53 P. G. W. Glare, ed., *Oxford Latin Dictionary* (Oxford: Clarendon, 1982), s.v. *praedico*. Henceforth OLD.

54 OLD, s.v. *praeceptum*.

55 Ps 2:10.

of *domeras* introduces a productive ambiguity. Certainly, the kings are judges, as in the Latin. However, whereas the Latin has merely kings, emphasized by *omnes qui*, the Old English presents a clarification of who judges – both kings and judges. This addition corresponds to the wise English leaders in the preface to the *Pastoral Care*, to Asser's presentation of Alfred emphasizing the importance of judges being learned and, so presumably, to the larger Alfredian educational program, as well as to the prologue to the laws, which states that a judge needs no lawbooks other than the Golden Rule.[56]

These subtle changes do not so much alter the meaning of the Psalm as shape how it is experienced, focusing and directing the audience's interpretation. The translation choices, especially the changes to the Latin text, draw attention to certain aspects of the Old English vocabulary. David as an anointed king teaches *æ*, he addresses *domeras* who *demað*, and returning to the introduction, there is an expression of empathizing with the king and of an awareness of enemies at home and from abroad. In short, the concerns expressed can be summarized as identification with the king, law, judges, and the people being unified in God's will – something they learn from their engagement with Scripture and from the king.

Terms for law, judges, and judgment are prevalent throughout the first fifty Psalms, but the English translation limits this vocabulary to the two terms identified: *æ* and *dom*. *Æ* is used fifteen times, translating Latin *lex*. *Dom* is used twelve times and *deman* is used ten times, translating Latin *iudicium* nineteen times and *lex* once. The remaining three uses are additions or clarifications to the Latin. *Domeras* is used once but is an addition to the Latin, and *demend* is used once to translate *iudex*. The difference between the terms for judges is that *domeras* refers to human judges, *demend* is used of God.

While these translation choices could be read as mere fidelity to the Latin text that they translate, comparison with English law, particularly with the prologue to Alfred's laws, demonstrates a clear alignment of the prose Psalms with English legal culture. Patrick Wormald identifies three terms referring to law in English: *þeaw*, *æ(w)*, and *dom*.[57] The first

56 MP 49.6.

57 Wormald, *Making of English Law*, 93–108. The term *riht* deserves some comment, although it is not directly relevant to the discussion here. *Riht-* appears in the prose Psalms only as an adjective, adverb, or in compounds. O'Neill, *Alfred's Old English Translation*, 319–20. *Riht* appears in the laws composed prior to the tenth century as noun, adjective, adverb and in compounds. Liebermann, *Gesetze*, 2: s.v. *riht*. Although the nominal uses have tended to receive the translation "law," most are probably better understood as "justice," "right," or, following Attenborough's translation of Wihtred 16.2 [L 21.1], "prerogatives."

two terms, *þeaw* and *æ(w)*, essentially refer to customary law. Although both are common in the corpus of Old English, they are relatively rare in law. *Þeaw* as a legal term appears before the tenth century only in the laws of Wihtred.[58] *Æ(w)* appears only four times in the legal corpus, once in the prologue to the seventh-century law code of Hlothere and Eadric, once in the prologue to Ine's laws, once in the first law of Ine's code, and once in the prologue to Alfred's laws.[59] Of these four uses in the legal corpus, *æ(w)* appears in the same clause as a form of *dom*.[60] *Æ(w)* appears on its own only in the prologue to Alfred's laws where, it is important to note, it does not refer to civil law but to divine – as is true in its use in the preface to the *Pastoral Care* and in prose Psalm 2:6.

The term *dom*, indicating a judgment or law, is far and away the most common term for civil law in the legal corpus, at least until the introduction of the terms *gerædnes* and *lagu* in the mid tenth century. *Dom-* appears in some form eight times in the prologue to Alfred's laws, and the verb *deman* six times.[61] Three of the appearances of *dom-* translate a Scriptural source directly:

MP 11 *domas* < *iudicia* Exodus 21:1–6

MP 21 *domes* < *sententiae* Exodus 21:31

MP 43 *dom* < *iudicio* Exodus 23:6

MP 49.6 directly translates Matthew 7:12 *lex* with *dom*, but then adds material, putting particular emphasis on legal vocabulary:

> Of ðissum anu*m* **dome** mon mæg geðencean, þæt he æghwelcne on ryht **gedemeð**; ne ðearf he nanra **domboca** oþerra. Geðence he, þæt he nanum men ne **deme** þæt he nolde ðæt he him **demde**, gif he ðone **dom** ofer hine sohte.

> From this one law can one be mindful that he judge each justly. Nor does he need any other lawbooks. Let him remember that he should

The Laws of the Earliest English Kings (Clark, NJ: The Lawbook Exchange, 2006). For a full discussion of *riht*, see Daniela Fruscione, "*Riht* in Earlier Anglo-Saxon Legislation: A Semasiological Approach," *Historical Research* 86 (2013), 498–504.

58 *Þær ða eadigan fundon mid ealra gemedum ðas domas 7 Cantwara rihtum þeawum æcton, swa hit hyr efter segeþ 7 cwyþ.* Wihtred Prol. [L. Wihtred Prol. 3].

59 Liebermann, *Gesetze*, 2: s.v. æ.

60 Hlothere and Eadric Prol., Ine Prol., Ine 1.1, MP 49.1.

61 *Dom-* appears in MP 11, 21, 40, 43, 49.6 (× 2), 49.8. *Domboc* appears once in MP 49.6. *Domeras* appears in MP 18. *Deman* appears in MP 43 (× 3) and 49.6 (× 3). There is one additional use of *dom* in the body of Alfred's laws, at Alfred 8 [L Alfred 7]. Interestingly, although Alfred's laws were referred to in subsequent legislation as *seo domboc*, at no point does his law code declare itself to be *æ*, *þeaw*, or *dom*.

judge no man as he would not want himself to be judged by him if he sought judgement over him.

Omnia ergo quaecumque vultis ut faciant vobis homines, et vos facite eis, haec est enim **lex** et prophetae.

All things therefore whatsoever you would that men should do to you, do you also to them, for this is the law and the prophets.[62]

Whereas Matthew 7:12 refers simply to the law, the insistent repetition of legal vocabulary in the prologue – the Old English translation uses *dom* twice, *domboc* once, and the verb *deman* three times – draws attention to what is probably the most significant assertion of legal judgment in the prologue.

The remaining uses of *dom* and *deman* do not directly translate the Latin. In MP 40, *domas* translates the sense of Exodus 23:1:

Leases monnes word ne rec ðu no þæs to [gehieranne],[63] ne his **domas** ne geðafa ðu, ne nane gewitnesse æfter him ne saga ðu.

Do not in any way give credence to the word of a false man, nor consent to his judgements, nor ever speak as a witness after him.

Non suscipies vocem mendacii, nec iunges manum tuam ut pro impio dicas falsum testimonium.

Thou shalt not receive the voice of a lie, neither shalt thou join thy hand to bear false witness for a wicked person.[64]

MP 49.8 lacks a scriptural source but explains how synods had made judgments that were then written down:

Hie ða on monegum senoðum monegra menniscra misdæda bote geset-ton, 7 on monega senoðbec hie writan, hwær anne **dom** hwær oþerne.

Then in many synods they established compensation for many human misdeeds, and they wrote in many synod books, here one judgement and there another.

The final uses of the verb *deman* make the connection between Christ's teaching, the Church's, and civil law:

[62] Angela M. Kinney, ed., *The Vulgate Bible, Volume VI: The New Testament* (Cambridge, MA: Harvard University Press, 2013), Mt 7:12.

[63] Jurasinski and Oliver have "geherianne"; the earliest manuscript of these laws, Cambridge, Corpus Christi College 173, records "gehieranne."

[64] Swift Edgar, ed., *The Vulgate Bible, Volume I: The Pentateuch* (Cambridge, MA: Harvard University Press, 2010), Exodus 23:1.

> Siððan ðæt þa gelamp, þæt monega ðeoda Cristes geleafan onfengon, þa wurdon monega seonoðas geond ealne middangeard gegaderode, 7 eac swa geond Angelcyn, siððan hie Cristes geleafan onfengon, halegra biscepa 7 eac oðerra geðungenra witena; hie ða gesetton for ðære mildheortnesse þe crist lærde, æt mæstra hwelcre misdæde þætte ða weoruldhlafordas moston mid hiora leafan buton synne æt þam forman gylte þære fiohbote onfon, þe hie ða gesettan; buton æt hlafordsearwe hie nane mildheortnesse ne dorston gecweðan, forþam ðe god ælmihtig þa*m* nane ne **gedemde** þe hine oferhogdon, ne crist godes sunu þam nane ne **gedemde** þe hine to deaðe sealde, 7 he bebead þone hlaford lufian swa hine.[65]

> After that it came to pass that many nations accepted the faith of Christ. Then many synods were assembled all over earth, even as far as among the English, who then accepted the faith of Christ. Then the holy bishops and other excellent counselors, decided, for the mild-heartedness Christ taught, that for the greatest misdeeds secular lords might, with their leave and without sin, accept monetary compensation for first offenses, which they then decreed, except in the case of betrayal of a lord, which they dared not resolve for any mild-heartedness, because almighty God did not judge any for them who despised Him, nor did Christ, God's son, judge any for him who condemned Him to death, and he commanded to love the lord as himself.

Domeras is also used once, apparently translating the sense of the Latin of Exodus 21:22–23 by combining the source noun and source verb:

> Gif hwa on cease eacniende wif gewerde, bete þone æwerdlan, swa him **domeras** gereccen. Gif hio dead sie, selle sawle wið sawle.[66]

> If one, in a quarrel, injures a pregnant woman, repay the injury as the judges order. If she is dead, give soul for soul.

> Si rixati fuerint viri et percusserit quis mulierem praegnantem et abortivum quidem fecerit sed ipsa vixerit, subiacebit damno quantum expetierit maritus mulieris et **arbitri iudicarint**. Sin autem mors eius fuerit subsecuta, reddet animam pro anima.

> If men quarrel and one strike a woman with child and she miscarry indeed but live herself, he shall be answerable for so much damage as the woman's husband shall require and arbiters shall award. But if her death ensue thereupon, he shall render life for life.

[65] MP 49.7.

[66] MP 18.

What we can see across these texts is the drawing together of divine and civil law primarily through the judgments (*domas/iudicia*) of judges (*domeras/iudices*). Perhaps contrary to what we might expect, the use of *æ* to translate *lex* and its association with divine law rather than civil, and the use of *dom* to translate *iudicium* do not show an emphasis on civil law as textual authority. Rather, textual authority as indicated by the Latin word *lex* (derived from *legere* "to read") is largely left to Scripture and customary law (*æ*) that has been handed down, hence the narrative of the law passing from God to Moses and so on in the prologue to Alfred's laws. Civil law (*dom*), which Alfred's prologue obviously means to be informed by divine law, still functions as a series of judgments derived from "legal proceedings before a *iudex*."[67] This is certainly an important point if we understand both the prose Psalms and the *domboc*, or at least the prologue, as participating in Alfred's educational program. It reminds the English nobles, who would have been taught to read in English and who would have been judges, that their decisions should be guided by both divine and civil law.

In conclusion, we should read the prose Psalms and the prologue to Alfred's laws together because they are the only two Alfredian texts that directly translate Scripture. Treating the introductions to the Psalms and the prologue to the laws as guides to the texts that follow, we can identify concerns that the texts amplify in their translation choices. A vocabulary of law, judges, identification with the king, and identification with a common national identity come to the fore. Moreover, the texts can tell us how they were deploying vocabulary to shape their audiences' ideas. When one pays particular attention to the translation, these two Old English texts grounded in Scripture appear to be remarkable guides for English nobles in a period of foreign incursion temporarily halted and a growing effort to expand West Saxon dominion over the other English kingdoms. They also offer their audiences a way to see themselves as a part of this new kingdom and state of affairs through their association with biblical figures. Although the commonalities of the texts' structures are more suggestive than concrete, the use of vocabulary strongly implies a common project between the prose Psalms and the prologue to Alfred's laws. Indeed, we may justly see shared legal concerns in the prologue to the laws and the introductions to the Psalms. The introductions to both (civil) legal and (religious) literary texts show a common interest in using law to shape textual interpretation and resulting behavior. The Alfredian educational project, then, has a clear role in shaping judges and guiding their thoughts when they must pass judgments; but the translation choices also indicate that the judges were not expected

[67] OLD, s.v. *iudicium* 1.

to rely, necessarily, on a set legal text but rather to follow the spirit of divine law. Returning then to the preface to the *Pastoral Care,* it is fair to say that the *domboc* and the prose Psalms provide the English with a model for how to return to rule by wise kings and judges that would unify them within a single kingdom.

2

Cynescipe, Bishop Æthelwold, and the Spread of Legal Language

Arendse Lund

In the tenth century, the Winchester school, led by Bishop Æthelwold, embarked on an ambitious mission: the standardization of Old English.[1] This lofty goal was attempted through a uniformity in word choice and the promotion of specific vocabulary. The undertaking was effected over the course of many years; with Winchester's role as an influential political, religious and cultural center, the success of this deliberate attempt to standardize vocabulary can be seen in the numerous charters, wills, diplomas, as well as the many manuscripts that the scriptorium produced. Closely associated scribal centers, such as Canterbury and Rochester, also felt the effects of these labors, as the Winchester vocabulary trickled into their writings – though not with as great a degree of regularity.[2] Over the past century, scholars such as Eduard Dietrich, Walter Hofstetter, Karl Jost, Josef Kirschner, Helmut Gneuss, and Celia and Kenneth Sisam, among others, have identified words promoted by the Old Minster, and the lasting impact this had on the writings of pupils, such as Ælfric of Eynsham, educated therein.[3] In noting striking similarities between the

[1] The emphasis on linguistic standardization espoused by the Winchester School, and the subsequent influence of this language, had long-lasting effects on scribes in early medieval England. Not only were the spelling and vocabulary standardized, but the script forms as well, in a deliberate attempt to achieve uniformity across working scribes. See Helmut Gneuss, "The Study of Language in Anglo-Saxon England," in *Language and History in Early England*, ed. Helmut Gneuss (Aldershot: Variorum, 1996), 3–32; Ursula Lenker, "The Monasteries of the Benedictine Reform and the 'Winchester School': Model Cases of Social Networks in Anglo-Saxon England?" *European Journal of English Studies* 4 (2000): 225–38; Lucia Kornexl, "Chapter 12: Standardization," in *The History of English*, Vol. 2, *Old English*, ed. Laurel Brinton and Alexander Bergs (The Hague: De Gruyter Mouton, 2017), 220–35; cf. notes 2 and 3 below.

[2] Walter Hofstetter, *Winchester und der spätaltenglische Sprachgebrauch: Untersuchungen zur geographischen und zeitlichen Verbreitung altenglischer Synonyme* (Munich: W. Fink, 1987), 14, particularly texts 16, 31, 59.

[3] Eduard Dietrich, "Abt Aelfrik. Zur Literatur-Geschichte der angelsächsischen Kirche," *Zeitschrift für historische Theologie* 25 (1855): 487–594, and 26 (1856):

English interlinear glosses in the psalter held by Lambeth Palace Library and those in a manuscript held by the British Library, Celia and Kenneth Sisam postulated an "influential monastic school in which these standard equivalents were taught."[4] We now know this to be Winchester.

I propose adding an additional term, *cynescipe*, to that list of Winchester vocabulary favored by Æthelwold and his circle. The word *cynescipe*, or "royal dignity," demonstrates how a term spread from legal to non-legal texts in tenth- and eleventh-century England. In this essay, I show how the promulgation of this term, so closely involved with the medieval ideas of kingship, is intricately tied to the influence of scribal communities and the role of monastic centers in the tenth century. Succinct analysis of the term is feasible because, according to the *Dictionary of Old English*, there are seventeen appearances of the word in the Old English corpus, the majority of which are in legal contexts; many of these occurrences are in legal prologues, paratextual spaces that straddle that same line between legal and literary genres through the expository prose that justifies and authorizes their texts.[5] While caution must always be urged at drawing firm conclusions from small bodies of work, the outstanding evidence points strongly toward a relationship with Winchester and specifically the bishop who headed the prestigious scriptorium. After all, the first appearance of the term *cynescipe* is in the mid tenth century during the reign of King Edgar the Peaceful. The word appears throughout Edgar's legislation, first in the Andover code, and then the *Wihtbordesstan* code. After this, we see the appearance of the word in two charters, one during Edgar's reign and one after, followed by its use in homiletic and biblical writings, and then reappearing in Cnut's law codes in the early eleventh century. In total, these occurrences span about sixty years. Although historically scholars have talked about it as if *cynescipe* were a popular term, I demonstrate below that all the uses are instead connected to Bishop Æthelwold of Winchester and his circle – with one exception.

163–256; Walter Hofstetter, "Winchester and the Standardization of Old English Vocabulary," *Anglo-Saxon England* 17 (1988): 139–61; Karl Jost, *Wulfstanstudien* (Bern: Francke, 1950), 176; Josef Kirschner, *Die Bezeichnungen für Kranz und Krone im Altenglischen* (Munich: Salzer, 1975), 215–16; Helmut Gneuss, *Hymnar und Hymnen im englischen Mittelalter: Studien zur Überlieferung, Glossierung und Übersetzung lateinischer Hymnen in England* (Tübingen: Max Niemeyer, 1968), 186–87, and Helmut Gneuss, "The Origin of Standard Old English and Æthelwold's School at Winchester," *Anglo-Saxon England* 1 (1972): 75–83; Celia Sisam and Kenneth Sisam, eds., *The Salisbury Psalter*, EETS, o.s. 242 (London: Oxford University Press, 1959).

4 Sisam and Sisam, *The Salisbury Psalter*, 74.

5 Although Gérard Genette wrote on paratexts in general, this applies particularly well to prologues; see Gérard Genette, *Paratexts: Thresholds of Interpretation*, trans. Jane E. Lewin (Cambridge: Cambridge University Press, 1997), 2.

Bishop Æthelwold and the Law

Æthelwold was one of the leaders of the tenth-century monastic reform movement in England. Originally from Winchester, he was involved with the royal courts from a young age, later teaching the future King Edgar and backing Edgar's succession to the throne.[6] Edgar was crowned in 959 and from 960 to 963 Æthelwold was in the king's personal service.[7] "There can be no doubt," Simon Keynes wrote of the relationship between the king and his bishop, "that Æthelwold enjoyed special standing in the early years of Edgar's reign at meetings of the king and his councilors, which at this stage makes him unique among heads of religious houses."[8] This close relationship led to Edgar appointing Æthelwold bishop of Winchester in late 963, a position Æthewold held until his death in 984.

In 960, while Æthelwold was in the personal service of Edgar, the king issued his Andover code containing the earliest appearance of the term *cynescipe*. The Andover code was the first major legislative effort of Edgar's reign and is also one of the best-attested pieces of early English legislation.[9] Two of the manuscripts containing the code include identically-worded prologues, which state: *Đis is seo gerædnes, þe Eadgar cyng mid witan geþeahte gerædde, Gode to lofe ⁊ him sylfum to cynescype ⁊ eallum his leodscype to þearfe.*[10] ("This is the ordinance which King Edgar decreed with the advice of his councilors, for the glory of God and his own royal dignity and for the benefit of all his people.") The term *cynescipe* should be understood as connoting royal power – with a particular focus in Edgar's laws on his rank as king. When the Andover code was translated into Latin, the single word *cynescipe* was expanded in the accusative as *regiam dignitatem*,

6 Julia Barrow, "The Ideology of the Tenth-Century English Benedictine 'Reform,'" in *Challenging the Boundaries of Medieval History: The Legacy of Timothy Reuter*, ed. Patricia Skinner (Turnhout: Brepols, 2009), 145.

7 Barbara Yorke, "Æthelwold [St Æthelwold, Ethelwold] (904×9–984), Abbot of Abingdon and Bishop of Winchester," in *Oxford Dictionary of National Biography* (23 September 2004), <https://www.oxforddnb.com>, accessed 12 March 2020.

8 Simon Keynes, "Edgar, *Rex Admirabilis*," in *Edgar, King of the English, 959–975: New Interpretations*, ed. Donald Scragg (Woodbridge: Boydell, 2014), 29.

9 While the Andover code itself does not specify the location of its issue, the *Wihtbordesstan* code cites it as *þe mine witan æt Andeferan gerædđon* ("what my councilors decreed at Andover"). See IV Edgar 1.4, ed. in Felix Liebermann, ed., *Die Gesetze der Angelsachsen*, 3 vols. (Halle: Max Niemeyer, 1903–16), 1:198. The law code survives in six manuscripts and Wormald argues that these form two or three transmission groups. For a full discussion of the scribal differences suggesting manuscript relationships, see Wormald, *Making of English Law*, 313–14.

10 II–III Edgar Prol.: *Gesetze* 1:194.

also meaning royal dignity.[11] While we frequently see glossators using several words to gloss a single Latin lemma in Old English, here we have the translator recognizing the two critical elements of the compound and using several words to convey the full meaning of *cynescipe*.[12] This strategy is often used with words that are not derived from Latin but are instead of English invention.[13]

Only three years after Edgar issued the Andover code, and while Æthelwold was still in his service, the king promulgated the *Wihtbordesstan* code. Once again, the prologue uses the same language to refer to the king:

> Woruldgerihta ic wille þæt standen on ælcum leodscipe swa gode swa hy mon betste aredian mæge, Gode to gecwemnysse 7 me to fullum cynescipe ... 7 to ælcere byrig 7 on ælcere scire hæbbe ic mines cynescipes gerihta, swa min fæder hæfde[14]

> I will that secular rights be in force amongst all my people as well as they can best be devised, to the satisfaction of God and for my full royal dignity ... and in every borough and in every shire I have the rights belonging to my complete royal dignity, just as my father had.

Cynescipe is used twice in short succession to emphasize Edgar's royal authority as stemming from both traditional authority and from divine will. The prefix *cyne* is often used by medieval writers as the first part of many words – *cynedom*, *cynehelm*, and *cynehlaford*, to name a few – and here it is combined with *scipe* as the second element. As a simplex, Bosworth-Toller takes *scipe* to mean "state, condition, dignity, office" and it is used to form many nouns.[15] Patrick Wormald translated this word as "kingship," encompassing the same idea – that a king's authority and kingship are explicitly linked. The writer of the *Wihtbordesstan* code connects Edgar's rights, his royal prerogatives, with his *cynescipe*.

Dorothy Whitelock noted that, thanks to the content and the homiletic style of the *Wihtbordesstan* code, "It is tempting to connect [the code] with

11 From *Quadripartitus*: *deo ad gloriam et sibi ad regiam dignitatem*; see *Gesetze* 1:195. As I mention below, I have translated *cynescipe* as "royal dignity" throughout, based on the *DOE*'s treatment of the word, as well as the two components of the term. The *Legend of the Seven Sleepers* is an exception to this rule, which will be discussed later (see note 47 below).

12 For the use of complex words as translation tools, see Jonathan Davis-Secord, *Joinings: Compound Words in Old English Literature* (Toronto: University of Toronto Press, 2016), 37–70.

13 Arendse Lund, "Law as Literature in the Vernacular Codes of Early Medieval England" (PhD diss., University College London, 2021), 203–23.

14 IV Edgar 2–2a: *Gesetze* 1:208.

15 Bosworth-Toller, s.v. *scipe*.

one of the great churchmen who surrounded King Edgar."[16] My research demonstrates that we can take this further: I propose that Æthelwold was involved in the creation of these codes.[17] Provided that the dating of the code is accurate to 963, which is consistent with the pestilence mentioned in the prologue, then Æthelwold is serving directly under King Edgar and likely involved with any creation of a legal code.[18] After all, not only was Æthelwold intricately involved with the goings-on of Edgar's court, but scholars have consistently linked him to the legal writings issued during his lifetime. We do know that Æthelwold is the scribe known as "Edgar A," responsible for a large number of the charters that survive from the first four years of the king's reign.[19] Moreover, as Barbara Yorke observes, there is a strong possibility that he is the same Æthelwold who appeared as a witness in charters in the years 932 and 934.[20] He is also often the only religious figure to serve as a witness and he continues to be linked to legal writings after being consecrated as bishop of Winchester.[21] When the synod in Winchester was held, sometime between 970 and 973, the attendees decided that all monastic communities in England would follow a common rule; this was the creation of the *Regularis concordia*, the customary adopted and written by Æthelwold himself.[22] As Yorke writes, "His

[16] Dorothy Whitelock, ed. and trans., *English Historical Documents. Volume I: c.500–1042*, 2nd ed. (London: Oxford University Press, 1979), 398.

[17] There was precedent for churchmen helping with the construction of royal codes as thirty years earlier Archbishop Wulfhelm had been involved in the composition of King Æthelstan's laws. *Gesetze* 1:146.

[18] Dorothy Whitelock dates the *Wihtbordesstan* code to *c.* 963 while Patrick Wormald places it later in Edgar's reign. I prefer the date of 963 as the pestilence mentioned at the time in the *Anglo-Saxon Chronicle* entry fits with the prologue to the code. While Wormald raises the question of Earl Oslac's presence in the northern recension of the *Anglo-Saxon Chronicle* – which has him appointed in 966 – that version was redacted in the later tenth or early eleventh century; furthermore, Oslac attested a diploma in 963 (see S 716) so a date of *c.* 963 for the code is entirely possible. See also Whitelock's *EHD* and Wormald's *Making of English Law* for their respective arguments.

[19] Yorke, "Æthelwold."

[20] S 417 and S 425. See Yorke, "Æthelwold."

[21] Simon Keynes, *An Atlas of Attestations in Anglo-Saxon Charters, c.670–1066* (Department of Anglo-Saxon, Norse, and Celtic, University of Cambridge, 1998).

[22] Thomas Symons, ed. and trans., *Regularis concordia Anglicae nationis monachorum sanctimonialiumque / The Monastic Agreement of the Monks and Nuns of the English Nation* (London: Thomas Nelson, 1953). See also, Dorothy Whitelock, Martin Brett, and Christopher N. L. Brooke, eds., *Councils and Synods, with Other Documents Relating to the English Church, 871–1204*, 2 vols. (Oxford: Clarendon, 1981). For manuscript evidence for the *Regularis concordia* and its association with Winchester, see Joyce M. Hill, "Æfric's 'Silent Days,'" in *Sources and*

pupil Ælfric identifies Æthelwold as the author in a composition he wrote for his own monks at Eynsham and there are also verbal links with other works attributed to Æthelwold."[23] Edgar's *Wihtbordesstan* code reflects many of the sentiments consistent with Edgar and Æthelwold's religious and political aims, and is very much aligned with their promotion of the Benedictine order. I contend that Æthelwold must have been involved.

If *cynescipe* were a widespread legal term, then we would expect to see the word used outside of Æthelwold's immediate circle, particularly since Edgar's *Wihtbordesstan* code includes a provision that multiple copies should be made and sent out "in all directions" so that the law may be known by rich and poor alike.[24] Assuming these manuscripts were indeed sent out and copies made, it is feasible that the term would catch on and begin to appear in other texts, legal or otherwise. However, in stark contrast to Edgar's Andover code, his *Wihtbordesstan* code is poorly attested and only survives in two manuscripts. Liebermann noted that these manuscripts share a textual kinship and Wormald argued that they "represent no more than a single line of transmission."[25] As such, we see no immediate evidence of the term spreading outside of Edgar's court.

Chronologically, the next time the term *cynescipe* is attested is in the opening to Ælfgifu's will when she leaves land to the Old Minster, Winchester, frees her slaves, and grants possessions to her relatives.[26] She opens the will with the statement: *þis ys Ælfgyfæ gegurning to hiræ cinehlafordæ; þæt is þæt heo hyne bitt for Godæs lufun and for cynescypæ þæt heo mote beon hyre cwydes wyrðæ.*[27] ("This is Ælfgifu's request of her royal lord, which is that she asks him on account of the love of God and on account of his royal dignity, that she may be entitled to make her will.") This opening connects the king's royal dignity with his role as *cynehlaford*, or royal lord.

Relations: Studies in Honour of J. E. Cross, ed. Marie Collins, Jocelyn Price and Andrew Hamer, Leeds Studies in English, n.s. 16 (Leeds: University of Leeds, School of English, 1985), 123–25.

23 Yorke, "Æthelwold."

24 This is the first time that we are given insight into the process of transmission the king mandates for the law code, as it is codified directly into the legislation itself. King Edgar orders that *write man manega gewrita be ðisum 7 sende ægðer ge to Ælfere ealdormen ge to Ægelwine ealdorman, 7 hi gehwyder, þæt ðes ræd cuð sy ægðer ge earmum ge eadigum* ("many document copies should be written of this and sent to both Ealdorman Ælfhere and Ealdorman Æthelwine, and they are to send them in all directions that this measure may be known to both the poor and the rich"). IV Edgar 15.1: *Gesetze* 1:214. Wormald, *Making of English Law*, 317.

25 Wormald, *Making of English Law*, 317.

26 S 1484, dated to 966 × 975. Ælfgifu has not been positively identified. See Richard Marsden, "The Will of Ælfgifu," in *The Old English Reader*, 2nd ed. (Cambridge: Cambridge University Press, 2015), 128–31.

27 S 1484.

The pressing question here becomes: how does *cynescipe* come to be in this will when it has only been attested in Edgar's law codes so far? The answer lies with Bishop Æthelwold. By 966, Edgar had appointed Æthelwold to the vacant see of Winchester, and the newly consecrated bishop expelled the clerics of the Old and New Minsters and replaced them with monks. Æthelwold's influence extended to Nunnaminster as well; Yorke describes how "Nunnaminster in Winchester and probably other nunneries in the Winchester diocese were also affected by Æthelwold's zeal" as they were "enclosed by walls at this time."[28] Alongside Ælfgifu's land grant, she makes a personal grant and plea to Æthelwold, writing: *And ic ann Æþelwoldæ bisceopæ þæs landæs æt Tæafersceat. And bidde hinæ þæt hæ symlie þingiæ for minæ modor an for me.*[29] ("I grant to Bishop Æthelwold the estate at Tæafersceat and ask him that he will always intercede for my mother and me.") She also grants land to the Old Minster, New Minster, and Nunnaminster – all places Æthelwold had a personal interest in. A strong possibility is that Æthelwold himself may have brought the term with him back to Winchester and influenced the phrasing of the will. Yorke describes Æthelwold's literary legacy, saying "His vernacular writings show a concern with clarity and with defining a precise Old English vocabulary which is believed to have played an important role in the development of Standard Old English."[30] To further underline this, we know that Æthelwold was highly involved with the scriptorium at Winchester as he commissioned manuscripts and the Winchester school of manuscript illumination reached its peak while he was bishop. One manuscript, the Benedictional of Saint Æthelwold, even includes a Latin inscription describing how Bishop Æthelwold commissioned its creation.[31]

In 984, Bishop Æthelwold died. Of the bishop's literary legacy and his efforts at standardization, Hofstetter writes that Æthelwold "was the decisive force behind the development of a new usage which, after an initial or intermediate stage, attained full maturity in the generation of his pupils."[32] We see that same pattern with the development of *cynescipe*. At some point after 987, one of the king's followers, a different Æthelwold, had his will recorded, where he directed his possessions to his wife with reversion to New Minster upon her death. The will opens with the statement: *Ðis is Aþelwoldis cwyde. þæt is ærest þæt he bitt his cynehlaford for Godes lufon 7 for his cynescipe þæt his cwyde standen mote on þæm þingon þe he æt þe gegearnod hæfþ 7 æt þinum foregengan* ("This is Æthelwold's will, which is first that he asks of his royal lord on account of God's love and on account of his royal

[28] Yorke, "Æthelwold."
[29] S 1484.
[30] Yorke, "Æthelwold."
[31] BL, Additional MS 49598.
[32] Hofstetter, "Standardization of Old English," 157.

dignity that his will relating to those things which he has acquired from you and your predecessors may stand").[33] Both Ælfgifu and Æthelwold's wills open with quasi-formulaic requests that the king support them; and in making their requests, they both make reference to God's love, the king's royal dignity, and refer to the king as *cynehlaford*. The phrasing of these two requests is too close to be coincidental, and yet there are no other wills containing this exact language. It is of course possible that there were other wills with similar language that have simply been lost to time, but the extant evidence all points to efforts made by the scriptorium at the Old Minster. Outside of Winchester, wills contain similar openings but with different diction: *ic bidde minne leouan hlaford for godes lufun. þæt min cwyde standan mote* ("I ask my dear lord on account of God's love that my will may stand").[34] This does not include a reference to *cynescipe* nor would we expect it to since the charter has no connection with Winchester. Instead the solidification of this term into a formulaic phrase provides insight into the ongoing regularization of Old English vocabulary at the end of the tenth century. The use of *cynescipe* in these charters, both at Winchester, Æthelwold's seat, is unlikely to be coincidence.

Ælfric, Wulfstan, and Æthelwold's Legacy

Next time we meet *cynescipe*, it is in the writings of one of Æthelwold's pupils where the term has moved from the legal to the non-legal realm. In the late 990s, Ælfric composed his *Catholic Homilies*, wherein he states: *Ne mæg nan eorðlic cyning cynelic lybban. Buton he hæbbe ðegenas 7 swa gelogodne hired swa his cynescipe gerisan mæge*.[35] ("No worldly king may live royally unless he has retainers and a household regulated in such a way as may befit his royal dignity.") Consistent with its use in legal writing, the term *cynescipe* appears as part of a possessive; here a king's royal power derives from his *cynescipe*.[36] Ælfric's use of the word is almost unsurprising: the connection between Æthelwold and Ælfric is well known, as Ælfric was educated *in scola Adelwoldi* ("in Æthelwold's school").[37] Ælfric's *Grammar*

33 S 1505.

34 S 1494.

35 Homily VIII, "Third Sunday after Epiphany," edited in Peter Clemoes, ed., *Ælfric's Catholic Homilies: The First Series, Text*, EETS, s.s. 17 (Oxford: Oxford University Press, 1997), 533 (this alternative text is found in Cambridge, Corpus Christi College 188).

36 Carola Trips, *Lexical Semantics and Diachronic Morphology: The Development of -hood, -dom and -ship in the History of English* (Berlin: Walter de Gruyter, 2009), 174.

37 Julius Zupitza, ed., *Ælfrics Grammatik und Glossar*, 2nd ed. with contributions

also seems to hint at grammatical studies at Winchester in the last third of the tenth century; Ælfric followed in his mentor's footsteps, and "continued Æthelwold's concern with grammatical correctness in Old English and with the translation of Latin texts into the vernacular."[38] He went on to become one of the most prolific Old English writers. In these writings, he employed Winchester vocabulary with "a remarkable degree of consistency" as he had "acquired this vocabulary as an essential element of the education which he received at the Old Minster at Winchester."[39] Like many of the other words he harnessed in his writings, Ælfric would have been exposed to the term *cynescipe* during his time at Winchester and influenced by Æthelwold's usage of it.

Ælfric uses *cynescipe* a number of times in his non-legal writings, developing it in subtle ways beyond its strictly legal role. In his adaptation of the *Book of Kings*, Ælfric wields the term as a double-edged sword, writing of a sinful king: *þa asende him God to swyðlice steore, swa þæt him comon to ða Chaldeiscan leoda and hine gebundenne geleddon to Babiloniscre byrig, and on cwearterne bescufon to sceame his kynescipe.*[40] ("Then God sent him a severe punishment, so that the Chaldean people came to him and brought him bound to the city of Babylon, and threw him in prison to shame his royal dignity.") The link between kingship and divine will is maintained as it is God who sends the king a punishment resulting in him understanding how his royal dignity is connected to good deeds and the divine; in the passage that follows this one, the king repents of his sins, performs penance, and God restores him to his kingdom, and his *cynescipe* is presumably once more intact. Showing a stylistic preference for the term, Ælfric also uses the term as an opportunity for emphasis through alliteration. This is the first time we find this positive term for kingship being abused, a connection that is highlighted through the alliteration of *cwearterne* and *kynescipe*. Although a change from the legal uses of the previous decades, as no law code places royal power in a negative context, Ælfric makes these words his own, tweaking their use to suit his purposes.

By contrast, in Ælfric's summary of the biblical story of Esther, the king's mercy is shown through his great *cynescipe*. Ælfric wrote the Old English version sometime around the turn of the first millennium.[41] In

---

by Helmut Gneuss (Berlin: Weidmann, 1966), 1. Gneuss presented further evidence for the connection of the two men in "The Origin of Standard Old English and Æthelwold's School at Winchester," *Anglo-Saxon England* 1 (1972): 63–85.

38 Yorke, "Æthelwold."

39 Hofstetter, "Standardization of Old English," 161 and 157.

40 Ælfric's *Book of Kings*, edited in W. W. Skeat, ed., *Ælfric's Lives of Saints* (London: N. Trübner, 1881), 384–413, "Item 18: From the Book of Kings," lines 437–40.

41 Katrina M. Wilkins, "On Esther," *Journal of Languages, Texts, and Society* 2 (2018): 130.

the story, the king's chief minister, Haman, attempts to massacre the Jews throughout the empire; following an intervention by Esther, the king's new wife, the king is convinced to belay the command. In a passage after the king thwarts Haman's plan to hang the Jewish courtier Mordecai, Esther's cousin, the king announces: *þæt þa Iudeiscan moston for his micclan cynescipe beon ealle on friðe 7 unforhte* ("that the Jews might all – because of his great royal dignity – be peaceful and unafraid").[42] In Ælfric's writings, *cynescipe* then carries a more explicit obligation, one that allows for a king's royal dignity to remain intact as long as his will is in line with God's will. Sinning, such as the example in Ælfric's *Book of Kings*, carries a forfeit of the king's *cynescipe*, without which he is stripped of his kingship and thrown in jail. By repenting and again aligning his will with God's will, the king's *cynescipe* is restored. In both these examples, which are biblical in nature, Ælfric is more concerned with emphasizing how kingship is beholden to divine will, rather than flaunting kingship as rationale for passing royal legislation.

All the instances of *cynescipe* up to this point have originated from Æthelwold and his circle, yet there exists a curious outlier with the use of the term in the Old English version of the *Legend of the Seven Sleepers*. The story goes back to the early Church and the motif survives in European folktales such as the German Peter Klaus story (re-written by Washington Irving as *Rip van Winkle*): A group of men refuse to cease worshipping God despite the Roman emperor's orders. In order to escape the emperor, they hide in a cave and God puts them to sleep for 372 years. When they awaken, they are hailed as resurrected martyrs in a thoroughly Christianized society.[43] The author of the Old English version is anonymous – although writers in the eleventh and twelfth centuries attributed the work to Ælfric – and this leaves us with contradictory evidence.[44]

42 Wilkins, "On Esther," 150; line 244 in Stuart D. Lee, ed., *Ælfric's Homilies on 'Judith,' 'Esther' and 'The Maccabees'* (1999) <http://users.ox.ac.uk/~stuart/kings>, accessed 30 June 2021. All subsequent citations to *Esther* are from this edition.

43 Eileen Joy, "The Old English Seven Sleepers, Eros, and the Unincorporable Infinite of the Human Person," in *Anonymous Interpolations in Ælfric's Lives of Saints*, ed. Robin Norris (Kalamazoo: Medieval Institute Publications, 2011), 71–96.

44 The text of the Old English *Legend of the Seven Sleepers* appears in BL, Cotton Julius E.vii, fols. 207v–222v; it can also be found in a fragmentary state in BL, Cotton Otho B.x, which was severely damaged by fire in the eighteenth century. Traditionally the Old English version of the *Seven Sleepers* has been attributed to Ælfric, and the work appears interpolated with Ælfric's *Lives of Saints* in its manuscript context; however, the prevailing view has shifted in the past two decades, and I follow Hugh Magennis in considering the work to be by an anonymous author. For the full argument, see Hugh Magennis, ed., *The Anonymous Old English "Legend of the Seven Sleepers" and its Latin Source*

The first use of the term *cynescipe* is in a description of Emperor Decius' legacy: *feala oðra casera æfter him rixodon ælc æfter oðrum on heora cynescipes wuldre, and on heora anwealdes myrhþe* ("many other emperors ruled after him, each after the others with glory in their royal dignity, and joy in their authority").[45] There are four appearances of the term in the *Seven Sleepers*; however, the use above is most consistent with the Winchester wills and Ælfric's literary uses in his *Lives of Saints*. This changes notably in the next three uses, where *cynescipe* has a very different meaning. First, we have the line: *Ealra manna hlaford geond þas widan worulde, we biddað þinne cynescipe þæt þu nan ðingc ne beo dreorig oððe sarig for ðan geongan cnihton…* ("Lord of all men throughout this wide world, we ask your royal majesty that you are not cruel or hurtful to the young warrior…").[46] Here, *cynescipe* translates more closely as "royal majesty" rather than "royal dignity".[47] The term follows *þinne*, the second-person singular possessive, as well as the predicate *biddað*, where its usage has changed to form instead a title involving direct address. As Carola Trips notes, "this is a metonymic shift arising from the salient meaning of *-scipe* [as] 'dignity'."[48] It is this meaning of *cynescipe* that is prevalent throughout the *Seven Sleepers*, which we can see in the speech a few lines later: *…gyf ðin cynescipe swa cwyð, hit geworden bið sona þæt man heora magas gelangie, and hi man stiðlice ðreatige* ("…if your royal majesty says so, it will straightaway happen that their kinsmen will be sent for and they will be severely threatened").[49] Again, the word *cynescipe* stands in as a title and a term of respect in direct address, rather than simply a quality associated with kingship. Toward the end of the *Seven Sleepers*, that trend has crystalized: *ic grete þe, leof, eadmodlice, and ic bidde þinne þrymfullan cynescype, þæt þu to us cume swa þu raþost mæge.*[50] ("I greet you, Sir, humbly, and I ask your glorious royal majesty that you come to us as quickly as you can"). The inclusion of *leof*, which is also used as a form of direct address, emphasizes the focus on *cynescipe* in this speech through the flowery references to the king; the

(Durham UK: Department of English Studies, 1994), 33–57. Ælfric was certainly aware of the *Seven Sleepers* and referenced it elsewhere. See Hugh Magennis, "The Anonymous Old English 'Legend of the Seven Sleepers' and its Latin Source," *Leeds Studies in English* 22 (1991): 43–56.

45 Magennis, ed., *Seven Sleepers*, lines 319–20. For the full text, see Magennis, ed., *Seven Sleepers*, 33–57.

46 Ibid., lines 256–58.

47 For this passage, the *DOE* inputs a new meaning of *cynescipe* as "(your) majesty." This shift is one that persists in more literary uses of the term, especially the forms of direct address. I translate *cynescipe* here as "royal majesty" instead to maintain the focus on the *cyne* component.

48 Trips, *Lexical Semantics and Diachronic Morphology*, 174.

49 Magennis, ed., *Seven Sleepers*, lines 265–66.

50 Ibid., lines 728–30.

adjective *þrymfullan* further modifies the title, thus highlighting the status of the *cynescipe*. The anonymous author plays with the term, adjusting the meaning to fit the dialogue. In the legal uses of *cynescipe*, there is a clear pattern of use by Æthelwold's circle; non-legal uses also show a strong connection with Æthelwold's circle, with only the *Seven Sleepers* having no apparent connection to it.

The final occurrences of the word *cynescipe* appear in the writings of Archbishop Wulfstan, the other major vernacular writer in early eleventh-century England. In his *Institutes of Polity*, Wulfstan depicts the bishop as a pillar of society and teacher of God's law, yet he balances the bishop's role with that of the king, with whom earthly power rests.[51] In the incipit, he uses the term that we have come to associate with Æthelwold and his Winchester circle:

> Bisceopum gebyrað þæt hi mid geþylde geþolian þæt hi sylfe gebetan ne magan, oð þæt hit þam cyncge gecyþed weorðe; 7 bete he syððan Godes æbylhþe þær bisceop ne mæge, gif he Godes willan rihte wylle wyrcean 7 his agene cynescype rihtlice aræran.[52]
>
> It is fitting for bishops that they tolerate with patience what they themselves cannot amend, until it is reported to the king, and he is afterwards to amend the offence against God where the bishop cannot, if he wishes to do God's will and rightly to elevate his own royal dignity.

Wulfstan relies on the early legal use of *cynescipe* as a characteristic of kingship here, and further ties the king's power and his royal dignity to God's will. Wulfstan's traditional use of words like *cynescipe* allow his audience to anticipate his narrative and thereby familiarize themselves with the basic tenets of his sermons.[53]

51 Andrew Rabin, ed. and trans., *The Political Writings of Archbishop Wulfstan of York* (Manchester: Manchester University Press, 2015); Andrew Rabin, ed. and trans., *Wulfstan: Old English Legal Writings* (Cambridge, MA: Harvard University Press, 2020); Karl Jost, ed., *Die "Institutes of Polity, Civil and Ecclesiastical": Ein Werk Erzbischof Wulfstans von York* (Bern: Francke, 1959), 62; see also the mention of Wulfstan in Dominik Wassenhoven, "The Role of the Bishop in Anglo-Saxon Succession Struggles," in *Leaders of the Anglo-Saxon Church: From Bede to Stigand*, ed. Alexander R. Rumble (Woodbridge: Boydell, 2012), 107.

52 See Whitelock, Brett and Brooke, *Councils and Synods*, 412–13 (no. 54). Also Jost, *Institutes of Polity*, 210–16.

53 In multiple homilies, his *Institutes of Polity*, and the law codes he authored, Wulfstan uses strikingly similar language and ideas. This restraint had a singular purpose: to make his topic more familiar to his audience. Andy Orchard describes "emphasis through repetition" as the "essence" of Wulfstan's style. Here we see that in effect. The audience of his writings, whether legal or homiletic, heard the same ideas often expressed in the same words. Familiarity was

Wulfstan's involvement in composing Cnut's laws allowed him to reuse the term he had surely seen in the law codes of Edgar. First, the term appears in the opening to the prologue to Cnut's Winchester code, which states:

> Ðis is seo gerednes, þe Cnut cyning, ealles Englalandes cycningc 7 Dena cyningc 7 Norþrigena cyninge, gerædde, 7 his witan, Gode to lofe 7 him sylfum to cynescipe 7 to þearfe, rade swa hwæðer swa man wille.[54]
>
> This is the ordinance which King Cnut, king of the land of the English and king of the Danes and king of the Norwegians, decreed, and his councilors, for the glory of God and for his own royal dignity and benefit.

This is nearly identical to the phrase in Edgar's code. Cnut's Winchester code survives in three Old English manuscripts, in addition to later, post-Conquest Latin codes. Even accounting for the manuscript variance, and the significantly different prologues between the manuscripts, the term *cynescipe* persists in them all. Similarly, Cnut's Letter of 1020 is a statement on lawgiving for both ecclesiastical and secular people, wherein the term *cynescipe* is used twice in short succession:

> … eac minum ealdormannum ic beode, þæt hy fylstan þam biscopum to Godes gerihtum 7 to minum kynescype 7 to ealles folces þearfe. Gif hwa swa dyrstig sy, gehadod oððe læwede, Denisc oððe Englisc, þæt ongean Godes lage ga 7 ongean minne cynescype oððe ongean woroldriht, 7 nelle betan 7 geswican æfter minra biscopa tæcinge, þonne bidde ic Þurcyl eorl 7 eac beode, þæt he ðæne unrihtwisan to rihte gebige, gyf he mæge.[55]
>
> I also command my ealdormen that they help the bishops in furthering God's rights and my royal dignity and the benefit to all the people. If there is anyone, ecclesiastical or lay, Danish or English, so rash as to go against God's law and against my royal dignity or against the secular law, and will not reform and cease according to the teaching of my bishops, then I pray and command Earl Thorkell, if he can, that he cause the unrighteous to do right.

The tying together of earthly and divine power is made explicit in phrases with parallel structure such as these. Cnut's law codes borrow heavily from Edgar's codes, and we know that Wulfstan relied upon and annotated the

---

the key strategy for Wulfstan's religious campaign. Andy Orchard, "Wulfstan as Reader, Writer, Rewriter," in *The Old English Homily: Precedent, Practice, and Appropriation*, ed. Aaron J. Kleist (Turnhout: Brepols, 2007), 320.

54 I Cnut Prol.: *Gesetze* 1:278; Rabin, *Wulfstan: Old English Legal Writings*, 232.

55 Cnut 1020, 9: *Gesetze* 1:274; Cnut 1020, 3–4 in Rabin, *Wulfstan: Old English Legal Writings*, 228.

manuscripts containing Edgar's laws. In drafting the Winchester code and Cnut's Letter of 1020, along with his *Institute of Polity,* Wulfstan reused the term that was closely associated with Bishop Æthelwold, showing the enduring influence of early medieval literary and legal circles, and of Bishop Æthelwold in particular.

Æthelwold's favored position in King Edgar's court and his installation at Winchester with oversight of the prestigious scriptorium meant that his deliberate efforts to regularize vocabulary had far-reaching consequences. The predominance of the term *cynescipe* in texts associated with Winchester, whether that be through authorship or content, reveals the success of those endeavors. Throughout this essay, we have seen the term *cynescipe* used in Edgar's law codes, two wills, a homily by Ælfric along with his *Lives of Saints,* and the anonymous *Legend of the Seven Sleepers;* finally, we saw the term in Wulfstan's *Institutes of Polity,* and returned to its legal context in Cnut's Winchester code and Letter of 1020. These occurrences span no more than sixty years and, instead of a popular Old English term for kingship, the evidence suggests the word had a limited range of influence, with Bishop Æthelwold serving as an important point of connection. Æthelwold's return to Winchester and close involvement with the scriptorium there presented an opportunity to introduce a new term, one which influenced his pupil Ælfric as well as legal writers composing charters in Winchester's scriptorium. His influence over the Old English language, enacted through that very same scriptorium and through his close relationship with King Edgar, ensured his literary legacy. The term *cynescipe* proves to be yet another word preferred by the bishop, and promoted through the Winchester school, to underscore the responsibilities of a king and provide an idealized view of kingship – a word that achieves additional heights through the writings of his pupils. Both Ælfric and Wulfstan use the word *cynescipe* to express their views – often explicitly, sometimes not – of a king's responsibilities to his people, and conversely, the people's responsibility to their king. Over the term's short lifespan, *cynescipe* developed from a word that mainly emphasized authority to one drawing more on the aspect of royal dignity, and finally solidified into a formulaic and titulary expression.

3

Traces and Supplements: Literary Prose in Sawyer 404

Scott T. Smith

The charter known as Sawyer 404, dated to 930, presents a diplomatic puzzle in which multiple traditions, events, and interventions converge in a single document.[1] While the authenticity of the text remains uncertain, the charter does show elements of several established diplomatic traditions, all of which share an interest in artful prose. Moreover, S 404 contains two short supplements to the original act of donation, one from King Æthelstan (r. 924–39) in a postscript, and one from King Edgar (r. 959–75) in a final addendum. In the context of its archive, the charter deals with a property that is also at issue in two other later documents and seems to take measures to safeguard against potential complications from a past forfeiture. This difficult charter, then, is a multivocal text that shows an accumulation of several diplomatic styles and tenurial interests.

S 404 can best be seen as an accumulative text, carrying traces and supplements of texts and events that both precede and follow its given date of 930. The history of the involved property is somewhat complex, but it can be summarized as follows:[2]

- King Æthelstan grants the Dumbleton (Gloucestershire) estate to Cynath, abbot of Evesham (Worcestershire), in 930.[3]

[1] All charters are cited by their number in P. H. Sawyer, *Anglo-Saxon Charters: An Annotated List and Bibliography* (London: Royal Historical Society, 1968), hereafter abbreviated as S. A revised and updated version of Sawyer is available at https://esawyer.lib.cam.ac.uk/. See also Simon Keynes, "Church Councils, Royal Assemblies, and Anglo-Saxon Royal Diplomas," in *Kingship, Legislation and Power in Anglo-Saxon England*, ed. Gale R. Owen-Crocker and Brian W. Schneider (Woodbridge: Boydell, 2013), 17–182. The most recent edition of S 404 appears in S. E. Kelly, ed., *Charters of Abingdon Abbey*, 2 vols. (Oxford: Oxford University Press, 2000), 92–99 (no. 22).

[2] This summary is drawn from Kelly, *Abingdon*, 94–95.

[3] Evesham is not named in the document. The Abingdon Chronicle wrongly names Cynath as an early abbot, claiming that he gave the land directly to Abingdon (Kelly, *Abingdon*, 98).

- Cynath later transfers the property to Osulf, bishop of Ramsbury (Wiltshire), whose possession is later confirmed by King Edgar, as affirmed in the postscript to S 404.
- The property is forfeited into the possession of King Æthelred II, who sells the land to Archbishop Ælfric in 1002.[4]
- Ælfric bequeaths the Dumbleton estate, with newly added lands, to Abingdon (Berkshire), sometime between 1002 and 1005.[5]

Clearly, such a history would require careful documentation to ensure against future competing claims. Susan Kelly has aptly observed that S 404 "has evidently been reworked, perhaps on several occasions, and may have reached its present form in the eleventh century." This reworking most likely occurred when the land passed from Archbishop Ælfric to Abingdon, with earlier documentation feeding into the finished product of S 404.[6] This composite text was then incorporated into two Abingdon cartularies, in somewhat modified form. The earlier cartulary-chronicle (British Library, Cotton Claudius C.ix, written *c.* 1170) contains the charter with an abbreviated witness list and no boundary clause.[7] The later recension (British Library, Cotton Claudius B.vi, written in the early thirteenth century) introduces new documents and expands many of the pre-Conquest charters (including S 404) that are abbreviated in the earlier cartulary-chronicle, along with some revision of narrative content to fit contemporary needs and perceptions.[8] Another key witness to the 'original' S 404 is a transcript of a single-sheet version that is now lost, made by Robert Talbot in the mid sixteenth century.[9] Talbot's copy uniquely

4 These events are recorded in S 901 (Kelly, *Abingdon*, 512–17, no. 132). The land was forfeited by a woman accused of adultery (*fornicaria preuaricatione*). Kelly suggests that "she had inherited the estate from Bishop Osulf (who died in 970) or from one of his heirs," adding that S 404 "contains a suspicious passage governing what was to happen to the estate in the case of forfeiture" (517). Clearly, this past forfeiture required some management in S 404.

5 The vernacular will survives in a thirteenth-century copy (S 1488; Kelly, *Abingdon*, 517–22, no. 133), with a Latin translation in the twelfth-century Abingdon Chronicle. See John Hudson, ed. and trans., *Historia ecclesie Abbendonensis: The History of the Church of Abingdon*, vol. 1 (Oxford: Clarendon, 2007), 168–71.

6 Kelly, *Abingdon*, 95 and 98.

7 The abbreviated witness list ends after the subscription of archbishops Wulfhelm (Canterbury) and Hrothweard (York), followed by the collective episcopal subscription *ceterisque pontificibus*. The vernacular bounds appear elsewhere in the manuscript, within a collection of boundary clauses gathered in the final quire of the manuscript. See Kelly, *Abingdon*, liii–lviii. For an edition of BL, Cotton Claudius C.ix, see Hudson, *Abingdon*.

8 Kelly, *Abingdon*, xlviii–l.

9 Ibid., xlvii. Talbot's transcripts are preserved in Cambridge, Corpus Christi

contains the postscript from King Edgar. His source document apparently contained an abbreviated witness list, but Talbot later squeezed an expanded list between the original shortened list and Edgar's postscript, which follows immediately after the abbreviated witnesses.[10] The Talbot transcript accordingly preserves an intermediate form of the archival material that was available to the Abingdon compilers.

S 404 was apparently worked up from a set of earlier records (many of which are now lost) into a finished text, with its distinct style being something of a joining mechanism. This style, moreover, is reminiscent of several diplomatic traditions known for their literary ambitions. Susan Kelly has called attention to the text's affiliations with earlier Mercian diplomatic, as well as the distinct style of the "Æthelstan A" charters (produced between 928 and 935) and the group collectively known as the "alliterative charters" (produced in the 940s and 950s); at the same time, Kelly makes the valuable point that S 404 is "essentially unique," despite its links with other charter traditions.[11] This amalgamation of styles in a unique document creates an aesthetic that is tailored for reminiscence, drawing upon multiple precedents and traditions in its cultivation of a style that presents itself as appropriate to its claimed place, time, and purpose. In this way, the charter uses literary performance as a means of claiming documentary legitimacy. This essay examines how S 404 achieves this performance through its measured use of techniques common to tenth-century literary charters specifically, and to artistic Latin prose generally. An initial survey of some of these techniques and precedents provides necessary context for the analysis of S 404.

Artful Prose

One ornamental prose technique is the use of *cursus*, the practice of ending clauses (and even smaller units within a sentence) with favored cadences.[12] Classical authors like Cicero used quantitative rhythms based on

College 111, pp. 139–78. The copy of S 404 appears at pp. 171–73.

10 Kelly suggests that Talbot incorporated these additions "from another source (or perhaps from an addition on the dorse)": *Abingdon*, 95–96. The full witness list is also preserved in the thirteenth-century copy. The complete list contains many subscriptions that are impossible for the assigned date of 930. Kelly suggests, however, that the expanded list was culled from a later charter and then added to S 404 at a later stage. While such a scenario would improve its claims to authenticity, the text's style suggests a composition date of *c.* 950, which accords well with the terms of office in the expanded witnesses.

11 Kelly, *Abingdon*, 96–97.

12 For *cursus* in general, see Gudrun Lindholm, *Studien zum mittellateinischen*

sequences of long and short syllables, a system which gradually gave way to a practice based on stress patterns. In medieval writers, these rhythms were typically based on syllable count and accentuation, most often (but not always) involving the last two words of a clause or sentence (also known as a clausula). To mark these units, this essay uses the notational system developed by Tore Janson, in which a paroxytone (a word accented on the penult, i.e., the second syllable from the end) is marked as *p*, while a proparoxytone (a word accented on the antepenult, i.e., the third syllable from the end) is marked as *pp*.[13] The provided notation also indicates the number of syllables in the final word of the clausula. The most common forms of *cursus* in early medieval texts are the *planus*: p 3p (σ́σ σσ́σ), *tardus*: p 4pp (σ́σ σσ́σσ); *uelox*: pp 4p (σ́σσ σσσ́σ); and *trispondaicus*: p 4p (σ́σ σσσ́σ).[14] There are variations for each of these forms, but the sequence of accented and unaccented syllables for the most part remains regular.[15] *Cursus* was frequently employed by Latin authors in early medieval England as a device to enhance their prose. Consider the following sentence from Bede, in which he describes the grief at the death of Abbot Ceolfrith after he fell ill on the way to Rome:

> Neque enim facile quisquam lacrimas tenere potuit, uidens comites ipsius *partim* patre amisso coeptum iter agere, *partim* mutata intentione qua Romam ire desiderant domum magis qua hunc sepultum nuntiarent reuerti; *partim* ad tumbam defuncti inter eos quorum nec linguam nouerant pro inextinguibili patris affectu residere.

> No one found it easy to keep back their tears as they saw some of his companions carrying on the journey they had begun, with their father-abbot gone, while some of them changed their minds and preferred to turn back for home where they could relate the news of his burial, rather than wanting to go on to Rome; some of them stayed by

---

Prosarhythmus: seine Entwicklung und sein Abklingen in der Briefliteratur Italiens (Stockholm: Almqvist & Wiksell, 1963); Dag Norberg, *Manuel pratique de latin médiéval* (Paris: Picard, 1968), 86–88; Sten Eklund, "The Use and Abuse of Cursus in Textual Criticism," *Archivum Latinitatis Medii Aevi* 43 (1984): 27–56; and Terence O. Tunberg, "Prose Styles and Cursus," in *Medieval Latin: An Introduction and Bibliographical Guide*, ed. F. A. C. Mantello and A. G. Rigg (Washington, D.C.: Catholic University of America Press, 1996), 111–21.

13 Tore Janson, *Prose Rhythm in Medieval Latin from the 9th to the 13th Century* (Stockholm: Almqvist & Wiksell, 1975).

14 In this notation each sigma represents a syllable, with accents marked.

15 For example, a *cursus tardus* could also consist of one proparoxytone (pp) followed by a trisyllabic proparoxytone (3pp). In this case, the sequence and number of accented and unaccented syllables would be the same as a p 4pp clausula (σ́σ σσ́σσ), but the caesura would fall after the third syllable rather than the second.

> the dead man's tomb among people whose language they did not know, because of their inextinguishable devotion to their father-abbot.[16]

The first two clausulae, *tenére pótuit* and *íter ágere,* are both *cursus medius* (p 3pp), an accentual cadence modeled on a quantitative trochee-cretic.[17] Each unit marks the end of a clause, indicating a pause in the progression of the sentence. The second *medius* clausula follows the first of three uses of *partim* (here in a medial position) to recount the responses of the grieving *comites*. The third clausula, *nuntiárent reuérti,* introduces the more common *planus* (p 3p), with the final clausula, *afféctu resídere,* presenting a *tardus* (p 4pp). Accordingly, each of the final three clauses, each marked with *partim* – prominently moved to initial position in the third and fourth clause – features a different cadence in its clausula. Bede uses *cursus* as a means of embellishment as well as a way to measure and mark the syntax of a sentence.

We can draw another Anglo-Latin example of *cursus* from Wulfstan of Winchester's *Vita sancti Æthelwoldi,* written sometime around 996. In the following passage, Wulfstan ends each clausula with an appropriate cadence, with some attention to specific patterns and placements.

> Erat namque sanctus Æthelwoldus ecclesiarum ac diuersorum operum magnus aedifactor, et dum esset abbas et cum esset episcopus. Vnde tetendit ei communis aduersarius solitas suae malignitatis insidias ut eum si ullo modo posset extingueret. Nam quadam die, dum uir Dei in structura laboraret, ingens postis super *eum cecidit* et in quandam foueam deiecit confregitque paene omnes costas eius ex *uno latere,* ita ut nisi fouea illum susciperet totus quassaretur.

> St Æthelwold was a great builder of churches and other buildings, both as abbot and bishop. It was from this direction that the enemy of us all laid a typically malign trap, hoping if at all possible to kill him. One day, when the man of God was toiling at building work, a huge post fell on

16 Christopher Grocock and I. N. Wood, ed. and trans., *Abbots of Wearmouth and Jarrow* (Oxford: Clarendon, 2013), 70–73. Emphasis added.

17 There was an early transitional mode known as *cursus mixtus,* which often sought correspondence of accent and ictus and thus accommodated cadences beyond the basic *planus, tardus,* and *uelox* types. This style was practiced prominently in late antiquity and survived into the early medieval period, with a gradual drift away from the quantitative forms. See Steven M. Oberhelman, *Rhetoric and Homiletics in Fourth-Century Christian Literature: Prose Rhythm, Oratorical Style, and Preaching in the Works of Ambrose, Jerome, and Augustine* (Atlanta, GA: Scholars Press, 1991); and Giovanni Orlandi, "Metrical and Rhythmical Clausulae in Medieval Latin Prose: Some Aspects and Problems," in *Aspects of the Language of Latin Prose,* ed. Tobias Reinhardt, Michael Lapidge, and J. N. Adams (Oxford: Oxford University Press, 2005), 395–412.

> him, knocking him into a pit. He broke almost all his ribs on one side, and would have been completely shattered but for the pit breaking his fall.[18]

In the first sentence each clausula ends with a different cadence, with a nominative noun in final position: *mágnus aedifáctor* (p 4p) and *ésset epíscopus* (p 4pp). This balance of parallel syntax and measured rhythm is supported by other embellishments, such as the repetition of "et dum esset" and "et cum esset" near the end of the sentence. As the mood shifts to the sinister, however, the clausulae change to *cursus trispondaicus* (p 4p), bringing a change in rhythm alongside a turn in action.[19] Moreover, setting aside the initial ablative absolute, the final sentence shows something of a chiastic arrangement in its cadences: *structúra laboráret* (p 4p), *éum cécidit* (p 3pp), *fóueam deiécit* (pp 3p), *úno látere* (p 3pp), and *tótus quassarétur* (p 4p). In other words, an opening and closing *trispondaicus* bracket two *cursus medius*, with a variant *trispondaicus* nested within them.[20] One might see a structural parallel between the placement of the central clausula and the sheltering pit that saves Æthelwold's life. At any rate, this passage shows how prose rhythms can inform the shape and meaning of a sentence, with cadences occurring not only at the end of a sentence or clause, but also within it.

Another prominent literary device in S 404 is the repetition of sound, especially alliteration. Alliteration was, of course, commonly employed by Anglo-Saxon writers throughout the period, both in the vernacular and in Latin.[21] Bede includes the device in his textbook of rhetorical figures (under the name of paromoeon) and we can see the technique in active use across many Anglo-Latin texts.[22] Aldhelm, whose style was a clear influence on tenth-century Anglo-Latin writers, famously displayed the device with characteristic panache in the opening sentence of his Letter to

18 Wulfstan of Winchester, *The Life of St Æthelwold*, ed. Michael Lapidge and Michael Winterbottom (Oxford: Clarendon, 1991), 28–29. Emphasis added.

19 The clausulae *pósset extinguéret, structúra laboráret,* and *tótus quassarétur* all show the *trispondaicus* cadence, although *extinguēret* and *quāssaretur* require vocal contraction to fit this scansion. For vowel contraction in two adjacent syllables, see Dag Norberg, *An Introduction to the Study of Medieval Latin Versification*, translated by Grant C. Roti and Jacqueline de La Chapelle Skubly (Washington, D.C.: Catholic University of America Press, 2004), 23–25.

20 In Janson's system the *trispondaicus* can be represented as pp 3p or p 4p, both of which have a cadence of σ́σσσσ́σ.

21 Andy Orchard, "Artful Alliteration in Anglo-Saxon Song and Story," *Anglia* 113 (1995): 429–63.

22 Bede, "De schematibus et tropis," in *Bedae Venerabilis Opera, Pars I: Opera didascalica*, ed. Calvin B. Kendall, Corpus Christianorum Series Latina 123A (Turnhout: Brepols, 1975), 148–49 (section 11).

Heahfrith, a text commonly studied in Anglo-Saxon schools as an exemplar of high style.[23]

> Primitus pantorum procerum praetorumque pio potissimum paternoque praesertim privilegio panagericum poemataque passim prosatori sub polo promulgantes stridula vocum simphonia et melodiae cantilenaeque carmine modulaturi ymnizemus, praecipue quia tandem almae editum puerperae sobolem ob inextricabile sons protoplaustorum piaculum priscorumque cirografum oblitteraturum terris tantundem destinare dignatus est, luridum qui linguis celydrum trisulcis rancida virulentaque vomentem per aevum venena torrentia tetrae tortionis in tartara trusit et, ubi pridem eiusdem nefandae natricis ermula cervulusque cruda fanis colebantur stoliditate in profanis, versa vice discipulorum gurgustia, immo almae oraminum aedes architecti ingenio fabre conduntur.[24]

> Principally, with particularly pious and paternal privilege, publicly proffering beneath the pole panegyric and poems promiscuously to the Procreator of all princes and praetors, let us raise a hymn in measured rhythms with a loud blending of voices and with song of melodious music, especially because He who thrust into Tartarus of terrible torture the ghastly three-tongued serpent who vomits torrents of rank and virulent poisons through the ages deigned in like measure to send to earth the offspring begotten of holy parturition in order to obliterate from the earth the criminal offense of first matter and the record of the first men on account of their inextricable sin; and (because), where once the crude pillars of the same foul snake and the stag were worshipped with coarse stupidity in profane shrines, in their place dwellings for students, not to mention holy houses of prayer, are constructed skillfully by the talents of the architect.[25]

The most conspicuous effect in this passage is its sustained burst of alliteration, with fifteen of the first sixteen words beginning with *p*. The sentence also contains more subtle uses of the technique, however, such as alliter-

[23] See Michael Lapidge and Michael Herren, trans., *Aldhelm: The Prose Works* (Cambridge: Cambridge University Press, 1979), 143–46; Scott Gwara, "A Record of Anglo-Saxon Pedagogy: Aldhelm's 'Epistola ad Heahfridum' and its Gloss," *Journal of Medieval Latin* 6 (1996): 84–134; and Mechthild Gretsch, *The Intellectual Foundations of the English Benedictine Reform* (Cambridge: Cambridge University Press, 1999), 362–65. The letter survives in five manuscripts from the Anglo-Saxon period. In four of these manuscripts the letter is paired with the prose *De uirginitate*. See Helmut Gneuss and Michael Lapidge, *Anglo-Saxon Manuscripts: A Bibliographical Handlist of Manuscripts and Manuscript Fragments Written or Owned in England up to 1100* (Toronto: University of Toronto Press, 2014), nos. 464, 473, 613, and 707.

[24] Rudolf Ehwald, ed., *Aldhelmi opera*, Monumenta Germaniae Historica, Auctores antiquissimi 15 (Berlin: Weidmann, 1919), 488–89.

[25] Aldhelm, *Prose Works*, 160–61.

ative pairs, some of them consecutive (*terris tantundem destinare dignatus*), as well as chiastic alliteration (*melodiae cantilenaeque carmine modulaturi*). Aldhelm would have provided a ready model for ornamental sound play in Latin prose.

The influence of Aldhelm is especially strong in the charters attributed to the draftsman known as "Æthelstan A," who produced a series of extraordinary documents under King Æthelstan between the years 928 and 935.[26] The following proem gives a good representation of the draftsman's distinctive style.

> Flebilia fortiter detestanda . totillantis sæculi piacula . diris obscenæ horrendæque mortalitatis . circumsepta latratibus . non nos patria indoeptæ pacis securos . sed quasi foetidæ corruptelæ in voraginem casuros . provocando ammonent . ut ea toto mentis conamine cum casibus suis . non solum despiciendo . sed etiam velud fastidiosam melancoliæ nausiam . abhominando fugiamus . tendentes ad illud evvangelicum; "date et dabitur vobis"; Qua de ré infima . quasi peripsema . quisquiliarum abiciens . superna ad instar pretiosorum monilium eligens . animum sempiternis in gaudiis figens . ad adipiscendam mellifluæ dulcedinis misericordiam . perfruendamque infinit[ae] letitiæ jucunditatem.[27]

> The woeful sins – which must be strongly abhorred – of the tottering world, encompassed by the dire howling of foul and horrible death, by their challenge remind us – we who are not secure in the peace obtained in the homeland, but rather about to plummet into an abyss of stinking corruption – to shun them with their calamities through a full effort of mind, not only by despising them but also by loathing them as if the nauseating vomit of biliousness, aiming for the gospel, "Give and it will be given to you," and therefore casting off the basest things as if the off-scouring of waste, choosing heavenly things in the likeness of costly necklaces and fixing the mind in never-ending joy on gaining the mercy of honeyed sweetness and on enjoying fully the delight of infinite happiness.

This proem has been analyzed in detail elsewhere, but we might quickly note instances of alliteration (*flebilia fortiter*), end rhyme (*fastidiosam melancoliæ nausiam*), and chiasmus (*adipiscendam mellifluæ dulcedinis misericor-*

[26] For the style of these charters, see Scott T. Smith, *Land and Book: Literature and Land Tenure in Anglo-Saxon England* (Toronto: University of Toronto Press, 2012), 35–46; D. A. Woodman, "'Æthelstan A' and the Rhetoric of Rule," *Anglo-Saxon England* 42 (2013), 217–48; and Ben Snook, *The Anglo-Saxon Chancery: The History, Language and Production of Anglo-Saxon Charters from Alfred to Edgar* (Woodbridge: Boydell, 2015), 86–124.

[27] S 416. Walter de Gray Birch, ed., *Cartularium Saxonicum: A Collection of Charters Relating to Anglo-Saxon History, Vol. 2: A.D. 840–947* (London: Whiting, 1887), 363 (no. 677).

diam), all devices favored by Aldhelm. The pointing in the contemporary single-sheet manuscript, reproduced above, however, also directs attention to other techniques. Many of the marked word units show distinct *cursus* patterns.

cursus tardus (p 4pp): *circumsépta latrátibus, quisquiliárum abíciens*
cursus planus (p 3p): *pácis secúres, provocándo ammónent*
cursus trispondaicus (p 4p / pp 3p): *quási peripséma, voráginem casúros, abhominándo fugiámus*
cursus uelox (pp 4p): *fórtiter detestánda*
Rarer *tardus* (pp 3pp): *melancóliæ naúsiam, monílium éligens*
Rarer *uelox* (p 5p): *horrendáeque mortalitátis, sólum despiciéndo*

In addition to this proliferation of clausulae, all marked off by pointing in the single-sheet manuscript, there is a pronounced degree of rhythmical patterning across the first three marked units. Each of the first two units – *flebilia fortiter detestanda* and *totillantis sæculi piacula* – contains three words totaling eleven syllables, in a grouping of 4-3-4. And while the two groups are not isotonic, they do show a chiastic pattern of accentuation:

flebilia fortiter detestanda (σσ́σσ σ́σσ σσσ́σ / ABC)
totillantis sæculi piacula (σσσ́σ σ́σσ σσ́σσ / CBA)

Moreover, each three-word group is internally chiastic in its accentuation, proliferating the effect.[28] Finally, the third unit – *diris obscenæ horrendæque mortalitatis* – features a long syllabic crescendo, in an ascending sequence of 2-3-4-5. Such a profusion of rhythmic effects fits well with Æthelstan A's propensity for exuberant expansion and literary showmanship.

The closest precedent for the style of S 404, however, can be found in the distinct group of tenth-century diplomas now generally known as the "alliterative charters." The approximately twenty charters in the group were produced throughout the 940s and into the 950s under kings Edmund (r. 939–46) and Eadred (r. 946–55), with the final diploma in the series being issued by King Eadwig in 956.[29] The alliterative charters contain several distinguishing features, but most important for our pur-

[28] A similar pattern appears in the proem's final word group, "perfruendamque infinitæ letitiæ jucunditatem" (σσσσ́σ σσσ́σ σσ́σσ σσσσ́σ), with a 5-4-4-5 arrangement. The middle two words contain significant sound repetition on medial -*t*- and final *ae*, and also show a chiastic pattern of accentuation. The first and last words in the group are isotonic, thereby marking the beginning and end of the unit.

[29] The alliterative group includes S 392, 404, 472, 473, 479, 484, 1606, 1497, 520, 544, 549, 548, 550, 552a, 556, 557, 569, 572, 566, 574, 633, 1290, and 931.

poses here is their use of alliteration and rhythmic effects.[30] The group can be represented here by a proem from S 549, dated to 949.

> Cunctis catholice conuersantibus certum est quod omnis sapiencia a domino constat esse concessa sagacibus . Quapropter studendum est toto mentis iam conamine illius opitulante prerogatiua qui euuangelico paradigmate protulit dicens ; discite a me quia mitis sum et humilis corde . discere . intelligere . et perseuerare . quia perseuerantibus ; finetinus salus promissa est perpetua.[31]

> To all those who abide by the Catholic faith, it is certain that all wisdom is agreed to have been granted to the wise by the Lord. Wherefore, it must be pursued with the full power of the mind, with the primary help of the one who pronounced in evangelical example, "Learn from me because I am mild and humble in heart."[32] Learning. Understanding. Being steadfast. Because for those who are steadfast, the salvation promised is forever eternal.

This short opening statement contains a remarkable level of ornamentation, primarily in its sound repetitions and rhythmic patterning. Alliteration is prominent throughout the proem. The first clause features words beginning with *c*, for example, with six words of fourteen participating; the alliteration is especially clustered at the beginning and end of the clause. The second and third clauses feature alliteration on *p*, with clusters of that sound framing the embedded biblical verse. Furthermore, the final four words can be arranged in two units of five syllables each, with sound repetitions in initial, medial, and final positions (*salus promissa / est perpetua*). Finally, the only words in the proem that begin with *d* together outline a theological maxim: *domino, dicens, discite/discere*; that is, God speaks and the faithful learn. The proem to S 549 shows remarkable sound repetitions and patterning.

[30] For the alliterative charters, see Simon Keynes, "King Athelstan's Books," in *Learning and Literature in Anglo-Saxon England: Studies Presented to Peter Clemoes*, ed. Michael Lapidge and Helmut Gneuss (Cambridge: Cambridge University Press, 1985), 153–59; Cyril Hart, "Danelaw and Mercian Charters of the Mid Tenth Century," in *The Danelaw* (London: Hambledon, 1992), 431–53; S. E. Kelly, ed., *Charters of Glastonbury Abbey* (Oxford: Oxford University Press, 2012), 376–77 and 382–84; and Charles Insley, "Collapse, Reconfiguration or Renegotiation? The Strange End of the Mercian Kingdom, 850–924," *Reti Medievali Rivista* 17 (2016): 231–49. The alliterative charters are most often described as "alliterative and rhythmical" with little elaboration. For some discussion of the learned vocabulary in the alliterative charters, see Snook, *Anglo-Saxon Chancery*, 138–43.

[31] P. H. Sawyer, ed., *Charters of Burton Abbey* (Oxford: Oxford University Press, 1979), 13–14 (no. 8).

[32] Matthew 11:29.

The proem also displays several notable rhythmical effects. First, the final three words of the first clause (*esse concéssa sagácibus*) are arranged in ascending order of syllable count (2-3-4), with the clausula showing *cursus tardus* (p 4pp). This confluence of rhythmical ornament – in combination with the repetition of *s* across the three words in initial, medial, and final positions – provides a stylistic punctuation to the end of the first sentence. Second, the proximate phrases *opitulante prerogatiua* and *euuangelico paradigmate* show parallel word order (adjective-noun) in isosyllabic units (each word has five syllables), perhaps as an elevated introduction for the biblical citation that follows. Notably, this rhythmical effect is complemented by vocalic and consonantal alliteration, while the like endings of *opitulante* and *paradigmate* bracket the unit with end rhyme. Third, the string of infinitives that follows the biblical verse (*discere. intelligere. et perseuerare*) features homoeoteleuton (the repetition of identical or like endings), combining grammatical and sound repetition across three units of rising syllable count (3-5-6). Moreover, polyptoton links the following casual clause to the infinitives (*perseuerare / perseuerantibus*), with three consecutive words in that clause ending in *-us*. The proem of S 549 exhibits a clear fondness for different kinds of ornamental patterning, especially in groups of three. This short analysis gives some idea of the general style of the alliterative charters, parts of which also appear prominently in S 404.

Putting it all Together

We begin our consideration of the literary elements in S 404 by examining its proem, which immediately follows the conventional sign of the Cross. Proems commonly provide an occasion for a preliminary statement – often delivered in elevated terms and style – before the document moves to the business of property. Accordingly, the somewhat short proem in S 404 packs a remarkable amount of ornamentation into a small space.

> Summa polorum cacumina, ima quoque solorum fundamina, tetra necnon baratrorum tragoedia almę trinitatis monarchia regnando ac regendo premendoque auctor omnium Deus gubernat æthraliter, cuius uidelicet largifluę liberalitatis munificentia Æthelstanum regem Albionis præstantissimum solio sublimauit paterno ac triquadri orbis rumigerula prȩceteris ampliauit prerogatiua.[33]

> God, the author of all things – not the gloomy drama of the abyss – governs from above the highest summits of the heavens and the deepest foundations of the earth, reigning, guiding, and controlling by rule of the

[33] Kelly, *Abingdon*, 92–93.

> blessed Trinity. His munificence of flowing generosity, it is clear to see, elevated Æthelstan, most excellent king of Albion, to his ancestral seat, and increased privileges celebrated above all others of the tripartite orb.

This opening sentence shows clear attention to symmetry and rhythm. The first two noun phrases are parallel in terms of grammar, number, and syllable count, with end rhyme linking the units: *summa polorum cacumina* and *ima solorum fundamina*. Each phrase can be parsed as follows: accusative plural adjective – genitive plural noun – accusative plural noun. Furthermore, if we remove *quoque*, each phrase is isosyllabic, with three words containing a total of nine syllables in a neatly ascendant grouping of 2-3-4; the first two phrases are likewise isotonic, as they show identical patterns of stress (σ́σσσ́σσσ́σσ). And if we designate *necnon* as hypermetrical, the third noun phrase (*tetra … baratrorum tragoedia*) has a very similar syllable count and accentuation pattern, with a difference of a single additional syllable. Rhyme across the first three phrases is restricted to the recurrent *-orum* in medial position, with the first and third words each ending in *-a*, resulting in a proximate sound repetition of final sounds across all three phrases. These subtle differences signal a shift in case, as this third noun phrase is declined nominative. Small variation here keeps the prose from becoming overly rigid, avoiding excessive expansion and overdetermined pattern. Taken together, these stylistic devices show a deliberate attention to ornament and symmetry, with a measured unrolling of the document's opening sentence.

After the initial sequence of rhythmic and rhyming noun phrases, the sentence presents a gerund phrase, describing an attendant condition for the grammatical action that has yet to be specified. Notably, the noun phrase *álmę trinitátis monárchia* (in the ablative) shares the same syllable count and accentuation as the preceding noun phrase (*tétra … baratrórum tragóedia*), along with a repetition of final *-ia*. Even as these shared elements connect the new construction to the sentence's opening noun phrases, the phrase does not continue the precedent of the medial *-orum*, breaking that pattern as it changes to the singular number. Consequently, the sentence maintains some continuity even as it signals a change in sound and syntax while it continues to develop meaning incrementally. The construction ends in a sequence of three gerunds, the first two of which (*regnando* and *regendo*) provide the proem's first instance of proximate alliteration. Moreover, the two words are nearly identical in spelling, even though they are formed from two different but closely related verbs, which, in an extreme case of paronomasia, extends the repetition of sound across the words.[34] The final gerund in the sequence (*premendo*) likewise introduces a prefix that will

[34] Paronomasia can be defined as a repetition in which different words that are similar in sound appear close together. In this case, the relevant words

be repeated prominently in the second clause. Accordingly, the ablative construction both continues established patterns and anticipates new techniques to come later in the document's opening statement.

The first clause ends with its finite verb and agent: "auctor omnium Deus gubernat æthraliter." This word order artfully delays both the subject and its verb until the end of the clause. Moreover, the sense here is exceptionally clear and direct, with no ornamentation to obscure or delay meaning. The phrase *auctor omnium* also reverses the genitive-nominative word order evident in all preceding noun phrases, with the appositive addition of *Deus* followed by the adverb *æthraliter*. These elements all introduce variation at the end of the clause without taxing sense or syntax. Finally, the last three words in the clause (*Deus gubernat æthraliter*) present a threefold crescendo in terms of syllable count, in an ascending pattern of 2-3-4, with *cursus tardus* (p 4pp) marking the end of the clause. Fancy.

The second clause, however, is somewhat more modest in ornamentation. Its final four words, for example, *rumigerula pręceteris ampliauit prerogatiua*, show a chiastic arrangement in terms of syllable count (5-4-4-5) but not in accentuation.[35] Likewise, the first and final words in this group share initial (*r-*), medial (*-g-* and *-r-*) and final (*-a*) sounds, whereas the two middle words show little sound repetition of any kind. There are other notable but modest embellishments in the clause, including two alliterative word pairs (*largifluę liberalitatis* and *solio sublimauit*) and the threefold repetition of the prefix *prae-*, all of which extend sounds and techniques present in the three gerunds from the first clause. These several groupings of three complement the appearance of a 'three-group' word in both the first and second clauses (*trinitatis* and *triquadri*), each of which is declined as genitive singular. The proem, consisting of a single sentence, compresses a significant number of literary devices within a limited space.

The next section of the document, which states the grant of property, adjusts the balance of the stylistic embellishments present in the proem. As in the proem, there is some rhythmical patterning, but on a much more modest scale. At the same time, the disposition amplifies the use of alliteration considerably, going well beyond the level of use evident in the proem.

> Tali namque sceptrorum suffultus diademate patronus regię dignitatis pannagericus gratuita cordis generositate Cynatho monasticę conuersationis archimandritę proprię possessionis tellurem duobus in locis iure hereditario perpetualiter condonauit, ac pręfato abbati suisque post

are the verbs are *regnare* (ā-stem, first conjugation) and *regere* (e-stem, third conjugation).

35 This patterning might explain why *praeceteris* is written as a single word rather than as a proper prepositional phrase (*prae ceteris*).

> se heredibus, euuangelico prouocatus paradigmate taliter promulgante 'Omni habenti dabitur et habundabit,' perhenniter possidendam firmauerat. Hoc denique imperator magnanimus non pretio philargirię sed longeuæ prosperitatis patrocinio ac paradisiacę amęnitatis mercimonio more solito prestauerat gratis.[36]
>
> Born up by such a crown of scepters, this celebrated patron of royal dignity, in the free generosity of his heart gave land of his own property in two places, perpetually and in hereditary right, to Cynath, abbot of monastic life, and, inspired by the evangelical example that so proclaims, "To each who has, it shall be given, and he shall prosper," he confirmed the possession eternally for the aforementioned abbot and his heirs after him. Finally, the magnanimous ruler in his usual way affirmed this freely, not for the love of money but for the support of lasting prosperity and the goods of paradisiacal comfort.

The first two clauses end in distinct cadences: *perpetuáliter condonáuit* (pp 4p, *uelox*) and *possidéndam firmáuerat* (p 4pp, *tardus*). Such *cursus* patterns, as we have seen, indicate an elevated register, and in this case their application underscores the security and perpetuity of the recorded grant of land. The final clause in the disposition, however, does not show *cursus* in its ending. Indeed, the lack of a standard rhythmic ending here is somewhat conspicuous, as the presence of the adverb *gratis* disrupts both a potential *cursus uelox* (*sólito prestauérat gratis*) and a syllabic crescendo in a 2-3-4 grouping (*more solito prestauerat*), a device which appears at the end of the proem's first clause (*Deus gubernat æthraliter*). In other words, the presence of *gratis* disturbs two different rhythmic patterns established earlier in the charter. What might be the significance of this disruption? One explanation would be that the shift is simply an insignificant accident, although the presence of two broken patterns would suggest some deliberation on the part of the draftsman. Another interpretation would be that the unconventional placement of *gratis* calls attention to itself, signaling special import for the statement as a whole and for the significance of that one word.[37] The clarification that the king received no payment may be an important part of the property's history before it made its way into the possession of Abingdon, perhaps to remove it more securely from potential competing claims, but the exact circumstances remain uncertain.

Finally, there is another aspect that might support a deliberate shift in rhythmic ornament in the final clause. Instead of *cursus*, the last sentence features two parallel phrases near its end (coming, in fact, immediately before the near occurrence of *cursus uelox*). The appositive phrases

[36] Kelly, *Abingdon*, 93.

[37] It should be noted as well that the first two clauses in the disposition both end with a finite verb.

"longeuæ prosperitatis patrocinio ac paradisiacę amęnitatis mercimonio" are parallel in syntax (genitive singular adjective and noun / dative singular noun), with the last two words of each phrase being isotonic (σσσσ́σ σσσ́σσ). The last two words of each phrase also demonstrate homoeoteleuton, the repetition of like endings (*-itatis* and *-nio*), which neatly fortifies the syntactic and accentual parallels with multisyllabic end rhyme across the two phrases.

Alliteration and other sound repetitions also contribute considerably to the passage's elevated style. There is sustained alliteration on *p* throughout the passage, with fifteen words participating in the pattern, recalling the bravado alliteration in Aldhelm's Letter to Heahfrith, but on a more modest scale. The charter's alliteration on *p* also clusters especially around its biblical citation, providing an ornamental frame for the quotation: "euuangelico **p**rouoca**t**us **p**aradigm<u>ate</u> tal*iter* **p**romul<u>gante</u> 'Omni habenti dabitur et habundabit,' **p**erh<u>enn</u>*iter* **p**ossid<u>en</u>dam firmauerat." Additional sound repetitions include the end rhyme of *-iter* (again bracketing the biblical verse); the near rhyme of *-ate* and *-ante*, near final *-t-*, and medial *-g-* in the first group; and medial *-en-* in the second, with that sound receiving the accent in both occurrences. Moreover, the *p* sound notably does not appear in the citation, which sets the biblical text apart even more. Finally, aside from *paradigmate*, the *p*-words in the passage are isosyllabic, and all but one of those (*perhenniter*) isotonic, with a cadence of σσσ́σ. Again, repetitions of sound and rhythm collaborate to create an embellished prose style.

Other cases of alliteration appear in the passage, as in first sentence: "**s**ceptrorum **s**uffultus **d**iademate **p**atronus regię **d**ignit<u>atis</u> **p**annagericus **g**ratu<u>ita</u> **c**ordis **g**enerosit<u>ate</u> **C**ynatho monasticę **c**onuers<u>ati</u>onis." The distribution of alliteration here pleases in its variety, especially in the interlaced series of *d-p-*[x]*-d-p* and *g-c-g-c*. The end of the final sentence likewise displays a saturation of sound play: "**p**retio **p**hilargirię sed longeuæ **p**rosperitatis **p**atrocinio ac **p**aradisiācę a**m**ęnitatis **m**erci**m**onio **m**ore <u>s</u>oli**t**o pre<u>s</u>**t**auera**t** grati<u>s</u>." After the string of alliteration on *p*, the passage clusters repetitions in initial, medial, and final positions: first *m* and then *t*, with the last three words containing *s* in initial, medial, and final position. Additionally, the passage features five consecutive words of five syllables each, excluding *ac*: "prosperitatis patrocinio ~~ac~~ paradisiācę amęnitatis mercimonio." The disposition provides an impressive display of artful prose, incorporating a range of techniques distinguished in their facility and variation.

Another remarkable concentration of ornamentation, again built upon repetitions of rhythm and sound, appears in the document's expansive dating clause.

> Hec nempe condonatio peracta est nongentesimo atque tricesimo laterculo Iesualis infantię summique prolis essentię, ac ter assis indictio copulatim coniungitur. Huius pro certo largifluę dapsilitatis locupletatio firma senatorum adstipulatione atque rata adsertione, uti infra karaxatur, quinto anno ex quo nobilissime gloriosus rex Angolsaxones regaliter gubernabat tertioque postquam authentice Northanhymbrorum Cumbrorumque blanda mirifici conditoris beniuolentia patrocinando sceptrine gubernaculum perceperat uirgę constat esse Christo to theon suffragante salubriter adimpleta ac prisco certissimę diriuationis confinio circumcincta hoc modo dinoscitur.[38]

> For in fact this grant was completed in the 930th year of Jesus's infancy and the essence of a highest offspring, and the indiction of a cycle thrice joined together. In truth, this enrichment of flowing munificence was beneficially done, with the secure confirmation and fixed affirmation of nobles, as written below, five years from when the most nobly glorious king of the Anglo-Saxons governed royally, and three years after he had authoritatively secured the guidance of the sceptral rod over the Northumbrians and Cumbrians, with the aid of the gentle benevolence of the wondrous Founder, and the support of Christ God. And it is established to be encircled as follows by ancient bounds of most certain derivation.

Susan Kelly has called attention to "the consciously literary language" in this dating clause, along with several parallels between it and the alliterative charters.[39] Going beyond this general observation, we can note a proliferation of embellishments in this passage featuring patterned repetitions of sound and rhythm. In terms of word order and syntax, we might note the parallel genitive phrases in the first sentence (*Iesualis infantię* and *prolis essentię*),[40] or hyperbaton in the phrase "sceptrine gubernaculum perceperat uirgę," with its separation of adjective and noun by a finite verb and its object.[41] It is in its rhythmical clausulae and patterned sound repetitions, however, that the dating clause shows its most ambitious literary effects. The first sentence, for example, contains three cases of *cursus tardus* (p 4pp):

> Hec nempe condonatio peracta est nongentesimo atque tricesimo laterculo Iesuális infántię summique prólis esséntię, ac ter assis indictio copulátim coniúngitur.

[38] Kelly, *Abingdon*, 93.

[39] Ibid., 97.

[40] The isotonic *infantię* and *essentię* (σσ́σσ) also feature disyllabic rhyme.

[41] Hyperbaton is a rhetorical device that features the disruption of natural or expected word order.

The number of clausulae here extends the document's interest in groupings of three, most evident in the proem. Here the desired cadence adorns two key noun phrases – both of which observe the birth of Christ – as well as the end of the clause. *Cursus* continues throughout the section, with examples of *tardus* (*módo dinóscitur* = p 4pp), *uelox* (*regáliter gubernábat, salúbriter adimpléta* = pp 4p), rarer *uelox* (*ráta adsertióne* = p 5p), and *trispondaicus* (*ínfra karaxátur* = p 4p). These cadences typically fall at the end of clauses, but in one case round out a noun phrase that also features trisyllabic rhyme in words with a shared prefix, along with repetition of several prominent sounds, especially in medial positions: "firma senatorum adstipulatione atque rata adsertione."[42] In this case, rhythm collaborates with other techniques to achieve an elevated style within a single phrase.

The dating clause also features several instances of patterned alliteration and other sound repetitions. At first glance, alliteration in the passage might seem somewhat limited. There are three alliterative pairs, for example, but none of the sustained repetitions evident in earlier sections of the document. Instead, alliteration is present in several patterned sequences, as evident in the clause "gloriosus rex Angolsaxones regaliter gubernabat." As previously noted, this clause ends in a *cursus uelox*, which in this case fortifies a chiastic sequence of alliteration, with *Angolsaxones* in a non-participating middle position; moreover, there is some parallelism in syntax as a modifier immediately precedes the word it modifies in both the initial (noun) and final (verb) phrases. We also see alliteration correspond with concord in the phrase "blanda mirifici conditoris beniuolentia," with *b*- alliteration linking adjective and modified noun; similarly, the embedded genitive phrase shows a possible sound link, set at the end and beginning of the words, with the support of *r* sounds (mirifici conditoris) in a chiastic pattern. Finally, the final clause of the section, which introduces the boundary clause, contains staggered repetition of *c* and *d* in initial and medial positions, with a measured repetition of final *o* (three times, of course) in supporting position: "prisco certissimę diriuationis confinio circumcincta hoc modo dinoscitur."[43] Taken together,

[42] It is possible that final *m* would be suppressed before an initial vowel through elision.

[43] A general guideline for the pronunciation of medieval Latin holds that *c* was pronounced as [s] or [tʃ] before front vowels. Early Anglo-Latin writers such as Aldhelm and Alcuin, however, seem generally, like the early Irish, to have pronounced *c* as [k] before any vowel. This practice was resilient enough to prompt questions about the proper pronunciation of *c* from Abbo's students at Ramsey in the 980s. See G. Herbert Fowler, "Notes on the Pronunciation of Medieval Latin in England," *History* n.s. 22 (1937): 99–100; Norberg, *Medieval Latin Versification*, 45–46; and Roger Wright, "Abbo of Fleury in Ramsey (985–87)," in

these several examples show careful combinations of rhythm and sound in service of ornamentation.

After the vernacular boundary clause, the document includes a supplement that was most likely included to circumvent future claims against the estate due to its past forfeiture. This content is delivered in artful prose, using techniques common to previous sections, but with some new devices and variations.

> Hoc supplementum quoque huic singraphę rex famosissimus augmentabat ut ne aliquis fraudulenta seductione hunc codicellum uetustis euincere ualeat libellulis. Si quis quod absit possessor agelluli fas diuinum profanando seu ius humanum uiolando deliquerit, alius eiusdem genealogiæ rationabilius agens regi supradicto in longinquam perfruatur retributionem. Augentibus uero hoc regale donatiuum dupla Deus adaugebat bona, minuentibus necnon Satan cum satellitibus inferat dampna. Det Deus ne proueniat. Pax in euum seruantibus.[44]

> Furthermore, the renowned king added this supplement to this charter, lest someone through fraudulent deception should avail to annul this document by means of older deeds. If there is anything that the land's owner should lose by profaning divine law or forfeit by violating human law, another of the same kindred, by acting more reasonably with the aforementioned king, may have it in long-lasting recompense. For those enlarging this royal grant, God increased goods twice over, while for those diminishing it may Satan with his subordinates inflict losses. God grant that it not come to pass. Peace be always to the faithful.

This section contains some notable alliteration, mostly in its final clauses,[45] but the technique is more constrained here than in the proem and disposition. Still, the supplement does contain several other instances of ornamentation. There are two cases of hyperbaton, for example. Rather than grouping a noun and its modifying adjective together (as in *fraudulenta seductione*), the line "uetustis euincere ualeat libellulis" splits those words with a verbal phrase (typically, the finite verb would appear at the end of the clause). Likewise, the line "in longinquam perfruatur retributionem" inserts a finite verb within a prepositional phrase, an atypical placement. These two uses of artificial word order lend the prose a literary register.

Conceptualizing Multilingualism in England, c.800–c.1250, ed. Elizabeth M. Tyler (Turnhout: Brepols, 2011), 113–14. While acknowledging the complexity of the question, my analysis here reads *c* as sounding as [k].

44 Kelly, *Abingdon*, 93–94.

45 Note especially *donatiuum dupla Deus*, another grouping of three. In contrast, Satan receives a lesser alliterative grouping of two (*Satan cum satellitibus*).

There are also two cases of parallel syntax in the passage, both of which feature end rhyme. Such careful patterning continues the document's cultivation of artful prose.

(1) *fas diuinum profanando seu ius humanum uiolando*

Omitting the conjunction, the two phrases are isotonic (σ́ σσ́σ σσσ́σ), with the last two words of each phrase creating a *cursus trispondaicus* (p 4p). These shared rhythms effectively complement the parallel syntax of the group.

(2) *Augentibus uero hoc regale donatiuum dupla Deus adaugebat bona, / minuentibus necnon Satan cum satellitibus inferat dampna.*

In this case, the parallels fall at the beginning and end of the clauses (ablative plural participle / adverb … finite verb / accusative plural noun), with ornamental alliteration clustered within those parameters. Finally, the section concludes in two octosyllabic lines:

Det Deus ne ***prouéniat*** .
Pax *in euum seruántibus* .

These lines show several striking features. First, the lines are linked by cross alliteration, following the initial alliterative pair of *Det Deus*. Also, each line contains four words, with the first three words constituting four syllables in total distributed in different sequences: *Det Deus ne* (1-2-1) and *Pax in euum* (1-1-2). This pattern allows variation even as it continues the attention to parallelism evident throughout the charter. Additionally, the three words in each unit contain a total of nine letters. This might be an incidental detail, but repetition of the reversed common sounds in *ne* and *in* would suggest something more deliberate, as would the appearance of *e* in each word of the first line, nearly always in medial position. At any rate, the two lines function unequivocally as rhythmical verse, scanned as consecutive 8pp lines.[46] This technique concludes the section with a literary flourish, as the charter briefly incorporates a verse form into its performance of artful prose.

This attention to style is also manifest in the last section of the charter, in which King Edgar confirms Bishop's Osulf's possession of land as he received it from Abbot Cynath. As indicated earlier, this addendum

[46] In rhythmical verse the line is determined by syllable count and stress accent, most often in the last word in a line or period, rather than by quantity of syllables. See Norberg, *Medieval Latin Versification*, 81–186; Andy Orchard, *The Poetic Art of Aldhelm* (Cambridge: Cambridge University Press, 1994), 19–72; and Brent Miles, "The *Carmina Rhythmica* of Æthilwald: Edition, Translation, and Commentary," *Journal of Medieval Latin* 14 (2004): 73–117.

appears only in the Talbot transcript. Susan Kelly suggests that the Abingdon compilers suppressed the Edgar content, most likely to obscure potentially problematic aspects of the estate's history.[47] The addition was most likely included in S 404 to guard against complications arising from the past forfeiture that had occurred before the land made its way to Abingdon. Still, the section does disrupt the temporal integrity of the document, and since the original compilers wrongly assumed that Cynath had been an early abbot at Abingdon, its content might have raised unwelcome questions. Despite any uneasiness the compilers may have felt as they worked S 404 into their cartulary-chronicle, however, it seems that the charter itself was composed originally as a single piece.

> + Ego Eadgar Christi annuente gratia Anglorum basileus largifluam huius territorii confirmationem Osulfo præsuli, uti a Cynatho abbate ei pridem concessa fuerat, crucis taumate optimatum meorum utens consilio, restaurando perpetim corroboraui.[48]

> I, Edgar, king of the English, as affirmed by the favor of Christ, with the sign of the cross and in consultation with my worthies, confirmed the generous ratification of this land in everlasting renewal to Bishop Osulf, as it had been given him by Abbot Cynath.

The addition shows many of the same techniques that are evident in the main body of the charter, but their application here is more subdued. For example, the passage contains evenly distributed alliteration on *c* but without the more elaborate patterns we have noted elsewhere in the charter. The sentence also contains rhythmical clausulae, the first two with *cursus planus* and the final with *uelox*, a cadence often favored for the end of a sentence. The most elaborate ornamentation in the addition would be the opening noun phrase, which shows both hyperbaton (with separation of the appositive nominative nouns *Eadgar* and *basileus*) and chiastic word order (nominative noun – genitive noun – ablative absolute – genitive noun – nominative noun). In addition to these stylistic continuities, the postscript also shares vocabulary with other sections of the document, most notably *largifluam*, which also appears in the proem and dating clause (as *largifluę*), providing a lexical link across the charter. Despite its more muted style, then, and its use of some hermeneutic vocabulary not found elsewhere in the charter (*basileus* and *taumate*), the Edgar addition seems to have been written (or revised) to accord with the earlier material.

If S 404 was created from a set of documentary materials prior to its arrival at Abingdon, as Susan Kelly has suggested, then we can see its

[47] Kelly, *Abingdon*, lxii. Kelly observes that the compiler of BL, Cotton Claudius B.vi was especially "on his guard against difficult and sensitive material."

[48] Ibid., 94.

style as a crucial ingredient in that archival alchemy. Rebecca Stephenson and Emily Thornbury, along with their contributors, have usefully demonstrated that "Anglo-Latin authors were acutely conscious of style as a performance of affinities."[49] The Latinity of royal diplomas, especially those issued in the first half of the tenth century, is no exception. In the case of S 404, its author (or authors over time) infused the diplomatic text with those literary elements that were especially distinctive of Mercian charters produced between the 930s and 950s, as would be appropriate for its given date of 930. Through its conspicuous display of such elements, S 404 carefully situates itself within that diplomatic tradition, thus asserting both its artistic and documentary legitimacy.

49 Rebecca Stephenson and Emily V. Thornbury, eds., *Latinity and Identity in Anglo-Saxon Literature* (Toronto: University of Toronto Press, 2016), 5.

4

The Curious Incident of the Monster in the Night-Time: Circumstantial Evidence in Law and Poetry

Anya Adair

> [Detective Gregory:] "Is there any other point to which you would wish to draw my attention?"
> [Sherlock Holmes:] "To the curious incident of the dog in the night-time."
> "The dog did nothing in the night-time."
> "That was the curious incident," remarked Sherlock Holmes.

Thus the famous presentation of circumstantial evidence to the modern imagination in Arthur Conan Doyle's *The Adventure of the Silver Blaze*.[1] Following this exchange, Holmes deduces from the circumstance of the dog's nocturnal silence the fact that it must have known whomever entered the stables when a prized horse went missing; he is therefore able to narrow his field of suspects. His less perspicacious foil Detective Gregory fails to appreciate the full consequence of this curious circumstance – for Gregory, as Holmes laments, is not "gifted with imagination."[2] As is typical of circumstantial evidence, the issue here turns on the discernment of acts no longer to be seen: the truth of what happened can only be constructed from inferences made after the event.[3] The problem posed by the fate of

1 Arthur Conan Doyle, "The Adventure of the Silver Blaze," in *The Strand Magazine*, ed. George Newnes, vol. 4, July to December (London: George Newnes Ltd., 1892), 656–57.

2 Ibid., 649.

3 For the purposes of this chapter, "circumstantial evidence" may broadly be understood as following the standard definition of *Black's Law Dictionary*: "Evidence based on inference and not on personal knowledge or observation." Henry Campbell Black, *Black's Law Dictionary*, ed. Bryan A. Garner (St. Paul, MN: Thomson Reuters, 2019). Black's second definition captures also the breadth of this form of evidence, defining it against the narrow evidentiary category that it is not: "All evidence that is not given by eyewitness testimony." In practical terms, the signs and traces upon which the workings of inference are to take effect range from fingerprints and smoking guns to the signifier in Thoreau's famous comment on adulterated milk: "Some circumstantial evidence is very strong, as when you find a trout in the milk." Henry

the horse with the silver blaze is one that the Old English law-writers would have appreciated, concerned as their codes are with animals stolen, straying, or disappearing only to re-appear in the form of their butchered and hidden remains.[4] But (in the absence of a reliable witness to the moment of disappearance) how would the pre-Conquest English subject and legal process have gone about solving this or an equivalent crime? Were public oaths or recourse to oath-helpers, and submission to the hot iron or boiling water, their only practical methods of arriving at the truth? Or might they have made use of our modern detective's methods – the application of reasoning, logic and imagination to what material evidence remains (or is significantly absent)?[5] This chapter makes an argument for the importance of the role of circumstantial evidence in the truth-seeking endeavors of the Old English legal system, and finds traces even in the decrees of the law codes to suggest that this approach to discovery was a widespread and accepted one in the legal field, adapted to a range of criminal and legal circumstances.[6] The same interest in deliberate observation

---

David Thoreau, "Journal, 11 Nov. 1850," in *The Journal of Henry D. Thoreau*, ed. Bradford Torrey and Francis H. Allen (New York: Dover, 1962), 94. Modern legal definitions also acknowledge the element of probability that obtains with circumstantial or indirect evidence, as in Richardson's law-school standard: "Evidence of some collateral fact, from which the existence or non-existence of some fact in question may be inferred *as a probable consequence*, is termed circumstantial evidence" (my emphasis). William Payson Richardson and Jerome Prince, *The Law of Evidence*, 7th ed. (New York: Brooklyn Law School, 1948), 88.

4 See, e.g., the laws relating to stolen cattle in Ine 46, II Edmund 6, IV Edgar 14, and II Æthelred 7; the laws relating to straying cattle in Ine 40, 42 and 42.1, VI Æthelstan 8.7 and 8.8; the laws relating to the tracing of stolen or strayed cattle in II Edward 4, V Æthelstan 2, VI Æthelstan 8.4, and III Edmund 6, 6.1 and 6.2; and the laws relating to the discovery of meat from stolen beasts in Ine 17 and 57. Citations from law codes throughout follow the conventions established in Felix Liebermann, ed., *Die Gesetze der Angelsachsen*, vol. 1 (Halle: Max Niemeyer, 1903–16), xi.

5 For the history of forensic death investigation in the post-Conquest period, see Sara M. Butler, *Forensic Medicine and Death Investigation in Medieval England* (New York: Routledge, 2015), esp. 125–75. And on the probable testimony of medical professionals as part of pre-Conquest personal injury hearings, see Lisi Oliver, *The Body Legal in Barbarian Law* (Toronto: University of Toronto Press, 2011), 42.

6 The question of how representative Old English law codes are of actual legal practice remains open. The seeming failure of early English litigation to take any notice of written law is a particular challenge to the idea that royal codes had practical efficacy and impact – as extensively canvassed by Wormald, *Making of English Law*, esp. 148. Though elsewhere Wormald somewhat contradicts this pessimistic view: Patrick Wormald, "Giving God and King their Due: Conflict and its Regulation in the Early English State," in Wormald, *Legal Culture*, 348. For a summary of the state of scholarship on this question, see Stefan Jurasinski and Lisi Oliver, eds., *The Laws of Alfred: The Domboc and the Making of Anglo-Saxon Law*

and telling inference emerges too in Old English poetry, which reveals in some of its narratives a dramatic reliance upon analogous truth-finding processes – *Beowulf* is the chosen exemplar here.[7] These genres demonstrate shared (and perhaps mutually influential) intellectual and cultural approaches to truth-finding and truth-proving, particularly in situations involving criminal or legal activity – and both, as I will argue, involve the imagination in the sense used by Sherlock Holmes above.

At the apparent procedural and epistemological center of pre-Conquest secular law are two forms of proof centered upon the institutional mobilization of God's omniscient knowledge of human action and thought.[8]

(Cambridge: Cambridge University Press, 2021), 78–81. Whatever the precise relation of the written laws recorded as royal codes to the procedures of legal practice in reality, text survival from the period has left us with an undoubted evidentiary lacuna between code and court: what Wormald calls the "zone of silence" in early English law (Wormald, *Making of English Law*, 160).

7 The interest of the *Beowulf*-poet in law and legal thought has been frequently noted, though as Stefan Jurasinski has observed, analogues for the claimed legalities of the poem (especially in earlier scholarship) are often sought in the imagined misty past of Germanic antiquity rather than in the recorded legal texts of the pre-Conquest period: *Ancient Privileges: Beowulf, Law and the Making of Germanic Antiquity* (Morgantown: West Virginia University Press, 2006), esp. 150. Grimm's *Rechtsalterthümer* is a representative and formative example of the argument for the poem's grounding in ancient Germanic legal custom: see Jacob Grimm, *Deutsche Rechtsaltertümer*, 2 vols. (Göttingen: Dieterichsche Buchhandlung, 1828). But the *Beowulf*-poet's knowledge and sensitive application of contemporary principles and ideas across a range of legal topics (ranging from property ownership and disposal to theft and the laws governing feud) is also clear, and has been elaborated by periodic scholarly interest over the past century: see, e.g., Dorothy Whitelock, "Beowulf 2444–2471," *Medium Ævum* 8 (1939): 198–204; Joseph L. Baird, "Grendel the Exile," *Neuphilologische Mitteilungen* 67 (1966): 375–81; Morton W. Bloomfield, "Beowulf, Byrhtnoth, and the Judgment of God: Trial by Combat in Anglo-Saxon England," *Speculum* 44 (1969): 545–59; Earl R. Anderson, "Treasure Trove in Beowulf: A Legal View of the Dragon's Hoard," *Mediaevalia* 3 (1977): 141–64; Theodore M. Andersson, "The Thief in Beowulf," *Speculum* 59 (1984): 493–508; John Hill, *The Cultural World in Beowulf* (Toronto: University of Toronto Press, 1995), esp. chapters 1 and 3; David D. Day, "Hands across the Hall: The Legalities of Beowulf's Fight with Grendel," *JEGP* 98 (1999): 313–24; Jurasinski, *Ancient Privileges*, 79–148; Nathan Breen, "The King's Closest Counselor: The Legal Basis of Wealhtheow's Comments to Hrothgar, *Beowulf* 1169–87," *The Heroic Age* 14 (2010); Leslie Lockett, "The Role of Grendel's Arm in Feud, Law, and the Narrative Strategy of *Beowulf*," in *Latin Learning and English Lore: Studies in Anglo-Saxon Literature for Michael Lapidge*, ed. Katherine O'Brien O'Keeffe and Andy Orchard (Toronto: University of Toronto Press, 2016).

8 An account of the ways in which this orientation to God's omniscience is implicated in myriad aspects of concealment and secrecy in the period can be found in Benjamin A. Saltzman, *Bonds of Secrecy: Law, Spirituality, and the*

Both the oath and the ordeal, which lie at the heart of our own modern imaginary of pre-Conquest law, operate via a highly formal and even ritualized procedure, in which human reasoning, supposition and imagination are supplanted (in intention at least) by the finality offered by the ultimate judgment of God.[9] As Andrew Rabin points out in his discussion of the ordeal in this volume, modern critical fascination (and bafflement) has long been caught by the seeming primitivisms of a proof that so subordinates the rationality of probable fact to the visceral manifestation of divine judgment.[10] For all the vividness with which these processes capture modern interest and criticism, it is important to recall that neither ordeal nor oath (central though they were) comprehended the full range of early English law and legal procedure, nor represented the only modes of attaining legal truth. But commentators have in general been reluctant to read into pre-Conquest law any officially sanctioned form of fact-finding beyond them – at least within the total process of what we would now think of as a criminal trial. Pollock and Maitland's view, though it has been both nuanced and challenged by a number of more recent commentators, remains an influential summation of this process.

> As to procedure, the forms were sometimes complicated, always stiff and unbending. Mistakes in form were probably fatal at every stage. Trial of questions of fact, in anything like the modern sense, was unknown. Archaic rules of evidence make no attempt to apply any measure of probability to individual cases. Oath was the primary mode

Literature of Concealment in Early Medieval England (Philadelphia: University of Pennsylvania Press, 2019), esp. 6–61.

9 Frederick Pollock and Frederic W. Maitland, *The History of English Law before the Time of Edward I*, 2nd ed., 2 vols. (Washington, D.C.: Lawyers' Literary Club, 1959 [repr. of 2nd ed., Cambridge: Cambridge University Press: 1898]), 2:598. Bartlett too notes the similarly divine appeal of both processes: the oath "was, in some sense, an ordeal, but one which relied upon God's eventual rather than his immediate judgment." Robert Bartlett, *Trial by Fire and Water: The Medieval Judicial Ordeal* (Oxford: Clarendon, 1986), 30.

10 See Rabin, "Uncertain Judgment: The Ordeal in Hagiography and Law" in this volume, esp. 115–19 and note 4. On the early English procedures of ordeal and their interpretation, see Bartlett, *Trial by Fire*; Margaret H. Kerr, Richard D. Forsyth, and Michael J. Plyley, "Cold Water and Hot Iron: Trial by Ordeal in England," *The Journal of Interdisciplinary History* 22 (1992): 573–95; H. L. Ho, "The Legitimacy of Medieval Proof," *Journal of Law and Religion* 19 (2004): 259–98; John Hudson, *The Formation of English Common Law: Law and Society in England from the Norman Conquest to Magna Carta*, 2nd ed. (New York: Routledge, 2018), 61–64; John Hudson, *The Oxford History of the Laws of England, Volume II: 871–1216* (Oxford: Oxford University Press, 2012), 84–87, 325–27; Jurasinski and Oliver, *The Laws of Alfred*, 78–112.

of proof, an oath going not to the truth of specific fact, but to the justice of the claim or defence as a whole.[11]

Several elements here are significant for present purposes. First is the view that the trial itself was procedurally rigid and therefore that the issue of the "truth" in any given case was subordinate in importance to observation of the proper form. Second is the centrality of oath – a mode of proof that, crucially, does not divide matters of fact from matters of law. Justice is sought and delivered on the broader base of lawful character and reputation: the (alleged) offender's word.[12] And third is that the "questions of fact" and "evidence" that are here denied a place in legal procedure are taken to involve the question of probability. The implication is that circumstantial evidence (and so a focus on questions of empirically derived truth and probabilities) cannot be any significant part of the pre-Conquest legal process.[13]

11 Pollock and Maitland, *History of English Law,* 1:38–39. Pollock and Maitland here rely on Brunner's discussion of the role of evidence and probabilities: Heinrich Brunner, *Deutsche Rechtsgeschichte,* 2 vols., vol. 2 (Leipzig: Verlag von Duncker & Humblot, 1892), 375.

12 For an overview of the importance, nature and processes of oaths, oath-helpers, and compurgation, see Andrew Rabin, *Crime and Punishment in Anglo-Saxon England* (Cambridge: Cambridge University Press, 2020), 35–37; Matthias Ammon, "'Ge mid wedde ge mid aðe': The Functions of Oath and Pledge in Anglo-Saxon Legal Culture," *Historical Research* 86 (2013): 515–35; Hudson, *Oxford History of the Laws of England,* 81–84. On the oath of allegiance, see Patrick Wormald, *Papers Preparatory to The Making of English Law: King Alfred to the Twelfth Century, Vol. II: From God's Law to Common Law,* ed. Stephen Baxter and John Hudson (University of London: Early English Laws, 2014), 112–26. In the law codes, clauses relating to the taking of oaths are numerous; a sampling produces the following clauses: Wihtred 16, Ine 15.2, I Edward 1.2 (who, and under what circumstances, must or may proceed to oath); Alfred 4.2, 11.4 (compensatory value of oath); Wihtred 20, Alfred 33, III Edmund 2 (Latin) (where oath-taking may take place); Alfred-Guthrum 3, II Cnut 65 (number of compurgators required); Hlothere and Eadric 6.2, I Edward 1.5 (procedures involved in oath taking); and I Cnut 17 (when oaths may not be sworn).

13 For Paul Hyams, the notion of a process of determining facts (as distinct from determining the question of law to which these facts, once established, give rise) simply does not obtain in the period. The disappearance in Germanic systems of the Roman distinction between fact and law simply "never posed a problem in the Early Middle Ages because [these elements] were unknown to secular law. This was not merely a matter of the disappearance of Roman law from northern Europe but a function also of God's omniscience. Men conceptualized legal proof largely in terms of God's judgment…" Paul R. Hyams, *Rancor and Reconciliation in Medieval England* (Ithaca: Cornell University Press, 2018), 219. This position has a long history in legal scholarship, founded upon the principle of the fundamental and irreconcilable difference between the

Yet we have King Æthelstan, perhaps in the 930s, legislating the following: "If anyone traces cattle to another man's estate, he who owns the estate shall, if he can, follow the trail, until it passes beyond his boundary. If he cannot do so, the trail shall serve for the oath of accusation, if he [the plaintiff] charges anyone on the estate" (*7 se þe bespirige yrfe innan oþres land, aspirige hit ut se [þe] þæt lond age, gif he mæge; gif he ne mæge, stande þæt spor for þone foraþ, gif he ðærinne hwæne teo*).[14] The short code in which this directive is found (conventionally designated V Æthelstan) addresses serious and apparently ongoing breaches of the king's peace (*ure frið*), whose remedy is the responsibility of such royal legal representatives as reeve, bishop, and thegn. The neglect or corruption of these responsibilities was deemed *oferhyrnesse* ("disobedience," here meaning "insubordination to the king") and penalties were heavy: substantial fines, confiscation of all property, and permanent exile for serious offenders, even death for those who afterwards aid them.[15] This particular law addresses the responsibilities of the landholder over whose property the tracks of stolen cattle have been traced. These responsibilities would appear to have been twofold: to assist in the recovery of the cattle (in his capacity as legal officer of the king), and to clear himself (or his dependents) of any suspicion of guilt of their theft. Both objectives were to be achieved by a reading of the available physical evidence: tracks left by the missing stock. The landholder's assistance in tracing (with the cattle's owner?) the tracks of the animals which entered his property, and the following of them to their point of departure from it, would discharge his legal responsibility, and establish

machinery of the post-Conquest jury trial and the conceptual parameters of early medieval Germanic ideologies. Edward Manson's account is typical of the attitude of nineteenth-century legal scholarship to the "rude mind" of the early medieval subject and the "primitive" nature of their nations and laws; but despite the total re-evaluation of the former, and the significant recuperation of the latter, the terms of Manson's denial of circumstantial evidence have been remarkably stable. "We must bear in mind that the theory of circumstantial evidence is unknown, or at least impracticable, to nations in a primitive state. They do not possess the habit of mind necessary for sifting and weighing testimony and drawing inferences, and if they did, such a process would be deemed too dilatory and too doubtful. The Anglo-Saxon procedure allowed nothing but the testimony of eye-witnesses to be received, and this obtained until the reign of King John and later." Edward Manson, "Truth in Judicial Proceedings," *The Juridical Review* 7 (1895): 367–68.

[14] V Æthelstan 2. Old English text from *Gesetze*, 1:168. Liebermann's edition is used throughout for the text of the laws from Edward the Elder to Æthelred I–IV. The translation here is that of Frederick Levi Attenborough, *The Laws of the Earliest English Kings* (Cambridge: Cambridge University Press, 1922), 155. For the laws of Edward and Æthelstan throughout, the translations of Attenborough form the basis for my own.

[15] V Æthelstan Prol.

his personal and wider innocence in the matter. If, however, he cannot (because of a refusal to co-operate or because the tracks do not in fact leave his property), then the tracks themselves become grounds for the owner of the cattle to initiate legal proceeding against the landholder. In fact, such evidence is deemed equivalent to the *foraþ* ("fore-oath") itself.[16] This tantalizing acknowledgment in law of the power of observation, logic and imagination to reconstruct facts after the event, and even of the apparent relationship between these factual circumstances and legal procedure, open interesting prospects. Answering the questions "What happened?" and "How do you know?" were evidently issues of importance to early English law.

Circumstances and Evidence in the Written Law

The law codes in fact make relatively frequent reference to matters of circumstance where these might be seen to provide evidence of a degree of criminal responsibility. These include common-sense and specialist observations, the inference of guilt derived from silence or concealment, and the evidentiary significance of detectable physical signs. Law codes across the period also suggest a consistent concern to regulate situations (particularly relating to property exchange) so as to avoid the possibility of there *not* being evidence of some kind. Thus the series of laws in the codes of the tenth century and beyond that lay out with precision the nature of the witnessing required to demonstrate that a legitimate sale took place and that no theft was involved. These are detailed and specific as to correct procedure, and seek above all to avoid the situation of theft accusation without clear evidence in either direction.[17] Buying something outside town, while not necessarily presumptive of theft, tends to raise suspicion.[18] Not immediately announcing the source of one's new cows likewise leaves open the possibility that they were ill-gotten.[19] And the

16 On the *foraþ* as an oath of accusation preceding a suit, see Attenborough, *Laws,* 197 and 211. For two legislative examples of requirements for what appear to be procedural *foraþas,* see II Æthelstan 9 and 11.

17 IV Edgar 6 is a typical example: "And every man shall buy or sell in the presence of these witnesses all the goods which he buys or sells either in a borough or in a wapentake" (*7 ælc mon mid heora gewytnesse bigcge 7 sylle ælc þeora ceapa þe he bicgcge oððe wæpengetace*). This clause is followed by a further eight related provisions setting out the correct behavior of the witnesses, and dealing with situations in which impulse-buying complicates the arrangement of appropriate witnesses (IV Edgar 7, 8, 8.1, 9, 10, 11).

18 See, e.g., Hlothere and Eadric 16; Ine 25.1; Alfred 34.

19 See, e.g., IV Edgar 8–11.

word of the seller in the chain of swearing to warrant was an oath that went to matters of fact – evidence of fact, as opposed to attestations as to personal character via the performance of compurgation, was here valued as rendering unnecessary the initiation of involved (and possibly indecisive) public procedures.

This determination to ensure the presence of appropriate witnesses in order to provide the needful proof in the event of accusation extends to an insistence on the safeguarding of physical evidence also. III Æthelred 9 moves easily from the need for the presence of trustworthy witnesses at the lawful slaughter of a cow to the requirement that hide and head be preserved for a period of time after the killing: presumably as evidentiary tokens to be shown should the absence of the living cow raise comment. "And no-one shall kill a cow unless he has two trustworthy men as witnesses, and he shall keep the hide and the head for three days; and those of a sheep likewise" (*7 nan man hryðer ne slea, buton he habbe twegre trywra manna gewitnesse, 7 he healde III niht hyde 7 heafod; 7 sceapes eallswa*). The point of the clause is to ensure the preservation of that physical evidence capable of identifying the animals; the implication is that these tokens will either preclude accusation or allow for judgment in any potential legal dispute. So important is the need for this preservation that failing to do so carries a fine of 20 ores – perhaps significantly, the same fine as is levied in this code for failing to appear at a required ordeal.[20] All of this attention to the preservation of material for later examination offers at least a *prima facie* case for the importance of physical evidence to the totality of legal truth and judgment. And from this regulatory foundation to ensure the existence of evidence, it is no great distance to the regulation of the process of reasoning about the evidence itself.

It should not be a surprise, therefore, to find that elsewhere in the early laws reasoned observation is called on. In a range of situations, relevant factual circumstances are delimited in the codes. Ine 26 requires that fostered children be paid a maintenance which, after the third year, is increased or decreased "according to his appearance" (*be his wlite*);

[20] III Æthelred 4.2. Wormald dates this code to the mid 990s; it was promulgated at Wantage with particular reference to the Danelaw, and has a strong Scandinavian quality in both language and legal ideas. Wormald, *Making of English Law*, 320–22. An *ora* ("a species of money introduced by the Danes," Bosworth-Toller) is at the time of the *Domesday Book* calculated at about 16 pence (or 20 pence if silver). Neff summarizes the relative values at the time of III Æthelred: "There were 16 pence to an ora, 5 pence to the shilling and 48 shillings, or 240 pence and thus 15 ora to the pound." Charlotte Neff, "Scandinavian Elements in the Wantage Code of Æthelred II," *The Journal of Legal History* 10 (1989): 300–01.

observation and deduction are here legally required.[21] Ine's laws also interest themselves in the appearance of pigs: where the pasturage of pigs is paid in kind, the number of pigs owing depends upon the thickness of the bacon of the pastured animals – *fewer* pigs are given when the bacon lies thinner on their backs.[22] The reasoning does not go to the financial value of the pig as payment, but to how much their pannage is deduced to have cost the owner of the oak wood: fat pigs must have eaten more acorns. The thicker the bacon, therefore, the more of it is owing. The skills of animal husbandry are required for this deduction, and its acceptance as a transactional standard argues for the acceptance also of the validity of the logic involved.

As in Sherlock's *Silver Blaze* investigation, nocturnal silence is a telling factor in certain laws of Wihtred and Ine: "If a man [who is] come from afar or a stranger should go off the track, and he then neither calls out nor does he blow a horn, he is to be regarded as a thief (*for ðeof he bið to profianne*), either to be killed or to be redeemed" (*Gif feorran-cumen man oþþe fræmde buton wege gange, 7 he þonne nawðer ne hyrme ne he horn ne blawe, for ðeof he bið to profianne, oþþe to sleanne oþþe to alysenne*).[23] Sherlock's quiet

21 Attenborough is unsure of the meaning of this clause: "It is not clear to me what is meant – whether a strong healthy child needs more sustenance, or whether more should be paid for a child which appears to be of aristocratic origin": *Laws*, 186. Liebermann translates *wlite* as *Körperbeschaffenheit* – "physical condition," implying notice of constitution and physique. *Gesetze*, 1:101. As Liebermann notes, the *Quadripartitus* translator of this clause is influenced (in rendering *wlite*, inaccurately, as *pretium* "value") by VI Æthelstan 6.1, wherein the value of a horse is to be deduced from its *wlites wyrðe* ("the value suggested by its appearance"): 3:73. Whatever physical detail we understand *wlite* to draw our attention to in the case of the horse or the boy, the link between factual observation and legal consequence is central.

22 Ine 49.3. "If pasturage is paid in pigs: [if the bacon is] three fingers thick, every third [pig], at two-fingers, every fourth, at a thumb, every fifth." (*Gif mon nime æfesne on swynum: æt þryfingrum þæt ðridde, æt twyfingrum þæt feorðe, æt þymelum þæt fifte*). Text and translation from Jurasinski and Oliver, *The Laws of Alfred*, 181–437. This edition is used throughout for the text of Alfred and Ine's laws; Jurasinski and Oliver's translations form the basis for my own.

23 Wihtred 28 (Oliver numbers this clause Wihtred 23). See also Ine 20–21: "[20] If a man from afar, or a stranger, travels through a wood off the highway and neither shouts nor blows a horn, he shall be assumed to be a thief, and as such may be either slain or put to ransom. [21] If, however, anyone claims the slain man's wergild, he [who slew him] shall be allowed to declare that he slew him, presuming him to be a thief; and neither the associates of the slain man, nor his lord, shall be allowed to proceed to an oath" ([20] *Gif feorcund mon oððe fremde butan wege geond wudu gonge 7 ne hrieme ne horn blawe, for ðeof he bið to profianne, oððe to sleanne oððe to aliesanne.* [21] *Gif mon ðonne þæs ofslægnan weres bidde, he mot geþyncan, þæt he hine for ðeof ofsloge, nalles þæs ofslegenan gegildan ne his hlaford*). The crucial term in the first clause is *profian*, which Bosworth-

dog and Wihtred's unblown horn produce different conclusions, but both rely on inferences drawn from the evidence of circumstances. In the Old English laws, the silence of the traveler who strays from the path is not the action of an honest man who would loudly have announced his presence. This person went in silence; therefore, this person is (presumptively) a thief. The presumption is in fact so strong that no trial is needed: the local who discovers the silent prowler becomes judge, jury, and even executioner: the presumed thief "may be slain or put to ransom" (*oþþe to sleanne oþþe to alysenne*).[24] Such a law takes the evidence of circumstances very seriously indeed. And in Ine's code, which repeats the clause from Wihtred, an expansion stipulates that the same circumstances that so damned the traveling foreigner also operate on the killer: if, after striking down the presumptive thief, he then conceals it (*he hit ðonne dierneð*), and "it is revealed after a long while, then he clears the way to the oath [being sworn] for the dead man, so that his kinsmen may prove him innocent" (*7 weorðeð ymb long yppe, ðonne rymeð he ðam deadan to ðam aðe, þæt hine moton his mægas unsyngian*).[25] The consequences of secrecy in killings can be more severe still: as Pollock and Maitland recognized, in the law codes can be found "a rudiment of the modern distinction between murder and manslaughter, but the line is drawn not between willful and other killing, but between killing openly and in secret."[26] The *mens rea* for murder – the guilty mind – is there implied in the act of hiding the body. As Saltzman observes, such legal moments demonstrate that "concealment can radically change the nature of an action and its relation to the law. If a crime is concealed, it is reasoned and, in fact, proven to have been committed on unjustifiable grounds."[27] For Saltzman, this legal disposition is a function of early English political epistemology: attempts at concealment threaten sovereign power to regulate behavior; they therefore demand "intense

---

Toller defines as "to esteem or regard as"; Icelandic *prófaðr* ("convicted of") is offered as a cognate. Liebermann gives *zu erachten (anzunehmen)*: *Gesetze*, 2:177. The OED, matching Liebermann's definition, suggests that Old English *profian* ("to assume to be, take for") is a borrowing from Classical Latin *probāre* specifically for use as a legal term (OED, s.v. "prove, v."); Ferdinand Holthausen agrees: *Altenglisches etymologisches Wörterbuch* (Heidelberg: C. Winter, 1934), s.v. "profian." And as Saltzman notes, though the primary sense of the Latin *probare* is "to try, test, examine, inspect, judge…," it carries also "the juridical sense of 'to prove or demonstrate' or to put to the test/prove by a judicial process such as the ordeal." Saltzman, *Bonds of Secrecy*, 259n46. Once more, the evidence of circumstances is couched in a language that moves close to the orbit of the major procedural forms of proof.

24 Wihtred 28, and see Ine 20.

25 Ine 21.1.

26 Pollock and Maitland, *History of English Law*, 1:52.

27 Saltzman, *Bonds of Secrecy*, 30.

legal prosecution."[28] But there is another and more pragmatic level of thought in operation here: one that is interested in the factual and legal meanings of the circumstances surrounding an act – and in the evidentiary value of that which is left behind after an (as yet uninterpreted) moment of human action.

In these legal clauses, circumstances trump even oath-helpers in imposing legal significance upon the signs arising from an act. In the case of Ine's expansion, the precise nature of the *hit* ("it") that is concealed is also significant: Liebermann translates literally as "it" (*es*); Attenborough broadly as "fact"; and Jurasinski and Oliver supply "[the killing]."[29] But the realities of homicide dictate what must (at least) have been hidden: the body. Once more, the law seeks to avoid the loss of physical remains, and its interest in this preservation is primarily procedural. The circumstance of publicizing the killing – and I would submit as a likely corollary, the physical details of the nature of that killing, written on the body of the dead foreigner to whose corpse the killer's announcement would call public attention – was the element that demonstrated innocence, and precluded the kin of the slain from recovering *wergild*. It is only when an emphatically long period (*ymb lang*) has passed that another form of proof (proceeding to oath) becomes available to replace what has been lost to time.

It is in some of the numerous laws relating to cattle that many of the elements so far examined come together to establish what are arguably patterns of legal process that assume or exploit the possibilities of circumstantial evidence. This is particularly the case with the tracking of stolen cattle. We find there the evidentiary significance of signs in both investigation and accusation: these signs offer certitude to the investigating expert, carry value within the legal process, and imply ways of thinking about evidence and conclusion. Cattle tracking appears for the first time in II Edward 4:

> Eac ic wille, þæt ælc man hæbbe symle þa men gearowe on his lande, ðe lædan ða men ðe heora agen secan willen, ⁊ hy for nanum medsceattum ne werian, ne ful nawar friðian ne feormian willes ne gewealdnes.
>
> It is my will also that everyone shall always have ready on his estate men who will guide others wishing to follow up their own [cattle]; and they [who guide] shall not for any bribes whatsoever hinder them; nor shall they anywhere shield crime, nor willingly and deliberately harbor [a criminal].[30]

[28] Ibid., 9 and see generally 19–61.

[29] *Gesetze*, 1:99; Attenborough, *Laws*, 43; Jurasinski and Oliver, *Laws of Alfred*, 385.

[30] This law is the subject of some discussion in Mechthild Gretsch, "The Fonthill

The preamble to this law has Edward exhort (*myngode*) his *witan* to consider how they might better preserve the public peace for which they are responsible (*heora frið*).[31] And as with V Æthelstan 2 discussed above, II Edward's laws are directed at the higher officials whose responsibility it is "that no man shall withhold from another his rights" (*ðæt nan man oðrum ryhtes ne wyrne*).[32] The aim of the code is to establish the means to achieve this lofty ideal. The law here requires landholders (of substantial estates?) to appoint or continue to maintain men whose job it is to assist those seeking missing cattle (where tracks need to be followed up) without fear or favor: taking bribes to protect or harbor the guilty is particularly to be guarded against. What is of particular interest is the implied possibility that the men who are to guide the seekers of the missing cattle may themselves possess the relevant skills for the particular task: cattle-detectives, as it were, whose role in the legal process is here almost formalized. If this is so, then there is the equal possibility that the owner-tracker of the missing stock might himself be represented by a similarly skilled agent from his estate. Explicit evidence is lacking however, both here and in the further reference to such guiding or supervisory activities detailed in VI Æthelstan 8.4. But the inference that such men as are named in the law here would have experience with livestock is a safe one; equally safe is the inference that their skills as livestock-handlers would include the ability to identify and follow the tracks of that livestock.[33] Further, the landholder

Letter: Language, Law and the Discourse of Disciplines," *Anglia* 123 (2006): 672 and 675–77. Here, one concern for Gretsch is to distinguish the "men on his estate who will guide others" (*þa men… on his lande, ðe lædan ða men*; i.e. "guides") of II Edward 4 from the *speremon* (allegedly "tracker" or perhaps "drover") in the Fonthill Letter, 10.3. While uncertainty still surrounds these terms (and the existence of the 'professions' they might imply), my point as to the physical evidence that men must trace or guide others in tracing is not substantially affected.

31 II Edward 1. "King Edward exhorted all his councilors, when they were at Exeter, to consider how the public peace for which they were responsible could be kept better than it had been, because it seemed to him that his previous orders had not been carried out so well as they ought to have been." (*Eadweard cyning myngode his wytan, þa hy æt Exanceastre wæron, þæt hy smeadon ealle, hu heora frið betere beon mæhte, þonne hit ær ðam wæs; forðam him þuhte, þæt hit mæctor gelæst wære, þonne hit scolde, þæt he ær beboden hæfde.*)

32 II Edward 1.2.

33 The existence of Old English charms for the safe recovery of stolen or straying cattle suggests another possible skill in the repertoire of such agents: some knowledge of the supernatural (at least as relates to the rites and rituals of stock recovery). But even if the Old English cattle charms were among the tools of the professional tracker (rather than being the common cry of anxious owner and shepherd) a more down-to-earth skill set would certainly remain necessary to effect recovery. On these charms more generally, see Andrew Rabin,

expected to provide a guide to assist the owner or tracker of the missing cattle would be wise to ensure that *his* man was at least as skilled as his neighbor's to forestall partisan or malicious interpretation of the evidence.

Outside the law codes, the *Fonthill Letter* (S 1445) contains the clearest example of the use of physical evidence in articulating guilt in the surviving Old English legal corpus – and missing cows are again at the center of the drama. This much-discussed document dates from the reign of Edward the Elder (899–924), and provides an account of a long-running dispute over property in Wiltshire, in which dispute the composer of the letter, an ealdorman named Ordlaf, is closely concerned. In his account, one incident is of particular interest: a thegn named Helmstan (godson of Ordlaf) was found guilty of an act of cattle theft.[34] The facts upon which Helmstan's guilt is based are interesting for what they reveal about the role of physical evidence.[35]

> Ða onufan ðæt ymban oðer healf gear nat ic hweðer ðe ymb tua, ða forstæl he ða unlædan oxan æt Funtial, ðe he mid ealle fore forwearð, 7 draf to Cytlid; 7 hine mon ðæræt aparade. 7 his speremon ahredde ða sporwreclas. Ða he fleah, ða torypte hine an breber ofer ðæt nebb; ða he ætsacan wolde, ða sæde him mon ðat to tacne.

> Then on top of that – I do not know whether it was a year and a half or two years later – he stole the untended oxen at Fonthill, by which he was completely ruined, and drove them to Chicklade, and there he was discovered, and the man who tracked him rescued the traced cattle [?]. When he fled, a bramble scratched him in the face; and when he wished to deny it, that was brought as evidence against him.[36]

"Ritual Magic or Legal Performance? Reconsidering An Old English Charm Against Theft," in *English Law Before Magna Carta: Felix Liebermann and Die Gesetze der Angelsachsen*, ed. Stefan Jurasinski, Lisi Oliver, and Andrew Rabin (Leiden: Brill, 2010), 179–80. Stephanie Hollis argues that these charms were "texts for ritual performances which were believed to be nebulously efficacious in the recovery of missing possessions." "Old English 'Cattle-Theft Charms': Manuscript Contexts and Social Uses," *Anglia* 115 (1997): 151.

34 On the *Fonthill Letter*, see Simon Keynes, "The Fonthill Letter," in *Words, Texts and Manuscripts: Studies in Anglo-Saxon Culture Presented to Helmut Gneuss on the Occasion of his Sixty-Fifth Birthday*, ed. Michael Korhammer (Cambridge: D. S. Brewer, 1992), 53–97; Andrew Rabin, "Testimony and Authority in Old English Law: Writing the Subject in the 'Fonthill Letter,'" in *Law and Sovereignty in the Middle Ages and the Renaissance*, ed. Robert Sturges (Tempe: Arizona Center for Medieval and Renaissance Studies), 147–69.

35 The nature of this physical evidence, and its relation to oral and written testimony in the legal process, is considered in Rabin, "Testimony and Authority," 166–67.

36 Translation from Dorothy Whitelock, ed. and trans., *English Historical*

It is the final sentence that is the most important for my purposes. The *to tacne* ("as evidence") is a reference that is both relevant to the question of fact in that it makes a positive claim as to the probative value of the circumstantial evidence, and relevant to the question of law in that it implies an evidentiary procedure in which consideration of physical evidence forms part of the 'trial' and is at least in part determinative of the final verdict.

Helmstan, some two years earlier, had been convicted of stealing a belt, by which conviction he lost his status as oath-worthy (*að-wyrðe*), one able to give his oath in legal cases, which may explain either why the physical evidence was found sufficient for conviction, or why physical evidence (rather than statements relating to oaths) was set out at all as part of the narrative of the case. The *Fonthill Letter*'s brief summation of the evidence suggests that Helmstan was caught red-handed in possession of cattle, fled the scene through a bramble-patch, and when apprehended, was found to bear the marks of his hasty escape on his face. Niles's reading of *aparade* as suggesting a kind of red-handed discovery of the criminal in the act of committing his crime is convincing.[37] What is perhaps most notable is the ready acceptance by Ordlaf of the guilt implied by the scratch. As Niles notes, Ordlaf certainly does not wish to challenge the outcome of

---

Documents. Volume I: c.500–1042, 2nd ed. (London: Oxford University Press, 1979) (*EHD*), 580 (Item 102). Whitelock's translation differs from that in the more recent edition of Nicholas P. Brooks and S. E. Kelly, *Charters of Christ Church, Canterbury,* 2 vols. (Oxford: Oxford University Press, 2013), 2:852–62. Brooks and Kelly give for the penultimate sentence "and drove them to Chicklade, where he was apprehended; and his spear-man [*or* 'trace-man'] recovered the goads [*or* 'trace-?s']" (2:855). In this, they respond to a debate that centers on the meaning and significance of the phrase ⁊ *his speremon ahredde ða sporwreclas*: both *speremon* and *sporwreclas* are *hapax legomena,* and the verb *ahreddan* is challengingly polysemous. Attempts to clarify the terms are made in Mechthild Gretsch, "The Language of the 'Fonthill Letter,'" *Anglo-Saxon England* 23 (1994): 57–102; Carole A. Hough, "Cattle-Tracking in the Fonthill Letter," *English Historical Review* 115 (2000): 864–92; and Gretsch, "The Fonthill Letter." The two scholars disagree; Brooks and Kelly follow the conclusions of Gretsch. For a useful summation of the issue, see John D. Niles, "The Fonthill Ghost Word, the Fonthill Thief, and Early West Saxon Scribal Culture," in *The Genesis of Books: Studies in the Scribal Culture of Medieval England in Honour of A. N. Doane,* ed. Matthew T. Hussey and John D. Niles (Turnhout: Brepols, 2012). Niles, influenced by the arguments of Hough, offers a persuasive emendation and alternative translation – one that emphasizes more strongly even than Whitelock's version the centrality of the act of tracking the footsteps of cattle and thief: "and drove them to Chicklade, *and thereat he was apprehended, and the man who traced him* [that is, who traced his prior route with the cattle] *recovered the wily twists and turns* ['**spor-wrencas*'] *of the track*" (88–89).

37 Niles, "Fonthill Ghost Word," 84.

this particular case – it makes up part of the body of facts upon which his ownership of certain contested land depends.[38] But even taking into account this possibly partisan context, there is a clear connection between physical evidence and inference of guilt in fact.[39]

Circumstantial evidence, then (particularly as seen in the many laws relating to cattle theft and tracking), was used to uncover crime, as well as to demonstrate publicly the guilt of the accused. In Helmstan's adventure, trace evidence has investigative as well as adjudicatory value. The direct tracking of the cattle, presumably by means of hoofprints and other signs of their passage, was what led (both literally and by evidentiary inference) to the guilty thief. The *Fonthill Letter* confirms that tracking stray or lost cattle was a widely accepted and legally pertinent method of finding and rectifying cattle theft, and of bringing the thieves to justice; and it demonstrates that circumstantial evidence carried weight even at a second remove from the initial discovery: the scratches on Helmstan's face linked him to the man who fled through brambles, and the man who fled through brambles was identified as Helmstan by the original trackers or pursuers of the lost beasts.

Dramatic Circumstances and Evidentiary Imagination in Beowulf

What is sought in *Beowulf* is these kinds of imaginative reasonings situated in contexts suggestive of legal processes or the detection of criminal activity. Accordingly, Beowulf's fight with Grendel and its aftermath is my focus: in this passage, hints of legal thinking are particularly thick in the poet's language choices, metaphors, and narrative structures.[40] These busy

[38] Ibid., 72. On the rhetorical artifice with which Ordlaf builds his case, see Scott T. Smith, "Of Kings and Cattle Thieves: The Rhetorical Work of the Fonthill Letter," *JEGP* 106 (2007): 447–67.

[39] The idea that physical evidence in the form of the appearance of a defendant could under certain circumstances be probative in the pre-Conquest legal process has been argued in J. Laurence Laughlin, "The Anglo-Saxon Legal Procedure," in *Essays in Anglo-Saxon Law*, ed. Henry Adams (Boston: Little Brown, 1876), 183–306: he writes that a presumption of the defendant's guilt was established when "a criminal caught in the act was pursued with the hue and cry, and brought before the court with evident marks of crime about him," since the guilt of this party "under the circumstances seemed most probable" (295). More recently, O'Keeffe has demonstrated a range of ways in which pre-Conquest law considered the body itself as capable of offering testimony to legal authority. Katherine O'Brien O'Keeffe, "Body and Law in Late Anglo-Saxon England," *Anglo-Saxon England* 27 (1998): 209–32.

[40] For a survey of these, see in particular Lockett, "Role of Grendel's Arm"; Hill, *The Cultural World in Beowulf*, 70–85; and Day, "Hands across the Hall."

scenes of declaration, display, discovery, and deduction exploit lexical and ideological elements from many fields of social action: the language of feuding and battle on the one hand, and the imagery of hunting and tracking on the other, are particularly prominent. But they also contain another and less frequently noted dimension of meaning, and one that is used by the poet to add considerably to the dramatic tensions there created. Physical evidence and its interpretation are often at the center of the narrative – a borrowing, I suggest, from the cultural domain of crime, its discovery, and its prosecution. It is the process of deductive reasoning from physical remains (the life-blood of circumstantial evidence) that is of particular interest here, as is its role in the provision of the underlying structure of the developing narrative.

In his depredations, Grendel (kin, we have been told twenty lines earlier, to the arch-criminal Cain) leaves all-too-tangible signs of his fatal presence in the world of men.

> Đa wæs on uhtan mid ærdæge
> Grendles guðcræft gumum undyrne;
> þa wæs æfter wiste wop up ahafen
> micel morgensweg. Mære þeoden
> æþeling ærgod unbliðe sæt,
> þolode ðryðswyð þegnsorge dreah
> syðþan hie þæs laðan last sceawedon,
> wergan gastes; wæs þæt gewin to strang
> lað ond longsum.

> Then in the early dawn before the day, Grendel's war-strength was revealed to the men; then after feasting, lament was lifted up: a great morning-cry. The renowned lord, a prince good since old times, sat in sorrow, the mighty one suffered, endured the anguish of thane-loss when they examined the tracks of the despised one, the wicked demon; that affliction was too strong, loathsome and lingering. (126a–134a)[41]

As the earliest rays of pre-dawn light illuminate to the survivors the horrors of the night, characteristic parataxis (Then… then…) builds the crescendo of discovery, the emotional effects of which proceed from the sighting of the physical evidence of slaughter and missing men. As the war-strength of Grendel is *undyrne* ("revealed"; lit. "un-hidden") their grief bursts out. To heighten its effect, it is paired and contrasted with memories of the recent feast: "then after feasting, lament was lifted up" (*þa wæs æfter wiste wop up ahafen*) – that is to say, where once there was feasting, now there is weeping. The deployment of this joy-sorrow trope

[41] Old English text of *Beowulf* from *Klaeber 4*; unless otherwise noted, translations are my own.

is here surely augmented by a fleeting pun – *æfter wiste* ("after feast") suggests *æfter wiste* ("after he knew"), a verb of knowing (*witan*) with the particular sense of becoming aware of facts. The terrible fact of which Hrothgar becomes aware as day dawns is that it is Grendel who has feasted – the more apparent paronomastic sense of this bitter *wiste*.[42] The dense drama of discovery reaches its catastrophe as Hrothgar and his men examine the tracks of Grendel (*last sceawedon*) – and it is then that the king is utterly oppressed with grief. This verb *sceawian* is the most active in the passage, and carries far stronger senses of scrutiny, inspection, and careful examination than would the equally metrical **last gesawon* (= *geseon*, "to see"). Upon this verb hangs the revelation and emotion of the scene: it is the disclosure of *sceawedon*, built upon the physical evidence left by the criminal monster, that provides the forensic structure of the unfolding drama.

With this dramatic discovery of crime to begin the interaction, it is fitting that the poet's narration of the twelve-year period of repeated incursions by Grendel into the great hall of the Danes should be framed as a criminal enterprise. Lines 134b–163b describe his actions as "murder" (*morðbeala* 136a) and "crime" (*fyrene* 137a), and recount that the monster "fought against justice" (*wið rihte wan* 144b) and would not "negotiate settlement" (*fea þingian* 156b). To crown the unlawful whole, the poet records with wry understatement that Hrothgar's *witan* had "no need to expect gleaming compensation" (*ne... wenan þorfte / beorhte bote* 157–58) from him. The horror of Grendel is augmented by the fact that he cannot be brought within the confines of the law. As this long terror plays out, the poet's interest remains upon evidence and its interpretation. We witness with the Danes the clear signs (*sweotolan tacne* 141b) of Grendel's malice:

> Þa wæs eaðfynde   þe him elles hwær
> gerumlicor   ræste sohte,
> bed æfter burum,   ða him gebeacnod wæs,
> gesægd soðlice   sweotolan tacne
> heal-ðegnes hate...

> Then it was easy to find one who found himself a resting-place elsewhere, far away, a bed among the private chambers, when the hall-thane's [Grendel's] hatred was made known to him, truly expressed by clear signs... (138a–142a)

[42] For the view that *wiste* here refers to Grendel's feast, see Jun Terasawa, "*Beowulf* 128: *æfter wiste*," in *"And gladly wolde he lerne and gladly teche": Essays on Medieval English presented to Professor Matsuji Tajima on his Sixtieth Birthday*, ed. Yoko Iyeiri and Margaret Connolly (Tokyo: Kaibunsha, 2002), 147–54.

Once again, the action depends upon the interpretation of physical evidence, as the structure of the "Then… when" (*Þa…ða*) sequence rivets sign to reaction. Here, interpretation is all too easy: the *sweotolan tacne* are missing men and the gore of Grendel's depredations. These clear tokens themselves "pointed out" (*gebeacnod* [*beacnian*]) and "expressed" (*gesægd* [*gesecgan*]) their message actively – and truly (*soðlice*) – to the men. No deduction is necessary; the evidence is so clear that it speaks its own incontrovertible truth: Grendel's leavings and his tracks serve as the accusation against him.

A number of critical accounts have demonstrated that the series of careful steps by which Beowulf approaches Heorot before being granted the right to "have… and hold" (*Hafa… ond geheald*) the hall by Hrothgar are thoroughly imbued with legal language and ideas.[43] As Hill argues, "Beowulf's progress from Hygelac's shores to Hrothgar's hall is a movement toward Hrothgar's official, legal permission to hold Heorot against Grendel."[44] Even without returning to Grimm's enthusiastic embrace of such binomials as "have and hold" as ancient Germanic legal formulae (and the concomitant bonding of poetry and law taken to be implied by their alliterative force),[45] it is at least clear that the language of *hafa ond geheald* comprehends a dispositive dimension that sits easily under a legal rubric.[46] The result, Day argues, is that the transfer of Heorot from Hrothgar to Beowulf is a robustly legal one, resulting in Beowulf's "formal legal control over the hall."[47] With his own right thus established, the legal opposition between

43 Notably Day, "Hands across the Hall," 313–15 and Hill, *The Cultural World in Beowulf*, 70–80.

44 *The Cultural World in Beowulf*, 70.

45 Grimm's introductory remarks in his *Deutsche Rechtsalterthümer* hang the weight of his argument for the connection of poetry, language and law upon these alliterating binomials: *Deutsche Rechtsaltertümer*, 8. The fundamentally coterminous nature of poetry and law was advanced by Grimm in 1815: "Von der Poesie im Recht," in *Zeitschrift für geschichtliche Rechtswissenschaft* (Digitale Bibliothek des Max-Planck-Instituts für Europäische Rechtsgeschichte, 1816), 27–30.

46 Although Schaefer is ultimately agnostic about the potential for specifically legal origins or associations of this binomial, she acknowledges the evident "socio-moral" and "dispositive" dimensions of the phrase. Ursula Schaefer, "On the Linguistic and Social Development of a Binomial: The Example of to Have and to Hold," in *Binomials in the History of English: Fixed and Flexible*, ed. Hans Sauer and Joanna Kopaczyk (Cambridge: Cambridge University Press, 2017), 328.

47 Day, "Hands across the Hall," 313. This control Day links to the "ancient concept" of *mund* in Germanic law: "a house-holder's power of possession and protection over both the persons of his household and its physical space" (315, and generally 315–20). For Day, the legal nature of the transfer gives to Beowulf a particular claim to right in the ensuing battle; it also renders the play on hand and hand-grip "an elaborate legal metaphor," implying "a legal battle over the

the two figures becomes an important dimension of the action.[48] On this level, Beowulf, noble hero protectively watching through the night, stands against the unrighteous criminal Grendel, sneaking through the darkness in silence. This stealth, as we have seen in the law codes, is itself damning evidence of ill intent and murder most foul.

Alongside the poet's interest in Beowulf as hero, and as a notable element of that hero's performance and control of legal right, is an interest in Beowulf and others as quasi-legal agents fulfilling an almost detectival role in the pursuit of truth.[49] Beowulf's heroic actions also embody his culture's belief in the power of speech and the integrity of his reputation and standing, and he is aware of the force of argument from circumstantial evidence with respect to the securing of both. Chief among this evidence is the arm and, later, head of Grendel, given as proof of his claims. The questions that drive the drama of these early scenes are those asked of this physical evidence (and their answers thereby dramatized): Are Beowulf's boasts true? Is Grendel dead? Are we safe? The key to the suspense in such passages is, of course, not what the audience knows, but what the characters within the poem do not. Lockett's account finds an intense "period of suspense" between the two battles; and, as she argues, it is the ambiguity of the "so-called 'clear sign'" of Grendel's severed arm that gives this suspense its force.[50] In these passages, it is not the word of the hero that impresses the men, nor attracts the main interest of the poet, but the circumstantial evidence of the monster's presence and departure, and the deduced probability of his consequent death.[51] None of these

---

rights of who should 'have and hold' the great hall" (323–24). Beowulf wins, in other words, because he has the law on his side.

48 Katherine O'Brien O'Keeffe's assessment of the opposition between Beowulf and Grendel identifies a series of poetic choices through which Grendel is given an increasingly human form as he approaches the hall: "Beowulf, Lines 702b–836: Transformations and the Limits of the Human," *Texas Studies in Literature and Language* 23 (1981): 484–94); this process emphasizes the nature of the conflict as one taking place in a world whose evils are of a human and criminal, rather than distantly monstrous, kind. In the context of this presentation, O'Keeffe argues, "the description of Grendel as an enemy of mankind, a dark solitary goer ... assumes sinister accuracy, since his love of murder and disregard of *feoh* (154b–158b, here, payment to settle a feud) make community impossible" (491).

49 Hrothgar's "long admonitory address" to Beowulf (1700–84) opens its section of praise for the hero by uniting *soð ond riht* ("truth and right" 1700b) to ground the acclamation that *ðes eorl wære / geboren betera* ("this man was born superior" 1702b–1703a): *Klaeber 4*, 213. Status, truth and *riht* go hand-in-hand.

50 For Lockett, this is a suspense that involves the early English audience of the poem, as much as it does the characters within: "Role of Grendel's Arm," 380.

51 That Grendel is already dead when Beowulf later beheads him in the mere at 1590 is indicated by the phrase *æfter deaðe* ("after death," 1589) and the

events is seen by actual witnesses in the poem. In fact, a major purpose of the 'morning after' passage (837–990) that follows Beowulf's engagement with Grendel is to follow how those who arrived after the event reconstructed the momentous doings of that dark night. We, the audience, though ourselves in possession of all the facts, watch those arriving at Heorot work it out for themselves, reading the sign of the severed arm and creating from the pattern of blood-spatter and the tracks of the fleeing monster the narrative of the battle and its successful outcome. Deductive reasoning is to underpin the imaginative reconstruction of the events.

Line 837a opens on the morning; the preceding lines 833b–834b prepare the evidence for the light of dawn. The "clear sign" (*tacen sweotol*) is now turned on the monster: it is Grendel's probable death that the visible sign of his hand and arm most immediately betokens.

Þæt wæs tacen sweotol
syþðan hildedeor hond alegde,
earm ond eaxle —þær wæs eal geador
Grendles grape— under geapne hrof.

That was a clear sign, when the battle-brave one set hand, arm and shoulder—all of Grendel's grasp there together—under the vaulted roof. (833b–836b)

The precise detail of where the arm is, and who exactly put it there, has generated some debate.[52] But for my purposes (and, I would suggest,

description of his body as *aldorleasne* ("lifeless," 1587). Fulk, confirming for his own part that this final blow dealt by Beowulf was "posthumous," notes the existence of the alternative reading that the monster survives until he is beheaded. R. D. Fulk, "Some Emendations and Non-Emendations in 'Beowulf' (Verses 600a, 976a, 1585b, 1663b, 1740a, 2525b, 2771a, and 3060a)," *Studies in Philology* 104 (2007): 164–67; the point is repeated in *Klaeber 4*, 165. Fulk chiefly ascribes this alternate reading to Alfred Bammesberger, who is in fact innocent of any such conjecture: he too accepts that the beheading was post-mortem: "Grendel's Death (Beowulf 850–852)," *Neophilologus* 86 (2002): 467–69. It is worth noting that in many versions of the Germanic "Bear's Son" folktale tradition that is often posited as a Beowulfian analogue, the pursuing hero does find the monster alive in its abode, and so does need to complete the killing. It may be significant that the poet of *Beowulf* departs markedly from the folktale tradition in this aspect, a narrative choice that renders the visible results of the first encounter all the more significant. See *Klaeber 4*, xxxvii–xxxviii; and for the legal implications of this analogue, John D. Niles, "The Myth of the Feud in Anglo-Saxon England," *JEGP* 114 (2015): 191–92.

52 For a summary of the issues, see Larry J. Swain, "Of Hands, Halls, and Heroes: Grendel's Hand, Hroþgar's Power, and the Problem of *stapol* in *Beowulf*," *Anglia* 134 (2016): 260–84. For the argument that it is not Beowulf but in fact Grendel who has "set" (*alegde*) the hand where it is found in the morning, see Bruce

for the poet's) the key here is the physical evidence of the arm itself – the *tacen sweotol*. Lockett notes significantly that, unlike the other references in the poem to *tacen*, no specific referent is given to this sign by the poet.[53] This is of course precisely the point: the evidence is still not interpreted; the tracks have not been followed. The mystery of what happened in the darkness of the night has not been solved – yet. And for this *tacen*, the list of possible significations and solutions is long. Lockett provides at least eight possibilities, both legal and symbolic;[54] a survey of other commentators reveals a still greater embarrassment of interpretive riches.[55] But one layer of meaning has been missing from these accounts – hiding in plain sight, perhaps, as the critics themselves work to interpret this very aspect of the arm. The shoulder, arm, and hand of Grendel is evidence – and the evidence is clear because the arm is enormous. What it means, however, is left by the poet to the reasoning of the characters in the poem.

Mitchell and Fred C. Robinson, eds., *Beowulf: An Edition with Relevant Shorter Texts* (Oxford: Blackwell, 1998), 122; J. G. Johansen, "Grendel the Brave? *Beowulf*, line 834," *English Studies* 63 (1982): 193–97; Rolf H. Bremmer, "Grendel's Arm and the Law," in *Doubt Wisely: Papers in Honour of E. G. Stanley*, ed. M. J. Toswell and E. M. Tyler (London: Routledge, 1996). For the argument that the hand is not hung on high, but merely "in the hall" see Mitchell, Robinson, and Webster, *Beowulf*, 122–23. But the arm appears to be hung on high by 925, and certainly is by 980. If it is not deliberately displayed by Beowulf, the poet is silent about who is responsible for its exhibition.

53 The significations of other *tacen* in the poem are specified by the poet: evidence of "the hall-thane's [Grendel's] hate" at 141–42, and "glory" at 1654.

54 Lockett, "Role of Grendel's Arm" understands these battle scenes as relating to the legal framework and discourse of feud. She shows that the arm might function to inspire awe for Beowulf (371), or satisfy a morbid curiosity (371), or offer a metonymic association – the hand is severed that did the damage at Heorot (375), or suggest a version of legal punishment in the form of public mutilation (377), or stand as a payment of compensation for feud – paid, as it were, in kind (375), or present a token of the ongoing feud that will goad a family member to continue it (379), or by open display demonstrate the legitimacy of the homicide (372). For a re-evaluation of the modern concept of feud as the legal basis for violence in *Beowulf*, see Niles, "The Myth of the Feud," 163–200, esp. 183–94.

55 *Klaeber 4* offers "that was clearly proved" for *Þæt wæs tacen sweotol*, suggesting that the immediate referent of the arm as token is the fulfillment of those elements most recently mentioned: Beowulf's oath (*gilp gelæsted* 829b) and his remedying the suffering (*oncyþðe ealle gebette* 830) of the Danes. But the editors note also that the arm might be "a sign of victory" (164). Elsewhere, it has suggested to commentators (among many other things) "the superiority of the victor over the victim" and "[c]orporal punishment" (Bremmer, "Grendel's Arm and the Law," 126); "the physical symbol of … wrongful control [of *mund*]" (Day, "Hands across the Hall," 323); "purification" and "signs and tokens of the creature's death […] safe in their symbolism and inactivity." Seth Lerer, "Grendel's Glove," *English Literary History* 61 (1994): 739–40.

The solution, and the process by which it is arrived at, is presented by the men who arrive to witness the aftermath of the events: the chain of circumstances becomes a complete narrative of the night and the nature of the vanquished monster. The physical remains of the arm is not the only piece of evidence they examine; indeed, its meaning is not articulated by the collective until all other traces have been followed.

> Đa wæs on morgen mine gefræge
> ymb þa gifhealle guðrinc monig;
> ferdon folctogan feorran ond nean
> geond widwegas wundor sceawian,
> laþes lastas.

> Then in the morning, as I have heard, many warriors, folk-chiefs, arrived about the gift-hall from far and near across long distances to behold (*sceawian*) the wonder, the foe's foot-prints (*lastas*). (837a–841a)

The great tracks of Grendel first capture the attention of the gathering group, and the poet moves our gaze away from the arm in order to follow a bloody trail with the warriors.[56] Physical evidence, observation, and conclusion tumble over one another as this passage flows rapidly from Heorot to the mere along the track of the wounded monster.

> No his lifgedal
> sarlic þuhte secga ænegum
> þara þe tirleases trode sceawode,
> hu he werigmod on weg þanon,
> niða ofercumen, on nicera mere
> fæge ond geflymed feorhlastas bær.
> Đær wæs on blode brim weallende,
> atol yða geswing eal gemenged
> haton heolfre, heorodreore weol.
> Deaðfæge deog siððan dreama leas
> in fenfreoðo feorh alegde...

> His parting from life did not seem mournful to any man of those who observed (*sceawode*) the track (*trode*) of the glory-less one, how he, weary in spirit, overcome by violence, away thence (doomed and driven back to the water-monster's mere) left behind life-trails (*feorh-lastas*). There the water boiled with blood, a horrible swirling of waves all mingled

56 Perhaps surprised by this narrative choice, some early commentators were inclined to take *lastas* here as a reference to the great hand and arm. See, e.g., P. G. Thomas, "Further Notes on 'Beowulf,'" *The Modern Language Review* 22 (1927): 71. But Grendel's large tracks "might well have been thought a *wundor* 840^{b}, especially if blood-stained." *Klaeber 4*, 164.

with hot gore, it welled with battle-blood. Doomed to death he hid himself, then, deprived of joy, in his fen-refuge he laid down his life… (841b–851b)

The men construct from the bloody tracks the how (*hu*) of the monster's retreat, and then witness in the welling of hot blood on the surface of swirling water the probable (though unseen) truth of Grendel's death deep below. In a move that has emerged as characteristic of the poet's method in such evidentiary moments (seen above at 129b–133a and 138a–142a), we begin with the emotional conclusion – *No his lifgedal / sarlic þuhte* ("his parting from life did not seem mournful" 841b–842a) – before being presented with the circumstances and deductions that gave rise to it. The first evidentiary conclusion suggested by the displayed arm has been reached: Grendel is dead.

Upon their return to Heorot, the collective voice of the interpreting community at last articulates the meaning of the arm itself. The poet illuminates the arm once more for this important viewing: *Ða wæs morgenleoht / scofen ond scynded* ("Then the morning-light was advanced and heightened" 917b–918a). At least four levels of attention are placed upon the token. The attention of the poem's audience as interpreter of evidence is of course crucial; the audience's scrutiny is guided by a sequence of observers within the poem. In the first of these, many men go to the hall to view this "curious wonder" (*searowundor*). The king, in stately ceremony, then approaches formally to examine the hand (920b–927b). And finally, Beowulf himself comments upon the evidence:

Uþe ic swiþor
þæt ðu hine selfne geseon moste,
feond on frætewum fylwerigne.

I would rather you had been able to see the enemy himself in his gear, fall-weary. (960b–962b)

Beowulf here regrets that there can be no viewing of Grendel's whole body (*hine selfne*) rather than just his arm;[57] it is Grendel's corpse, not the living monster in battle, that he wishes the king could have seen: *fylwerigne* ("fall-weary") means "killed."[58] But the hero recognizes, too, that once the arm has been observed (again the verb is *sceawedon*) there is no need of repetitive boasting. The reason for this emerges from the forensic scrutiny to which the nobles now subject the dead monster's hand.

[57] See *Klaeber 4*, 174.

[58] See ibid., 381.

Ða wæs swigra secg, sunu Eclafes,
on gylpspræce guðgeweorca,
siþðan æþelingas eorles cræfte
ofer heanne hrof hand sceawedon,
feondes fingras; foran æghwylc wæs,
steda nægla gehwylc, style gelicost,
hæþenes handsporu, hilderinces,
egl' unheoru. Æghwylc gecwæð
þæt him heardra nan hrinan wolde
iren ærgod, þæt ðæs ahlæcan
blodge beadufolme onberan wolde.

Then the man was the quieter, the son of Ecglaf, in boasting of warlike deeds, after the nobles observed the hand, over the high roof by the man's strength, the enemy's fingers. At the end of each was, all the places of the nails, very like steel, the horrible, disagreeable hand-vestiges of the heathen combatant. Everyone said that no iron of hardy ones, good from old, would touch him in such a way that it would weaken the troublemaker's bloody battle-hand. (980a–990b)[59]

The precise sense and grammatical detail of this passage (and especially 984–87) is somewhat obscure. But although modern commentators find the details of finger, nail, and hand difficult to parse, and the relation of *eorles cræfte* ("the man's strength") to all of these difficult to reconstruct,[60] no such interpretive problem existed for the nobles in the poem. Their judgment is by consensus – *Æghwylc gecwæð* ("everyone said") – and is made in considered fashion, in the context of procession, royal speech, and formal response at the steps of the great hall. The close analysis of the physical and material details of the hand lead to the conclusion that no iron could have harmed the monster. The group has arrived through deduction at the very conclusion offered by the omniscience of the poet some 200 lines earlier: "no paragon of irons over the earth, of war-swords, would affect the criminal marauder" (*þone synscaðan / ænig ofer eorþan irenna cyst, / guðbilla nan, gretan nolde*, 801–03). What the poet (and the audience) knew then, we now watch Hrothgar's nobles deduce from the *blodge beadufolme* ("bloody battle-arm"). And the deduction vindicates Beowulf's boasts, even to the prescience or good fortune of the boast that he *hine sweorde swebban nelle* ("shall not slay him [Grendel] with sword"

59 The translation here largely follows R. D. Fulk, ed., *The Beowulf Manuscript: Complete Texts and The Fight at Finnsburg* (Cambridge, MA: Harvard University Press, 2010), 151.

60 For an account of the difficulties, see *Klaeber 4*, 175: the problems of interpretation have been ascribed either to the "unfamiliar idiom" or "textual corruption" of the passage: *Klaeber 4*, 175.

679). Elsewhere in this speech (675–87), Beowulf shows himself to be ignorant of Grendel's magical defense against weaponry: he claims that he could easily kill Grendel with a sword (680). For Bjork, this unfulfillable boast signifies the "restricted nature of humankind's knowledge";[61] under such a disadvantage, the Danes (repeatedly attempting defense with sword) "are as much victims to their lack of knowledge as to their adversary."[62] This second evidentiary conclusion about Grendel is thus a major one: he was untouchable by sword all along; and only Beowulf, therefore, fighting as his courage prompted him to fight, could have emerged victorious. The result of the hero's valor and strength are manifest in the evidence of the arm, which stands for the boast of prowess that Beowulf no longer needs to make.

Summation of Evidence

The *Beowulf*-poet's dramatization of the answers to the questions "What happened?" and "How do you know?" depend heavily upon an exploitation of the possibilities of deductive reasoning in legal and quasi-legal contexts. A similar dependence has been seen in the events recorded in the *Fonthill Letter* and certain law codes. It is perhaps doubtful that enough evidence for the use of circumstantial evidence can be found in either the law codes or the literature of early England seriously to disturb the judgment of Maitland: "Oath was the primary mode of proof, an oath going not to the truth of specific fact, but to the justice of the claim or defence as a whole."[63] But there are grounds for more than the suspicion that underpinning the forms of legal process lay depths of cultural experience (and a business of human action) whose application of a fundamentally forensic process was as influential to actual inquest as it was under-represented in written records. In the tracking of cattle, in the thinking about scratches, even in the fatness of pastured pigs, there is legislative and procedural evidence of an interest in the persuasions of probative logic, and the existence of voices to speak to its relevance. And when to that is added the entry of that imaginative reasoning into formal procedure – *stande þæt spor for þone foraþ* ("the trail shall stand for the oath of accusation") – then a significant jurisprudential step has been taken. It is a move similar to that which the *Beowulf*-poet dramatizes as we follow the trail left by the mortally wounded Grendel, and it is the sequence described by Ordlaf in the case against Helmstan: there is

[61] Robert E. Bjork, "Speech as Gift in *Beowulf*," *Speculum* 69 (1994): 1004.

[62] Ibid., 1005.

[63] Pollock and Maitland, *History of English Law*, 1:39.

the hunt for evidence, the inferential nature of the evidence as discovered, and its final acceptance as proof of significant fact. This alliance of rational, investigative, and imaginative activity suggests a legal and literary culture more than capable of adapting for dramatic and forensic effect the potential of inference and probable consequence to resolve conflict and achieve justice.

5

Uncertain Judgment: The Ordeal in Hagiography and Law

Andrew Rabin

It is with typically measured prose that Michael Lapidge concludes that Bishop Swithun of Winchester "can justly be regarded as a saint of the universal church."[1] Lapidge's comprehensive survey of the texts and traditions associated with Swithun's veneration amply justifies this assessment: in his *Cult of St Swithun*, Lapidge and his collaborators range widely from the ninth to the sixteenth centuries; from Winchester to Dublin, Helsinki, and Évreux; and from history into chronicle, hagiography, liturgy, poetry, musical composition, and artistic production, all to demonstrate the influence of Swithun's cult on medieval religious and cultural life.[2] Indeed, there appears to be only one major area of early medieval culture omitted from this list, namely, the law. For as legal historians well know, the earliest life of Swithun, Lantfred's late tenth-century *Translatio et miracula s. Swithuni*, occupies an important place in the history of pre-Conquest legal practice as one of the few surviving narrative records of an Anglo-Saxon ordeal by hot iron.[3] This chapter will focus on this episode in order to

1 Michael Lapidge, *The Cult of St Swithun*, Winchester Studies (Oxford: Clarendon, 2003), 61.

2 See the contributions to Lapidge, *Cult of St Swithun* by John Crook, Robert Deshman, and Susan Rankin.

3 Paul R. Hyams, "Trial by Ordeal: The Key to Proof in Early Common Law," in *On the Laws and Customs of England: Essays in Honor of Samuel E. Thorne*, ed. Morris S. Arnold et al. (Chapel Hill: University of North Carolina Press, 1981), 93–95; David Pelteret, *Slavery in Early Mediaeval England* (Woodbridge: Boydell, 1995), 59; Ian C. Pilarczyk, "Between a Rock and a Hot Place: The Role of Subjectivity and Rationality in the Medieval Ordeal by Hot Iron," *Anglo-American Law Review* 25 (1996): 94–96; Katherine O'Brien O'Keeffe, "Body and Law in Late Anglo-Saxon England," *Anglo-Saxon England* 27 (1998): 224–25; Catherine Cubitt, "'As the Lawbook Teaches': Reeves, Lawbooks and Urban Life in the Anonymous Old English Legend of the Seven Sleepers," *English Historical Review* 124 (2009): 1040; John Hudson, *The Oxford History of the Laws of England, Volume II: 871–1216* (Oxford: Oxford University Press, 2012), 68–73; Helen Foxhall Forbes, *Heaven and Earth in Anglo-Saxon England: Theology and Society in an Age of Faith* (Aldershot: Ashgate, 2013), 169–71; Helen Foxhall

reassess the role of hagiographic narrative in both the history and practice of the ordeal and the composition of legal narratives more generally.

The ordeal, in its foreignness and seeming barbarity, has long been a problem for those seeking to understand the mentality of early medieval law.[4] As William Ian Miller has written, "It appalls and intrigues. We marvel at the mentality of those cultures that officialize it; we feel a sense of horror as we imagine ourselves intimately involved with boiling water or glowing irons. And we don't feel quite up to it. So our terror and cowardice become their brutality and irrationality."[5] For earlier historians of English law, such as T. F. T. Plucknett and Frederick Pollock, the ordeal served as a marker of the primitivism they saw as characteristic of English law before the so-called "great leap forward" of the twelfth century.[6] More

Forbes, "Making Manifest God's Judgement: Interpreting Ordeals in Anglo-Saxon England," in *Writing, Kingship, and Power in Anglo-Saxon England* ed. Rory Naismith and David A. Woodman (Cambridge: Cambridge University Press, 2018), 269–70; Nicholas Karn, *Kings, Lords, and Courts in Anglo-Norman England* (Woodbridge: Boydell, 2020), 38–40.

4 The literature on this topic is vast, but see esp. John W. Baldwin, "The Intellectual Preparation for the Canon of 1215 Against Ordeals," *Speculum* 36 (1961): 613–36; Rebecca V. Colman, "Reason and Unreason in Early Medieval Law," *The Journal of Interdisciplinary History* 4 (1974): 571–91; Charles M. Radding, "Superstition to Science: Nature, Fortune, and the Passing of the Medieval Ordeal," *The American Historical Review* 84 (1979): 945–69; Robert Bartlett, *Trial by Fire and Water: The Medieval Judicial Ordeal* (Oxford: Clarendon, 1986); William Ian Miller, "Ordeal in Iceland," *Scandinavian Studies* 60 (1988): 189–218; Margaret H. Kerr, Richard D. Forsyth, and Michael J. Plyley, "Cold Water and Hot Iron: Trial by Ordeal in England," *The Journal of Interdisciplinary History* 22 (1992): 573–95; Stephen D. White, "Proposing the Ordeal and Avoiding It: Strategy and Power in Western French Litigation, 1050–1110," in *Cultures of Power: Lordship, Status, and Process in Twelfth-Century Europe*, ed. Thomas N. Bisson (Philadelphia: University of Pennsylvania Press, 1995), 89–123; Finbarr McAuley, "Canon Law and the End of the Ordeal," *Oxford Journal of Legal Studies* 26 (2006): 473–513; Peter T. Leeson, "Ordeals," *The Journal of Law and Economics* 55 (2012): 691–714; Stefan Jurasinski and Lisi Oliver, eds., *The Laws of Alfred: The Domboc and the Making of Anglo-Saxon Law* (Cambridge: Cambridge University Press, 2021), 78–112.

5 Miller, "Ordeal in Iceland," 189.

6 T. F. T. Plucknett, *Edward I and Criminal Law* (Cambridge: Cambridge University Press, 1960), 69–74. This view is criticized in Colman, "Reason," 571–78, 590–91; Radding, "Superstition to Science," 946–47; Hyams, "Trial by Ordeal," 98–99; Bartlett, *Trial by Fire*, 101–02; David Rollason, *Two Anglo-Saxon Rituals: The Dedication of a Church and the Judicial Ordeal*, Fifth Brixworth Lecture (Brixworth: Friends of All Saints Church, Brixworth, 1988), 13–14; Pilarczyk, "Rock and a Hot Place," 106–09; Wormald, *Making of English Law*, 26; Vickie L. Ziegler, *Trial by Fire and Battle in Medieval German Literature* (Rochester: Camden House, 2004), 1–20; Levi Roach, *Kingship and Consent in Anglo-Saxon England,*

recently, following the work of Rebecca Colman and Paul Hyams, scholars have instead adopted what has been referred to as a "functionalist" approach, focusing, in Colman's words, on the "functional relationship between certain legal procedures and their particular social context."[7] Influenced by social anthropology, the functionalist argument highlights the ordeal's potential to generate consensus in small communities. As a flexible procedure that framed the communal interpretation of a wounded body as the manifestation of divine judgment, it became, as Peter Brown writes, "a theatrical device by which to contain disruptive conflict."[8] The functionalist argument has not gone unchallenged, most famously by Robert Bartlett who saw the ordeal instead as a coercive means of asserting social control.[9] More recently, James Q. Whitman has compellingly suggested that the ordeal was not part of a discovery process at all, but rather served as what he calls a "comfort procedure" intended to eliminate ambiguity from the sentencing phase of a trial and thus anticipating the development of the doctrine of reasonable doubt.[10]

871–978: Assemblies and the State in the Early Middle Ages (Cambridge: Cambridge University Press, 2013), 118–19. For more recent characterizations of the ordeal as irrational, "a-rational," or primitive, see Naomi D. Hurnard, *The King's Pardon for Homicide Before A.D. 1307* (Oxford: Clarendon, 1969), 342; Alan Harding, *The Law Courts of Medieval England* (London: Allen & Unwin, 1973), 25–26; John H. Langbein, *Torture and the Law of Proof: Europe and England in the Ancien Régime*, 2nd ed. (Chicago: University of Chicago Press, 1976), 6; R. C. Van Caenegem, *The Birth of the English Common Law*, 2nd ed. (Cambridge: Cambridge University Press, 1988), 64–67; R. C. Van Caenegem, "Methods of Proof in Western Medieval Law," in *Legal History: A European Perspective* (London: Hambledon, 1991), 73–74; Jeffrey A. Bowman, *Shifting Landmarks: Property, Proof, and Dispute in Catalonia around the Year 1000* (Ithaca: Cornell University Press, 2004), 119–40; William Ian Miller, *Eye for an Eye* (Cambridge: Cambridge University Press, 2006), 3; James Q. Whitman, *The Origins of Reasonable Doubt: Theological Roots of the Criminal Trial* (New Haven: Yale University Press, 2008), 53–56; Leeson, "Ordeals," 691–93.

7 Colman, "Reason," 571–72. See also Radding, "Superstition to Science," 948–50; Hyams, "Trial by Ordeal," 90–126; Leeson, "Ordeals," 692n3.

8 Peter Brown, "Society and the Supernatural: A Medieval Change," *Daedalus* 104 (1975): 137.

9 Bartlett, *Trial by Fire*, 34–35, 42. See also Robin Chapman Stacey, *The Road to Judgment: From Custom to Court in Medieval Ireland and Wales* (Philadelphia: University of Pennsylvania Press, 1994), 199–200; Sarah Larratt Keefer, "*Ðonne se cirlisce man ordales weddieð*: The Anglo-Saxon Lay Ordeal," in *Early Medieval Studies in Memory of Patrick Wormald*, ed. Stephen Baxter et al. (Farnham: Ashgate, 2009), 363. Critiques of both positions can be found in Miller, "Ordeal in Iceland," 190–91; Pilarczyk, "Rock and a Hot Place," 93–94.

10 Whitman, *Origins*, 9–27, esp. 12–13. For his critique of Bartlett, see Whitman, *Origins*, 67–71. Similar, if less elaborate, characterizations of the ordeal can be found in Thomas Andrew Green, *Verdict According to Conscience: Perspectives on*

This chapter will approach the ordeal from a different angle. Rather than asking whether the ordeal represents a rational response to problems of criminal behavior and justice administration, it will focus instead on the ways in which the ordeal – and, no less importantly, the narrative record of an ordeal – contributed to the norms by which law was made, practiced, and internalized by an early medieval community.[11] As ritualized as an ordeal proceeding could be, these rituals concealed significant flexibility in both procedure and interpretation. As a result, the manner in which an ordeal transpired, like other aspects of early medieval law, was determined by the norms of the community within which it occurred, and its "success" as a legal proceeding depended in large part on the extent to which its procedures and outcomes coincided with those norms.[12] This emphasis on communal norms extended to written accounts of the ordeal as well. That is, the records of ordeals were composed, less to accurately transcribe a legal proceeding, than to shape readers' memories of the event and their views of the legal authority that authorized it.

Yet legal records – including those of ordeals – do more than reflect the norms according to which a dispute was resolved: they actively participate in the reinforcement of those norms in the legal consciousness of the community. In this sense, Warren Brown's comments about the land disputes recorded in early medieval charters should be taken as equally applicable to the records of ordeals, namely, that "[E]ach reflects a conscious or unconscious effort to select and organize information from the past for the needs of the present, each reflects an effort to select and organize information from the present for the possible needs of the future."[13] Accordingly, we must be wary of treating the ordeal narrative in Lantfred as – in the words of one reader – "an actual criminal trial" or comparing it, as does another reader, with the stories of Arthur Conan Doyle, only to conclude, "Unlike the detective novels, unlike the mysteries of Sherlock Holmes, of

---

the English Criminal Trial Jury, 1200–1800 (Chicago: University of Chicago Press, 1985), 14; Forbes, *Heaven and Earth*, 158–98.

11 John Hudson, "Court Cases and Legal Arguments in England, *c.*1066–1166," *TRHS*, 6th series, 10 (2000): 92–93; Paul R. Hyams, "Norms and Legal Argument Before 1150," in *Law and History*, ed. Andrew Lewis and Michael Lobban (Oxford: Oxford University Press, 2004), 41–61; Levi Roach, "Law Codes and Legal Norms in Later Anglo-Saxon England," *Historical Research* 86 (2013): 465–86; Andrew Rabin, *Crime and Punishment in Anglo-Saxon England* (Cambridge: Cambridge University Press, 2020), 3–6, 21–24.

12 Colman, "Reason," 581; Brown, "Society and the Supernatural," 137; Richard Firth Green, *A Crisis of Truth: Literature and Law in Ricardian England* (Philadelphia: University of Pennsylvania Press, 1999),109; Paul Friedland, *Seeing Justice Done: The Age of Spectacular Capital Punishment in France* (Oxford: Oxford University Press, 2012), 11.

13 On this point, see also Friedland, *Seeing Justice Done*, 11.

course, the ordeal happened."[14] To do either assumes a narrative transparency that directs the reader away from the tale's miraculous content – thereby relegating to the margins of our analysis those devotional features of the narrative which its initial readers viewed as most important – while also overlooking the way in which the narrative has been shaped in order to influence communal norms regarding the relationship between ecclesiastical authority and the administration of secular justice. The goal of this chapter, then, must be to rethink the role of the ordeal in the eyes – and the *minds* – of its beholders.

I

Perhaps the greatest hindrance to understanding the medieval ordeal lies in the contradictory evidence of its use. Most scholarly treatments locate the ordeal either in the pretrial investigation of wrongdoing or in the presentation of evidence at the trial itself.[15] Whitman departs from this consensus in assigning the ordeal to the sentencing phase as confirmation of the verdict.[16] The few surviving records of ordeals do not fit easily with either of these claims, however. Little reliable evidence beyond legal clauses and anecdotes survives from pre-Conquest England, though later records are telling. For instance, Eadmer's *Historia novorum in Anglia* records an incident in 1098 in which fifty defendants, all members of what had been the Anglo-Saxon nobility, were accused by William II of poaching the king's deer, though all were exonerated after undergoing the ordeal of hot iron.[17] *Domesday Book* records twenty-one instances of

14 Brown, "Society and the Supernatural," 136.

15 Julius Goebel, *Felony and Misdemeanor: A Study in the History of Criminal Law* (Philadelphia: University of Pennsylvania Press, 1976 [orig. publ. 1937]), 69–70; H. R. Loyn, *The Governance of Anglo-Saxon England, 500–1087* (Stanford: Stanford University Press, 1984), 139; Bartlett, *Trial by Fire*, 13–33; Sarah Larratt Keefer, "*Ut in omnibus honorificetur Deus*: The *Corsnæd* Ordeal in Anglo-Saxon England," in *The Community, the Family and the Saint: Patterns of Power in Early Medieval Europe*, ed. Joyce M. Hill and Mary Swan (Turnhout: Brepols, 1998), 238–39; Warren Brown, *Unjust Seizure: Conflict, Interest, and Authority in an Early Medieval Society* (Ithaca: Cornell University Press, 2001), 207; Bowman, *Shifting Landmarks*, 133, 140; Richard Huscroft, *Making England, 796–1042* (New York: Routledge, 2019), 79.

16 Whitman, *Origins*, 7. Surviving legislation from Catalonia differs from both positions by characterizing the ordeal as a form of punishment. Bowman, *Shifting Landmarks*, 130.

17 Martin Rule, *Eadmeri historia novorum in Anglia, et opuscula duo de vita Sancti Anselmi et quibusdam miraculis ejus*, Rolls Series (London: Longman, 1884), 102. See Van Caenegem, *Birth of the English Common Law*, 69; Pilarczyk, "Rock and a

property holders offering to undergo ordeals in order to prove their rights as landowners, but little survives to suggest that such offers were routinely taken up.[18] Rather, the offer seems to have functioned as a rhetorical formula intended to demonstrate the seriousness of the landowner's intent to defend his claim.[19] Later evidence reflects a similar pattern: between 1194 and 1208, 275 documented ordeals yielded a mere eight convictions, seven of which only occurred because the defendant confessed before the ordeal could be carried out.[20] Likewise, in surveying pleas from the early thirteenth century, Frederic William Maitland found only one instance of a conviction by ordeal.[21] Further afield, the entire corpus of Icelandic sagas contains only ten references to ordeals, of which a mere seven are ultimately carried out.[22] Catalonian legal records from the years between 900 and 1100 likewise mention only ten instances of the ordeal.[23] In eastern Europe, a legal register from the Hungarian city of Várad includes roughly 300 ordeals between 1208 and 1235, yet only seventy-eight of these led to a conviction. In those cases in which the ordeal resulted in a trial rather than an out-of-court settlement, the seventy-eight convictions were far

Hot Place," 99–100; H. R. Loyn, *The English Church, 940–1154* (Harlow: Pearson, 1999), 100; Green, *Crisis of Truth*, 107; Whitman, *Origins*, 65; Hudson, *Oxford History of the Laws of England*, 326–27. There is evidence that the results of the ordeal could also be used to manufacture guilt. See Robin Fleming, *Domesday Book and the Law: Society and Legal Custom in Early Medieval England* (Cambridge: Cambridge University Press, 1998), 18–19.

18 Colman, "Reason," 586; John Hudson, *The Formation of English Common Law: Law and Society in England from the Norman Conquest to Magna Carta*, 2nd ed. (New York: Routledge, 2018), 62–63; James A. Brundage, *The Medieval Origins of the Legal Profession: Canonists, Civilians, and Courts* (Chicago: University of Chicago Press, 2008), 54–55; Sally Harvey, *Domesday: Book of Judgment* (Oxford: Oxford University Press, 2014), 284–85. Interestingly, seventeen of the twenty-one survive in Little Domesday, and thirteen of these were from Norfolk. Harvey, *Domesday*, 285. For a broader discussion of ordeals offered but not carried out, see White, "Proposing the Ordeal," 89–123.

19 Harvey, *Domesday*, 281. See Bowman, *Shifting Landmarks*, 123.

20 James Masschaele, *Jury, State, and Society in Medieval England* (New York: Palgrave Macmillan, 2008), 84.

21 Frederic William Maitland, *Select Pleas of the Crown, Vol. I: A.D. 1200–1225*, Selden Society (London: Bernard Quaritch, 1887). See also Kerr, et al., "Cold Water," 576. Bartlett notes that ordeals are mentioned in the pipe rolls for the reign of Henry II and Exchequer accounts from the reign of Richard I, though the records are so fragmentary as to make it nearly impossible to determine the ratio of convictions to acquittals. Bartlett, *Trial by Fire*, 65–66.

22 William Ian Miller, *Bloodtaking and Peacemaking: Feud, Law, and Society in Saga Iceland* (Chicago: University of Chicago Press, 1990), 250. See also Miller, "Ordeal in Iceland," 193–94.

23 Bowman, *Shifting Landmarks*, 135.

outstripped by the number of acquittals (130).[24] As is often the case with medieval legal records, it is difficult to determine whether these data are representative. Nonetheless, the apparent consistency across time and distance suggests that they cannot simply be dismissed. On one hand, the high percentage of exonerations reflected in these statistics suggest that Whitman may have overstated the extent to which the ordeal served as a "comfort procedure" to reassure judges and juries of the defendant's guilt. At the same time, the low rate of convictions suggests that the ordeal was not simply an evidentiary procedure either. Indeed, the incidence of exoneration suggests the ordeal may have served much the same purpose as jury nullification, found disproportionately in capital cases of the period.[25] Much as juries returned acquittals despite manifest evidence of the defendant's guilt in order to ensure the autonomy of local justice over the harsher law of the king, so the ordeal may have been used as a means of avoiding punishment rather than confirming it.[26] A motive of this sort might well explain Eadmer's account of the fifty acquitted Anglo-Saxon noblemen, a narrative predicated on the hostility of the native aristocracy toward their Norman conquerors.

Yet arguably the most important consequence of the ordeal's apparent bias for acquittal is the implication that its result was governed, at least in part, by the norms of the community in which it took place. Much like jury nullification, success in an ordeal provided communities with a means of asserting the superiority of local knowledge and local practices – what Rebecca Colman calls "the discretionary power of local communities"[27] –

[24] Imre Zajtay, "Le Registre de Várad: Un monument judiciaire du début du XIIIe siècle," *Revue historique de droit français et étranger* 31 (1954): 527–62. See also Brown, "Society and the Supernatural," 139; Bartlett, *Trial by Fire,* 63; Wendy Davies and Paul Fouracre, "Procedure and Practice in the Settlement of Disputes," in *The Settlement of Disputes in Early Medieval Europe,* ed. Wendy Davies and Paul Fouracre (Cambridge: Cambridge University Press, 1986), 222; Van Caenegem, *Birth of the English Common Law,* 68; Van Caenegem, "Methods of Proof," 75–76; Green, *Crisis of Truth,* 84, 107.

[25] Green, *Verdict According to Conscience,* 22–28. See also Bowman, *Shifting Landmarks,* 125; Masschaele, *Jury, State, and Society,* 76–77, 82–84; Andrew Rabin, "Capital Punishment and the Anglo-Saxon Judicial Apparatus: A Maximum View?" in *Capital and Corporal Punishment in Anglo-Saxon England,* ed. Jay Paul Gates and Nicole Marafioti (Woodbridge: Boydell, 2014), 181–200.

[26] Frederick Pollock and Frederic William Maitland, *The History of English Law Before the Time of Edward I,* 2nd ed., 2 vols. (Cambridge: Cambridge University Press, 1911), 1:xxiv, 2:599; Bartlett, *Trial by Fire,* 80; Green, *Verdict According to Conscience,* 52; Kerr, et al., "Cold Water," 574; H. L. Ho, "The Legitimacy of Medieval Proof," *Journal of Law and Religion* 19 (2004): 272–74; R. H. Helmholz, *The Spirit of Classical Canon Law* (Athens: University of Georgia Press, 1996), 159; Leeson, "Ordeals," 692, 705–08.

[27] Colman, "Reason," 589. See also William Chester Jordan, "A Fresh Look at

over the legal mandates of an external authority.[28] Likewise, this prioritization of the local furnished the context within which the minority who failed at their ordeals were to be judged: insofar as the ordeal functioned as an expression of local legal norms, failure reflected a violation of those norms as much as, if not more than, a violation of any supercessionary authority.[29] It may be for this reason that – unlike most pre-Conquest legal rituals – the codification of the ordeal in royal legislation is complemented by its regulation in two non-legislative texts, *Ordal* (*The Ordeal*) and *Blaserum* (*On Incendiaries*), neither of which bears any indication that it was issued by the king, his council, or other centralized legal authority.[30] The emphasis on the normative function of the ordeal highlights its character as one of the most community-oriented of pre-Conquest legal rituals. Practices such as the swearing of oaths of loyalty, enrollment in a hundred, and the payment of dues and tithes all served as a means of mediating the relationship between the individual and the legal sovereignty of Church or king. In contrast, although the procedures for ordeals are prescribed in royal legislation, oversight of the ordeal is the prerogative of the Church rather than a reeve or other royal representative, criteria for judging the results of an ordeal are not stipulated, and the decision regarding those subject to the ordeal – including unknown or foreign individuals and those of suspicious character – rests on the judgment of the community.[31]

Medieval Sanctuary," in *Law and the Illicit in Medieval Europe*, ed. Ruth Mazo Karras, Joel Kaye, and E. Ann Matter (Philadelphia: University of Pennsylvania Press, 2008), 24.

28 Andrew Reynolds explicitly identifies the ordeal as a "guilt-absolving mechanism." *Anglo-Saxon Deviant Burial Practices* (Oxford: Oxford University Press, 2009), 22. See also Harding, *Law Courts*, 40; Colman, "Reason," 578–79; Green, *Verdict According to Conscience*, 52; Hudson, *Formation of the English Common Law*, 5–6; Fleming, *Domesday Book and the Law*, 17; Green, *Crisis of Truth*, 109; Ho, "Legitimacy," 274; John Blair, *The Church in Anglo-Saxon Society* (Oxford: Oxford University Press, 2005), 448; Wolfgang Müller, *The Criminalization of Abortion in the West* (Ithaca: Cornell University Press, 2012), 46; Elizabeth Papp Kamali, *Felony and the Guilty Mind in Medieval England* (Cambridge: Cambridge University Press, 2019), 246.

29 See also Bartlett, *Trial by Fire*, 37; Green, *Crisis of Truth*, 109–10; Blair, *Church in Anglo-Saxon Society*, 448; Jordan, "Fresh Look," 30.

30 On these texts, see also Wormald, *Making of English Law*, 367–68, 373–74; Forbes, "Making Manifest," 261; Huscroft, *Making England*, 166.

31 Colman, "Reason," 584; Frank Barlow, *The English Church 1000–1066: A Constitutional History* (New York: Longman, 1979), 147; Miller, "Ordeal in Iceland," 198; Hudson, *Formation of the English Common Law*, 62–64; Keefer, "The *Corsnæd* Ordeal," 239–40; O'Keeffe, "Body and Law," 224–25; Green, *Crisis of Truth*, 96; Ho, "Legitimacy," 255; P. S. Barnwell, "The Early Frankish *Mallus*: Its Nature, Participants, and Practices," in *Assembly Places and Practices in Medieval Europe*, ed. Aliki Pantos and Sarah Semple (Dublin: Four Courts

The ordeal has been described as the substitute for an oath in the absence of any other means of verification, but the need for verification itself only occurs when the potential proband does not conform to communal norms.[32] The ordeal thus functioned, depending on the circumstances, as a means of situating the individual in relationship to the legal norms of the community or as a means of asserting those norms when they are at risk of being supplanted.

The ordeal's contribution to the establishment of legal norms rests upon its character as a form of juridical performance.[33] As Peter Brown writes, "Seen from the outside, the ordeal was a *spectaculum* to which everyone flocked."[34] The performative aspect of the ordeal emerges in the legislation outlining the various rituals associated with its practice, which diagram the actions demanded of supervisor and proband with an unusual degree of specificity. The significance attached to this specificity was such that errors in the administration of ordeals were themselves punishable by law.[35] The surviving records of Anglo-Saxon oathtaking procedures offer little evidence of how the oath was administered or performed beyond a limited number of verbal formulae. But for the ordeal, the records furnish far greater detail. Old English *Ordal* specifies that the proband in an ordeal by hot iron must walk with the iron nine feet from the stake; the circumstances under which a proband in an ordeal by water must submerge his hand to the wrist or the elbow; the point during an ordeal at which two men from either party may test the water or iron; the position at which these witnesses must stand in relation to the ordeal, along with similar stipulations regarding the actions of the other

Press, 2004), 241; Ziegler, *Trial by Fire*, 5–6; Reynolds, *Anglo-Saxon Deviant Burial Practices*, 21; Hudson, *Oxford History of the Laws of England*, 325.

32 Harding, *Law Courts*, 27–28; Bartlett, *Trial by Fire*, 30–31; Brundage, *Medieval Origins of the Legal Profession*, 54; Jurasinski and Oliver, *Laws of Alfred*, 89–91, 102–11; Whitman, *Origins*, 59–66. I have written elsewhere of the similarities between oath-taking rituals, the casting of charms for legal purposes, and the ordeal. See Andrew Rabin, "Ritual Magic or Legal Performance? Reconsidering an Old English Charm Against Theft," in *English Law Before Magna Carta: Felix Liebermann and Die Gesetze der Angelsachsen*, ed. Stefan Jurasinski, Lisi Oliver, and Andrew Rabin (Leiden: Brill, 2010), 179, 191–92; Rabin, *Crime and Punishment*, 45–46.

33 Friedland, *Seeing Justice Done*, 94, 101. On the role of performance in public ritual, see M. Bradford Bedingfield, *The Dramatic Liturgy of Anglo-Saxon England* (Woodbridge: Boydell, 2002), 1–24.

34 Brown, "Society and the Supernatural," 138.

35 *Ordal* 1.6 and III Æthelred 6.2. All quotations from the laws are drawn from Felix Liebermann, *Die Gesetze der Angelsachsen*, 3 vols. (Halle: Max Niemeyer, 1903–16). Translations are my own. On the penalties for erring when administering an ordeal, see Ho, "Legitimacy," 277; Tom Lambert, *Law and Order in Anglo-Saxon England* (Oxford: Oxford University Press, 2017), 173.

witnesses present at the ritual.[36] *Blaserum* likewise specifies who must be present at an ordeal; the procedures by which an ordeal by iron or water may be selected; and the procedural differences between a singlefold and threefold ordeal. II Æthelstan 23.1 stipulates the ritual preparations a proband must undergo before an ordeal, while II Cnut 30 provides the rituals and procedures that must be used to open an ordeal proceeding.[37] In short, whereas the procedures attending most other pre-Conquest legal rituals remain vague in the surviving textual record, the documentary evidence concerning the performance of ordeals is anomalously specific. If other legal practices have rules, ordeals have what might be called, for lack of a better term, stage directions.

The performative features of the ordeal highlight the fact that it was directed as much at the spectators to the ritual as it was at the court or proband.[38] As David Rollason has observed, the language of ordeal rituals is fraught with "authoritarian imagery."[39] *Ordal*, for instance, dictates not just where those witnessing the ordeal were permitted to stand, but also the purification rituals they must undergo – fasting, sexual abstention, the sprinkling with and tasting of holy water, and the kissing of cross and Bible – in order to be present.[40] That these rituals are identical to

[36] On the unusually elaborate rules governing ordeals, see Ho, "Legitimacy," 266–67; Keefer, "The *Corsnæd* Ordeal," 240–41, 250; Keefer, "Anglo-Saxon Lay Ordeal," 355–56; Forbes, "Making Manifest," 266–69. A different view arguing that ordeal rituals did not necessarily adhere to strict instructions, see Hyams, "Trial by Ordeal," 96–98, 109–10. On the absence of procedural detail regarding oathtaking rituals, see Hudson, *Oxford History of the Laws of England*, 86; Helen Gittos, *Liturgy, Architecture, and Sacred Places in Anglo-Saxon England* (Oxford: Oxford University Press, 2013), 17. Similarly detailed instructions can be found in Frankish formularies as well. See Barnwell, "Early Frankish Mallus," 242.

[37] The links between *Ordal, Blaserum*, and the legislation of Æthelstan has been discussed in Wormald, *Making of English Law*, 367, 373. On these clauses, see Colman, "Reason," 583–84; Wormald, *Making of English Law*, 304–05; Green, *Crisis of Truth*, 62–63; Hudson, *Oxford History of the Laws of England*, 86; Rabin, "Capital Punishment," 191; Lambert, *Law and Order*, 173; Forbes, "Making Manifest," 261–62; Huscroft, *Making England*, 79, 157. *Ine* 66 (numbered 62 by Liebermann) has been understood as a measure concerning the use of ordeals, although as demonstrated recently by Stefan Jurasinski and Lisi Oliver, this reading is not tenable. See Jurasinski and Oliver, *Laws of Alfred*, 91–98.

[38] Brown, "Society and the Supernatural," 138; Stacey, *The Road to Judgment*, 33; Friedland, *Seeing Justice Done*, 94, 107; Lars Hermanson, "How to Legitimate Rebellion and Condemn Usurpation of the Crown: Discourses of Fidelity and Treason in the *Gesta Danorum* of Saxo Grammaticus," in *Disputing Strategies in Medieval Scandinavia*, ed. Kim Esmark et al. (Leiden: Brill, 2013), 132.

[39] David Rollason, *Saints and Relics in Anglo-Saxon England* (Oxford: Basil Blackwell, 1989), 171.

[40] *Ordal* 1.4.

those required of the proband indicates the degree to which those present are implicated in the ritual.[41] In this sense, the regulations concerning the ordeal's spectators reflect what Peter Goodrich has called the law's "governance of perception, the direction of thought through control of the visual."[42] Insofar as the ordeal invites the divine to intervene in the workings of human justice, the detailed strictures concerning how the ordeal may be, not just undergone, but *seen* to be undergone marks the community as the subject of the ordeal ritual, no less than the proband. All involved are supplicants under the gaze of God and the authority of the officiating clergy.

Within this context, it is striking that the one feature of the ordeal left unspecified in surviving regulations is the criteria by which the results were to be interpreted. For instance, in the ordeal by hot iron, it is unclear whether the hand is to show no injury at all, or simply no sign of infection.[43] Considering the potential gradations of injury that a hand subjected to this sort of test might exhibit, likewise unclear is the point at which the proband was deemed to have "passed" or "failed."[44] A "lack of quantitative precision," in Colman's words, is a common feature of ordeal formularies and a number of texts testify to the confusion such ambiguity might produce.[45] The thirteenth-century *Ljósvetninga saga*, for instance, recounts an ordeal by hot iron in which, following the unwrapping of the proband's hand, the accuser demands of the administering priest, "What kind of bastard are you, that you do not declare her badly burned immediately?" (*Hví ert þú svo mikill verrfeðrungur að segja eigi að hún er brunnin?*)[46] To which the priest replied, "It is presumptuous to seize the

41 Cf. II Æthelstan 23, 23.2, and *Ordal* 1.4.

42 Peter Goodrich, *Oedipus Lex: Psychoanalysis, History, Law* (Berkeley: University of California Press, 1995), x.

43 Kerr, Forsyth, and Plyley note that it is unusual for burns to show visible signs of infection before the fifth day, thus making the time between ordeal and inspection crucial to the question of whether a proband passed or failed. See "Cold Water," 593.

44 See also John Hudson, *Land, Law, and Lordship in Anglo-Norman England* (Oxford: Oxford University Press, 1994), 29.

45 Colman, "Reason," 589. See also Hyams, "Trial by Ordeal," 104–05; Pilarczyk, "Rock and a Hot Place," 96–98; Green, *Crisis of Truth*, 84; Forbes, "Making Manifest," 260, 265–66; Kamali, *Felony*, 303.

46 All quotations from *Ljósvetninga saga* are taken from Björn Sigfússon, *Ljósvetninga saga*, Íslenzk fornrit (Reykjavík: Hið Íslenzka Fornritafélag, 1940). Translations are my own. For an in-depth discussion of this episode, see Theodore M. Andersson and William Ian Miller, *Law and Literature in Medieval Iceland: Ljósvetninga saga and Valla-Ljósts saga* (Stanford: Stanford University Press, 1989), 32–43. See also Miller, "Ordeal in Iceland," 194–98. On the obligations of a cleric overseeing an ordeal, see Loyn, *English Church*, 7, 45.

prerogative to declare judgment for yourself when it is for me to make the decision. We must have a second and clearer proof" (*Nú fer óliðlega er þið dæmið og takið málið fyrir hendur mér fram er eg á atkvæðið að veita og skal vera enn tilraun önnur skírari*). This response is insufficient for the proband's advocate, however, who then accuses the priest of having taken bribes to delay the exoneration of the proband, for "the outcome could not be more obvious!" (*Eigi má skírari vera!*)[47] In this case, the dispute between parties undermined the efficacy of the ordeal: despite what would appear to be empirical evidence, the ritual produced neither an agreed-upon result nor, ultimately, an end to the feud itself.[48] Other factors also could obscure the results of the ritual. Some of these might be intentional: a text attributed (wrongly) to Albertus Magnus records a recipe for a lotion consisting of radish juice, egg whites, lime, and psyllium seeds that would protect the proband's hand against the heat of the iron.[49] Others simply reflected the realities of medieval life: one consequence of living in a society made up primarily of farm laborers, as no less an authority than Peter the Chanter complained, was that "innocence was too closely connected with calluses."[50] Legal precision is thus balanced by interpretive ambiguity.

This ambiguity invariably subjected the ordeal to the very aspect of law it was designed to eliminate: the inadequacy of human judgment. By inviting divine intervention into worldly law, the ordeal was intended to serve as a safeguard against judicial ignorance, bias, or self-interest.[51] As Whitman has shown, anxiety over the moral consequences of passing false judgment – particularly when clergy were involved – led to the development of the ordeal as a way of ensuring that those exercising judgment were unpolluted by the shedding of innocent blood.[52] The severity of

47 Maitland writes that "we cannot but guess that it was well to be good friends with the priest when one went to the ordeal." Frederic William Maitland, "Outlines of English Legal History, 500–1600," in *The Collected Papers of Frederic William Maitland*, ed. H. A. L. Fisher (Cambridge: Cambridge University Press, 1911), 448.

48 Miller, "Ordeal in Iceland," 198.

49 Albertus Magnus, *Liber de mirabilis mundi*, edited in Michael R. Best and Frank H. Brightman, eds., *The Book of Secrets of Albertus Magnus: Of the Virtues of Herbs, Stones, and Certain Beasts; Also a Book of the Marvels of the World* (Oxford: Clarendon, 1973), 109. Similar recipes are discussed in Forbes, "Making Manifest," 273–74.

50 Cited in Baldwin, "Intellectual Preparation," 626. See also Radding, "Superstition to Science," 945–46; Davies and Fouracre, "Procedure and Practice in the Settlement of Disputes," 214; Van Caenegem, *Birth of the English Common Law*, 69; Pilarczyk, "Rock and a Hot Place," 102; Bowman, *Shifting Landmarks*, 121, 137; Whitman, *Origins*, 89.

51 Wormald, *Making of English Law*, 159.

52 Whitman, *Origins*, 27–50; Kamali, *Felony*, 246. Sara Butler notes the link between

these concerns is not only reflected in admonitions such as those by Pope Gregory I that "it is grave and unseemly to pronounce a judgment that professes to be certain when the matter is in doubt" (*Grave satis est et indecens, ut in re dubia certa dicatur sententia*), but also in the close supervision exercised by King Alfred over the rulings issued by his judges, for whom "malice" (*malevolentiam*) or "ignorance" (*ignotiam*) were grounds for royal punishment.[53] Yet the ordeal's failure to resolve the problem of ambiguity was recognized early in its history. As Robert Bartlett has shrewdly pointed out, Charlemagne's command in 809 that the ordeal was to be believed "without any doubting" (*absque dubitatione*) indicates that there were enough skeptics of the ordeal to merit a royal decree.[54] The possibility that misinterpretation might implicate the priest overseeing the ordeal in the shedding of innocent blood likewise motivated the Fourth Lateran Council of 1215 to prohibit clerical participation in the ritual.[55] In short, the recognition of the ordeal's vulnerability to the very ambiguity its practitioners sought to eliminate was not a sudden discovery of the thirteenth or fourteenth centuries; rather, tension between belief and skepticism was

---

concepts of blood pollution – particularly as it relates to the ordeal – and the natural process of cruentation. Sara M. Butler, *Forensic Medicine and Death Investigation in Medieval England* (London: Routledge, 2015), 141. See also Loyn, *English Church*, 45.

53 Asser, *De rebus gestis Alfredi*, cap. 106, edited in William Henry Stevenson, ed., *Asser's Life of King Alfred* (Oxford: Clarendon, 1959), 93. On the problem of doubt, see also Andrew Rabin, "The Mound, the Altar, and the Tomb: Sanctuary, Jurisdiction, and Punishment in Early Medieval Hagiography," *Studies in Philology* 117 (2020): 442–43; Elizabeth Papp Kamali, "Trial by Ordeal by Jury in Medieval England, or Saints and Sinners in Literature and Law," in *Emotion, Violence, Vengeance and Law in the Middle Ages: Essays in Honor of William Ian Miller*, ed. Kate Gilbert and Stephen D. White (Leiden: Brill, 2018), 49–79, esp. 62–63. These concerns were hardly limited to Christian jurists. See Intisar A. Rabb, *Doubt in Islamic Law: A History of Legal Maxims, Interpretation, and Islamic Criminal Law* (Cambridge: Cambridge University Press, 2015).

54 Bartlett, *Trial by Fire*, 12. Carolingian critics of the ordeal include Agobard of Lyons, Atto of Vercelli, and Ivo of Chartres. See Radding, "Superstition to Science," 946–47; Wormald, *Making of English Law*, 48, 71; Brown, *Unjust Seizure*, 208; Bowman, *Shifting Landmarks*, 121; Harvey, *Domesday*, 282–83.

55 Baldwin, "Intellectual Preparation," 613–36; Brown, "Society and the Supernatural," 136; Langbein, *Torture and the Law of Proof: Europe and England in the Ancien Régime*, 56; Bartlett, *Trial by Fire*, 89–98; Green, *Crisis of Truth*, 108; R. H. Helmholz, *The Ius Commune in England: Four Studies* (New York: Oxford University Press, 2001), 92–93; McAuley, "Canon Law and the End of the Ordeal," 473–513; Whitman, *Origins*, 48–49, 53–59; Harvey, *Domesday*. On the impact of the Fourth Lateran Council on English ordeal usage, see Bartlett, *Trial by Fire*, 133; S. F. C. Milsom, *A Natural History of the Common Law* (New York: Columbia University Press, 2003), 6; Masschaele, *Jury, State, and Society*, 74–75; Müller, *Abortion*, 67; Harvey, *Domesday*, 282–84; Kamali, *Felony*, 22.

a constant presence in the ordeal's history.[56] Indeed, it was this tension that made the ordeal a useful tool in the enforcement of communal norms. If belief in the ritual's efficacy encouraged its performance, skepticism regarding the accuracy of its verdict undermined its authority, thus introducing the ambiguity that invited – and even required – onlookers and participants to interpret the ordeal according to the norms of the community.[57] In the words of Richard Firth Green, the ordeal represented "the judgment of God manipulated to make it consonant with the communal will."[58] This aspect of the ordeal, particularly in light of its public nature, suggests that it was less a means of determining fact – especially when the guilt or innocence of the proband was already known – than it was a way of reinforcing the normativity of legal customs and (when appropriate) purging their violation.[59]

The imperative that the ordeal's verdict be certain (or, at least, perceived as such) necessarily excluded from those legal texts governing the ritual any acknowledgment of bias, ambiguity, or subjective judgment.[60] This necessity explains in part the excessively detailed instructions concerning the administration of the ordeal. It also explains the predominance in non-legal narrative texts (including Lantfred's *Miracula s. Swithuni*) of "tricked" ordeals, that is, those in which the result has been surreptitiously manipulated by divine or human actors.[61] In his classic study of equivocal ordeals, Ralph Hexter attributes the popularity of such texts to "human nature": "most people enjoy hearing about any sort of trickery, especially if it is at the expense of a sacred institution."[62] Although the attractiveness of a well-executed narrative twist cannot be denied, the tricked ordeal serves as a form of legal commentary as well. In other words, while traditional legal texts portray the ordeal as the unerring intervention of the divine in worldly justice, accounts found in other genres provide a crucial counternarrative, one which accentuates the ordeal's vulnerability

56 Colman, "Reason," 582; Bartlett, *Trial by Fire*, 99; Huw Pryce, *Native Law and the Welsh Church* (Oxford: Oxford University Press, 1993), 37–38; Green, *Crisis of Truth*, 110; Leeson, "Ordeals," 703–04.

57 On this point, see also Colman, "Reason," 589; Brown, "Society and the Supernatural," 139–40; Bartlett, *Trial by Fire*, 80, 97; Miller, "Ordeal in Iceland," 199; Fleming, *Domesday Book and the Law*, 54; Bowman, *Shifting Landmarks*, 127, 37; Friedland, *Seeing Justice Done*, 11.

58 Green, *Crisis of Truth*, 109.

59 Colman, "Reason," 589; Friedland, *Seeing Justice Done*, 99. For a contrary reading, see Bartlett, *Trial by Fire*, 65.

60 On this, see also Ralph J. Hexter, *Equivocal Oaths and Ordeals in Medieval Literature* (Cambridge, MA: Harvard University Press, 1975), 6–7; Green, *Crisis of Truth*, 110; Keefer, "Anglo-Saxon Lay Ordeal," 367.

61 See also Bowman, *Shifting Landmarks*, 137.

62 Hexter, *Equivocal Oaths*, 9.

to manipulation. Later in the Middle Ages, tricked ordeals – especially in the Arthurian cycle – served as a means of highlighting the conflict between illicit love and public morality.[63] Earlier, however, ordeal narratives, particularly those found in hagiographical texts, were intended to contrast the limits of worldly law with the infallible justice of heaven.[64] Narratives of failed or manipulated ordeals emphasized the power and mercy of the divine, while also, in Bartlett's words, "cast[ing] doubt on the trustworthiness of ordeal verdicts."[65] That is, narratives of tricked ordeals provide a means of exploring the ritual's limitations in a manner that more traditional legal texts cannot. Tales of this sort thus mark the boundary between conventional (in some cases, externally imposed) codified law and a more intangible concept of authority. In acceding to the righteousness of that authority, the reader also accepts the cultural norm – the web of belief, custom, ethics, and identity – that it represents.

In short, then, whether we accept Hyams's claim that the ordeal was a ritual designed to "reestablish a workable peace in small communities" or Whitman's assertion that the ordeal was a "comfort procedure" designed to displace judges' feelings of guilt when passing harsh sentences, one crucial point stands out: the balance between specificity and ambiguity in the ordeal's performance enabled the ritual to reassert the legal norms *of* the community *to* the community by investing the court with the interpretive flexibility to judge according to those norms, and the ritual precision to ensure that those judgments possessed the authority of divine sanction. In other words, ritual *objectivity* makes possible interpretive *subjectivity*. As a ritual only adopted in extreme cases, the ordeal thus became a performance of legal identity intended to reaffirm shared beliefs, traditions, and traditional structures of juridical authority.

63 As, for instance, in narratives concerning Tristan and Isolde as well as Lancelot and Guinevere. Hexter, *Equivocal Oaths*, 16–45; Brown, "Society and the Supernatural," 139; Green, *Crisis of Truth*, 106–07.

64 Harding, *Law Courts*, 46–48; Frank Barlow, *The English Church 1066–1154* (New York: Longman, 1979), 151; Rollason, *Saints and Relics*, 164, 171–72; Brown, *Unjust Seizure*, 4; Brundage, *Medieval Origins of the Legal Profession*, 68; Harvey, *Domesday*, 280–81; Bruce C. Brasington, *Order in the Court: Medieval Procedural Treatises in Translation* (Leiden: Brill, 2016), 45–47. For a broader discussion of this point, see Andrew Rabin, "Holy Bodies, Legal Matters: Reaction and Reform in Ælfric's *Eugenia* and the Ely Privilege," *Studies in Philology* 110 (2013): 220–65; Rabin, "Jurisdiction and Punishment," 439–68.

65 Bartlett, *Trial by Fire*, 80.

II

Bearing these points in mind, we turn now to the episode recounted by Lantfred in the *Miracula s. Swithuni*.[66] The narrative comprises the twenty-fifth chapter of the *Miracula*, titled "About the man who, in his bare hand, carried red hot metal" (*De homine qui nuda manu ignitum calibem portavit*).[67] According to the text, a merchant named Flodoald sent his servant from Winchester to Calne, where he was arrested by Eadric, the local reeve, "for some offense" (*pro quodam facinore*). The reeve, for reasons unspecified, ordered the servant to undergo the ordeal of hot iron. As a result, Flodoald journeyed to Calne and engaged in an extensive, through fruitless, series of negotiations with Eadric in an attempt to save the servant.[68] Finally, the reeve, "taking too much pride in his worldly authority" (*ultramodum superbiens pro mundanis fascibus*) ordered the ordeal to proceed, increasing the weight and heat of the iron to an unusual degree as he did so. Disappointed, Flodoald and his companions prayed to Saint Swithun for help. And, when the servant's hand is unwrapped, they found the saint had granted their prayers: although they perceived a suppurating wound – the sign of the servant's guilt – the reeve saw only a clean hand. Rejoicing, they returned to Winchester, where the servant was given by Flodoald into the service of the saint.

As an account – albeit fictional – of a legal procedure, Lantfred's narrative is puzzling in several ways, not least because it omits any justification for the ordeal itself.[69] The text does not entertain any doubt regarding the servant's guilt, nor – if we accept Whitman's view of the ordeal as a "comfort procedure" for squeamish judges – does the reeve "taking too much pride in his worldly authority" appear to require spiritual consolation to support his prosecution. One possible justification for the use of the ordeal, however, is suggested by the identities of the narrative's protagonists. As several commentators have noted, Flodoald's name indicates that he may have been of Norman or Picard origin, possibly a member of the community of foreign merchants that had developed in Winchester over the course of the tenth century.[70] A number of scholars, most notably

66 Quotations from Lantfred's *Miracula* are taken from Lapidge, *Cult of St Swithun*, 252–334. All translations are my own. The episode in question can be found in cap. 25 (pp. 308–11).

67 See also O'Keeffe, "Body and Law," 222–24.

68 David Pelteret notes that Flodoald's efforts at negotiation suggest a "genuine affection" for his slave. Pelteret, *Slavery in Early Mediaeval England*, 59.

69 Forbes, *Heaven and Earth*, 169–70; Forbes, "Making Manifest," 260; Huscroft, *Making England*, 254.

70 Lapidge, *Cult of St Swithun*, 308n227; Patrick Wormald, *Papers Preparatory to the Making of English Law: King Alfred to the Twelfth Century, Vol. II: From God's Law*

David Pelteret, have also commented on the fact that it was a slave who was targeted by Eadric for the ordeal.[71] Equally significant, though – and a point which has not figured into the scholarship on this text – is the fact that the arrest and subsequent ordeal took place in the jurisdiction of Calne, not Winchester. Calne is located some fifty miles from Winchester at the far northwestern end of Wessex, roughly two days' journey. Removing the narrative from Winchester to Calne highlights the foreignness of both the slave and Flodoald, his master. Their status as foreigners – both of the kingdom and the jurisdiction – leaves them more exposed to the ordeal than they would have been as natives or locals. As decreed in II Cnut 35, "If a person who is friendless or come from afar is so bereft of friends as to lack a surety, on the first accusation he is to be suspended in chains and there abide until he undergoes God's ordeal, and there suffer what he may..." (*gyf freondleas man oððe feorrancuman swa geswenced weorðe þurh freondleaste, þæt he borh næbbe, æt frymtyhtlan þonne gebuge he hengenne and þær gebide oð ðæt he ga to Godes ordale, and gefare ðær þæt he mæge*).[72] In such a situation, the ordeal serves as a means of subordinating the alien proband to the legal norms and rituals of the community. In effect, God serves as the surety that the proband cannot himself provide.[73] Bearing witness to the judgment of God thereby enables those members of the community present at the ordeal to *know* the character of the proband in a way that his foreignness would otherwise prevent and situate him within a recognizable and commonly accepted legal framework. Viewed from this perspective, Lantfred's decision to highlight the foreignness of Flodoald and his servant frames his narrative as an *exemplum* exploring the application of legal norms and practices to those alien to a community's jurisdiction.

Yet adherence to these norms is not merely a matter for the outsider: they also govern the actions of those tasked with enforcing them. The subsequent clause in II Cnut 35.1 reads, "Truly, whoever hands down a more severe sentence on the friendless or those come from afar than upon his own companions does injury to himself" (*Witodlice, se ðe freondleasan and feorrancumenan wyrsan dom demeð þonne his geferan, he dereð him sylfum*). Like so many of the legal texts attributable to Archbishop Wulfstan of York, this clause is better read as a statement of ethical principle than prescriptive legislation: the clause begins with the quasi-homiletic "Witodlice" (*Truly*); prohibits "more severe" judgments (*wyrsan dom*) without clarifying the

to Common Law, ed. Stephen Baxter and John Hudson (University of London: Early English Laws, 2014), 73.

71 Pelteret, *Slavery in Early Mediaeval England*, 59; Karn, *Kings*, 39.

72 On this clause, see Bartlett, *Trial by Fire*, 31.

73 Keefer, "Anglo-Saxon Lay Ordeal," 353; Whitman, *Origins*, 63; Jurasinski and Oliver, *Laws of Alfred*, 102–11.

criteria according to which a judgment might be considered overly severe, and concludes with the oddly inoperable penalty that a judge guilty of such harsh verdicts "does injury to himself," without clarifying the nature of the injury or the mechanism by which the injury was to be delivered. In short, this is a clause that traffics in legal norms rather than the specific enforceable regulation of judicial behavior that would make it functional as law. However, amorphous as it is, this clause describes precisely the violation of legal norms of which the reeve is guilty. Notably, the text does not criticize Eadric's decision to apprehend the servant or to make him undergo the ordeal. Lapidge wonders if Eadric's fault lay in the fact that "he prescribed the ordeal for a crime which did not necessarily demand the death penalty if the accused were found guilty,"[74] yet nothing in the text suggests as much, and the term *facinus*, which Lapidge translates with the relatively innocuous "misdeed," can encompass a wide variety of offenses, from petty theft to homicide. Instead, the text's accusation that Eadric is excessively proud in the execution of his office is linked, not to his prescription of an ordeal, but to his refusal to negotiate with Flodoald over compensation for the servant's crime and his insistence on the use of *eximiae molis feruentem* ("a mass of iron of unusual/remarkable size").[75] Eadric's fault is not so much substantive as comparative. In other words, the text condemns not his authority itself, but his excessive use of it as being *ultramodum* ("too much").[76] The text here dramatizes the discussion of ordeals in II Cnut 35–35.1: as foreigners, Flodoald and his servant fall under that category of those for whom the ordeal may be appropriate in order to find a means of judging non-normative subjects according to communal norms and practices; in exceeding his authority, however, Eadric violates the very norms that the ordeal ritual is designed to ratify.

It is the need to reinstate these norms that shapes the miracle with which the narrative culminates. In response to the prayers of Flodoald and his companions, Swithun clouded the judge's perception, so that "the man's defenders witnessed the blisters and swelling, while the accusers perceived his hand to be as well healed as if it had never touched the hot iron" (*fautores arsuram et inflationem conspiciebant, criminatores ita sanam etenim uidebant palmam quasi penitus forum non tetigisset ferrum*). Appropriately, Lantfred characterizes this difference in perception as "too much" (*ultramodum*) to be believed, drawing an implicit contrast between

[74] Lapidge, *Cult of St Swithun*, 309n233.

[75] On the importance of pretrial negotiation and the opprobrium attached to those who failed to engage in it, see Hudson, *Formation of the English Common Law*, 6–13.

[76] Hyams, "Trial by Ordeal," 93–94; Hudson, *Land, Law, and Lordship*, 29; Forbes, *Heaven and Earth*, 169–70; Huscroft, *Making England*, 254. See also Cubitt, "As the Lawbook Teaches," 1040.

the excessive pride of the reeve and the miraculous power of the saint.[77] Yet it is important to note that the saint does not exercise his power to exonerate the servant: Swithun does not heal the servant, nor even protect him from the pain of "the terrible burn that covered the whole palm of his scorched hand with its inflammation" (*manu calibem eximie molis feruentem multoque carbone rubentem*).[78] Rather, the different perception afforded the partisans of secular law on the one hand and divine authority on the other reflects the superior spiritual discernment – the capacity to be, in Augustine's words, an "oracle of the law" (*oraculum legis*)[79] – claimed by the Church as the foundation of episcopal participation in judicial matters.[80] More pertinent, though, is the fact that the different perceptions of the proband's hand echo the potential for multiple interpretations intrinsic to the ordeal ritual itself. Indeed, the seemingly miraculous ending to Lantfred's narrative bears a striking resemblance to the conclusion of the ordeal recounted in *Ljósvetninga saga*.[81] In both instances, the witnesses' different perceptions of the proband's wounds reflect their differing views of the judicial authority administering the ordeal and the legal norms according to which it was conducted. In Lantfred's case, however, these differing perceptions are not merely a matter of interpretation but a means of reaffirming the legal principles upon which a Christian community is founded. The proband's wounds testify to the effectiveness of the ordeal and the capacity of the divine judge to render a just verdict; in contrast, the reeve's failure of perception indicates the degree to which his severity exceeded the norms of appropriate judgment, thus making it impossible for him to perceive the evidence of guilt directly in front of him. His blindness to his pride is matched by his blindness to the norms he transgressed; he has, metaphorically, done himself the injury hinted at in Wulfstan of York's moral penalty. Implicitly, a functioning legal system demands, not simply justice, but judgment rendered according to juridical norms and Christian principles.

77 For a comparable dispute between secular and divine authority, see Rabin, "Jurisdiction and Punishment," 439–68.

78 Given the painful punishment suffered by the servant, Nicholas Karn suggests that the miracle should be understood as the result of Flodoard's piety rather than the unjust treatment of the accused: *Kings*, 40. See also Forbes, "Making Manifest," 271. For analogous uses of judicial ambiguity, see Kamali, "Trial by Jury," 54, 63; Rabin, "Mound," 462.

79 Alois Goldbacher, ed., *Augustinus: Epistulae (ep. 185–270)* (Vienna: Austrian Academy of Sciences, 1911), 616 (ep. 260).

80 Barlow notes the similarity of this result with the ordeal of one William Pantolf in 1080: *English Church*, 161.

81 Elizabeth Papp Kamali has examined a narrative concerning Saint William of York that likewise shares many of these same themes. See Kamali "Trial by Ordeal," 52–53.

Viewed from this perspective, three conclusions may be drawn concerning the role played by both ordeals and ordeal narratives in the legal consciousness of an early medieval community. First, the ordeal, as a juridical procedure, was fundamentally an exercise in legal epistemology. Its reliance upon divine intervention in worldly justice served as a mechanism to render the foreign, the marginalized, or the unknown knowable, thereby subordinating the unusual or unknown to the norms of the community.[82] Second, whether we understand the ordeal as an evidentiary procedure or a confirmative procedure, its primary function was to reaffirm communal legal norms in unusual circumstances through the interplay of ritual precision and interpretive flexibility. Third, Lantfred's *Miracula s. Swithuni* was, among other things, a strong confirmation of the legitimacy of the ordeal itself, and, more importantly, of the legal norms it miraculously endorsed. It achieved this by dramatizing the (near-fatal) consequences of discarding those norms in favor of individual prejudice or personal desire. In this sense, it was not merely the proband who was on trial, but also those witnesses who, in affirming the results of the ordeal, affirmed also the laws, rules, and norms by which the community was governed. They may not have been the ones holding the hot iron, but it was their justice, their interpretation of the ordeal, and the rightfulness of their verdict that would determine, not just the fate of the accused, but the legal identity of the community itself.

[82] See also Bartlett, *Trial by Fire*, 31, 37.

PART II

LITERATURE AND LAW: NORMATIVE RENEWALS

6

The Historical and Literary Context of the *Legatine Capitulary* of 786 in England and Abroad

Kristen Carella

The *Legatine Capitulary* of 786 has often been dismissed as the product of a fleeting papal mission reflecting primarily, if not exclusively, the legislative sensibilities of foreigners who lacked a clear understanding of Anglo-Saxon law and cultural practices. Scholars have tended to disregard it as an irrelevant one-off that, while perhaps containing a few details of historical interest, possessed no bearing on local affairs, let alone matters farther afield. As a result, there has been a general lack of interest regarding its importance for early medieval Northumbrian, Anglo-Saxon, and European legal history. This oversight is entirely unwarranted, as I have argued at length elsewhere.[1] Taking my lead from Catherine Cubitt's work in *Anglo-Saxon Church Councils, c.650–c.850*,[2] I have shown in several articles that the text was composed, or at least formatively influenced by Alcuin, a native Northumbrian; and, moreover, that it draws upon language and procedures deeply rooted in English customary law.[3] The *Legatine Capitulary* stands out, therefore, not merely as a rare example of a legal document composed by a Northumbrian legislating for his own people in his native country, but as a Northumbrian law code in its own right.[4] As such, it provides an uncommon glimpse into Anglo-Saxon legal

[1] See Bryan Carella [who now publishes as Kristen Carella], "The Earliest Expression for Outlawry in Anglo-Saxon Law," *Traditio* 70 (2015): 111–43; Carella, "Alcuin and the Legatine Capitulary of 786: The Evidence of Scriptural Citations," *Journal of Medieval Latin* 22 (2012): 221–56.

[2] Catherine Cubitt, *Anglo-Saxon Church Councils, c.650–c.850* (London: Leicester University Press, 1995).

[3] Carella, "The Earliest Expression for Outlawry," and Carella, "Alcuin and the Legatine Capitulary of 786."

[4] Consider also the *Dialogue of Ecgberht* (also known *Succinctus dialogus ecclesiasticae institutionis*), a short treatise consisting of sixteen sections that address legal matters pertinent mostly to the clergy and, at times, elements of society with whom they interacted. It is the only one of several works (all of which save the *Dialogus* are considered to be spurious) attributed to Ecgberht, archbishop

practices, both ecclesiastical and secular, during the gap of more than a century between the Laws of Ine and the Laws of Alfred to which no surviving vernacular law code bears witness. These facts demand a re-evaluation of the document's significance for Northumbrian and Anglo-Saxon legal history.

Even less appreciated is the significance of the *Legatine Capitulary* for continental European legal history. While I have considered its bearing on English affairs in several prior articles,[5] this chapter will focus on its importance in Francia. The document emerged during a period when the Carolingian reimagining of the capitulary tradition was barely in its nascence. Indeed, the *Legatine Capitulary* would appear to have played a formative role in that transformation. Charlemagne's increased reliance on capitularies as the main expression of his reform agenda is usually traced to the *Admonitio generalis* of 789, a document also composed, in part, by Alcuin just three years after he drafted the *Legatine Capitulary*. Given this timing, it is tempting to view the *Legatine Capitulary* as a kind of dry run in which Alcuin first began to reimagine the capitulary as a genre specifically designed to articulate the sweeping cultural reforms of the Carolingian *Renovatio*.

Noteworthy in both texts is Alcuin's hortatory approach to legislation, drawing on rhetoric more typical of sermons and homilies than the more common language of either ecclesiastical or secular legal documents of his era, including earlier capitularies. This novel approach was typified in the main by pious exhortation to moral behavior, not by threats of temporal sanctions. When Alcuin mentions punishments at all, they are typically divine in nature, such as anathema or damnation; not punitive action applied by secular authorities. Instead, he tends to justify legal precepts on the basis of Scripture alone, not with citations from ecclesiastical authorities conciliar, patristic, papal, or otherwise that might entail worldly sanction (as opposed to purely spiritual consequences), as was typical of his contemporaries. We first see this distinctive approach to lawgiving in the *Legatine Capitulary*. A few years later, it appeared fully formed in the early Carolingian capitulary tradition, specifically in the *Admonitio generalis*. Tracing these themes, this chapter will examine the literary and historical context of the *Legatine Capitulary* in the late eighth century, focusing on Francia. In particular, I shall describe how Alcuin reimagined the capitulary as a genre suited to express the spirit

of York (d. 766). See Kristen Carella, "Northumbrian Law before the Vikings: A Preliminary Assessment of the Evidence," in *Languages of the Law in Early Medieval England: Essays in Memory of Lisi Oliver*, ed. Andrew Rabin and Stefan Jurasinski (Leuven: Peeters, 2019), 45–58.

5 See notes 1 and 4 for my work examining the significance of the *Legatine Capitulary* for Anglo-Saxon legal history.

of Charlemagne's political and cultural reform agenda by drawing on language and methods more commonly found in sermons and homilies than in legal documents to address real-world matters of policy.

The Legatine Capitulary of 786 in Anglo-Saxon England

I shall begin by providing some background on the *Legatine Capitulary*. As the epistolary preface of the document relates, Pope Hadrian dispatched a mission of legates

> ... trans mare in gentem Anglorum peragrare debuissemus, ut si qua zizania messem optimo semine satam, quam beatus Gregorius papa per os sancti Agustini seminavit, inritasset, funditus eradicare quod noxium et fructum saluberrimum stabilire summon conamine studuissemus.[6]

> ... to travel across the sea to the land of the English, "so that, if anywhere tares had spoiled the harvest, sown with the best seed" [Matthew 13:25–30], which the blessed Gregory sowed through the mouth of Saint Augustine, we might strive with the greatest effort to root up from below anything which might be harmful, and secure a most salvific fruit.[7]

The contingent was led by George, bishop of Ostia, a trusted and experienced diplomat who had served on various missions at the behest of papal and continental authorities since the 750s. He was joined by Theophylact of Todi, once head of the papal library who served as papal legate on multiple occasions, and a Frankish bishop by the name of Wigbod, best known for his biblical commentary entitled *Quaestiones in Octateuchum*.[8] The legation first arrived in Kent, where they were received by Archbishop Iænbert of Canterbury. Iænbert arranged a meeting with Cynewulf, king

6 MGH Epp. IV, Alcuini, ep. 3, p. 20, lines 12–15.

7 All translations, unless otherwise specified, are my own.

8 PL 93.233–430 (ed. Herwagen, 1563), PL 96.1101–1168 (ed. Martène, 1723). See also Michael Gorman, "Commentaries from Isidore to Wigbod: A Guide to Manuscripts, Editions and Bibliography" <http://ccat.sas.upenn.edu/jod/genesis>, accessed 30 June 2021; and see Michael Gorman, "Wigbod, Charlemagne's Commentator: the Quaestiunculae super Euangelium," *Revue Bénédictine* 114 (2004): 5–74; Michael Gorman, "Wigbod and the Lectiones on the Hexateuch attributed to Bede in Paris, Lat. 2342," *Revue Bénédictine* 105 (1995): 310–47; Michael Gorman, "The Encyclopedic Commentary on Genesis Prepared for Charlemagne by Wigbod," *Recherches Augustiniennes et Patristiques* 17 (1982): 173–201. It is likely that Wigbod also prepared, at Charlemagne's request, a still unpublished commentary on the Gospels. See Michael Gorman, "Wigbod and Biblical Studies under Charlemagne," *Revue Bénédictine* 107 (1997): 40–41.

of Wessex and Offa, king of Mercia as well as the leading men of both realms. At this gathering, a letter sent from the pope was read aloud that admonished the English and sought to bring them into compliance with orthodox practices. That letter and its contents are lost to history.

After this gathering, the mission split its effort. Theophylact headed west into Mercia and the British-speaking parts of the island, while George and Wigbod went north across the Humber to meet with King Ælfwald of Northumbria and Archbishop Eanbald. Ælfwald was delayed for a period, however, during which time Alcuin and another cleric named Pyttel joined the legation as *lectores* (though it is unclear what responsibilities their role entailed). During this time as well, the legation learned about sinful behaviors in the local culture above and beyond those addressed in Pope Hadrian's letter. So, they wrote a capitulary to address these abuses:

> audientibus nobis relatum est, quod reliqua uicia non minima ibi necessaria erant ad corrigendum, quia, ut scitis, a tempore sancti Agustini pontificis sacerdos Romanus nullus illuc missus est nisi nos. Scripsimus namque capitulare de singulis rebus et per ordinem cuncta disserentes auribus illorum protulimus.[9]

> It was related to us in our hearing that other not trivial vices were in need of correction there, since, as you know, from the time of the holy bishop Saint Augustine, no Roman priest has been sent there except ourselves. We wrote a capitulary concerning the individual matters and, treating everything in order, made them known in their hearing.

This document is the so-called *Legatine Capitulary* of 786, a collection of twenty chapters written onsite, in Northumbria to correct abuses the legation learned about while they were there. Next, the legation headed south again to meet Offa, king of Mercia. A second council was held, wherein, we are told, the same *capitula* were read aloud both in Latin and the vernacular. All present signed the document and promised to obey. Afterwards, the mission came to an end.

The Legatine Capitulary of 786 in Carolingian Francia

Let me now turn to the role of the *Legatine Capitulary* in Carolingian history. While Alcuin's presence in the legation is significant, especially given the evidence that he authored the *Legatine Capitulary*, it may have been important for other reasons as well. Was Alcuin representing Charlemagne's interests on some level? This question warrants further examination. The

[9] MGH Epp. IV, Alcuini ep. 3, p. 21, lines 1–5.

text is silent about whether Alcuin was an official part of the mission. Likewise, it is unclear whether this occasion was Alcuin's first return to Northumbria since leaving for Charlemagne's court, or if he had not yet departed. Either way, his connections with the Carolingian intellectual milieu and with Charlemagne himself were well established by 786. The legation proper, in any case, would appear to have been handpicked to promote, or at least protect, Carolingian interests. Its leader, Bishop George of Ostia, was deeply ensconced in the diplomatic and political affairs of Charlemagne's court dating from at least the early 750s, to the extent that Levison described his activities as "belonging to the Frankish kingdom as well as to Italy."[10] Abbot Wigbod, likewise, was chosen for his connections with Aachen. Not only was he included as a primary member of the legation to serve as Charlemagne's representative,[11] but also, as Michael Gorman has argued, Wigbod's "diplomatic and exegetical work may have placed [him] in Charlemagne's inner circle."[12] Given Wigbod's exegetical skills, his presence may have been significant for the composition of the *Legatine Capitulary*.

Though unprovable, it seems highly possible that the inclusion of two prominent scholars from Charlemagne's inner circle in the legation was not mere happenstance. It may be that they were dispatched not merely to protect Frankish interests, but perhaps also to promote a specific agenda. If so, we might doubt the claim made in the capitulary itself (quoted above) that the motivation to write it arose purely in response to what the legates witnessed on the ground once they arrived in Northumbria. It is more likely in my view that Alcuin seized upon this opportunity to address long-standing concerns he had about cultural practices in his homeland. I suspect as well that he had already been working on a draft of what became the *Legatine Capitulary* well before the legation arrived.

We might also ask if Charlemagne's interests extended beyond the mere correction of abuses in England. The presence of two well-respected and well-connected scholars representing his concerns during the production and dissemination of the *Legatine Capitulary* throughout the main centers of Anglo-Saxon England certainly raises that possibility. Did Charlemagne have plans that in some way included spreading his reform agenda to England via ecclesiastical channels? While any such claim is unknowable without further evidence, circumstances suggest it is possible. In any case, the onset of the Viking invasions, beginning with the sacking of Lindisfarne barely six years later, would have put an end to any such putative agenda. Whatever the extent of Charlemagne's interests

10 Wilhelm Levison, *England and the Continent in the Eighth Century* (Oxford: Clarendon, 1946), 128.

11 Ibid., 16. See also Gorman, "Wigbod and Biblical Studies," 52, 54–55.

12 Gorman, "The Encyclopedic Commentary on Genesis," 175.

in Anglo-Saxon England, the influence of the *Legatine Capitulary* soon extended to the European continent. There, it laid the groundwork for the transformation of the Carolingian capitulary tradition into a primary mechanism for projecting the reform agenda of the Carolingian *Renovatio*. This transformation was inaugurated with the release of the celebrated *Admonitio generalis* of 789, a document also authored (in part) by Alcuin, and which covered much of the same ground.[13]

For what follows, it is important to understand the cultural and political *mise-en-scène* out of which the *Legatine Capitulary* emerged: the Golden Age of Northumbria had barely crested. York was still a center of learning on a continental scale, and thus a focal point of intellectual affairs across Western Europe. The foundations of what became the Carolingian *Renovatio* were being laid. At this point, a legation of diplomats and intellectuals arrived in England ostensibly at the behest of the pope, though its membership clearly represented Carolingian interests as well, if not primarily. The list of corrections they were sent to deliver to Anglo-Saxon magnates is lost to history. What survives instead is an elegantly written legal document – a first of its kind – demonstrably composed by Alcuin, a Northumbrian and an Anglo-Saxon to be sure, but one with close and emergent connections to Charlemagne's inner circle. What is more, the document known as the *Legatine Capitulary* was composed in the presence of two other prominent individuals with loyalty to Francia: George, a diplomat long in the service of Carolingian kings, and Wigbod, an abbot and scholar who, like Alcuin, was also closely connected with Charlemagne's inner circle. When we see anything like the *Legatine Capitulary* again, it is the *Admonitio generalis*, also composed by Alcuin (in part) three years later, this time for a Carolingian audience. Given these carefully orchestrated circumstances, I speculate that the *Legatine Capitulary* was not composed merely as an *ad hoc* response to address abuses the legates witnessed once they arrived in Northumbria, but also as a calculated gesture to assert Carolingian interests in a prominent political and cultural center of Anglo-Saxon England and Western Europe. Even more importantly, the *Legatine Capitulary* laid the groundwork for the transformation of the capitulary as the primary mode for Charlemagne to project his reform agenda in what became the Carolingian *Renovatio*. In what follows, I will focus on the literary context of the *Legatine Capitulary*.

13 Carella, "Alcuin and the Legatine Capitulary of 786," 232–33.

The Literary Context of the Legatine Capitulary of 786

A number of factors warrant comparing the *Legatine Capitulary* to the *Admonitio generalis* of 789, the second portion of which (§§ 59–80) has been firmly attributed to Alcuin.[14] Not only was it composed roughly three years after the *Legatine Capitulary*, but also – rather unusually for capitularies of this period – it addressed both laymen and clergy simultaneously. There is no question that the two documents are similar:

> While the *Admonitio* proposes a more ambitious agenda, the basic principles underlying both documents have much in common. Their similarities, however, are not limited merely to shared ideology. The two documents also exhibit points of contact in style and, occasionally, in content. For example, both documents legislate against certain offences rarely treated in canon law during this period (notably usury and the unjust use of weights and measures); and each, in places, shares nearly identical phrasing.[15]

Most significantly for the present study, it took a hortatory, sermonizing approach aimed at far-reaching social reform. As Cubitt states:

> The homiletic character of the second part [of the *Admonitio*], more concerned with general moral principles than with the punishment of specific offences, and replete with biblical quotations, is unprecedented in

[14] For a discussion of the scholarship relating to Alcuin's authorship of the *Admonitio generalis*, see Cubitt, *Anglo-Saxon Church Councils*, 161–65. In particular, see F.-C. Scheibe, "Alcuin und die *Admonitio Generalis*," *Deutsches Archiv für Erforschung des Mittelalters* 14 (1958): 221–29; F.-C. Scheibe, "Alcuin und die Briefe Karls des Grosen," *Deutsches Archiv für Erforschung des Mittelalters* 15 (1959), 181–93; Rosamond McKitterick, *The Frankish Church and the Carolingian Reforms 789–895* (London: Royal Historical Society, 1977) 1–2 and note 2; Luitpold Wallach, *Alcuin and Charlemagne: Studies in Carolingian History and Literature* (Ithaca: Cornell University Press, 1959), 147–68; D. A. Bullough, "Alcuin and the Kingdom of Heaven: Liturgy, Theology, and the Carolingian Age," in *Carolingian Renewal*, ed. D. A. Bullough (Manchester: Manchester University Press, 1991), 22 and note 44; Hubert Mordek, "Karolingische Kapitularien," in *Überlieferung und Geltung normativer Texte des frühen und hohen Mittelalters*, ed. Hubert Mordek (Sigmaringen: Thorbecke, 1986), 41 and note 88; D. A. Bullough, *Alcuin: Achievement and Reputation* (Leiden: Brill, 2004), 379–84; Hubert Mordek, Klaus Zechiel-Eckes, and Michael Glattaar, eds. and trans., *Die Admonitio generalis Karls des Großen* (Hannover: Hahnsche Buchhandlung, 2012), 1–17 and 47–63; Thomas Martin Buck, *Admonitio und Praedicatio: Zur religiös-pastoralen Dimension von Kapitularien und kapitulariennahen Texten (507–814)* (Frankfurt am Main: Lang, 1997), 80n59; 85–86; 100–01; and 112n280.

[15] Carella, "Alcuin and the Legatine Capitulary of 786," 232. See also Cubitt, *Anglo-Saxon Church Councils*, 163.

> Frankish legislation and is strongly reminiscent of the legatine decrees. Both the canons of the *Admonitio* and the legatine decrees frequently begin *capitula* with the enunciation of a moral precept, sometimes in the form of a scriptural quotation, and proceed to elaborate upon this with a great weight of biblical citations.[16]

Not only were the *Legatine Capitulary* and the *Admonitio generalis* composed just three years apart, but they also agree on points ranging from minor statutory details to overall jurisprudential ideology. Importantly for my present argument, both documents display a similar stylistic approach to lawgiving that was deeply influenced by preaching. Since this approach is more fully developed in the *Admonitio generalis*, I will begin by discussing this later text and then proceed to compare it with the *Legatine Capitulary*, showing that Alcuin was already experimenting with this novel approach in the earlier document, his first known legislative effort.

Let us take a closer look at the homiletic features of the *Admonitio generalis*. Addressing bishops first, Alcuin commences by addressing this audience as parishioners, adopting a marked homiletic tone and deploying language typical of the genre, urging the faithful proactively to embrace righteous behavior:

> **Haec enim, dilectissimi, pio studio et magna dilectionis intentione** vestram unianimitatem ammonere studuimus, quae magis necessaria videbantur, ut sanctorum patrum canonicis institutis inherentes praemia cum illis aeternae felicitates accipere mereamini. Scit namque prudentia vestra, quam terribili anathematis censura feriuntur, qui praesumptiose contra statua universalium conciliorum venire audeunt. Quapropter et vos diligentius ammonemus, ut omni intentione illud horribile execrationis iudicium vobis cavere studeatis, sed magis canonica instituta sequentes et pacifica unitate nitentes ad aeterna pacis gaudia pervenire dignemini.[17]

> **Now, we have been at pains, most beloved, with pious zeal and greatly loving devotion** to recall to your concord those matters which seemed particularly necessary, to the end that, cleaving to the canonical provisions of the holy fathers, you may be counted worthy to receive, with them, the rewards of eternal felicity. For your prudence knows how terrible is the sentence of anathema which strikes those who dare presumptuously to contravene the decrees of the universal councils. Wherefore we also admonish you that more diligently in order that you may strive with all devotion to guard yourselves against that dreadful judgement of execration and, conforming to the provisions of the canons

16 Cubitt, *Anglo-Saxon Church Councils*, 161.
17 Mordek et al., *Die Admonitio generalis*, 208.

> flourishing in peaceloving unity, may rather be thought worthy to attain the eternal joys of peace.[18]

This language marks an abrupt change from the language of prior sections of the *Admonitio generalis*. The former section typically consists of tersely worded provisions that appeal primarily to Church councils and papal decrees as authorities. As an example, consider the four sections immediately prior to the one just quoted (i.e., from the portion not attributed to Alcuin):

> 56. Episcopis. In decretis Leonis papae, sicut et in Sardicense concilio, ut episcopi alterius clericum ad se non sollicitent nec ordinent.
> 57. Episcopis. Item eiusdem, ut nullus episcopus servum alterius ad clericatus officium sine domini sui voluntate promovere praesumat. Et hoc Gangarense Concilium prohibit.
> 58. Episcopis. Item eiusdem, ut si quis sacerdotum contra constituta decretalia praesumptiose agat et corrigi nolens, ab officio suo submoveatur.
> 59. Episcopis. In decretis Gelasii papae, ut nullus episcopus viduas velare praesunt.[19]
>
> 56. To bishops. In the decrees of pope Leo, as also in the council of Sardica: that bishops are not to entice to themselves, or ordain, another's cleric.
> 57. To bishops. Further, from the same: that no bishop is to presume to advance someone else's *servus* to clerical office without his lord's approval. The council of Gangra also prohibits this.
> 58. To bishops. Further, from the same: that any *sacerdos* who presumptuously contravenes the decretal ordinances and refuses to be corrected is to be removed from office.
> 59. To bishops. In the decrees of the pope Gelasius: that no bishop is to presume to veil a widow.[20]

Generally speaking, the language of the first portion of the *Admonitio generalis* is typical of most ecclesiastical legislation of its era, both earlier and, to a large extent, thereafter. It prescribes or prohibits specific behaviors, citing the authority of prior ecclesiastical legislation. Alcuin's approach is substantially different.

Alcuin's portion commences with *Haec enim, dilectissimi...*, addressing the faithful with language echoing sermonistic or homiletic exordia. Rather than enumerating provisions and their support by authorities

[18] P. D. King, trans. *Charlemagne: Translated Sources* (Lambrigg: P. D. King, 1987), 214.

[19] Mordek et al., *Die Admonitio generalis*, 206–07.

[20] King, *Charlemagne*, 213–14.

drawn from prior ecclesiastical law, Alcuin urges his subjects to embrace a moral life by direct appeal to Scripture, relying on its authority almost exclusively. Notably also, the Alcuinian section concludes on the same homiletic note, invoking the language of peroration:

> Et hoc ideo diligentius iniungimus vestrae caritati, quia scimus temporibus novissimis pseudodoctores esse venturos, sicut ipse dominus in evangelio praedixit et apostolus Paulus ad Timotheum testatur. **Ideo, dilectissimi,** toto corde praeparemus nos scientia veritatis, ut possimus contradicentibus veritati resistere, et divina donante gratia verbum dei crescat et currat multiplicetur in profectum sanctae dei ecclesiae et salute animarum nostrarum et laudem et gloriam nominis domini nostril Iesu Christi. **Pax praedicantibus, gratia oboedientibus, gloria domino nostro Iesu Christo. Amen.**[21]

> And we enjoin this the more diligently upon your lovingness because we know that in the last days there will appear false teachers, as the Lord Himself foretold in the gospel and as the apostle Paul testifies to Timothy. **Wherefore, most beloved,** let us prepare ourselves with all our heart in knowledge and truth, that we may be able to resist those who oppose the truth and that, by the gift of divine grace, the word of God may flourish and become general and spread, to the benefit of God's holy church and the salvation of our souls and the praise and glory of the name of Lord Jesus Christ. **Peace to those who preach, grace to those who obey, glory to our Lord Jesus Christ. Amen.**[22]

Alcuin's rhetoric in this passage echoes the language of sermons that urge the faithful toward embracing moral behavior of their own volition. At the same time, he refrains from merely cataloging required reforms enforced by threats of temporal sanction. Rather, he seeks to inspire the audience to join in the reforms with religious fervor. This novel approach to lawgiving provides insight into his views about reform. It suggests that Alcuin, who is not typically remembered as a legislator, envisioned law as a fundamental element of Charlemagne's larger agenda. Specifically, it shows that he viewed the capitulary, reimagined in this way, as a genre especially well suited to express the magnitude and spirit of the Carolingian *Renovatio*.

Overall, Alcuin's portion of the *Admonitio generalis* represents a novel approach to legislation that laid the groundwork for Charlemagne's reliance on the capitulary as a primary means of projecting his moral vision throughout Carolingian society. While less fully developed, the *Legatine Capitulary* anticipates this gesture. There, we observe the same hortatory, moralizing approach to legislation, a comparable use of sermonistic lan-

[21] Mordek et al., *Die Admonitio generalis*, 238.

[22] King, *Charlemagne*, 220.

guage and structure, and the same, nearly exclusive reliance on Scripture as an authority. I will consider each of these features in turn.

First of all, the hortatory approach typical of preaching clearly informs the *Legatine Capitulary* in much the same way as in the *Admonitio generalis*. Alcuin's predilection toward sermonistic language is apparent throughout the text. Consider, as one example, *capitulum* XX:

> XX. Vigesimum caput. Omnibus generaliter intimavimus, ut iuxta propheticam vocem agere decertent, quae ait "Nolite tardare converti ad Dominum nec differatis de diem." Et alibi: "Convertimini ad me in toto corde vestro, in ieiunio fletu et planctu." Item: "Convertimini ad me et ego convertar ad vos." Et iuxta apostolum: "Confitemini alter alteri peccata vestra et orate pro invicem, ut salvemini," ne ullum (quod absit) subitanea mors imparatum inveniat. Et iuxta iudicium sacerdotum et modum culpae eucharistiam sumite et fructus dignos poenitentiae facite, fructuosa namque poenitentia est admissa deflere et fleta in postmodum non admittere. Si quis autem (quod abist) sine poenitentia aut confessione de hac luce discessit, pro eo minime orandum est. Nullus enim nostrum absque peccato est, nec infans unius diei dicente apostolo: "Si dixerimus, quia peccatum non habemus, ipsi nos seducimus et veritas in nobis non est." Penitemini igitur et convertimini, quia "mors non tardat," ut deleantur nostra peccata et illa vita sine fine mansura cum angelis sanctis perfrui mereamini per eum, qui vivit et regnat in secula seculorum.[23]

> XX. The twentieth chapter: We announced to all generally that they should strive to act according to the prophetic voice, which says: "Do not delay to repent before the Lord, and do not defer it from day to day" [Ecclus 5.8]. And elsewhere: "Repent before me with all your heart, in fasting, and in weeping, and in mourning" [Joel 2.12]. And elsewhere, "Repent before me, and I will turn to you" [Zach 1.3]. And, according to the Apostle, "Confess your sins to one another and pray for one another so that you may be saved" [James 5.16], lest ([God] forbid) a sudden death should find anyone unprepared. And receive the eucharist according to the judgment of priests and the degree of guilt, and make fruits worthy of penance, for it is a productive penance to weep over your misdeeds, and, having wept over them, not to commit them afterwards. If, however, anyone ([God] forbid) passes from this light without penance or confession, there should be no prayers for him. For none of us is without sin, not even an infant who is only a day old, as the Apostle says: "If we say that we do not have sin, we deceive ourselves, and the truth is not in us" [I Ioh 1.8]. Do penance, therefore, and repent, "because death is not slow" [Ecclus 14.12], so that your sins might be

[23] MGH Epp. IV, Alcuini ep. 3, p. 27, lines 14–27.

wiped away and so that you may deserve to enjoy that life with the holy angels enduring without end, forever and ever.

Capitulum XX, urging the faithful to repent and ask forgiveness for their sins before time runs out, expresses this common theme in early medieval sermon literature. What is more, it relies heavily on a homily on Ecclesiasticus (Sirach) 5:8 which Alcuin knew and used elsewhere,[24] clearly showing that Alcuin was thinking about sermons when he composed the *Legatine Capitulary*. As such, it hardly reads as legislation at all, but rather more like a moralizing entreaty to virtuous behavior merely contextualized within a legal framework.

Second, the language and content of the *Legatine Capitulary* is organized and presented in a manner clearly informed by preaching. Both sections of ten *capitula* – the first group addressed to clergy, the second to lay magnates – culminate with language that invokes a homiletic peroration. For example, the last part of *capitulum* X reads:

> Obsecravimus etiam, ut assidue preces fierent pro ecclesia Dei, ut Deus et dominus noster Iesus Christus exaltet, corroboret, protegat et defendat, conservet immaculatam ad laudem et gloriam nominis sui in omnia secula seculorum, Amen.[25]
>
> We also implored that prayers be made assiduously for the Church of God, so that God and our Lord Jesus Christ may exalt, strengthen, protect, defend, and preserve the Church immaculate for the praise and glory of His name, in all things forever and ever. Amen.

Similarly, the last part of *capitulum* XX reads:

> Penitemini igitur et convertimini, quia "mors non tardat," ut deleantur nostra peccata et illa vita sine fine mansura cum angelis sanctis perfrui mereamini per eum, qui vivit et regnat in secula seculorum.[26]
>
> Do penance, therefore, and repent, because "death is not slow" [Ecclus 14.12], so that our sins might be wiped away and so that you may deserve to enjoy that life with the holy angels enduring without end, forever and ever.

[24] This homily, ultimately based on two sermons of Caesarius of Arles, is attested in at least seven witnesses. I have reconstructed its contents from the surviving evidence in Bryan Carella [who now publishes as Kristen Carella], "Reconstructing a Lost Latin Homily on Ecclesiasticus (Sirach) 5:8," *Revue Bénédictine* 117 (2007): 261–93.

[25] MGH Epp. IV, Alcuini ep. 3, p. 23, lines 12–15.

[26] MGH Epp. IV, Alcuini ep. 3, p. 27, lines 25–27.

Both sections, thus, end on a note that recalls a homiletic peroration more than a legal tract. What about the beginning? The text of the *Legatine Capitulary* survives only as it was embedded in an epistolary report from the head of the legation, Bishop George of Ostia, to Pope Hadrian, describing the results of the mission. George records only the *capitula*. If these chapters were framed by an exordium-style introduction of the kind we see in the *Admonitio generalis*, it is lost to history.

Third, a distinguishing feature of both Alcuin's portion of the *Admonitio generalis* and the *Legatine Capitulary* is their heavy reliance on Scripture as the primary authority of their provisions. A few statistics will suffice to make the point. In the roughly 2,240 words in the Alcuinian portion of the *Admonitio generalis* there are, by my count, forty-three direct citations of and twenty-five references to Scripture. Appeals to other kinds of authorities are correspondingly rare. I have identified only eleven, ranging from allusions to the writings of the Church Fathers to prayers of the Divine Office. One finds a similar ratio of scriptural to non-scriptural authorities in the *Legatine Capitulary*. Indeed, I count eighty-three biblical references in the roughly 3,800 words of text that constitute the document, and only eighteen appeals to other authorities. Non-scriptural authorities, moreover, consist mainly of vague references, although a handful of direct citations appear as well. For example, the text includes several citations of Augustine, a certain *sapiens* I am unable to identify, and a non-standard citation of Prudentius' *Diptychon* I.3.[27] The remaining non-scriptural references are very generalized. They include a reference to the Nicene Council[28] (admonishing that it be upheld), to the six ecumenical councils,[29] and even more nebulous appeals ecclesiastical law of various kinds.

Both the *Legatine Capitulary* and the Alcuinian portion of the *Admonitio generalis* witness a novel approach to lawgiving. Both texts transform the legalistic genre of the capitulary, reimagining it as a hortatory document deeply informed by the rhetoric of preaching. This new approach relied heavily on Scripture as a basic authority as well as the language and certain structural elements of sermons and homilies. As such, the capitulary was specially adapted to project a moral vision aimed at societal reform. Significantly, Alcuin's first known experiment with this gesture is first attested in late eighth-century Northumbria. We see it next approximately three years later in Carolingian Francia, where Alcuin deploys it as one of the early legislative efforts of the nascent Carolingian *Renovatio*. Ultimately, it is in this context that we may best understand the reasons for Alcuin's development of the capitulary in this distinctive manner.

[27] MGH Epp. IV, Alcuini ep. 3, p. 26, line 44.

[28] MGH Epp. IV, Alcuini ep. 3, p. 21, line 10.

[29] MGH Epp. IV, Alcuini ep. 3, p. 23, lines 14 and 16; MGH Epp. IV, Alcuini ep. 3, p. 22, lines 20–21.

The *Legatine Capitulary* of 786 stands out as an important document in early Anglo-Saxon legal history, a substantially innovative document with a direct bearing not only on affairs in Northumbria but throughout the major political centers of England, where it was read aloud and endorsed by the leading magnates of the day. At the same time, the *Legatine Capitulary* of 786 played a significant role in Carolingian legal history. Given the makeup of the legation that drafted it and their roles in the nascent reforms on the continent, it is possible the document reflects Charlemagne's interest in Anglo-Saxon, or at least English, affairs; at least while York remained a center of European learning. Whatever the nature and extent of his agenda abroad, it must have been snuffed out soon after by the Viking invasions which devasted Northumbria in the late eighth century and thereafter. On the European continent, the *Legatine Capitulary* laid the groundwork for the transformation of the capitulary into a primary mechanism for projecting Charlemagne's reform agenda. Experimenting first in the *Legatine Capitulary* and then developing his ideology and compositional approach still further in *Admonitio generalis*, Alcuin reimagined the capitulary, drawing heavily on the language and techniques of preaching. The specifics of Alcuin's transformation of the genre – specifically his nearly exclusive reliance on Scripture as an authority and his reliance on sermonistic language and structures – are not well attested in later Carolingian capitularies. What is preserved, however, is the spirit of Alcuin's approach, calling on all Christians to participate willingly and ardently in Charlemagne's reform agenda. Very notably, this essential part of the Carolingian *Renovatio* emerged initially in Northumbria and was first conceived and set to vellum by Alcuin.

7

Liturgy as Law: Coronation *Ordines* in Tenth-Century England[1]

Nicole Marafioti

Royal coronation *ordines* occupy a peculiar place in the historiography of early English law, kingship, and ecclesiastical culture. As liturgical formulae, they offer instructions for religious speech and ritual action, codifying the particulars of a rite that would be employed sporadically – perhaps as rarely as once or twice in living memory. These texts are remarkable for their preservation of ritual dialogue and choreography, as well as their particularly ecclesiastical vision of Christian kingship and royal obligation.[2] However, the *ordines* as written do not capture the full nuance of a royal coronation in practice. The distance between text and ritual is largely unknowable; we cannot reconstruct the full range of speech and action taken by the principals in or witnesses to the rite.[3] The written *ordines* do not reveal whether their language could be modified or expanded upon; they do not specify whether portions of their liturgical Latin were rendered into Old English; and their logistical details are far from exhaustive. Although they provide an invaluable impression of how ecclesiastical authors envisioned the coronation rite, the written formulae are textual creations which delineate the priorities, ideologies, and aspirations of their creators.

1 Research for this essay was generously supported by an ACLS Burkhardt Fellowship, the National Humanities Center, Cornell University's Medieval Studies Program, and Trinity University.

2 Janet L. Nelson's seminal work on English coronation *ordines* is collected in her *Politics and Ritual in Early Medieval Europe* (London: Hambledon, 1986); and see now David Pratt, "The Making of the Second English Coronation *Ordo*," *Anglo-Saxon England* 46 (2017): 147–258. On liturgical drama more generally, see M. Bradford Bedingfield, *The Dramatic Liturgy of Anglo-Saxon England* (Woodbridge: Boydell, 2002), 1–24.

3 Carol Symes, "Liturgical Texts and Performance Practices," in *Understanding Medieval Liturgy: Essays in Interpretation*, ed. Helen Gittos and Sarah Hamilton (Farnham: Ashgate, 2016), 239–67.

In their status as textual artifacts, pre-Conquest coronation *ordines* are remarkably similar to early English law codes. Both genres articulate instructions and ideologies which were likely enacted to some extent, even if the degree of correlation between text and practice is now irrecoverable.[4] Both represent acts of speech and consensus: royal decrees ostensibly preserve agreements among the kingdom's governing elites, while the *ordines* codify verbal expressions of ecclesiastical approval and public acclamation of a new king.[5] Both seek to define and elevate the king's authority, in part by placing royal and ecclesiastical obligations in conversation.[6] And both emerged in the ninth century as prominent genres of political literature: Alfred (r. 871–99) revived vernacular written law after a centuries-long hiatus, while the earliest extant English *ordines* are associated with the reign of his father Æthelwulf (r. 839–58) and stepmother Judith.[7] New laws and revised *ordines* were disseminated across the tenth and eleventh centuries, and the fact that the liturgical rites and royal decrees were both penned – and, to various degrees, formulated – by elite clergymen affirms that the two genres emerged from the same political-literary sphere.[8]

This is not to suggest that coronation rites and royal decrees were fully aligned in their content or objectives. Each genre aimed to accomplish highly specific work, and this reality has led these texts to be treated in relative isolation from the wider corpus of pre-Conquest literature (and each other). Yet although they are presented as practical documents – instructions for administering ecclesiastical ritual and maintaining earthly order – they should also be understood as literary creations. Their authors crafted rhetorical arguments, couching political theory and ideologies of

4 Symes, "Liturgical Texts," 239–43; Patrick Wormald, "*Lex scripta* and *verbum regis*: Legislation and Germanic Kingship, from Euric to Cnut," in Wormald, *Legal Culture*, 1–43.

5 Levi Roach, *Kingship and Consent in Anglo-Saxon England* (Cambridge: Cambridge University Press, 2013), 104–12.

6 Wormald, *Making of English Law*, 416–65, esp. 446–48.

7 There is no textual record of royal decrees issued between *c.* 700 and Alfred's *domboc*. On the dating of the *ordo*, see Nelson, *Politics and Ritual*, 341–60; Pratt, "Coronation *Ordo*," 155–57.

8 For royal law and coronation *ordines* as complementary, see Janet L. Nelson, "Liturgy or Law: Misconceived Alternatives?" in *Early Medieval Studies in Memory of Patrick Wormald*, ed. Stephen Baxter et al. (Farnham: Ashgate, 2009), 433–47. For possible authors of the early tenth-century coronation rite, see Pratt, "Coronation *Ordo*," 206–10; Janet L. Nelson, "The First Use of the Second Anglo-Saxon *Ordo*," in *Myth, Rulership, Church and Charters: Essays in Honour of Nicholas Brooks*, ed. Julia Barrow and Andrew Wareham (Aldershot: Ashgate, 2008), 117–26. For bishops as legislators in this period, see Wormald, *Making of English Law*, esp. 299–300, 310, 330–39, and 449–65.

kingship in liturgical or legal language. The varied sets of decrees collectively identified as "law codes" were dynamic and innovative texts, and many drew upon literary precedents – biblical and historical, insular and continental – as they codified legal custom, articulated ideals of justice and social order, and projected royal authority. Preserved predominantly in Old English and presented as collective agreements among the king and his councilors, these texts were tailored for broad consumption among the English-speaking population and copied widely.[9] By contrast, pre-Conquest coronation *ordines* survive in just a handful of ecclesiastical handbooks. The relative scarcity of these texts in England and their preservation in liturgical Latin indicates a smaller audience than the laws aspired to – although a partial Old English rendering of the rite, which circulated *c.* 1000, may speak to broader public interest in the text.[10] Still, the Latin *ordines* circulated persistently in ecclesiastical circles, codified in pontificals and pastoral compilations alongside rites for consecrating churches, creating bishops, and burying the dead. There are literary echoes of the coronation *ordines* in contemporary texts, indicating that familiarity with the liturgical language may have been more widespread than the narrow manuscript record suggests.[11]

Interest in the English coronation liturgy is most evident, however, in the repeated reworkings of the text itself between the ninth and eleventh centuries. Four discrete versions of the rite have been identified in this period. The "first English *ordo*" (which I will refer to here as *Ordo* 1) was almost certainly used for the coronation of Æthelwulf as king of the West Saxons and, later, the coronations of his sons; but it is probable that the rite

9 For editions of ninth- and tenth-century royal laws, see Stefan Jurasinski and Lisi Oliver, eds., *The Laws of Alfred: The Domboc and the Making of Anglo-Saxon Law* (Cambridge: Cambridge University Press, 2021); Felix Liebermann, ed., *Die Gesetze der Angelsachsen*, 3 vols. (Halle: Max Niemeyer, 1903–16). I follow Jurasinski and Oliver's edition and enumeration for the laws of Alfred and Ine (with Liebermann's enumeration in parentheses, when the two editions diverge); and Liebermann's for the laws of other pre-Conquest kings, unless otherwise noted.

10 Mary Clayton, "The Old English *Promissio regis*," *Anglo-Saxon England* 37 (2008): 91–150.

11 For example, Byrhtferth's *Vita Oswaldi* and the *Encomium Emmae Reginae* incorporate language from the English coronation *ordo*: Michael Lapidge, ed. and trans., *Byrhtferth of Ramsey: The Lives of St Oswald and St Ecgwine* (Oxford: Clarendon, 2009), 106–11; Alistair Campbell, ed., *Encomium Emmae Reginae* (London: Cambridge University Press, 1998 [orig. publ. 1949]), 22–23; J. Armitage Robinson, "The Coronation Order in the Tenth Century," *Journal of Theological Studies* 19 (1917): 56–72. The language of coronation *ordines* was also adapted in charters: Levi Roach, *Æthelred the Unready* (New Haven: Yale University Press, 2016), 154–56.

itself was considerably older.[12] A new version, known to scholars as the first recension of the "second English *ordo*" (*Ordo* 2A), emerged around the turn of the tenth century, although it is debated whether it was compiled during the reign of Alfred for the coronation of his son Edward the Elder (r. 899–924), or in Edward's reign for his son Æthelstan (r. 924/5–39).[13] *Ordo* 2A incorporated elements from *Ordo* 1 but significantly adapted and expanded the earlier text, relying heavily – though not exclusively – upon recent continental exempla for its new content, particularly the Erdmann and Leiden *ordines*.[14] *Ordo* 2A was further developed in the later tenth century, into a set of texts known as the second recension of the "second

12 *Ordo* 1 survives in three manuscripts: the Leofric Missal A (Bodl., MS Bodley 579), the Egbert Pontifical (Paris, Bibliothèque Nationale, MS Lat. 10575), and the Lanalet Pontifical (Rouen, Bibliothèque Municipale, MS 368 [A.27]). For manuscripts, dating, and context, see Nelson, "Earliest Royal *Ordo*," 351–53; Nelson, "First Use," 118–29; Pratt, "Coronation *Ordo*," 154–61; David Pratt, *The Political Thought of King Alfred the Great* (Cambridge: Cambridge University Press, 2007), 72–78. The text is edited in Nicholas Orchard, ed., *The Leofric Missal*, 2 vols. (London: Boydell, 2002), 2:429–32, with introductory material at 1:99–105.

13 The revised rite of *c.* 900 (*Ordo* 2A) survives in twenty Continental manuscripts produced between the tenth and seventeenth centuries. Janet Nelson once proposed that *Ordo* 2A was intended for Edward the Elder's accession, but she has since argued that Æthelstan's coronation was a likelier occasion: Nelson, "The Second English *Ordo*," in *Politics and Ritual in Early Medieval Europe* (London: Hambledon, 1986), 361–74; Nelson, "First Use," 121–26. Since then, David Pratt has proposed that the rite was composed during Alfred's reign, for Edward: Pratt, "Coronation *Ordo*"; and compare also Anton Scharer, "A New Second 'English' *Ordo*?" in *Changing Perspectives on England and the Continent in the Early Middle Ages* (Farnham: Ashgate, 2014), 1–11 (no. IX). In my discussion below, I rely on the earliest manuscript, the Ratold Sacramentary (Paris, Bibliothèque Nationale, MS lat. 12052), compiled in the later tenth century and edited in Nicholas Orchard, ed., *The Sacramentary of Ratoldus (Paris, Bibliothèque nationale de France, lat. 12052)* (London: Boydell, 2005), 47–55, with context at xcvi–xcvii and cxxix–cxxxvi. For other manuscripts, see Richard A. Jackson, ed., *Ordines Coronationis Franciae, Volume 1: Texts and Ordines for the Coronation of Frankish and French Kings and Queens in the Middle Ages* (Philadelphia: University of Pennsylvania Press, 1995), 5–172.

14 The Erdmann *Ordo* of *c.* 900 survives in two manuscripts: a Sens pontifical *c.* 900 (Saint Petersburg, National Library of Russia at Saint Petersburg, MS. Lat. Q.v.I, no. 35); and a twelfth-century Nevers pontifical (Paris, Bibliothèque Nationale, MS lat. 17333). The Leiden *Ordo* (so named by David Pratt) is a shorter, early version of the Frankish text known conventionally as the "*Ordo* of Seven Forms" or "*Ordo* of Eleven Forms": it is preserved in a single manuscript, compiled *c.* 1000 (Leiden, Rijksuniversitet Bibl., MS Vossianus lat. Q.13). Pratt argues that the Leiden *Ordo* was employed in Charles the Straightforward's 893 coronation and used as a source for *Ordo* 2A soon after. Pratt, "Coronation *Ordo*," esp. 151–52, 172–75, and 178–94; Nelson, "Second English Ordo," 361–65; but compare Nelson, "First Use," 123–26. Both texts are edited in Jackson,

English *Ordo*" (*Ordo* 2B).[15] This revision was almost certainly produced for King Edgar (r. 959–75) and used into the next century, with part of the text rendered into Old English.[16] Finally, a "third English *ordo*" (*Ordo* 3) modified the language surrounding dynastic legitimacy and hereditary right, perhaps in anticipation of a dynastic shift; the text may have been used in the 1066 coronations of Harold Godwineson and William I.[17]

The present chapter will focus on *Ordo* 2A. This text was composed at a time when West Saxon kings were consolidating territory, assigning themselves ever-greater legal and judicial authority, and claiming extensive governing powers over previously disparate populations.[18] In this same period, bishops and clergy were negotiating the role of the Church in this new political order, after a century of Viking disruptions and generations of (what ecclesiastical records construe as) secular encroachment on the property and legal rights of churches.[19] In this context, the new version of the coronation *ordo* should be read as a liturgical expression of political ideology, articulated by churchmen who were closely involved with royal governance.[20] The author (or authors) of *Ordo* 2A introduced Frankish elements into the established language of West Saxon coronations, expanding the older English rite to give it new ceremonial weight. The resulting text integrated West Saxon tradition with continental inno-

---

Ordines: Erdmann at 142–53 and Leiden (as manuscript A of "*Ordo* of Eleven Forms") at 154–67.

15 Two versions of *Ordo* 2B are attested: the earlier survives exclusively in the Benedictional of Archbishop Robert, while the later sub-version is preserved in five pre-Conquest English pontificals: Nelson, "Second English *Ordo*," 369–74, with a list of manuscripts at 363.

16 The later tenth-century redaction (*Ordo* 2B), represented by two sub-versions, survives in six English manuscripts from the tenth and eleventh centuries. Janet Nelson argues that both sub-versions of *Ordo* 2B were produced for Edgar, for his two coronations in *c.* 960 and 973: Nelson, "Second English *Ordo*," 368–74. For Archbishop Wulfstan of York's (r. 1002–23) authorship of the Old English rendering, see Clayton, "*Promissio regis*."

17 Nelson, "The Rites of the Conqueror," in *Politics and Ritual in Early Medieval Europe* (London: Hambledon, 1986), 375–401; but compare George Garnett, "The Third Recension of the English Coronation *Ordo*: The Manuscripts," *Haskins Society Journal* 11 (1998): 43–71.

18 George Molyneaux, *The Formation of the English Kingdom in the Tenth Century* (Oxford: Oxford University Press, 2015), 1–3.

19 See esp. Robin Fleming, "Monastic Lands and England's Defence in the Viking Age," *English Historical Review* 100 (1985): 247–65; Catherine Cubitt, *Anglo-Saxon Church Councils c.650–c.850* (London: Leicester University Press, 1995), 230–40.

20 Pratt, "Coronation *Ordo*," 224–38. Recently, Grimbald of Saint-Bertin (d. *c.* 901) and Archbishop Athelm of Canterbury (r. 923–26) have been associated with the rite: Pratt, "Coronation *Ordo*," 48–53 and 60–64; Nelson, "First Use," 126.

vations, emphasizing the king's singular status as anointed ruler and buttressing the broader political ambitions of Alfred and his descendants. For a generation of rulers who looked beyond Wessex to present themselves as kings of the English, this new coronation liturgy could only enhance their claims to wide-ranging, legitimate authority.[21] *Ordo* 2A was designed as a performative text, which joined liturgical drama to the various forms of political theater surrounding royal succession.[22] Its vision of Christian rulership was tailored for a public ritual of transformation, in which the act of ecclesiastical consecration turned a man into a king.

Read through a political lens, *Ordo* 2A seems to exemplify ideological alignment between the new king and his ecclesiastical advisors, with Christian rhetoric deployed in support of royal political goals.[23] Yet the text also imposes conditions and obligations, which speak to the concerns and priorities of religious leaders – and which occasionally diverge from the picture of royal authority presented in the law codes. Even as it affirms divine and ecclesiastical support for his rule, the *ordo* delineates the king's responsibilities toward his subjects and the institutional Church, grounding these requirements in the language of law and justice. Accordingly, I propose that *Ordo* 2A should be understood as legal as well as political and liturgical literature: a compact between the new ruler and the clergy, which delineated the king's obligations and limitations in future interactions with the Church, its property, and its personnel. In particular, the rite defines the limits of royal power in relation to the earthly Church, defines the nature of the royal office in relation to God and the clergy, and confirms the importance of bishops to the kingdom's governance.

In the following pages, I consider three passages of *Ordo* 2A which exemplify this legal approach: the *ordo*'s opening section, in which the king renders a promise of support to the bishops; the *Sta et retine*, which accompanies the moment of enthronement; and the concluding "three precepts," which delineate the king's obligations to his subjects. These new additions to the English coronation rite incorporated Frankish diction alongside original material, confirming the king's obligations before God, the presiding bishops, and the assembled witnesses. Though presented in liturgical language, these passages should not be interpreted merely as religious blessings or expressions of ecclesiastical approval. They must

21 Sarah Foot, "The Making of *Angelcynn*: English Identity Before the Norman Conquest," *TRHS*, 6th series, 6 (1996): 25–49; Simon Keynes, "Edward, King of the Anglo-Saxons," in *Edward the Elder, 899–924*, ed. N. J. Higham and D. H. Hill (London: Routledge, 2001), 40–66; Pratt, *Political Thought*, 105–11; Pratt, "Coronation *Ordo*," 149 and 224–38.

22 For royal transitions, see Nicole Marafioti, *The King's Body: Burial and Succession in Late Anglo-Saxon England* (Toronto: University of Toronto Press, 2014).

23 Pratt, "Coronation *Ordo*," 224–30.

also be understood as formal commitments, which established a legal framework for Christian kingship.

This chapter approaches *Ordo* 2A as a complement to late ninth- and early tenth-century royal decrees, contending that the rite provides a rationale for the laws' religious regulations.[24] The *ordo* requires the king to guarantee ecclesiastical rights and privileges in the secular sphere, and indeed, the royal law codes of this period recognize the Church as autonomous in spiritual and canonical matters – even as they confirm the king's patronage and protection.[25] According to the logic of *Ordo* 2A, royal support for the Church was not a matter of personal piety but a legal obligation. Care for the Church was a binding commitment, a condition of a king's rule.

* * *

Ordo 2A introduces a new beginning for the English coronation rite, which foregrounds episcopal authority and ecclesiastical rights. After a detailed *incipit*, the text opens with a petition by the presiding bishops: they request a promise from the king, who affirms the Church's rights and protections. The bishops then request the assembly's approval; once granted, two bishops lead the king by the hands to the altar, where he prostrates himself as *Te Deum Laudamus* is chanted.[26] The petition, response, and instructions for prayer are adapted from the Frankish Erdmann *ordo*, yet the *incipit* and king's prostration are original to *Ordo* 2A.[27] There is no parallel for any of this material in the earlier English *Ordo* 1, which begins with the title "Blessings upon a newly chosen king," and then proceeds to invoke God directly.[28] By contrast, the new opening of *Ordo* 2A is a preamble to the rite proper, which eventually begins with *Ordo* 1's prayer of invocation.[29]

This new introductory section creates a heightened moment of dramatic tension between the king and bishops. The opening rubric of *Ordo* 2A, which has no known source, is uniquely descriptive. It encapsulates

[24] Connections with pre-Conquest law have been noted but not thoroughly examined: Nelson, "Liturgy or Law"; Pratt, "Coronation *Ordo*," 224–25; Tom Lambert, *Law and Order in Anglo-Saxon England* (Oxford: Oxford University Press, 2017), 205–06.

[25] Nicole Marafioti, "Crime and Sin in the Laws of Alfred," in *Languages of the Law in Early Medieval England: Essays in Memory of Lisi Oliver*, ed. Stefan Jurasinski and Andrew Rabin (Leuven: Peeters, 2019), 59–84; Nicole Marafioti, "Unconsecrated Burial and Excommunication in Anglo-Saxon England: A Reassessment," *Traditio* 74 (2019): 55–123.

[26] Orchard, *Ratoldus*, 47–48.

[27] Jackson, *Ordines*, 147.

[28] *Benedictiones super regem nouiter electum*: Orchard, *Leofric*, 2:429.

[29] *Te inuocamus domine sanctae*...: Orchard, *Ratoldus*, 48; Orchard, *Leofric*, 2:429.

the process of royal election, with an emphasis on the role of bishops and (to a lesser extent) other clergy and the people:

> Incipit percunctatio siue electio episcoporum ac clericorum necnon populorum ad regem consecrandum siue benedicendum. Ammonitio episcoporum uel clericorum seu populorum ad regem, dicenda ita, legatur ab uno episcopo coram omnibus.[30]

> Here begins – through the inquiry or election of the bishops and clergy, and also the people – the consecration or blessing of the king. The admonition of the bishops or the clergy or the people is to be spoken to the king, thus to be read by one bishop in the presence of all.[31]

Bishops are identified here as participants in the king's selection (*electio*) and facilitators of the admonition (*ammonitio*) to which he must agree. This detailed explication contextualizes the new ritual elements which follow, clarifying for English bishops their role in an unprecedented set of petitions and responses. At the same time, the rubric construes the bishops' endorsement – alongside that of the clergy and people – as a precondition for the king's accession.[32] As written, the rite cannot continue without the king's commitment to ecclesiastical interests and the assembly's subsequent approval of the royal candidate, all to be mediated by the presiding bishops. This is a striking development from *Ordo* 1, which takes the king's accession for granted and requires no preliminary commitment.

Where *Ordo* 2A begins by citing the collective consent of the bishops, clergy, and people, this balance soon skews in favor of episcopal authority. The *populus* must participate in the king's selection, according to the opening rubric, and will later approve his consecration; yet their consent will be sought only after the royal candidate has formally accepted the conditions imposed by the bishops. Following the Frankish Erdmann *ordo*, the bishops' admonition focuses on the privileges and autonomy of the Church:[33]

30 *Vel clericorum seu populorum* is present in the Ratold Sacramentary but omitted in most manuscripts: Jackson, *Ordines*, 177–78.

31 Orchard, *Ratoldus*, 47. In the Ratold Sacramentary (fol. 21v), these two sentences are rubricated: <gallica.bnf.fr/ark:/12148/btv1b84274539>. Compare the brief rubricated *incipit* of *Ordo* 1 in the Leofric Missal (fol. 302v): <https://digital.bodleian.ox.ac.uk/objects/97b5f725-af6d-4934-ad75-575eb081838f/>.

32 Conditionality in the opening promise is noted by Pratt, "Coronation *Ordo*," 150; Nelson, "Second English *Ordo*," 369–70.

33 There is no parallel in *Ordo* 1. For the corresponding passage in the Erdmann *ordo* and other analogues, see Jackson, *Ordines*, 117–18 and 147.

> A uobis perdonari petimus, ut unicuique de nobis, et ecclesiis nobis commissis, canonicum priuilegium ac debitam legem, atque iustitiam conseruetis, et defensionem exibeatis, sicut rex in suo regno unicuique episcopo et ecclesiae sibi commissae per rectum exibere debet.[34]

> We request that you grant that for each of us [bishops] and for the churches entrusted to us, you shall preserve the privilege of the canons, and due law, and justice, and dispense protection – just as a king, out of justice, ought to grant to every bishop in his kingdom and to the churches committed to them.

The king then repeats this language verbatim, opening his response with the phrase "I promise and grant you" and affirming that he will fulfill these obligations "as much as I am able, with the Lord's help."[35] Where *Ordo* 1 opens directly with a prayer for the king's prosperity and his subjects' safety, *Ordo* 2A asserts that the king's primary obligation – indeed, the condition for his consecration – was to guarantee the earthly protections and privileges of bishops and their churches.[36]

This promise was concerned with the Church's legal rights, which the king could ostensibly guarantee. Indeed, each of these commitments was consistent with principles which underpinned English royal decrees, even though the language was drawn from a Frankish source.[37] The most straightforward obligation – *defensio*, protection – was a standard element of royal law from the seventh century.[38] Around the time this rite was committed to parchment, the concepts of sanctuary and church-peace were being defined and codified in royal decrees, alongside penalties for

34 Orchard, *Ratoldus*, 47.

35 *Responsio regis. Promitto uobis et perdono… quantum potuero adiuuante domino.* Orchard, *Ratoldus*, 47–48.

36 Orchard, *Leofric*, 2:429.

37 A connection between *Ordo* 2A and Alfredian law is suggested by Pratt, "Coronation *Ordo*," 162 and 225; Wormald, *Making of English Law*, 446–48.

38 Ecclesiastical protections appear in royal laws from the seventh century: see Æthelberht 1–6 (=L 1) and Wihtred 1–2, edited in Lisi Oliver, ed., *The Beginnings of English Law* (Toronto: University of Toronto Press, 2002), 60–61 and 152–53; Ine 5–5.1 and 6.1. Compare the early eleventh-century tract *Grið*, which compiles earlier royal decrees: Liebermann, *Gesetze*, 1:470–73; Andrew Rabin, ed. and trans., *The Political Writings of Archbishop Wulfstan of York* (Manchester: Manchester University Press, 2015), 76–81. See also 41.2 of the *Hibernensis*, a canon law collection composed 669 × 748: "that defenders (*defensores*) must be sought to protect the Church," with episcopal oversight; Roy Flechner, *The Hibernensis: A Study and Edition*, 2 vols. (Washington, D.C.: Catholic University of America Press, 2019), 1:314 with translation at 2:706 and dating at 1:59–61. For the early-medieval use of *defensio* for legal protections, see Barbara Rosenwein, *Negotiating Space: Power, Restraint, and Privileges of Immunity in Early Medieval Europe* (Ithaca: Cornell University Press, 1999), 8 and 109–12.

violating ecclesiastical property.[39] Legal protections like these reinforced the Church's institutional integrity and its privileged status in the world, and as construed in *Ordo* 2A, it was the king's responsibility to actively dispense (*exibeatis*) such protections. The king's other obligations required him to preserve or maintain (*conseruetis*) established custom, including "due law and justice" for bishops and churches. This point guarantees legal rights and procedures, confirming that ecclesiastical entities would be entitled to the same law and justice as their secular counterparts – as plaintiffs or defendants in disputes, but perhaps more pertinently, as earthly administrators with their own judicial rights. This would ensure high-ranking clergy the ability to direct civil justice and collect judicial revenues, in their capacity as earthly administrators of churches and estates; this phrase seems to grant judicial privileges akin to "sake and soke."[40]

The king also commits to preserve "the privilege of the canons" (*canonicum priuilegium*), the first item listed in the promise. It is not entirely clear what this phrase meant *c.* 900. In later medieval canon law, canonical privilege (*privilegium canonis*) referred to the legal protection of clergy against violence, and it is possible that *Ordo* 2A anticipated this concept; certainly, such protections appear in English royal decrees of this period.[41] Yet I suspect that the *ordo*'s English author understood this phrase somewhat differently, with *canonicum priuilegium* referring to the unique legal status of ecclesiastical canons. Perhaps the phrase was meant to be read in opposition to "due law and justice," distinguishing ecclesiastical from secular systems of justice but guaranteeing the Church full access to each. Or perhaps these three elements – "the privilege of the canons and due law and justice" – were meant to be read as a single unit, with the king affirming ecclesiastical autonomy in all legal and judicial matters, including its right to administer ecclesiastical justice in accordance with the canons. In either interpretation, preserving "the privilege of the canons" aligns with the other royal obligations in this promise: each is presented as a legal right which the king could personally guarantee.

39 Especially Alfred 2, 5–5.4, 44.2 (=L 42.2); IV Æthelstan 6–6.1.

40 For judicial privileges granted to clergy or churches, see esp. Patrick Wormald, "Lordship and Justice in the Early English Kingdom: Oswaldslow Revisited," in Wormald, *Legal Culture*, 313–32; Stephen Baxter, "Lordship and Justice in Late Anglo-Saxon England: The Judicial Functions of Soke and Commendation Revisited," in *Early Medieval Studies in Memory of Patrick Wormald*, ed. Stephen Baxter et al. (Farnham: Ashgate, 2009), 383–419; Mary Frances Giandrea, *Episcopal Culture in Late Anglo-Saxon England* (Woodbridge: Boydell, 2007), 180–86; Lambert, *Law and Order*, 323–25; Molyneaux, *English Kingdom*, 175–77.

41 Alfred 3, 41 (=L 40). The Second Lateran Council of 1139 codified physical protections for the clergy: Norman P. Tanner, ed., *Decrees of the Ecumenical Councils*, vol. 1 (London: Sheed & Ward, 1990), 200 (canon 15).

The king's preliminary commitments in *Ordo* 2A thus articulate and affirm a set of legal principles pertaining to the Church, in its capacity as an earthly corporation. The promise requires the new king to acknowledge the Church as a legal entity, protected by earthly laws, rights, and privileges. Yet it also confirms that there were elements of ecclesiastical operation that required collaboration, oversight, or enforcement from secular partners – and *Ordo* 2A made a king's consecration conditional upon his pledge to serve as such a partner. In its English context, this passage formalizes the king's legal obligations to the institutional Church and its personnel. Where royal laws present ecclesiastical rights and protections as one-time initiatives issued by individual kings and their councilors, *Ordo* 2A envisions policies which attached to the royal office, transcending the reign of any single ruler and becoming a condition of consecrated kingship.

* * *

The bishops' first role in *Ordo* 2A is that of gatekeepers, for it is only after they secure the king's promise that his consecration can continue. The bishops' degree of control over the rite is especially prominent in the rubricated instructions which conclude the text's new opening sequence:

> Deinde alloquantur duo episcopi populum in ecclesia, inquirentes eorum uoluntatem. et si concordes fuerint, agant deo gratias omnipotenti decantantes, Te Deum Laudamus. et duo episcopi accipiant eum per manus, et deducant ante altare et prosternet se usque in finem Te Deum Laudamus.[42]
>
> Then let two bishops address the people in the church, asking their will, and if they are in agreement, let them thank almighty God, chanting *Te Deum Laudamus*. And let two bishops take him by the hands and lead him before the altar, and he shall prostrate himself until the end of *Te Deum Laudamus*.

The closing sentence of this passage, with bishops leading the king by the hands, is an original intervention by the author; it has no parallel in *Ordo* 1 or the Frankish rites. This new piece of ritual choreography marks a moment of transition, as the bishops physically guide the king into the heart of the church and bring him to prostration before the altar. Attention shifts from the king's legal obligations to his communion with the divine, as the preamble concludes and the liturgical prayers – the same as in *Ordo* 1 –

[42] Orchard, *Ratoldus*, 48. In the Ratold Sacramentary (fol. 22r), the passage is rubricated (except for the phrase *Te Deum Laudimus*) and capitalized: <gallica.bnf.fr/ark:/12148/btv1b84274539>.

finally begin.[43] It only now becomes evident that the preliminary promise was not rendered at the high altar but in a less central area of the church, perhaps even outside the building; only after agreeing to the bishops' conditions does the king progress further inside. When he eventually arrives at the altar, the king lies prostrate while the bishops (apparently) remain standing. If performed as choreographed, the king's submission before God may have looked to witnesses very much like submission to the bishops.

As the text transitions from preamble to prayer, bishops continue to direct the action – and logically so, given the rite's ecclesiastical setting.[44] They also serve as arbiters of popular will, soliciting the people's approval before proceeding with the consecration. Two of the officiating bishops are instructed to speak (*alloquantur*) directly to the assembly, request (*inquirentes*) a response, and then interpret and ratify the answer: they must determine if (*si*) the people agree and, if so, begin the liturgical prayers.[45] Unlike the king's promise at the beginning of *Ordo* 2A, there is no script for this exchange. Although the people's support is cited at the outset as a condition for the king's consecration, the absence of any formula for the assembly to express their will (*uoluntatem*) downplays the formality of their assent. If *Ordo* 2A were used in practice, these vague instructions would have allowed officiating bishops considerable latitude in phrasing the public's approval.

However these directions may have been adapted in practice, the written text is clear that the logistical aspects of the royal inauguration – including acclamation by the *populum* – are to be mediated by bishops. Popular consensus is construed as a reflection of God's approval, meriting a formal expression of thanks (*agant deo gratias*); but it is the bishops' recognition of this fact, rather than the assembly's verbal affirmation, which enables the ritual to proceed.[46] Likewise, it is the king's verbal and physical deference to the bishops throughout the rite's preamble which qualifies him for the prayers, investment, and anointing to follow. Collectively, bishops are presented in *Ordo* 2A not only as gatekeepers but as mediators between the principal parties: they facilitate interactions between the king and God, the king and the Church, and the king and the people. The *ordo*'s opening sequence presents bishops as holding authority over the

43 Orchard, *Ratoldus*, 48; Orchard, *Leofric*, 2:429.

44 For the bishops' elevated role in ninth-century Frankish coronation *ordines*, see Janet L. Nelson, "Kingship, Law and Liturgy in the Political Thought of Hincmar of Rheims," in *Politics and Ritual in Early Medieval Europe* (London: Hambledon, 1986), 139–54; Pratt, "Coronation *Ordo*," 172.

45 This follows the Erdmann *ordo*: Jackson, *Ordines*, 147.

46 This reading turns on the conditional phrase "if they are in agreement," quoted above.

kingdom's political future, with the power to advance (or deny) the king's consecration and accept (or reject) the people's will.

With its elevation of episcopal authority, the opening of *Ordo* 2A adopted the sensibilities of its Frankish sources, asserting a more expansive and authoritative role for the kingdom's bishops – a departure from the English *Ordo* 1, which envisioned greater balance between lay and ecclesiastical participation in the rite.[47] Yet in the West Saxon context in which *Ordo* 2A was composed *c.* 900, I suggest that the bishops' outsized power was also intended to counterbalance political transition and disruption. By definition, a royal consecration was the culmination of an interregnum: at the start of the ritual, there was no anointed king to wield divinely-sanctioned authority over the kingdom. *Ordo* 2A envisions bishops stepping into this political void as a collective, authoritative voice at the head of the kingdom. It is possible that the rite's author sought to provide a mechanism for stability in case of a prolonged or contentious transition, and indeed, this text was used during a period punctuated by sustained and violent succession disputes. Edward the Elder barely fended off a challenge from his first cousin, between 899 and 903; and his son Æthelstan was not crowned until 925, after fourteen months marked by conflict with his half-brothers. The author of *Ordo* 2A may well have anticipated such disputes among different branches of the ascendant royal family.[48] The text establishes bishops as trustees of the royal office, who must ratify the people's election and commit the new king to the responsibilities of his station. They not only provide religious legitimacy through the rite of ecclesiastical anointing, according to *Ordo* 2A, but also serve as guardians of the royal office and facilitators of royal succession.

Accordingly, *Ordo* 2A refers repeatedly to secular systems and procedures, couching matters of law and custom in liturgical language. This is particularly notable in the *Sta et retine* section, a moment of ritual climax which likely accompanied the king's enthronement. The passage appears toward the end of the text, after the king's investment with crown and regalia; its language adheres closely to the Frankish Leiden *ordo* and would be retained in later English versions of the coronation rite.[49] In *Ordo* 2A, subtle changes to the Frankish language are thought to reflect the immediate political considerations of the English author, and these are

47 For the bishops' enhanced role, see Pratt, "Coronation *Ordo*," 159–60; Nelson, "Symbols," 271–72; Nelson, "Kingship, Law and Liturgy," 139–54.

48 For *Ordo* 2A and West Saxon dynastic politics, see Pratt, "Coronation *Ordo*," 224–28; Nelson, "First Use," 122–24; Nelson, "Second English *Ordo*," 365–69.

49 Jackson, *Ordines*, 163. For correspondences between English and Frankish rites, see Nelson, "Second English *Ordo*," 362.

often cited in proposed datings of the text.[50] I suggest, however, that *Sta et retine* provides a legal framework for the king's exceptional status:

> Sta et retine ammodo quem hucusque paterna suggestione tenuisti hereditario iure tibi delegatum, per auctoritatem dei omnipotentis et per presentem traditionem nostram, omnium scilicet episcoporum ceterorumque dei seruorum, et quanto clerum sacris altaribus propinquiorem prospicis, tanto ei potiorem in locis congruis honorem impendere memineris, quatinus mediator dei et hominum te mediatorem cleri et plebis, in hoc regni solio confirmet, et in regnum aeternum secum regnare faciat. Iesus christus dominus noster, rex regum et dominus dominantium, qui cum deo patre et spiritu sancto.[51]

> Stand and keep henceforth – through the authority of almighty God and through our present tradition, namely of all the bishops and other servants of God – that which, until now, you have held by paternal suggestion, entrusted to you by the law of inheritance; and as much as you see clergy near the sacred altars, so much shall you remember to devote greater honor to them in appropriate places; and may our lord Jesus Christ, king of kings and lord of lords, who [reigns] with God the father and the holy spirit – as much the mediator between God and mankind, as you are the mediator between the clergy and the people – confirm you on the throne of this kingdom, and cause you to reign with him in the eternal kingdom.

Dating arguments typically focus on the phrase *paterna suggestione*, "paternal suggestion," paired here with *hereditario iure*, "the law of inheritance."[52] Since succession shifted from fratrilineal to patrilineal after Alfred's death in 899, the claim of paternal heredity may have been particularly pertinent to the sons and grandsons who succeeded him. This vocabulary diverged slightly from its Frankish source: the Leiden *ordo* used the phrase "paternal succession" (*paterna successione*), which was changed in *Ordo* 2A to "paternal suggestion" (*paterna suggestione*).[53] Although this slight change could reasonably be attributed to a stylistic choice or transcription error, given that the passage closely follows its source, I read it as a meaningful revision.[54] Where the diction of the Leiden *ordo* is redundant, with *paterna successione* and *hereditario iure* grounded in the same principle of dynastic inheritance, *Ordo* 2A creates a rhetorical opposition between suggestion

50 Nelson, "First Use," 123–25; Pratt, "Coronation *Ordo*," 186–87; Keynes, "Edward," 48–49; Garnett, "Third Recension," 63.

51 Orchard, *Ratoldus*, 54; Nelson, "Ritual and Reality," 334–35.

52 Above, note 50.

53 Like the Leiden *ordo*, all manuscripts of the *Ordo* of Eleven Forms use *successione*: Jackson, *Ordines*, 163.

54 Compare Pratt, "Coronation *Ordo*," 186n213.

(*suggestione*) and law (*iure*). Perhaps this revision aimed to distinguish informal and formal systems for choosing a king; or perhaps it sought to sidestep competing claims within the royal family, by downplaying the importance of paternal endorsement. Edward and Æthelstan each overcame challengers who were themselves sons of kings, and it is conceivable that the rite's author softened the Frankish diction in anticipation of intradynastic conflict.[55]

The larger point, however, is that these earthly systems – dynasty and law – required confirmation in the ecclesiastical and spiritual spheres, through liturgical consecration. "Paternal suggestion" and "the law of inheritance" are grouped together in this passage as preliminary qualifications, presented as tenuous or conditional. The king's formal inauguration – the means by which he can keep (*retine*) his office – is achieved by two religious confirmations: first, "through the authority of God almighty"; second, "through our present tradition," as directed by bishops and clergy. In this formulation, *Ordo* 2A expands its Frankish source with a second, grammatically unnecessary "through" (*per*), which construes God's authority and "our present tradition" as separate but parallel qualifications.[56] The overall effect is a differentiation of secular and religious spheres of activity, with the former (familial and legal) ratified by the latter (divine and ecclesiastical).[57] The passage thus creates a sense of indebtedness to the "bishops and other servants of God" who facilitate the rite in accordance with divine will, and there is an expectation of reciprocity. The king is offered clear guidance: whenever he encounters clergy at the altar – as during the coronation rite – he must remember to honor them appropriately. This mnemonic aimed to link altars with the consecration ritual, in the king's mind, so he would routinely recall his sworn commitments to the Church and clergy.

After this pointed reminder, however, *Sta et retine* concludes with a more holistic view of the king's place in Christian society: now anointed, crowned, and enthroned, he is designated "the mediator between the clergy and the people." The king is granted exceptional status, distinct from both clergy and *plebis*, and the gravity of this role is emphasized

[55] Edward and his cousin Æthelwold (d. 903) shared a paternal grandfather, with each of their fathers having reigned as king. Æthelstan and his half-brothers were all Edward's sons, by two successive wives.

[56] *Per auctoritatem dei omnipotentis et per presentem traditionem nostram*. Orchard, *Ratoldus*, 54 (my emphasis). There is no second *per* in the Leiden or Eleven Forms *ordines*, but it appears in all but one manuscript of *Ordo* 2A: Jackson, *Ordines*, 163 and 190.

[57] For broader discussion, see Janet L. Nelson, "National Synods, Kingship as Office, and Royal Anointing: An Early Medieval Syndrome," in *Politics and Ritual in Early Medieval Europe* (London: Hambledon, 1986), 248–49.

by comparison with Christ, "the mediator between God and mankind." Still, this comparison highlights a significant limitation of the royal office: despite his anointing, the king does not possess divine or priestly powers of mediation.[58] His job is not to intercede directly with God on behalf of the people, but to supervise and arbitrate relations between the groups under his direct authority. As explained earlier in *Ordo* 2A:

> … totius albionis ecclesiam deinceps cum plebibus sibi annexis ita enutriat, ac doceat, muniat, et instruat, contraque omnes uisibiles et inuisibiles hostes idem potenter regaliterque tuae uirtutis regimen amministret…[59]
>
> [May the king] – along with the people attached to him – hereafter nourish, and instruct, defend, and build the Church of all Albion; and may he forcefully and royally administer the exercise of your [i.e. God's] power against all visible and invisible enemies.

The king's duty, as delineated here, is to cultivate and administer "the Church of all Albion," construed as a single entity, coterminous with the kingdom. He is to provide logistical oversight as an administrator (*amministret*), enabling the Church to advance God's power on earth; and he is to nourish (*enutriat*) and guide (*doceat*) the institution, directing its earthly course so it may survive, grow, and prosper. Alongside the legal and religious autonomy the king initially promised to bishops, this formulation delineates the limits of the king's authority over the Church. He is obliged to provide legal and logistical support to the institution – and require his followers' cooperation in these efforts – but intervention in its spiritual mission, like direct intercession with God, is beyond his purview.

The king's mediation between clergy and laity, by contrast, is a central obligation of his office, and the conclusion of *Ordo* 2A frames it as a legal imperative. *Sta et retine* is followed by a final set of conditions adapted from the English *Ordo* 1: "the three precepts," which commit the king to enforcing peace and justice.[60] Where *Sta et retine* defines the king's role in relation to the clergy, the people, and God, this passage articulates the specific responsibilities of that role. "This is the obligation (*rectitudo*)

[58] As noted by Nelson, "Ritual and Reality," 334–35; Nelson, "National Synods," 249–51; Nelson, "Liturgy or Law," 439–40. The same was true in *Ordo* 1: Pratt, *Political Thought*, 77.

[59] Orchard, *Ratoldus*, 49. For the corresponding passage in the Leiden *ordo*, see Jackson, *Ordines*, 159–60.

[60] In *Ordo* 2B, the precepts replaced the opening promise of *Ordo* 2A. For the precepts and their development, see Nelson, "Second English *Ordo*," 369–70; Nelson, "Ritual and Reality," 336–38; Pratt, "Coronation *Ordo*," 163–64; Clayton, "*Promissio regis*," 107–13; Pauline Stafford, "The Laws of Cnut and the History of Anglo-Saxon Royal Promises," *Anglo-Saxon England* 10 (1982): 173–90.

of the king, newly ordained and raised to the throne: to command these three precepts to the Christian population subject to him," namely preserving the peace; prohibiting theft and wrongdoing; and ordering just and merciful judgments.[61] The diction of this passage adheres closely to *Ordo* 1, but with significant structural revisions. In *Ordo* 1, the assembly responds *amen* after each precept is recited.[62] In *Ordo* 2A, the responses are eliminated, so the precepts become simply a list of commands for the king to issue – all articulated by the officiant, with no affirmation by the king or assembly.[63] The precepts are no longer presented as a compact with the public, ratified with a collective *amen*, but as a set of directives imposed on the king by bishops.

Even as it dispenses with public assent, however, the precepts of *Ordo* 2A present the clergy and people as a collective group, from which the king is distinguished. This is clearest in subtle verbal revisions to the source text. In the first precept on peacekeeping:[64]

Table 7.1. *Ordo* 1 and *Ordo* 2A First Precept.

Ordo **1**	*Ordo* **2A**
First, that the Church of God and the entire Christian population <u>keep true peace, in God almighty</u>.	First, that the Church of God and the entire Christian population <u>is keeping true peace at all times</u>.
Inprimis, ut ecclesia dei, et omnis populus christianus, ueram pacem <u>seruent, in omnipotenti deo</u>.	in primis ut ecclesia dei et omnis populus christianus ueram pacem <u>seruens in omni tempore</u>.

In *Ordo* 1, the Church and the people are presented as two entities who must keep the peace "in God almighty," with the plural verb *seruent* indicating separate segments of the population. By contrast, *Ordo* 2A groups the Church and populace together as one unit, using the singular gerund *seruens*.[65] Additionally, the mention of God is replaced with the phrase

[61] *Rectitudo regis est nouiter ordinati, et in solium sublimati. Haec tria praecepta populo christiano sibi subdito praecipere*. Orchard, *Ratoldus*, 54. I read *rectitudo* here as a Latin cognate to Old English *riht*.

[62] Orchard, *Leofric*, 2:432.

[63] Orchard, *Ratoldus*, 54. Compare *Ordo* 2B, in which the king – not the bishop – recites the precepts: H. A. Wilson, ed., *The Benedictional of Archbishop Robert* (London: Henry Bradshaw Society, 1903), 140.

[64] Orchard, *Leofric*, 2:432; Orchard, *Ratoldus*, 54.

[65] Other copies of *Ordo* 2A also lump *ecclesia* and *populus* together, but they (like *Ordo* 2B) use the singular subjunctive *servet* instead of the Ratold Sacramentary's gerund *servens*: Jackson, *Ordines*, 191–2; Wilson, *Benedictional*, 140.

"at all times," thereby removing any religious invocation from the king's commands to the people. Like *Sta et retine*, the revised precept denies the king the role of mediator with the divine. Still, the king is set apart from the broader population of clergy and laity – the "Christian population subject to him" – who are collectively beholden to his commands.[66] This schema is reiterated at the end of the third precept:[67]

Table 7.2. *Ordo* 1 and *Ordo* 2A Third Precept.

Ordo **1**	*Ordo* **2A**
Third, that he instruct fairness and mercy in all judgments, so that clement and merciful God may indulge his mercy by this means upon us.	Third, that he instruct fairness and mercy in all judgments, so that clement and merciful God may indulge his mercy upon him and us.
Tertium est, ut in omnibus iudiciis, aequitatem et misericordiam precipiat, ut per hoc nobis indulgeat suam misericordiam clemens et misericors deus.	Tertium est, ut in omnibus iudiciis aequitatem et misericordiam praecipiat, ut illi et nobis indulgeat sua misericordia clemens et misericors deus.

Where the officiant in *Ordo* 1 asks God to extend mercy to "us," *Ordo* 2A has that mercy directed to "him and us." The king is not part of the wider population, in this construction, but his share of God's mercy depends on his efforts to keep his subjects – *nobis* – in peace and justice.

Read together, *Ordo* 2A's preliminary promise, *Sta et retine*, and three precepts establish parameters for the king's relationship with the Church, the clergy, and the kingdom's lay population. The most abstract of these groups is the *populus*. Set in rhetorical opposition to the clergy at various points in the text, "the people" are represented by witnesses to the coronation. Even though the *populus* is sidelined in the rite's choreography, care for the Christian population is envisioned as a central royal obligation. In particular, the precepts' focus on earthly law and justice – forbidding theft and wrongdoing, establishing fair and merciful judgments – pertains directly to the security and wellbeing of the lay population. Yet where *Ordo* 1 presents the king's inauguration as a compact with his subjects, *Ordo* 2A constructs this ceremony as a transaction between the king and the bishops, to be witnessed by the people and confirmed by God. This liturgical text creates an opportunity for bishops to establish the king's obligations to the Church, define his role in ecclesiastical affairs, and set firm limits on his status as consecrated ruler. If there were questions about how a king should support

[66] Above, note 61. The word *christiano* is new since *Ordo* 1: Orchard, *Leofric*, 2:432.
[67] Orchard, *Leofric*, 2:432; Orchard, *Ratoldus*, 54.

the Church, or how he should interact with the clergy, or whether his anointing made him an intercessor with God, *Ordo* 2A would provide the answers.

* * *

It is widely acknowledged that pre-Conquest law comprised more than the extant corpus of written Old English codes.[68] Dispute resolution, economic transactions, and peacekeeping were surely guided less by royal directives than by local judgment and custom – practices and principles which varied regionally and were not systematically committed to writing.[69] Most day-to-day applications of law and justice would have fallen under the jurisdiction of local authorities: laypeople, such as ealdormen and reeves, but also bishops, abbots, abbesses, and other clergy. As secular administrators, ecclesiastics would have been involved (to varying degrees) with the implementation of civil law and justice, in accordance with local custom or royal directives.[70] They also would have been guided by Latin canons, which governed spiritual affairs and ecclesiastical business – but which also set ground rules for interactions between clergy and laity, directed the administration of ecclesiastical justice, and steered the Church's earthly operations.[71] Canonical collections may be approached as legal texts in their own right, which established principles and procedures for the institutional Church, and which directly influenced laypeople as well.[72]

I suggest here that *Ordo* 2A – however it was interpreted or administered in practice – should likewise be read as an ecclesiastical text with legal bearing. This was not liturgical prayer divorced from the political realities of kingmaking, nor a vague set of religious exhortations or platitudes. Rather, *Ordo* 2A provided a legal framework for Christian kingship, grounded in the king's formal, binding acceptance of royal obligations related to the administration of law and justice, the autonomy of ecclesiastical governance and personnel, and the responsibilities and limitations

68 See especially Wormald, "*Lex Scripta*"; Lambert, *Law and Order*, 67–82; Kristen Carella, "Northumbrian Law Before the Vikings: A Preliminary Assessment of the Evidence," in *Languages of the Law in Early Medieval Europe: Essays in Memory of Lisi Oliver*, ed. Stefan Jurasinski and Andrew Rabin (Leuven: Peeters, 2019), 45–57.

69 Wormald, "Charters, Law and the Settlement of Disputes in Anglo-Saxon England," in Wormald, *Legal Culture*, 278–311; Wormald, *Making of English Law*, esp. 143–44; Lambert, *Law and Order*, esp. 136–46; Molyneaux, *English Kingdom*, 104–15.

70 Molyneaux, *English Kingdom*, 109–10.

71 Cubitt, *Anglo-Saxon Church Councils*, 65–74; Carella, "Northumbrian Law."

72 Cubitt, *Anglo-Saxon Church Councils*, 61–63 and 241–43; Carella, "Northumbrian Law."

of the royal office. This legalistic approach is especially evident in four areas. First is the text's conception of the "Church of God" or "Church of Albion" as a legal entity, with a corporate identity which encompassed individual clergy and churches. Even though its spiritual operations were to remain independent of lay control, this institutional Church was entitled to legal rights, protections, and privileges in the world, comparable to those enjoyed by its secular counterparts. Second, the text entrusts the king with a degree of authority over the institutional Church, along with an obligation to cultivate and administer it properly. Although his influence is limited to facilitating its logistical operations and guaranteeing its legal protections, it is the king – not lesser laypeople – who bears ultimate responsibility for the Church's autonomy, prosperity, and ability to fulfill its earthly mission. Third, the text confirms the role of bishops in the kingdom's governance, placing episcopal approval among the legal requirements for kingmaking. Alongside dynastic qualifications, the law of heredity, and popular acclamation, the bishops' endorsement of a new king is presented as an indispensable element of royal inaugurations. Moreover, the bishops' central role in the rite establishes them as both gatekeepers to the royal office and mediators with the divine, with real authority over the king and his subjects – especially during transitions between regimes. Fourth, *Ordo* 2A emphasizes the unique nature of the royal office while dismissing the possibility of an intercessory connection to God. The act of anointing distinguishes the king from other laypeople and signals divine approval of his accession, according to the text, but his role is fundamentally different from the clergy's. The king is a mediator only among humans.

For all the legal imperatives in *Ordo* 2A, there are no direct verbal links between this text and written royal law codes. Perhaps the *ordo*'s authors saw an opportunity, in revising the older rite, to advance ecclesiastical priorities on their own terms. Where the laws were presented as the king's will, articulated in the king's voice, the coronation *ordo* was meant to project the authority of the bishops and foreground the interests of the Church. This new coronation liturgy may have been designed (in part) as a formal confirmation of ecclesiastical prerogatives during a period when bishops seem to have produced little legal discourse of their own.[73] Still, the *ordo* did not emerge in an intellectual or political vacuum. Its key ideas – ecclesiastical autonomy, royal protection of the Church, episcopal participation in governance, and the king's role as mediator – are all reflected in royal decrees of this period. It is possible that *Ordo* 2A codified implicit principles of Christian kingship, which influenced but were not directly

[73] On the absence of synodial canons from the mid-ninth century, see Cubitt, *Anglo-Saxon Church Councils*, 235–40.

articulated in written laws. For example, Alfred's *domboc* – notwithstanding its iteration of biblical law and occasional calls for penance – is remarkably restrained in its religious regulation.[74] Nowhere does the text encroach on episcopal authority or threaten the spiritual integrity of the Church. On the contrary, the *domboc* embraces the principles of collaboration, protection, and mediation which were prioritized in the *ordo*. As other lawmaking kings had (and would), Alfred acknowledged the contribution of his counselors, a cohort which included religious advisors.[75] However, his laws go further than any earlier royal code in their articulation of episcopal rights and ecclesiastical autonomy. The *domboc* repeatedly awards compensation to bishops for violations of ecclesiastical rights or offenses against the clergy; it grants enhanced protections to consecrated churches, through the confirmation of church-peace; and it takes for granted that penitential procedures and canonical penalties would run parallel to secular systems of justice.[76] Moreover, the *domboc* integrates the episcopal administration of penance into secular judicial procedures:

> Gif he þonne þæs weddige þe hym riht sy to gelæstanne 7 þæt aleoge, selle mid eaðmedum his wæpn 7 his æhta his freondum to gehealdanne 7 beo feowertig nihta on carcerne on cyninges tune; ðrowige ðær swa biscep him scrife, 7 his mægas hine feden, gif he self mete næbbe.[77]

> If [someone] pledges something that is lawful for him to fulfill and repudiates it, let him humbly give his weapons and possessions to his friends to hold and spend forty nights in prison on an estate of the king; let him suffer there as the bishop prescribes for him, and let his family feed him, if he has no food himself.

This clause treats pledge-breaking as a twofold offense: it is a violation of royal law, punishable by imprisonment, but also a sin which merits penance.[78] The spiritual penalty is left entirely to the bishop's judgment, with the royal law governing only the practical conditions under which

74 Marafioti, "Laws of Alfred."

75 Alfred Prol. 49.9; Jurasinski and Oliver, *Laws of Alfred*, 281n9.

76 For compensation awarded to bishops for violations of episcopal protection, ecclesiastical property, and nuns: Alfred 3, 9, 17(=L 15), 41(=L 40). For sanctuary and church-peace (*cirican frið*): Alfred 2, 5–5.4, 44.2 (=L 42.2). For penance, confession, and excommunication: Alfred 1.2, 1.7–1.8, 5.4, 16 (=L 14). See also Alfred 25 (=L 21), which confirms the bishop's right to depose a homicidal priest. For further discussion, see Marafioti, "Laws of Alfred."

77 Alfred 1.2, and see also 1.7–1.8.

78 For imprisonment as penitential, see Daniel Thomas, "Incarceration as Judicial Punishment in Anglo-Saxon England," in *Capital and Corporal Punishment in Anglo-Saxon England*, ed. Jay Paul Gates and Nicole Marafioti (Woodbridge: Boydell, 2014), 92–112.

the offender's penance must be completed: forty days of confinement, provisioned by his family while under the king's protection. Alfred, as the putative author of this law, is situated as mediator between the people and the clergy, dictating the terms of legal reconciliation and facilitating interactions between the offender, his allies, and the clergy.[79] By providing logistical instructions and confirming the bishop's right to impose judgment, the king enables the smooth administration of ecclesiastical justice and affirms the need for sinners to submit to the clergy.

Regulations like these seem entirely in line with *Ordo* 2A's vision of the king as "mediator between the clergy and the people," who must "preserve the privilege of the canons, and due law, and justice, and dispense protection." Whether the *ordo* pre- or post-dated the compilation of the *domboc*, the two texts seem to share an understanding of royal obligation toward the Church. Yet *Ordo* 2A may have also aimed to restrain royal ambitions in religious affairs. Alfred's *domboc* framed royal lawmaking as a direct continuation of biblical tradition, and it is conceivable that this approach was regarded by some – perhaps even members of the king's inner circle – as presumption or overreach. Conspicuously, the decrees of Alfred's son Edward contain no references at all to religious matters. Even if Edward's written laws were intended to supplement (rather than replace) his father's, it is remarkable that his laws omit the religious rhetoric and attention to ecclesiastical rights which infused the *domboc*.[80] Framed as commands to his reeves or admonishments to the *witan*, his two extant law codes are predominantly concerned with secular judicial procedures.[81] However, his laws' focus on peace and justice aligns closely with the *ordo*'s three precepts, particularly in II Edward: after urging the assembly to consider "how their peace could be better than it was before," the text proclaims that no one may deprive another of justice, establishes rules for trying thieves, prohibits various subversions and evasions of the law, and orders regularly scheduled judicial assemblies so "everyone may be worthy of public justice."[82] This adheres closely to the requirements, in *Ordo* 2A, that the king command or instruct (*praecipere*) his subordinates to keep the peace, to prohibit "thefts and all wrongdoing," and to ensure fairness in all *iudiciis* – that is, judgments or judicial proceedings.[83] Even

79 See Alfred 1.4–1.8 for increasingly severe penalties for pledge-breakers who resist this sentence.

80 For Edward's laws as supplementary to Alfred's, see I Edward Prol.; II Edward 5; Wormald, *Making of English Law*, 286–90.

81 I Edward Prol.; II Edward Prol.

82 II Edward Prol.: *hu heora frið betere beon mæhte, þonne hit ær ðam wæs*. II Edward 8: *ðæt ælc man sy folcrihtes wyrðe*.

83 Orchard, *Ratoldus*, 54: *rapacitates et omnes iniquitates*.

without direct attention to the rights of the Church, Edward's laws fulfill the obligations laid out by the bishops at his consecration.

Religious policies revived under Æthelstan, with decrees which directly acknowledged the advice of bishops and reinforced ecclesiastical initiatives such as almsgiving, tithing, and penance.[84] As in Alfred's *domboc*, these policies governed the logistics of devotional activity and construed neglect of certain religious obligations as disobedience to the king.[85] However, in Æthelstan's laws, there is a more pronounced focus on the exceptionality of the royal office, with the king distinguished clearly from his clerical and lay subjects.[86] This effect is accomplished through the rhetorical pairing of bishops with their lay counterparts, and their collective differentiation from the king – an approach which echoes the groupings of "clergy and people" or "bishops or clergy and also the people" in *Ordo* 2A.[87] This division is sometimes articulated in Æthelstan's own voice, but subject communities also presented themselves as groups of clergy and laity, collectively beholden to the king.[88] The citizens of London, led by the city's "bishops and reeves," acknowledged the need to preserve "the peace and those pledges which we have given and which the king has asked of us"; while lay and clerical leaders in Kent thanked Æthelstan for his willingness "to instruct (*precipere*) us concerning our peace, and for inquiring and advising concerning our interests."[89] In these formulations, the king is presented as an outsider empowered to shape local policy – hierarchically superior, but with legal responsibility for the wellbeing of clergy and laity alike.

This brand of royal oversight may have been justified by the king's obligation to keep the peace, a central royal commitment in *Ordo* 2A

[84] Bishops are acknowledged in I Æthelstan Prol., Æthelstan Alms Prol., II Æthelstan Epil.; councilors are acknowledged in the prologues of IV and V Æthelstan. Policies for almsgiving and tithing are detailed in Æthelstan Alms and I Æthelstan. Penance for swearing falsely is prescribed in II Æthelstan 26–26.1: see Marafioti, "Unconsecrated Burial."

[85] Æthelstan Alms 2; I Æthelstan 5.

[86] As Patrick Wormald notes, Edward's decrees had already begun to construe the law as an expression of the king's will: *Making of English Law*, 288.

[87] Orchard, *Ratoldus*, 54 and 47: *Cleri et plebi*; *episcoporum ac clericorum necnon populorum*.

[88] I Æthelstan 1: "I want bishops and reeves to command this to everyone who must obey them" (*ic wille, þæt biscopas 7 þa gerefan hit beodan eallum þam þe him hiran sculon*).

[89] VI Æthelstan Prol. and 8.9: *þa biscopas 7 þa gerefan*; *þæs friðes 7 þæs weddes, þe we seald habbað 7 se cyng us beboden hafað*. III Æthelstan Prol.: *gratias agunt, quod nobis de pace nostra precipere uoluisti et de commodo nostro querere et consulere*. Compare the three precepts' requirement that the king command (*praecipere*) his subordinates: Orchard, *Ratoldus*, 54.

which was cited repeatedly in Æthelstan's laws, as it was in Edward's.[90] Yet Æthelstan's religious decrees also provide – for the first time in pre-Conquest law – an explicit justification for royal intervention in religious matters: the king is personally answerable to God. On the one hand, Æthelstan is presented as God's agent, whose religious mandates aligned with divine will: neglecting these policies would incur both judicial penalties and divine wrath (*Godes irre*).[91] On the other hand, Æthelstan is depicted as a human whose own salvation is at stake: he issued religious policies "for the remission of my sins and the acquisition of eternal life."[92] The king was not an intercessor with the divine, as *Ordo* 2A made clear, but Æthelstan's religious decrees tied his own salvation to his enforcement of God's commands and cultivation of the Church. This model of Christian kingship would gain force in the decades ahead, with later generations of English kings taking an active hand in the kingdom's religious reforms and presenting themselves as God's earthly advocates.[93] In the early tenth century, however, Æthelstan's decrees were novel in construing the act of lawmaking as an expression of royal piety – a formulation which closely followed the model of Christian kingship articulated in *Ordo* 2A.

The dating of *Ordo* 2A continues to be debated, but there is a strong likelihood that it was produced by Alfred's advisors, with his successors' coronations in mind.[94] Whether or not this text was employed for Edward's consecration, it seems to have been in use by the time Æthelstan was crowned in 925.[95] Whether it informed or reflected the priorities of royal legislation, *Ordo* 2A presented a vision of Christian kingship consistent with the written decrees of this period. The turn of the tenth century was an ambitious period of royal lawmaking, and it seems natural that

90 III Æthelstan Prol., V Æthelstan Prol., VI Æthelstan Prol. and 10.

91 I Æthelstan 5.

92 Æthelstan Alms Prol.: *ad remissionem peccatorum meorum et adquisitionem vitę ęternę*. Spiritual justification for religious policy is likewise provided in I Æthelstan 2–3. Compare also V Æthelstan 3, which commissions psalms to be sung weekly "for the king, and for everyone who wants what the king wants, and for others, as they deserve" (*for þone cyng 7 for ealle þe willaþ ðæt he wile 7 for þa oþre, swa hy geearnian*).

93 VIII Æthelred 2.1 states that "a Christian king is Christ's representative" (*Cristen cyning is Cristes gespelia*). See also I Edmund; II and IV Edgar; V–X Æthelred; and I Cnut. For ecclesiastical praise of royal intervention in monastic reform, see Nicole Marafioti, "The Legacy of King Edgar in the Laws of Archbishop Wulfstan," in *Remembering the Medieval Present: Generative Uses of England's Pre-Conquest Past, 10th to 15th Centuries*, ed. Jay Paul Gates and Brian T. O'Camb (Leiden: Brill, 2019), 21–50.

94 Pratt, "Coronation *Ordo*."

95 Nelson, "First Use." It is possible that Edward's coronation followed *Ordo* 1, which also included the three precepts: see above.

the ecclesiastical authors of a new coronation *ordo* would pursue a similarly ambitious approach, as they negotiated their own position – and the Church's – in response to royal expansion. It is possible that *Ordo* 2A was regarded as a radical document when it premiered, with its refashioning of the older English rite and its extensive use of Frankish content. The subtlety of verbal changes suggests that its sources' diction lent legitimacy to the new rite, yet *Ordo* 2A offered a fresh perspective by foregrounding the king's obligations to his subjects and the Church. The ambition of this approach may be gauged by subsequent revisions. In the later tenth century, the opening promises of *Ordo* 2A were omitted entirely from *Ordo* 2B and replaced with the three precepts: these were now spoken in the king's voice instead of a bishop's; and they were rendered after the king's prostration, not as a precondition of his anointing. Perhaps the opening section of *Ordo* 2A was considered controversial or presumptuous, with its elevation of episcopal authority and displays of royal deference. At the time of its composition, however, *Ordo* 2A may have reflected a new reliance on bishops as administrators of royal policies; or a tighter delineation of secular and ecclesiastical authority, in the wake of ninth-century disputes; or a reconceptualization of the political limits of the kingdom, with a corporate English Church mirroring the ideological (if not yet real) political consolidation to which Alfred and his descendants aspired. In any of these interpretations, *Ordo* 2A offers an important counterpoint to vernacular royal decrees. Where royal law codes present ecclesiastical rights and protections as one-time initiatives, issued by individual kings, *Ordo* 2A does something different: it creates ecclesiastical policy which attached to the royal office, transcending the reign of any single ruler and becoming a condition of legitimate, consecrated kingship.

8

The Passive Ealdorman? Juxtaposing the Later Old English Law Codes and the "Dispute Narratives"[1]

Mary Elizabeth Blanchard

Pre-Conquest ealdormen, and their eleventh-century counterpart earls, can cut dramatic figures in the surviving Old English and Latin corpora.[2] The *Anglo-Saxon Chronicle* often provides terse descriptions of military leaders and royal councilors engaging in acts of heroics, cowardice, or betrayal. Surviving saints' *vitae* and house chronicles frequently include these secular officials as side characters who either help or hinder the main saint or community depending on specific ealdormen's friendship to the protagonist. Close examination of these ecclesiastically centered works reveals that politics often had a more significant influence on how these secular men interacted with clerics or monastic houses than clerical authors openly acknowledge. Yet ealdormen often remain mysterious figures and the nature of their official duties, particularly in non-military situations, is often left vague or unsaid in the extant sources. To discover the possible duties of the ealdorman within the legal culture of the period, it is necessary to turn to the law codes from later pre-Conquest England (here defined as 871–1066) as well as the surviving records of litigation, some of which only survive in post-Conquest copies. These sources provide different and sometimes conflicting pictures, but taken together they offer a glimpse of the potential duties and legal responsibilities assigned to ealdormen. In the surviving laws, these secular leaders seem to be allocated a more passive role when compared with other appointed positions, specifically bishops and reeves. The litigation records, however, particularly the "dispute charters," portray ealdormen

1 An earlier version of this chapter was presented in 2018 at the International Congress on Medieval Studies at Kalamazoo. The author thanks all those in the audience who made comments and suggestions.

2 Despite a transition in the terminology used under Cnut from *ealdormann* to *eorl*, there is little evidence of substantial changes to the position itself except for the decreasing number of officials appointed through the eleventh century. Fewer earls led to increasingly large earldoms.

actively as witnesses, judges, and overseers of cases. These latter sources, while undoubtedly legal texts, also contain narrative literary elements, which are particularly apparent as they attempt to establish one official story to the exclusion of other potential contending accounts. In this more expansive narrative space, details emerge to suggest that ealdormen in the tenth and eleventh centuries took on a number of official roles and participated actively in a range of legal functions.

In terms of composition, these records of litigation do not always fall into standard charter forms. Some of the cases can only be found in post-Conquest monastic chronicles, or cartulary-chronicles as they are sometimes called, which already places them closer to narrative sources and less formulaic records.[3] Others take the form of letters or writs of personal statements providing one person's witness support of a claimant or version of the estate's history.[4] Even the single-sheet "dispute charters" examined below, which record quarrels and the resulting litigation, do not seamlessly fit with the more formulaic and generally shorter standard charters. The more "standard" charters often only record that an estate has been bought or given from one party to another while the "dispute" charters typically include narrative histories of the relevant estates. Sarah Foot has argued for the need to reconsider the approach to early English charters in general and analyze them as narrative sources.[5] Even though a charter describes a sequence of events through formulaic means this does not mean it is not a story if scholars "are satisfied it contains those elements we expect of a narrative: an opening and some form of end; a central subject (or subject matter) around which its story is told; a clear temporal location, albeit one not exclusive to a single time-frame (present, past, or future)."[6] While Foot analyzes the more standard pre-Conquest charters, her metric is especially applicable to the longer "dispute char-

3 Sarah Foot, "Reading Anglo-Saxon Charters: Memory, Record or Story?" in *Narrative and History in the Early Medieval West*, ed. Elizabeth M. Tyler and Ross Balzaretti (Turnhout: Brepols, 2006), 44. Part of the argument for this name is that these particular texts often interweave a religious house's history together with the basics of charters and wills in (or at least claimed to be in) the abbey's possession.

4 I am loosely following Simon Keynes's subdivisions of litigation records into (a) letters or personal statements, (b) impersonal or "institutional" statements about an estate's history, and (c) records of settlements of disputes, found in Simon Keynes, "The 'Cuckhamsley Chirograph,'" in *Languages of the Law in Early Medieval England: Essays in Memory of Lisi Oliver*, ed. Stefan Jurasinski and Andrew Rabin (Leuven: Peeters, 2019), 195–97 with a helpful chart at 210. Keynes, however, focuses on the Old English corpus and thus does not address cases from the *Liber Eliensis* or *Chronicon abbatiae Rameseiensis*.

5 Foot, "Reading Anglo-Saxon Charters," 46–49.

6 Ibid., 49.

ters." These charters were often written after competing claims on an estate led to an official legal process to determine the owner.

Therefore, the lawsuits under discussion offer limited subject matter: all revolve around varying claims to land. They thus tend to present a skewed picture of the general legal system, particularly in excluding the legal culture experienced by those below the land-owning elites. Tom Lambert, partially motivated by this concern, focuses less on the detail of land disputes in his account of local legal practices in pre-Conquest England.[7] This evidentiary choice may explain why he devotes less discussion to ealdormen and earls than previous historians and is disinclined to attribute many legal duties to them, particularly in the tenth century, emphasizing the local leaders of the new hundred court system as opposed to "royal agents" or a "network of officials."[8] Part of the difference in interpretation between Lambert and other scholars, best represented by Patrick Wormald, may lie in Lambert's focus on justice in local communities, whereas the latter often start with the king and his elite councilors. Ealdormen, as part of the aristocratic elite, may have had more interest in or even more duties in regard to who owned what in the areas within their ealdordoms. In fact, this chapter will suggest that ealdormen needed to keep track of who owned which estates in order to perform some of their official obligations.

This chapter demonstrates that the "dispute charters" challenge modern genre divisions between legal records and literary narrative. Indeed, while their format is comparable to the standard layout of authentic charters, their inclusion of narrative links them closely to chronicles. The cases examined below are formatted as chronicles, charters, and writs but they all share common elements which place them in what will be called "dispute narratives" in the following analysis. While these charters and writs are a part of legal culture they also contain narrative literary elements, particularly these documents' use of narrative attempts to establish the official story behind a disputed estate. These narratives were often (but not always) agreed upon by those involved after the case had

7 Tom Lambert, *Law and Order in Anglo-Saxon England* (Oxford: Oxford University Press, 2017), Chapter 6.

8 Ibid., 250, 293. Cf. Patrick Wormald, "Charters, Law and the Settlement of Disputes in Anglo-Saxon England," in Wormald, *Legal Culture*, 304; Levi Roach, *Kingship and Consent in Anglo-Saxon England, 871–978: Assemblies and the State in the Early Middle Ages* (Cambridge: Cambridge University Press, 2013), 144; George Molyneaux, *The Formation of the English Kingdom in the Tenth Century* (Oxford: Oxford University Press, 2015), 179–80; and Keynes, "Cuckhamsley Chirograph," 200. Wormald, Roach, Molyneaux, and Keynes all seem more inclined to assume ealdormen had duties beyond military leadership.

appeared before a royal, shire, or hundred court.[9] This is especially true of those disputes which span multiple years or generations, some of which begin with a different event not involving the estate itself. These litigation records are perhaps the most fascinating as they reveal familial if not communal history based on a combination of oral memory and written charter-deeds. As Foot points out, charters are not necessarily *the* story but rather one side's version of events which they are attempting to make the official account in the face of a competing history.[10] While all charters can be analyzed in this way, the dispute charters offer a clear example of how narrative could be used in early English legal culture. These disputes also augment the picture of high-ranking officials painted by the law codes as their narrative detail offers new insight into the larger legal activities of the kingdom.

Appearances in Old English Law Codes

A survey of the law codes for the duties specific to ealdormen, bishops, and reeves reveals an interesting pattern.[11] That is, the later in the pre-Conquest period a king issued a law code, the less direct mention of ealdormen it contains. Ealdormen (and earls) seem almost non-existent and bishops and reeves appear prominently in comparison. This survey helps to reveal which types of officials early English rulers tended to address or order to uphold the laws within the codes themselves. For brief comparative purposes, the late seventh-century laws of Ine are also included. While the laws of Ine were written in a different ecclesiastical-political environment, the same case can be made for Alfred's *domboc* in comparison to the majority of his successors, particularly those kings following Æthelstan. The point here is to highlight ealdormen's appearances in the Old English laws and to examine why, in spite of different political and social circumstances which could have changed the focus of the kingdom's laws, the trend throughout is that these officials appear less in the later codes.

The prologue to the laws of Ine states that the king along with his ealdormen and chief councilors gathered in order "that true law and true statutes might be established and strengthened throughout our people, so that none of the ealdormen or of our subjects might afterwards pervert

9 Certain cases appeared before all three until a decision was made.

10 Foot, "Reading Anglo-Saxon Charters," 63.

11 I have grouped these three officials together as they all appear to be acting in the name of someone else and the king had (at least nominally) a say in the appointment of all three positions.

these our decrees."[12] Two centuries later King Æthelstan commanded all bishops, ealdorman, and reeves to "observe the peace just as I and my councilors have enacted it."[13] According to III Edgar, the shire court should meet twice a year, convened in the presence of the bishop of the diocese and the ealdorman, and both were "to expound both the ecclesiastical and the secular law."[14] The third law code of Æthelred states "the peace which the ealdorman and the king's reeve give in the meeting of the Five Boroughs that is to be atoned for with twelve hundred."[15] Cnut's letter of 1020 sends greetings to his people, specifically his bishops, earls, and men of twelve hundred and two hundred wergilds.[16] Earls are mentioned only on one other occasion; after charging the prelates to be "zealous about God's dues" the king adds, "I charge all my ealdormen that they help the bishops in furthering God's rights and my royal dignity and the benefit of all the people."[17] The same king's second letter in 1027 exhorts, "I implore and command my councilors, to whom I have entrusted the councils of the kingdom, that from now on they shall not in any way either for fear of me or for the favor of any powerful person, consent to any injustice, or suffer it to flourish in any part of my kingdom."[18] Cnut's letter is unclear as to whether he meant secular and ecclesiastical persons but certainly makes no direct reference to reeves. Both letters do specifically address reeves in other sections, indicating that they should work in conjunction with bishops.[19] Cnut's laws, however, do not address or lay out any duties for earls specifically although bishops and reeves are mentioned in connection with collecting or paying fines.[20] Comparison with the early

[12] Laws of Ine, Prologue. For translation, see Dorothy Whitelock, ed. and trans., *English Historical Documents. Volume I: c.500–1042*, 2nd ed. (London: Oxford University Press, 1979), no. 32. (Unless otherwise noted, translations of laws come from *EHD*.) In many ways this statement reflects later tenth- and eleventh-century comments directed at reeves.

[13] VI Æthelstan 11. *EHD*, no. 37

[14] III Edgar 5.1–5.2. *EHD*, no. 40.

[15] III Æthelred 1.1. *EHD*, no. 43.

[16] Cnut 1020 1. *EHD*, no. 48.

[17] Cnut 1020, 8. The next two paragraphs do mention Earl Thorkel, commanding him "if he can, to cause the evil-doer to do right" (9). This exhortation comes after a comment that if someone will not make amends after breaking the law (secular or ecclesiastical) and does not desist at the bishop's direction then Thorkel was to step in. If the wrongdoer persisted, Thorkel "with the power of us both he shall destroy him in the land or drive him out of the land" (10). As this seems only to be directed at a specific official who was likely acting as regent of England at the time, I do not classify these comments in the same way as those more clearly addressed to ealdormen or earls in general.

[18] Cnut 1027, 11. *EHD*, no. 49.

[19] Cnut 1020, 11 and Cnut 1027, 11.

[20] See, e.g., II Cnut 8.2 and 48.1. *EHD*, no. 50.

laws of Ine highlights not only the expectation of early English kings that their officials to uphold the laws but also the fact that they did have concerns about secular officials abusing their positions of authority. By the later tenth century there was a distinctive shift in focus to lower-level offices which appears to coincide with the increase in the royal use of shire-reeves (*scirgerefa*).[21] Later pre-Conquest rulers worried about abuse of office but they directed their exhortations at their reeves.[22]

VI Æthelstan is particularly revealing, as the king commanded all three types of royal officials to uphold the peace but notably only threatened the reeve with punishment for failing to do so. If the reeve did not follow the dictates of his position, the king threatened to remove him from office and no longer offered friendship to the man.[23] The lack of directly stated consequences for bishops and ealdormen who also received commands to uphold justice may indicate that, in general, Æthelstan and his successors felt confident in explicit threats only against reeves' official positions.[24] The early English kings were not powerless against their other officials as there is evidence of royal orders to exile, maim, or even kill ealdormen; while bishops, although rarely removed from office, could find themselves banished from the royal court if they earned the king's displeasure. Explicit written threats, however, are lacking in the extant sources. Ealdormen and bishops were perhaps more difficult to remove from office than reeves, and drafting legislation that commanded without specifying a punishment may have allowed the king the flexibility to devise politically manageable chastisement or retribution for recalcitrant ealdormen. Bishops and ealdormen were powerful in their own right and could have strong local ties, based on either family or a long reign, and thus be entrenched in local society. The difficulties caused by such political and social ties are amply demonstrated by two brief examples. Eadwig's apparent exile of Bishop Cynsige of Lichfield from his court in the late 950s, after this particular bishop may have been involved in chastising the young king at his own coronation, shows a ruler likely able to bar a prelate from his court but not to remove him from office.[25] Eadric

21 See Molyneaux, *Formation of the English Kingdom*, 179–82; and Lambert, *Law and Order*, 293.

22 See IV Edgar 1.5; VIII Æthelred 32; Cnut 1020, 11; Cnut 1027, 12; II Æthelstan 25.

23 VI Æthelstan 11.

24 The laws of Ine is the only law code I have come across which has an explicit threat against ealdormen who do not properly perform their duties. Ine 36.1: "If he is an ealdorman [and lets a thief go], he is to lose his office, unless the king wishes to pardon him."

25 The exile of Cynsige is implied by his lack of attestations in the late 950s. See Simon Keynes, *An Atlas of Attestations in Anglo-Saxon Charters, c.670–1066* (Department of Anglo-Saxon, Norse and Celtic, University of Cambridge, 1998), Table XLVIII.

Streona's infamous changing allegiances between the Alfredian line and the invader Cnut was seemingly rewarded by Cnut's confirmation of the man as ealdorman of Mercia. Yet, Cnut's ordered execution of Eadric Streona a year later indicates not a true reward but a biding of time by the new king before he removed a powerful nobleman.[26]

Two possible reasons behind these pointed exhortations to reeves are that shire-reeves may have misused their powers more frequently than ealdormen, or that the higher officials may not have taken part regularly in local issues. Both may be true. Work by Nicole Marafioti and Alaric Trousdale on the laws of Alfred and his great-grandson Edmund respectively may offer a third possibility. Marafioti notes that fines concerning the violation of an archbishop or bishop's surety, peace, or dwelling reveal they were treated no differently than lay leaders of equivalent rank.[27] For example, a man drawing a weapon in the bishop's presence was fined based on the prelate's temporal standing (judged as equivalent to that of an ealdorman) not the spiritual nature of his office. Marafioti does not deny that ecclesiastical processes were present, in fact she argues that the *domboc* assumed such an infrastructure was in place with King Alfred appropriating the system "by deputizing the clergy in the process of secular law-enforcement."[28] If Marafioti is correct then the law codes might be expected to have increasing references to bishops as their place as deputies was normalized into the judicial system, something that does occur in the later laws.

This corresponds with Trousdale's work on the laws of Edmund. Examining the so-called *Chapters*, a tenth-century document by Archbishop Oda of Canterbury, alongside Edmund's three law codes, Trousdale comes to the conclusion that particularly I Edmund contains a "systematic approach at delineating the rights and obligations of bishops with respect to their local spheres of administration and their responsibilities to the king."[29] Both Alfred and Edmund were dealing with an expanded

[26] For Eadric Streona's confirmation as ealdorman of Mercia, see Katherine O'Brien O'Keeffe, ed., *The Anglo-Saxon Chronicle: A Collaborative Edition, Volume 5: MS. C* (Cambridge: D. S. Brewer, 2001), s.a. 1017. Unless otherwise noted, all Chronicle translations are based on Dorothy Whitelock, Susie I. Tucker and David C. Douglas, eds. and trans., *The Anglo-Saxon Chronicle: A Revised Translation* (London: Eyre & Spottiswoode, 1961).

[27] Nicole Marafioti, "Crime and Sin in the Laws of Alfred," in *Languages of the Law in Early Medieval England: Essays in Memory of Lisi Oliver*, ed. Stefan Jurasinski and Andrew Rabin (Leuven: Peeters, 2019), 63. Marafioti is referring specifically to Alfred 3, 15, 38.2, and 40.

[28] Marafioti, "Crime and Sin," 74.

[29] Alaric A. Trousdale, "Being Everywhere at Once: Delegation and Royal Authority in Late Anglo-Saxon England," in *Languages of the Law in Early Medieval England: Essays in Memory of Lisi Oliver*, ed. Stefan Jurasinski and Andrew Rabin (Leuven: Peeters, 2019), 280.

kingdom; Alfred's moves to encourage organization and local administrative self-sufficiency are particularly well documented.[30] Thus, bishops appear more frequently in the law codes of the early and mid-tenth century as they are incorporated more into the local legal culture under the auspices of the king.[31] This may well also explain the increasing frequency of reeves in the late tenth-century and eleventh-century legal codes. As kings introduced the further use of shire-reeves as administrators, their legal duties, particularly in the local community, may have required clear presentation and establishment via royal declaration. Pushing this idea slightly further, ealdormen's duties may not be mentioned because they had been part of the system long enough that it was unnecessary to tell the localities what they did.

Most of the laws which deal with or mention ealdormen emphasize their high social status. A running theme throughout many Old English law codes was that anyone who was caught forcibly entering an ealdormen's dwelling, drawing a weapon in his presence, or breaking his surety paid a fine.[32] Alfred's law code states: "If anyone fights or draws a weapon in the presence of the archbishop, he is to pay 150 shillings compensation; if this happens in the presence of another bishop or an ealdorman, he is to pay 100 shillings compensation."[33] Cnut's second law code commands, "if anyone violates a diocesan bishop's or an ealdorman's surety, he is to compensate for it with two pounds."[34] Furthermore, an ealdorman (or sometimes a bishop) could also receive a fine or portion of one from judicial proceedings. Payment of this type (a set of fines referred to as the third penny) was often a multiple of three, with two-thirds paid to the king and the final third given to the local ealdorman.[35] Again II Cnut provides a clear example: "And he who refuses to follow just law and just judgment, is to be liable to pay [a fine] in the area under English law to him who has a right to it, either to the king 120 shillings, or to the earl 60 shillings, or to

30 Ibid., 291.

31 There may have been interest in clear delineation of bishops' judicial duties by leading ecclesiastical figures in the buildup to the Benedictine reform during the mid-tenth century which may have also contributed to their more frequent appearances in the law codes. I would like to thank the editors of this volume for this suggestion.

32 See Ine 6.2, 45; Alfred 3, 15, 38–38.2, 40; III Æthelred 12; II Cnut 15.2, 30.6, 58.2, 71a.

33 Alfred 15.

34 II Cnut 58.2.

35 For a concise overview of the third penny in late pre-Conquest England, see Stephen Baxter, *The Earls of Mercia: Lordship and Power in Late Anglo-Saxon England* (Oxford: Oxford University Press, 2007), 89–97. Lambert offers thoughtful reinterpretations in *Law and Order*, 337–42, placing this fine alongside the evidence for other fines in the judicial system.

the hundred 30 shillings, or to each of them, if it so happens."[36] Between the third penny and the other laws which emphasize the ealdormen's status, it becomes clear that these royal officials were socially important men. Yet, the examples cited above provide something else as well, an image of ealdormen as passive members of the judicial system. Their status was defined in terms of fines and compensation owed to them but they themselves are generally prescribed no specific duty.

Active ealdormen in the royal law codes are more difficult to find. Examples do exist but in case of the later law codes it remains unclear if the duties applied to all ealdormen or just to a specific event in each individual case. The laws of Ine indicate that men involved in a lawsuit could intercede with the local ealdorman.[37] Alfred's law code provides a few more possible activities, including acting as a witness for a man who decided to seek a lord outside his own district and appointing a deputy to attend regional meetings for him.[38] This code additionally offers one other activity in which ealdormen may have participated – lending support to a man besieging another in order to obtain justice. It reads: "If he [the attacker] has not sufficient power to besiege him in his house, he is to ride to the ealdorman and ask him for support; if he will not give him support he is to ride to the king, before having recourse to fighting."[39] While an ealdorman's duties may have included providing help to those seeking justice at the local level from obstinate offenders, the final line here indicates the royal official did not always exert himself to do so. As the ealdordoms grew bigger the ealdormen may well have not been able to fulfill certain duties such as attending the two annual shire meetings in the various shires encompassed in their region. Perhaps, as Alfred's laws suggest, they then used their own family members or even their own reeves (as opposed to a royal reeve), as representatives.[40] Some duties formerly undertaken by ealdormen were likely shifted to shire-reeves, or, as the administrative apparatus evolved with an expanding kingdom, new

36 II Cn, 15.2.

37 Ine 50: "If a *gesith*-born man intercedes with the king or the king's ealdorman or with his lord for members of his household, slaves or freemen, he, the *gesith*, has no right to any fines, because he would not previously at home restrain them from wrong-doing."

38 Alfred 37 and 38.2.

39 Alfred 42.3.

40 See S 1472. Charters are cited from P. H. Sawyer, *Anglo-Saxon Charters: An Annotated List and Bibliography* (London: Royal Historical Society, 1968), revised S. E. Kelly, ed., *The Electronic Sawyer*, http://esawyer.org.uk/about /index.html. The case recorded in the Hereford Gospel includes among the witnesses "Eadwine, the ealdorman's [son]" (*Edwine þæs ealdormannes*). An Earl Hranig is also listed but this Eadwine is believed to be one of the sons of Earl Leofwine of Mercia, whose death is recorded in 1039.

duties were developed specifically for reeves and bishops. Cnut's first letter indicates that earls were still expected to help with obstinate local offenders, meaning some duties which appear in Alfred's laws continued into the eleventh century. The overall picture presented by later Old English law codes, however, is that of ealdormen and earls as passive, if high-ranking, figures within legal culture. The question remains whether the dispute narratives support this image.

Appearances in Dispute Narratives

The records of land disputes documented in letters, charters, writs, and house chronicles such as the *Liber Eliensis* and Ramsey Abbey's *Liber benefactorum* reveal an interesting pattern when placed in juxtaposition with the Old English law codes. In these texts, ealdormen appear actively as witnesses, judges, and overseers of cases. The ecclesiastical nature (and relatively late date) of these surviving sources likely cause a slightly skewed perspective since, particularly in those cases incorporated into the cartulary-chronicles, the clergy were often a claimant in the lawsuits. Understandably, a bishop (or abbot) could not be both judge and personally involved in the case.[41] The various litigation records reveal that the ealdormen could have extensive oversight of dispute settlement. Ealdormen do not appear in all lawsuit records, and they were not the only or perhaps even the primary judges in all cases. As Tom Lambert has pointed out, both lawmen (presumably those with knowledge of royal law codes) and judges are mentioned in the records but there is no indication these were always the men who presided over the meeting.[42] But even without making the litigation records stand as evidence for ealdormen habitually or frequently sitting in judgment, the significance of the opposition between the sources is clear. The law codes often indicate nothing beyond their status as important men, while the litigation records reveal they were present at and sometimes very active in lawsuits. A possible reason for this difference was canvassed above: the outcome of estate disputes may have been of more interest or fallen more securely

[41] If an ealdorman was a claimant he also does not appear to have sat in judgment on that particular case. The *Liber Eliensis* records the history of Hatfield (Herts) which became a disputed estate between Bishop Æthelwold (on behalf of his foundation at Ely) and Ealdorman Æthelwine and his brothers. This agreement took place in the presence of Ealdromen Ælfhere, Ælfric *Cild*, and Æthelwine as well as "the whole of the retinue accompanying them." See Janet Fairweather, trans., *Liber Eliensis: A History of the Isle of Ely from the Seventh Century to the Twelfth* (Woodbridge: Boydell, 2005), ii.7; hereafter *LE*.

[42] Lambert, *Law and Order*, 138–41.

under the purview of ealdormen as these cases involved not only higher status claimants but also necessitated clarifying who owned which estates within a specific official's ealdordom.

As Patrick Wormald noted, no surviving lawsuits actually cite a law.[43] There is good reason to believe, however, that informal negotiations took place ahead of the case appearing before the assembly (or perhaps even during the assembly); such negotiations were unlikely to be included in the written record except for the agreed-upon settlement in the "official" account.[44] The informal negotiations might have not only been between the different claimants but also involved important members of the assembly. Lambert points out that sometimes *who* the assembly decided could present proof of ownership determined who would win.[45] Levi Roach observes that absolute victory was not necessarily the end goal of these informal negotiations or the court cases but rather re-establishment or renegotiation of relations often ending with compromise.[46] Agreements were quite possibly negotiated once, or perhaps even before, the assembly decided who could present proof. The actual agreements made before the assemblies then become performative public acts in front of the community.[47] The final result of these informal negotiations became the official history of the estate, but for ealdormen what may have mattered the most was that a clear owner emerged rather than which side won the case. The additional concern of forfeiture for the stealing of an estate or another crime adds another layer to the proceedings. Penitent elements of submission in the relinquishing of a claim were countered by merciful or forgiving performance as the side that "won" the case publicly acknowledged satisfaction.[48] Properly performed, these elements would likely not only clear the air between the claimants but also show the assembly

43 Wormald, "Charters, Law, and the Settlement of Disputes," 304.

44 Roach, *Kingship and Consent*, 144. Roach notes that local law and justice "operated through a mix of formal and informal procedures which defy classification according to modern concepts of 'public and private.'"

45 Lambert, *Law and Order*, 267.

46 Roach, *Kingship and Consent*, 140.

47 Roach emphasizes the performative nature of assemblies in *Kingship and Consent*, esp. chapters 8 and 9, as well as in "Penance, Submission and *Deditio*: Religious Influences on Dispute Settlement in Later Anglo-Saxon England (871–1066)," *Anglo-Saxon England* 41 (2012): 343–71. Others have emphasized the communal nature of local justice in particular: see Lambert, *Law and Order*, esp. Chapter 6; and Alice Taylor, "*Lex Scripta* and the Problem of Enforcement: Anglo-Saxon, Welsh, and Scottish Law Compared," in *Legalism: Community and Justice*, ed. Fernanda Pirie and Judith Scheele (Oxford: Oxford University Press, 2014), 47–75.

48 Roach, "Penance, Submission and *Deditio*," 355–57 and 368.

the matter was clearly settled, the outcome in which ealdormen may have been the most invested.

From the case between the churches of Winchcombe and Worcester over land at Upton (Gloucestershire) in the late ninth century to the quarrel concerning Saint Mildrith's property between Ælfstan, abbot of Saint Augustine's, Canterbury, and the priest Leofwine in the 1040s, ealdormen made frequent appearances as important actors in the judicial system in terms of dispute settlement.[49] Following Foot's criteria, the Upton charter reveals all of the elements suggestive of narrative form: a beginning, end, temporal location, and central subject around which a story is told.[50] This story begins as a certain Wullaf came forward claiming his father had leased the land for three lives (a standard in many leases, the life of the original lease recipient plus the lives of two heirs) from two abbesses of Winchcombe.[51] We receive a temporal location in the past: the charging of Ealdorman Æthelwulf with ensuring the bequests in the will of King Cenwulf of Mercia (796–821) reached their intended recipients. This included Upton, which Cenwulf had left to Winchcombe stipulating it could only be held for one life. Here suddenly is an indication of multiple narratives, one version coinciding with royal will, and another, Wullaf's family history, backed up by title-deeds. While the Mercian *witan*, under the leadership of Ealdorman Æthelred, issued a judgment on the matter, it seems that Æthelwulf oversaw much of the case. It was to Æthelwulf that Wullaf delivered his title-deeds (which the Mercian *witan* had declared invalid). The charter itself that records the dispute, dated to 897, indicates that Æthelwulf ordered it to be made and given to Wullaf to replace those deeds he had handed over.[52] The charter does double duty: not only does it provide a clear narrative of the dispute, but the document is in itself the end of the tale. With such a set ending the written record becomes the official account, overwriting what Wullaf's family had previously said was the history and parameters of the estate lease. This charter provides a much longer and more detailed narrative than standard charters, supplying a clear beginning, temporal location, and ending, but it cannot be placed neatly into one genre or another. It is an official legal document, but it also tells a story and can (and perhaps should) be read also as a form of literature: dispute narratives. And within that narrative space Ealdorman Æthelwulf emerges not just as an active character in the story but a significant one from beginning to end. He is the one who accepts the invalidated title-deeds, destroying one version of the story, but he

[49] S 1442 and S 1472.

[50] Foot, "Reading Anglo-Saxon Charters," 49.

[51] Wullaf claimed both Cynethryth and Ælfflæd (King Cenwulf's daughter?) gave him title charters for three lives.

[52] S 1442: *Aedeluulfus ei istum postea scriber praecipiebat.*

also ensures the creation of a new charter thus perpetuating the official narrative with a clear ending.

The Upton charter is not unique in its storytelling nor in its depiction of active ealdormen. Sometime during Edgar's reign, a priest stole title-deeds for Snodland from the bishop of Rochester and sold them to Ælfric, Æscwyn's son. After the theft was discovered and the case brought before King Edgar and his councilors, the deeds were returned and Ælfric's widow forfeited her lands.[53] The widow then brought the title-deeds of Bromley and Fawkham to the bishop of Rochester. One infers she threw herself on the prelate's mercy, as he then proceeded to obtain the charters, which had been handed over to the king, "by means of argument and persuasion for 15 mancuses of gold and 130 pounds [of silver]."[54] The bishop now owned the estates but allowed the widow to remain on them. After King Edgar's death, the widow's kinsman persuaded her to take forceful possession of Bromley and Fawkham.[55] Ealdorman Eadwine "and the section of the public which was the adversary of God" were appealed to, likely at a shire or hundred assembly, and the bishop was compelled to give up the deeds.[56] The assembly did not allow the prelate the chance to offer any of the three forms of proof that would demonstrate his ownership and the community lost the estates. The bulk of the story takes place in the 960s or 970s but the extant record, found in a cartulary at Rochester, was likely written in the 980s as the then bishop of Rochester attempted to recover the estates.[57] Though the evidence in this case is less clear, Ealdorman Eadwine appears to have been overseeing the appeal made by the widow and, together with "the section of the public," to have decided in her favor. The detail provided by the cartulary offers scope for authorial judgment upon the justice of the decision and the piety of those making it; it also provides a narrative space within which the active intervention of the ealdorman in the full legal process is revealed. Cartularies are certainly closer to other narrative forms than the more formulaic charter documents but it is notable that this text contains many of the elements which appear in dispute records found in single-sheet charters. Here we also find the dramatic beginning – the theft of title-deeds; a central subject where various estates are reclaimed or exchange hands; and we also find the temporal location – that moment in the history of Rochester when it owned these estates, framed within both preceding and following events.

[53] S 1457. For full text and translation see A. J. Robertson, ed., *Anglo-Saxon Charters*, 2nd ed. (Cambridge: Cambridge University Press, 1956), no. 59; hereafter *AS Charters*.

[54] S 1457.

[55] S 1457.

[56] S 1457.

[57] Keynes, "Cuckhamsley Chirograph," 196.

There is also an end, though the composer of the cartulary takes care to leave open the possibility that the estates that have been lost to the community may yet be regained. The central subject is the community's claim to these lands. This is the Rochester community's version of the story but, by the comments within the text, we know that it was not the only version; it is indeed not even the official version, as the ealdormen and others, in determining not to allow the bishop to present his proof, had closed the case in favor of the widow.

Ealdormen do not appear as overseers in all dispute cases but in certain circumstances this may have been due to an absence of this particular type of official rather than a lack of interest or shirking of duty. The late tenth-century Cuckhamsley chirograph records the settlement of a dispute between Wynflæd and Leofwine over estates at Hagbourne and Bradfield (Berkshire). Wynflæd was very well connected and approached King Æthelred with four high-ranking witnesses: Archbishop Sigeric, Bishop Ordbriht, Ealdorman Ælfric, and Ælfthryth, the king's mother.[58] Her opponent, however, insisted the case be heard before the shire-meeting (*scirgemote*). Wynflæd and Leofwine presented their case to Bishop Æthelsige, Bishop Æscwig, Abbot Ælfric, and the whole shire.[59] Wynflæd was allowed to produce proof of ownership and was eventually awarded the estates, although the overseers of the case ordered her to give Leofwine the money his father had given her for the estate. Wynflæd reluctantly returned the money "as little as she dared" but Leofwine seemed unconvinced, demanding she swear an oath that it was the full sum.[60] Wynflæd responded that she could not swear such an oath, and nor could he (presumably that it was not the full price) and both the narrative and charter end there. This is the second time in this particular narrative that an oath is mentioned and then not sworn. The first occurs when Wynflæd presented her proof at the shire court alongside her numerous witnesses, after which the overseers of the case "declared that it would be better for the oath to be dispensed with rather than sworn, because thereafter friendship would be at an end [between them]."[61] The lack of oath-swearing combined with the seemingly very poorly performed public acts of reconciliation stand out among dispute narratives. The high status of

58 S 1454. For full text and translation see A. J. Robertson, ed. and trans., *Anglo-Saxon Charters*, 2nd ed. (Cambridge: Cambridge University Press, 1956), no. 66.*A*. For more on Ælfthryth's appearance in certain legal documents, see Andrew Rabin, "Female Advocacy and Royal Protection in Tenth-Century England: The Legal Career of Queen Ælfthryth," *Speculum* 84 (2009): 261–88.

59 S 1454.

60 S 1454: *þa dyde hio swa hio dorste*.

61 S 1454: *ðæt betere wære ðæt man þene aþ aweg lete þonne hine man sealde forþan þær syþþan nan freondscype nære*.

many of Wynflæd's witnesses may explain the anomaly but the lack of an ealdorman as one of the overseers does raise questions over whether secular officials were more interested in (and capable of enforcing) oaths being sworn in such cases. Like other disputes, this record indicates that an exchange or gift of land occurred at some point in the past but it was now being contested (temporal location). No ealdorman is named as one of the overseers alongside two bishops and an abbot, but Simon Keynes has pointed out that this is likely because there was no ealdorman for Berkshire at the time rather than a lack of participation from the highest lay official of the area.[62] Whether this lack of an ealdorman led to oaths not being sworn or perhaps why Leofwine wanted the case tried at the shire court is unclear but it does leave us with a narrative which employs some unique features and authorial commentary.

The dispute over the property of Saint Mildrith seems to indicate that ealdormen, or earls in this case, could still be given oversight of such matters in the mid-eleventh century. Although parts of the text are now illegible, it is still possible to find the basics of the story. The central subject revolves around the estate which the priest, Leofwine, claimed King Cnut sold him, while Abbot Ælfstan of Saint Augustine's asserted the same king had bestowed it on the monastery. It can be inferred that at some point in the past (temporal marker) the two parties had come into conflict, eventually requiring or going to a third party for resolution. Negotiations of some sort occurred, as the text records that Leofwine agreed to give up his claim in return for two sulungs elsewhere until his death and an annual payment of five pounds. Unlike the much earlier disputes, the charter contains no mention of any sort of gathering that could be construed as an assembly, either royal or local. Both Leofwine and Abbot Ælfstan, however, are said to have declared (*cænde*) their ownership so there may have been at least a local assembly involved. Except for the presence of Earl Godwine, this appears to have been a wholly ecclesiastical matter, as the document lists the witnesses as Archbishop Eadsige, Bishop Siweard, Earl Godwine, and the two communities of Saint Augustine's and Christ Church. Still, the earl appears as the active mediator among ecclesiastical royal officials. This particular charter states in three separate places that Earl Godwine made (*worhte*) the agreement between the two parties.[63] The document opens with this phrase and it is repeated before the negotiated outcome is listed: Leofwine giving up his claim for other land elsewhere and an annual payment. The text thus emphasizes Godwine's role as the maker of the agreement. The final time *worhte* appears is in the witness list itself. After Archbishop Eadsige and Bishop Siweard, the scribe wrote Earl

[62] Keynes, "Cuckhamsley Chirograph," 200.

[63] S 1472. For full text and translation, see *AS Charters*, no. 102.

Godwine "who made the settlement."[64] How the earl did this goes unsaid but we do see that there were two conflicting stories resolved through implied negotiations which seem to have taken place behind the scenes. The agreed-upon compromise also provides the clear ending of one party relinquishing their claim in exchange for land and money. The repeated use of *worhte* recalls the dispute narrative first discussed above in which the charter records that Æthelwulf ordered it to be made. However, Earl Godwine appears more active in this document than Æthelwulf did, as he is not following the decision of the Mercian *witan* but seems to be the one making the agreement. A group had made the decision on which story would be the official one in the Upton dispute, but for the Saint Mildrith estate it is the singular earl who made the agreement between the two parties. This charter may indicate the political power of Godwine in the 1040s but it also likely highlights the growth of this particular office within the expanded kingdom of England.

Earl Godwine also appears in a dispute narrative (also dated to the mid 1040s) between Ælfwold, bishop of Sherborne, and Care, son of Toki, and his brothers. The final arrangements were made at Exeter "before Earl Godwine and the whole shire" concerning Holcombe Rogus in Devon.[65] The parties reached a compromise with only one brother of Care remaining on the land which would pass to Sherborne Abbey after his death. The abbey had lost this particular estate during Æthelred's reign, as recorded in Bishop Æthelric's writ to Ealdorman Æthelmær in which the cleric complains he is not receiving the correct amount of ship-scot (*scypgesceote*).[66] Ship-scot and the related term ship-soke are related to either the building of ships or collection of money to build ships and man them for the defense of the kingdom. An ealdorman may well have needed to be informed that his ecclesiastical counterpart was experiencing issues raising the expected ship funds as this could impact regional or even kingdom-wide defense, particularly with the renewed Viking attacks in the late tenth and early eleventh centuries. Both underfunded ship-scot and the levying of troops would also be important to the king, which may explain why the various rulers placed land disputes under an ealdorman's oversight.

The history of Holcombe Rogus can be traced back slightly further, in that Edmund Ironside leased the land from the diocese early in the eleventh century. Both the dispute and the episcopal complaint offer their own short narrative; together, they tell a longer story. This longer narrative was perhaps not always the official story, but its details offer insight into the legal system, its negotiations, land holdings, and the potential other

[64] S 1472: *Godwine eorl þe ðone seht worhte.*

[65] S 1474. For translation, see *AS Charters*, no. 105.

[66] S 1383. For translation, see Florence E. Harmer, ed., *Anglo-Saxon Writs*, 2nd ed. (Stamford: Paul Watkins, 1989), no. 63.

duties and concerns for both bishops and ealdormen, in this case ship-scot. Once again, the role of the ealdorman in the narrative both lends authority to the legal actions (the phrase "before Earl Godwine" functions rhetorically to emphasize the legitimacy of proceedings although in this case he does not appear to be acting alone as he does for the Saint Mildrith estate) and reveals surprising details of the breadth of the ealdorman's legal concerns. Earl Godwine presided over proceedings, negotiating a complex compromise about landholdings; Ealdorman Æthelmær heard complaints about the payment of ship dues owed to a bishop. These are certainly the concerns of elite figures, but they also require action on the part of the relevant ealdorman. It also provides a glimpse into what Sherborne believed – or wished others to believe – was the history of the estate.

Holcombe Rogus was not the only estate with a long history of one or even multiple disputes. The mid-tenth-century dispute narrative concerning the estates at Send and Sunbury reveals a long-standing quarrel which rivals the information found in the *Fonthill Letter* and the convoluted claims in the *Liber Eliensis*.[67] Like the *Fonthill Letter*, the charter concerning Send and Sunbury begins with a theft – in this case of a slavewoman (Thurwif) by Æthelstan of Sunbury during the reign of King Eadred.[68] When called to clear himself, Æthelstan did not appear. Afterwards, Æthelstan returned the slavewoman and paid her owner two pounds in compensation. Ealdorman Brihtferth, however, ordered Æthelstan to pay his wergild because of his failure to appear before the local assembly on the appointed day. Unable to pay the wergild and unwilling to allow his brother Edward to do so, Æthelstan lost the estate. After the death of Eadred, however, he resumed residence on the land until King Eadwig gave it to Beornric who promptly ejected him. Æthelstan then took his case to Edgar after the kingdom split between the two royal brothers. Edgar and his Mercian councilors (*Myrcna witan*) were unsympathetic and ordered that he pay his wergild as he should have done to Eadred. Æthelstan was still unable to do so and again refused to have his brother pay it, resulting in the permanent loss of the estate from his family.

Edgar then gave the estate to Ealdorman Æthelstan "to be held and granted, during his lifetime or at his death, to anyone he pleased."[69] The ealdorman later sold the land to Ecgferth who then promised it to Archbishop Dunstan, if he would act as an advocate for Ecgferth's wife and child after his death. Upon Ecgferth's death, the king and his councilors declared the man's lands forfeit and gave the estate at Sunbury along with Ecgferth's land at Send to Ealdorman Ælfheah. The archbishop

[67] S 1447. S 1211, which records the history of an estate at Cooling, is also convoluted and covers several decades.

[68] S 1447.

[69] S 1447. For translation, see *AS Charters*, no. 44.

then offered to pay Ecgferth's wergild in order to gain control of the land but Edgar replied the money would only have been enough to buy a consecrated grave for Ecgferth and that "I have left the whole case to Ælfheah."[70] After six years, Dunstan approached Ælfheah and purchased both Send and Sunbury lands "uncontested and unopposed," enabling him to claim ownership.[71] Dunstan's final purchase of the land was the clear ending to a story that occurred over many years, but at the same time, was the beginning of the story in that this event prompted the drafting of the charter in the first place.

Although more convoluted than many land disputes, this particular charter, through its narrative, does allow us a glimpse of three ealdormen involved in the judicial process. Brihtferth appears acting at the regional level while Æthelstan and Ælfheah perform activities on a more kingdom-wide stage. We receive the impression that King Edgar grew tired of the case and twice gave the estate to an ealdorman in order not to have to deal with it anymore. Whatever the reason for the gifts, the ealdormen who are the recipients of such estates certainly appear to have taken part in judicial proceedings, including issuing decisions, and being placed in charge of long-contested estates. Many of the cases in the "dispute charters" or "dispute narratives" may well have first appeared before the local ealdorman, either presiding over an assembly or as a judge, and only after the disputes somehow garnered royal attention did they appear before the king and his councilors. Indeed some disputes recorded in surviving charters appear to have remained at the local level.[72] If a case did make it to a royal assembly, the king could make a decision, confirm a decision made by a local assembly, or hand the case back over to the important men at the regional level.[73] Disputes like Wynflæd's quarrel with Leofwine or those over the estates of Sunbury and Send reveal the importance of having powerful friends

70 S 1447: *ic hæbbe ealla þa spæce to Ælfhege læten.*

71 S 1447. This was not the only dispute Archbishop Dunstan was involved in. See S 1458 which recorded the history of Wouldham in Kent. The archbishop had to prove the estate had been given to St. Andrew's in Rochester in a will he had witnessed.

72 For example, see S 1460 involving Bishop Æthelstan of Hereford dated to the first quarter of the eleventh century. The prelate was a claimant of an estate in Worcestershire and thus appeared before the shire-meeting (*sciregemote*) at Worcester in the presence of Earls Leofwine and Hakon.

73 The surviving Anglo-Saxon writs give some insight into the first two options. See *AS Writs*. Edward the Confessor sometimes makes a decision (*Writs*, no. 62) and other times confirms the local decision (*Writs*, no. 35) or directs the local assembly to do so (*Writs*, no. 17).

to intercede for claimants or their families. While the law codes reveal the importance of ealdormen within the social hierarchy that governed legal processes, the recorded land disputes demonstrate not only a much more active presence by these officials but also a judicial system heavily influenced by personal relationships with important and powerful figures. The "dispute narratives" are stories usually written down as the official record but unable to hide that there had been conflicting claims and histories of the land in question. These texts provide insights into the legal system in action as well as how interested ealdormen may have been in the outcome – a clear end to the matter, perhaps more important than which side won. These secular officials actively helped in the official and unofficial negotiations of the matter as their other duties likely required an outcome to the conflict.

These active roles and influential relationships are confirmed by the more traditional narrative sources such as the house chronicles of Ely and Ramsey. The *Liber Eliensis* reveals that Ealdorman Æthelwine of East Anglia attended many shire and hundred meetings and often made decisions in favor of Ely during the last quarter of the tenth century.[74] Ealdorman Byrhtnoth of Essex appears less frequently but also apparently issued generally favorable decisions. Indeed, the monks called upon Byrhtnoth for assistance when Æthelwine did not recover lands as he had promised. This interaction was recorded in the case of the disputed estates at Hauxton and Newton (Cambridgeshire). Eadric, the owner of the estates, had left them to King Edgar on his death; the king eventually sold the land to Bishop Æthelwold for Ely. Ælfwold, the brother of Eadric, laid claim to the land and had possession of the title-deeds. The case apparently went on for many years and although Ealdorman Æthelwine "brought it to the attention of many witnesses" the bishop and abbot could not obtain the title-deeds.[75] Abbot Byrhtnoth of Ely then offered the ealdorman three hides at Wangford in order that Æthelwine would exert his influence and retrieve the charters for Ely. Æthelwine took the land at Wangford but did not obtain the deeds. After years of litigation, the abbot approached Ealdorman Byrhtnoth while he visited the monastery. Byrhtnoth, the ealdorman of Essex, then brokered a deal with Ælfwold who handed over the deeds to Hauxton and Newton in exchange for a charter relating to Ramsey (Essex) and Sproughton (Suffolk) and thirty mancuses of gold. When one high-ranking man failed to acquire a disputed estate for the community, they made use of their relationship with another to secure their claim.

74 For examples, see *LE*, ii.11, ii.11a, ii.12, and ii.24.

75 *LE*, ii.27.

The *Liber Eliensis* also reports that Æthelwine promised to settle a dispute over land at Horningsea (Cambridgeshire). In a disparaging note, the *Liber Eliensis* adds that Æthelwine's words "had no weight to them, and his promises never came to fruition."[76] It would appear that the ealdorman's failure to act successfully for Ely was a memory that rankled. Two points may be made here: first, that the role of ealdormen in the narrative sources is more complicated, particularly by local politics, than in the charters; and second, that the expectation from the community is that the ealdorman will take an active part in the legal process (at least in the case of land disputes and where he has been provided with sufficient financial inducement). Furthermore, the house chronicle reports that Siferth gave the long-disputed lands at Brandon and Livermere (Suffolk) to Bishop Æthelwold "against the will of Ealdorman Æthelwine and very many others."[77] Despite these negative comments, Æthelwine did maintain a relatively favorable relationship with Ely, including eventually paying the monks for the land at Wangford – a relationship with the local ealdorman worked to the monastery's legal advantage in most cases.[78]

Conclusion

Ealdormen certainly had military duties, but whether they also had significant legal responsibilities has been a more contentious question. As demonstrated above, law codes do not provide extensive support for ealdormen actively participating in the legal system. They are high-ranking important figures but appear fairly passive. However, the dispute narratives, whether formatted as a charter, chronicle, writ, or letter, reveal that ealdormen did participate in the legal system, at least when it came to land disputes. Tom Lambert has argued there is little to indicate ealdormen or earls were necessarily always present at local criminal cases.[79] There could be a number of reasons for this, but it may reasonably be associated in part with the expanded size of the Wessex kingdom, as well as the increased incorporation into the legal system of, first, bishops in the early tenth century and later shire-reeves in the second half of the same century. This can be seen in the increasing mention of bishops and then reeves in the law codes of the 900s. Yet, the few duties clearly assigned to

[76] *LE*, ii.49.

[77] *LE*, ii.35.

[78] This is not to say that ealdormen were the only important local figures to whom a monastic house could turn. For an example of Bishop Æthelwold's influence on behalf of Ely in a similar situation, see *LE*, ii.11.

[79] Lambert, "Law and Order," 142–46.

ealdormen in legal codes, in conjunction with their military obligations, may explain why ealdormen are more active in the dispute narratives. At a minimum, the highest-ranking lay officials in a region would of necessity be involved in land disputes, particularly within their ealdordoms, because they needed to know who owned what in order to perform their military obligations, if not other duties such as determining if someone had illegally occupied an estate.

As for military obligations, there is some debate over what calling up the *fyrd* actually meant in terms of whether ealdormen mostly used their own household troops supplemented by landowners who owed military service or all men from a region were expected to show up.[80] Whether it is men or paying their fees, the few glimpses we receive of the systems for levying troops and providing for them in the field are based on land ownership.[81] Therefore, an ealdormen needed to have an idea of who owned land and how much in order to know either the size of the *fyrd* or how much money for military stipends he could expect from those in his region. As discussed above in regard to the history of Holcombe Rogus, a similar situation may have involved ship-soke and ship-scot and the naval capability of a region or the kingdom to defend itself. Defending their region of influence or the kingdom as a whole was, after all, essential to the duties of ealdormen. An ealdorman needed to know the size of military stipends, the whereabouts of missing ships, and, where relevant, which local thegnly family needed to be held accountable for failing to pay their dues – if not through a sophisticated system of exact number and tallies, at least in general terms. The law codes, in their laconic clauses and steadily decreasing interest in ealdormen as subjects of punitive threat, do not make this role clear but the stories of the dispute narratives do.

I have attempted to reconcile the seemingly contradictory pictures presented of passive and active ealdormen in different types of legal documents. The law codes provide an ideal of the legal culture, generally a royal one, and while not necessarily inaccurate, they do offer a one-dimensional view of ealdormen. The narrative elements of the land disputes, on the other hand, offer hints of a dynamic legal activity, including listening to conflicting claims of ownership, negotiations, and performative acts

80 See, e.g., Richard Abels, *Lordship and Military Obligation in Anglo-Saxon England* (London, 1988); Richard Abels, "Household Men, Mercenaries and Vikings in Anglo-Saxon England," in *Mercenaries and Paid Men*, ed. John France (Leiden, 2008), 143–66; James Campbell, "Some Agents and Agencies of the Late-Anglo-Saxon State," in *The Anglo-Saxon State* (London: Hambledon, 2000), 201–26; and C. Warren Hollister, *Anglo-Saxon Military Institutions on the Eve of the Norman Conquest* (Oxford: Clarendon, 1962).

81 See John Morris et al., eds., *Domesday Book*, 35 vols. (Chichester: Phillimore, 1975–86), [Berkshire] i, 56v, and [Worcestershire] i, 172.

of compromise or resolution, all of which ealdormen participated in or presided over. Like cartulary-chronicles, dispute charters stand between the pragmatism of legal text and the emotive rhetoric of literary narrative. They offer insight into not just the legal culture but also into the differing histories behind each lawsuit which were (in intention at least) overwritten by the "official" story recorded in the charter. Together, law codes and dispute narratives make possible a better understanding of the activities of various ealdormen; close examination of their narrative detail offers a clearer view of the range of legal duties these men were obligated to perform.

9

Royal Reeves, Royal Authority, and the "Holy Society" in Archbishop Wulfstan's Writings

Chelsea Shields-Más

Wulfstan, archbishop of York between 1002 and 1023, held his office during an incredibly tumultuous time in English history.[1] Beginning in the 980s and continuing intermittently until the reign of Cnut in 1016, England suffered serious devastation at the hands of the Vikings.[2] These attacks had reached their pinnacle of destruction and brutality during the last decade of Æthelred II's reign, and with the English resistance amounting to something altogether ineffective, enormous sums of money were paid to the Danes in tribute on several occasions.[3] Contemporary sources suggest that this was a period when the people of England were plunged into despair and fear, with diminishing faith in their state and the ability of the king to defend it and its people.[4] As archbishop of York

1 Pauline Stafford, "Church and Society in the Age of Ælfric," in *The Old English Homily and its Backgrounds*, ed. Paul E. Szarmach and Bernard F. Huppé (Albany: State University of New York Press, 1978), 22–27; Joyce M. Hill, "Archbishop Wulfstan: Reformer?" in *Wulfstan, Archbishop of York: The Proceedings of the Second Alcuin Conference*, ed. Matthew Townend (Turnhout: Brepols, 2004), 309–13; Renée Trilling, "Sovereignty and Social Order: Archbishop Wulfstan and the *Institutes of Polity*," in *The Bishop Reformed: Studies in Episcopal Power and Culture in the Central Middle Ages*, ed. Anna T. Jones and John S. Ott (Aldershot: Ashgate, 2007), 58–60; Patrick Wormald, "Archbishop Wulfstan and the Holiness of Society," in Wormald, *Legal Culture*, 244–46; Simon Keynes, "An Abbot, an Archbishop, and the Viking Raids of 1006–7 and 1009–12," *Anglo-Saxon England* 36 (2007): 177–81 and 203–08.

2 Simon Keynes, "Apocalypse Then: England A.D. 1000," in *Europe Around the Year 1000*, ed. P. Urbańczyk (Warsaw: Institute of Archaeology and Ethnology, Polish Academy of Sciences, 2001), 259–60; Pauline Stafford, *Unification and Conquest: A Political and Social History of England in the Tenth and Eleventh Centuries* (London: E. Arnold, 1989), 63–67; Ann Williams, *Kingship and Government in Pre-Conquest England, c.500–1066* (London: MacMillan, 1999), 97–101; and Keynes, "An Abbot," 153.

3 Keynes, "An Abbot," 154, 156.

4 Keynes, "Apocalypse Then," 266–67; Keynes, "An Abbot," 154.

and close advisor to two kings, Wulfstan was well positioned to articulate measures intended to improve England's dire situation.[5] Wulfstan was deeply concerned for the state and wellbeing of the English people. The disasters they faced in the form of Viking attacks he viewed as a result of their having fallen away from God and Christian conduct; accordingly, Wulfstan believed it necessary to reform English society if it were to endure, and to regain God's favor. Wulfstan's writings suggest that the archbishop saw the restoration of order to society as the key to solving England's crises. He attempted, in his homiletic and legal works, to create prescriptions for an ordered, holy, Christian society in order to redeem the English in the eyes of God, and to ensure lasting peace and prosperity. The vision of an ordered, "holy society" that emerged from these works was multifaceted and its execution involved the work of both secular and ecclesiastical entities. This chapter demonstrates that the work of royal officials figured prominently in Wulfstan's vision of reform. In the centralization of these officials (and especially of the secular figure of the reeve) can be seen not only the archbishop's recognition of the importance of secular figures to the support of the Church within a holy society, but the varied legal and literary means by which Wulfstan wove the persuasions, exhortations, and regulations through which he sought to realize his vision.

Wulfstan, Reformer and Writer

Wulfstan first makes an appearance in the historical record in 996, when he was appointed as the bishop of London, though nothing about him prior to that year is known. While bishop of London, he composed a few homilies and penitential letters.[6] Andrew Rabin has demonstrated that this post and Wulfstan's activities while bishop of London had an important impact on his later thought and writings.[7] Wulfstan's tenure at the diocese of St. Paul's was influenced by the uniquely political nature of the bishop's role, as well as the circle of men with whom Wulfstan associated.[8] Importantly, Rabin has pointed out that the geographic location of St.

[5] Patrick Wormald, "Æthelred the Lawmaker," in *Ethelred the Unready: Papers from the Millenary Conference*, ed. David Hill (Oxford: British Archaeological Reports, 1978), 55.

[6] Patrick Wormald, "Archbishop Wulfstan: Eleventh-Century State-Builder," in *Wulfstan, Archbishop of York: The Proceedings of the Second Alcuin Conference*, ed. Matthew Townend (Turnhout: Brepols, 2004), 26–27.

[7] Andrew Rabin, "Wulfstan at London: Episcopal Politics in the Reign of Æthelred," *English Studies* 97 (2016): 188.

[8] Ibid., 189, 192, 194.

Paul's – an area of strategic importance, but also one which sat between what were once separate kingdoms (Essex and Wessex) – as well as the bishop's limited control over diocesan estates and wealth, meant that bishops of London were often deeply involved in secular, and especially royal, politics, alongside their religious obligations.[9] In fact, the bishop of London's political activities could at times even overshadow his religious functions.[10] Men who occupied this post often bore close ties to the king and relied on royal patronage for support, and accordingly, they would have had one foot in both the secular and ecclesiastical realms.[11] Based on an examination of the charters Wulfstan attested while bishop of London, Rabin contends that Wulfstan associated with a group of elite ecclesiastics at court who had been educated by the first generation of monastic reformers and who sought to cement and protect ecclesiastical privileges and to revive or re-establish "the affiliation between the king and the church that had been a central feature of the early Reform."[12] Thus, Rabin argues, it was both the unique nature of the diocese of St. Paul's – and the political experience which it entailed – paired with Wulfstan's engagement with a group of elite, reform-minded ecclesiastics, that prepared the ground (and indeed made him an appealing choice) for his elevation to the dual appointments of the sees of York and Worcester in 1002.[13]

Despite Wulfstan's impactful engagement in the political sphere during his tenure at St. Paul's, it is his role as archbishop of York that stands out in the historical – and literary – record. The years 1002 × 1023 marked the period in which he produced the majority of the wide and varied body of work for which he is best remembered. Wulfstan did not often sign his name to his work; yet it has been possible to ascribe to the archbishop a wide body of writings as a result not only of his distinctive style, but also the presence of his hand in myriad manuscripts associated with him.[14] The

9 Ibid., 188–91.

10 Ibid., 190.

11 Ibid., 189–90.

12 Ibid., 197.

13 Ibid., 192.

14 Dorothy Whitelock, ed., *Sermo Lupi ad Anglos*, 3rd ed. (Exeter: University of Exeter Press, 1980), 17–19; Dorothy Whitelock, "Archbishop Wulfstan, Homilist and Statesman," *TRHS*, 4th series, 24 (1942): 44–45; Eric Stanley, "Wulfstan and Ælfric: 'The True Difference between the Law and the Gospel,'" in *Wulfstan, Archbishop of York: The Proceedings of the Second Alcuin Conference*, ed. Matthew Townend (Turnhout: Brepols, 2004), 433–38; Wormald, "Archbishop Wulfstan: Eleventh-Century State-Builder," 10–12; Wormald, "Archbishop Wulfstan and the Holiness of Society," 225–29; Jonathan Wilcox, "The Wolf on Shepherds: Wulfstan, Bishops, and the Context of the *Sermo Lupi ad Anglos*," in *Old English Prose: Basic Readings*, ed. Paul E. Szarmach, with the assistance of Deborah A. Oosterhouse (New York: Garland Publishing, 2000), 395–97; Joyce Tally Lionarons,

complexities of this manuscript record, however, mean that defining the relationships among Wulfstan's works, and delineating the precise connections between his productions and those works upon which he drew, remains a challenge.[15] The early years of his tenure as archbishop saw the compilation of tracts on status and many homilies – Wulfstan's Old English homiletic writings number around forty, and he also composed legislation for Æthelred II and Cnut.[16] Other works are more difficult to categorize in terms of genre: *Institutes of Polity*, which arguably represents the culmination of Wulfstan's political thought,[17] details the duties of each member of society, from king to common folk, within the framework of a Christian polity. In form neither strictly legal nor homiletic, *Institutes of Polity* makes use of a number of textual modes to further its essentially didactic message. This is a text that Wulfstan appears to have been

---

The Homiletic Writings of Archbishop Wulfstan: A Critical Study (Cambridge: D. S. Brewer, 2010), 12–22. Wulfstan's hand is given detailed treatment in N. R. Ker, "The Handwriting of Archbishop Wulfstan," in *Books, Collectors and Libraries*, ed. A. Watson (London: The Hambledon Press, 1985), 9–26.

[15] Despite this, it has been possible, to some extent, to determine Wulfstan's sources and influences; some manuscripts associated with him contain what has been labeled "Wulfstan's commonplace book." See Lionarons, *Homiletic Writings*, 12–22; Wormald, "Archbishop Wulfstan and the Holiness of Society," 231–41; Jonathan Wilcox, "The Dissemination of Wulfstan's Homilies: The Wulfstan Tradition in Eleventh-Century Vernacular Preaching," in *England in the Eleventh Century: Proceedings of the 1990 Harlaxton Symposium*, ed. Carola Hicks (Stamford: Paul Watkins, 1992), 200. Commentators tend to be in agreement that the term "commonplace book" is somewhat of a misnomer, and that these are more correctly regarded as collections of texts of canon law, homilies, and letters, which Wulfstan perhaps considered of use as sources. Wormald, *Making of English Law*, 202; Whitelock, "Archbishop Wulfstan," 47; Wilcox, "The Dissemination of Wulfstan's Homilies," 200; Lionarons, *Homiletic Writings*, 12. Some of these sources include: "the canons of the Synod of *Celchyth* of 816, the synod of the Council of Hertford, papal letters, the *Constitutions* of Odo, several letters of Alcuin … a homily of Abbo of St Germain, Latin [homiletic] excerpts … the two pastoral letters written for Wulfstan by Ælfric, [and] two copies of the chapter of Amalarius which is the source of Wulfstan's *De regula canonicorum*" (Whitelock, "Archbishop Wulfstan," 47). The manuscripts associated with Wulfstan are: BL, Additional 38651; BL, Cotton MSS Cleopatra B.xiii, Nero A.i, Tiberius A.iii, Tiberius A.xiii, Vespasian A.xiv, Vespasian D.ii; Bodl., Barlow 37, Bodley 343, Hatton 113–14, Junius 121; Cambridge, Corpus Christi College MSS 190, 201, 265, 302, 419, 421; Copenhagen, Kongelige Bibliotek, Gl. Kgl. Sam. 1595; York, Minster Library, MS Add. 1. Lionarons summarizes the content of each of these manuscripts in *Homiletic Writings*, 12–22.

[16] Wilcox, "The Wolf on Shepherds," 395; Wormald, "Archbishop Wulfstan: Eleventh-Century State-Builder," 26.

[17] Andrew Rabin, ed. and trans., *Wulfstan: Old English Legal Writings* (Cambridge, MA: Harvard University Press, 2020), xvii.

working on and refining for much of his career as archbishop,[18] and, together with his homilies and legislation, it offers insight into both the role of royal officials in his program to reform English society, and the textual means by which Wulfstan constructed this program.

Wulfstan was dedicated to saving his country and people from what he presumed to be God's wrath at their failure to be a good Christian nation, and it is clear from his writings that he saw the path to this salvation through re-establishing an ordered Christian kingdom. We can see a precedent for this type of reaction in the law codes in IV Edgar 1, which dates to 962. This code references a plague which has befallen the country, and expresses the belief of the king and his councilors that it was the result of God's displeasure with the people and their sins.[19] The clauses under IV Edgar 1 thus aim to reform the people's actions and return them to God's favor. One particular grievance highlighted in Edgar's laws is the failure to pay proper church dues and tithes. This is outlined in his Andover code (II–III Edgar) and reiterated in IV Edgar: the English people have sinned and fallen away from God's commands, and they have failed to properly render church dues and tithes.[20] IV Edgar 1.1–2 draws a com-

18 Trilling, "Sovereignty and Social Order," 62–64; Wormald, "Archbishop Wulfstan: Eleventh-Century State-Builder," 19–20 and 26–27; Wormald, "Archbishop Wulfstan and the Holiness of Society," 244–46; Wilcox, "The Wolf on Shepherds," 400–01; Whitelock, *Sermo Lupi ad Anglos*, 25–27.

19 Felix Liebermann, ed., *Die Gesetze der Angelsachsen*, 3 vols. (Halle: Max Niemeyer, 1903–16), 1:206. See also A. J. Robertson, ed. and trans., *The Laws of the Kings of England from Edmund to Henry I* (Cambridge: Cambridge University Press, 1925), 29. *[IV Edgar:] Her is geswutelod on þisum gewrite, hu Eadgar cyncg wæs smeagende, hwæt to bote mihte æt þam færcwealme, þe his leodscype swyðe drehte 7 wanode, wide gynd his anweald. [IV Edgar 1:] Ðæt is þonne ærest, þæt him ðuhte 7 his witum, þæt ðus gerad ungelimp mid synnum 7 mid oferhyrnysse Godes beboda geearnod wære, 7 swyðost mid þam oftige þæs neadgafoles, þe Cristene men Gode gelæstan scoldon on heora teoðingsceattum.* ("[IV Edgar:] Notification is hereby given in this order, that King Eadgar has been considering what remedy could be found for the plague which has greatly afflicted and reduced his people throughout the length and breadth of his dominion. [IV Edgar 1:] In the first place, he and his councilors are of opinion that misfortune such as this has been merited because of sin and disregard of God's commands, and especially through the withholding of the tribute which Christian people should render to God by their tithes.") IV Edgar 1.4–5 consist of a call for God's dues to be paid as laid out in the Andover Code (II–III Edgar) and that reeves especially should enforce this. Here we can see the idea that the failure to pay God's dues (cast here as "withholding," suggesting deliberate malfeasance) invokes God's wrath. The method by which reeves should enforce and punish this is established in II Edgar 3.1: reeves are to obtain (forcibly, if necessary) what is owed God while also leaving the offender with only one-eighth of his original property.

20 On this see also Nicole Marafioti, "The Legacy of King Edgar in the Laws of Archbishop Wulfstan," in *Remembering the Medieval Present: Generative Uses of*

parison with payments owed by tenants to their lords: in such cases, the lord should endeavor to be merciful, but if the tenant fails to respect the lord's authority and render payment, then the lord may take his property and life. IV Edgar 1.3 states that God may act in the same way, when people fail to make their duty-bound payments of tithes and church dues. Edgar's reign, seen from the perspective of Wulfstan's era as a period of relative peace and stability – and one in which the Church was properly supported – provided a sharp contrast to the tumultuous decades that followed, under the reigns of his sons, Edward the Martyr (r. 975–78) and Æthelred II (r. 978–1016).[21] It is perhaps not surprising, therefore, that references to and citations of Edgar's laws are prominent among the methods used by Wulfstan to construct his vision of an ordered, holy nation. As Nicole Marafioti has it: "In a range of legal, political, and religious texts, Wulfstan cited "Edgar's law" as an ideal foundation for contemporary legislation and ecclesiastical regulation, thereby providing a model for a well-ordered society and establishing a sense of continuity with England's better past."[22]

The Elements of a "Holy Society" Across Wulfstan's Works

In Wulfstan's mind, it seems his goal was to be achieved through reinstating and revitalizing the appropriate ordering of society. The law was one of several practical textual means by which Wulfstan could work toward this goal – Jay Paul Gates contends that beginning with the Peace of Edward and Guthrum, "secular law is made the tool for enforcing church authority."[23] This text, dated by Gates to 1002 × 1008, has been established as both a forgery from Wulfstan's pen, and likely his earliest foray into writing legislative texts.[24] Gates sees this text, with its apparent reflection of elements of IV Edgar, as Wulfstan's "first effort to lay out his vision of the holy society, founding law and social order on a penitential model."[25] Wulfstan's work frequently touches on status and the proper ordering of society, and in particular, the necessity of the Three Pillars of Society

England's Pre-Conquest Past, 10th to 15th Centuries, ed. Jay Paul Gates and Brian T. O'Camb (Leiden: Brill, 2019), 22–23.

21 Ibid., 23–24.

22 Ibid., 28.

23 Jay Paul Gates, "Preaching, Politics and Episcopal Reform in Wulfstan's Early Writings," *Early Medieval Europe* 23 (2015): 110.

24 Ibid., 108. Rabin dates the text more narrowly, to 1002 × 1004. Andrew Rabin, ed. and trans., *The Political Writings of Archbishop Wulfstan of York* (Manchester: Manchester University Press, 2015), 55.

25 Gates, "Preaching, Politics and Episcopal Reform," 108.

to the proper functioning of the throne, which the archbishop saw as strengthened by both God's and secular law.[26] Chapter Four of *Institutes of Polity* focuses upon the Three Pillars of Society – *oratores, laboratores,* and *bellatores* – as essential support for a successful throne.[27] Wulfstan stresses the importance of the Three Pillars and that upholding them, with every person in their rightful place and role in society, would aid in maintaining the strength and unity of the kingdom.[28] These are presented as non-negotiable factors, and of course, they reinforce Wulfstan's picture of an ordered Christian nation.

Other important elements of his program were the elevation of God's law over secular law, the raising of the status of ecclesiastical officials over secular administrators, and royal agents' amplified role in protecting and supporting the Church.[29] Rabin argues that Wulfstan saw ecclesiastical and legislative roles as two halves of a single enterprise, with clergy and secular agents sharing the same obligations.[30] And reflecting on Wulfstan's praise of King Edgar in the 959 entry of the *Anglo-Saxon Chronicle,* Eric Stanley observes that "the laws of kings are to be seen as an appendage to and extension of the laws of God."[31] Throughout his writings, Wulfstan demonstrates a sustained interest in society as a unified entity, comprising both ecclesiastical and secular elements; it is no surprise, therefore, that the work of royal officials should be understood by him as integral to the realization of his holy society.

The totalizing nature of Wulfstan's reformist vision was to affect not only its conceptualization but also its textual realization. Across the corpus of his outputs, Wulfstan returns zealously to the idea of a system of justice and law over which God reigned supreme. Based on a phrase employed by Wulfstan in his *Sermo lupi ad Anglos* of 1014, Stanley argues that the English, and especially Wulfstan, viewed law and justice as closely linked with God.[32] A phrase Wulfstan uses in this text, *Godes gerihta mid rihte gelæste* (lit. 'justly render God's dues') indicates, according to Stanley,

[26] Rabin, *Political Writings,* 146–47.

[27] Karl Jost, ed., *Die "Institutes of Polity, Civil and Ecclesiastical": Ein Werk Erzbischof Wulfstans von York* (Bern: Francke, 1959), 55; and Rabin, *Political Writings,* 106–07. Cf. Michael Swanton, trans., *Anglo-Saxon Prose* (London: Dent, 1993), 189: "Those who pray, those who work, those who fight."

[28] T. E. Powell, "The 'Three Orders' of Society in Anglo-Saxon England," *Anglo-Saxon England* 23 (1994): 119. See also Swanton, *Anglo-Saxon Prose,* 189–90.

[29] Rabin, *Political Writings,* 127–29; and Rabin, *Wulfstan: Old English Legal Writings,* xvi.

[30] Rabin, *Wulfstan: Old English Legal Writings,* xiii. This is especially clear in the homily Napier 51, dating to either 1008 or 1014 and likely preached to the *witan*: see Rabin, *Political Writings,* 127–29.

[31] Stanley, "Wulfstan and Ælfric," 440.

[32] Ibid., 430.

more than mere legal obligation. God, supreme in the eternal arrangement of divine justice, is deserving of the people's "rightful service":[33] as well as "to pay," the verb *gelæstan* denotes "to serve" and even "to accompany."[34] On this reading, the term *gerihta* ("rights/dues") both denotes God's rights and implies the divine rightfulness of the service that constitutes them. Wulfstan's zeal for this concept is further revealed in *Institutes of Polity*, wherein he states one should *riht lufian for Gode and for worulde* ("love justice for the sake of God and the state").[35] In both homily and in political tract, his attitude regarding secular law's necessary connection with God's law and divine justice is clear. Joyce Lionarons states that, in fact, Wulfstan did not differentiate between law and homily in terms of content, only in terms of genre; thus, legislation was revised to adapt the material for oral delivery in another form.[36] These adaptations, Lionarons contends, would have had the advantage of making the law more accessible to the average lay person, while also serving as a reminder of good Christian conduct.[37] Whatever their precise function, it is certainly clear that Wulfstan saw the value of (and devoted his rhetorical effort to) more than one textual genre in furthering his reformist aims.

Direct attempts by Wulfstan to bring about the social order that he believed necessary to the nation's salvation may be found in the drafting of Cnut's legislation, which signaled an attempt to eradicate royal abuses of power and to return the nation to the "better days" of King Edgar's reign. In this connection, Pauline Stafford highlights Cnut's code of 1018, first recognized as a law code by A. G. Kennedy in 1983.[38] This code arose from a meeting of the Danes and the English at Oxford in 1018, wherein at the outset the code established the intent to return to and observe the laws of King Edgar.[39] II Cnut takes this further, with its clauses 69–83, which pledge to eliminate abuses of royal power.[40] All of this legislation – Cnut's 1018 code and I and II Cnut – was the work of Wulfstan, and had the ultimate goal of promoting and establishing good Christian kingship. Stafford contends that the adoption of the laws of a "good" king (Edgar), by a conqueror – Cnut – was in effect "guaranteeing the good laws of the

33 Ibid.
34 Bosworth-Toller, s.v. *gelæstan*.
35 Stanley, "Wulfstan and Ælfric," 439.
36 Lionarons, *Homiletic Writings*, 164.
37 Ibid., 168.
38 A. G. Kennedy, "Cnut's Law Code of 1018," *Anglo-Saxon England* 11 (1982): 58.
39 Pauline Stafford, "The Laws of Cnut and the History of Anglo-Saxon Royal Promises," *Anglo-Saxon England* 10 (1981): 173.
40 Ibid., 178.

past," while at the same time making royal rights and prerogatives clearly known, which was an important element of good Christian kingship.[41]

Napier Homily 50 functions in a similar vein; this text may have been preached to the *witan* assembled at the 1018 meeting at Oxford.[42] This homily represents another important strand in Wulfstan's efforts to repair English society.[43] It is the homily's focus on the duties and responsibilities of the secular officials that is of interest here, particularly in light of its connections with Cnut's code of 1018 and the fact that it may well have been preached to the *witan* assembled in Oxford. The 1018 code of Cnut is largely made up of clauses also found in V–VIII Æthelred and I–II Cnut, and is transmitted in Cambridge, Corpus Christi College 201, a manuscript with Wulfstanian connections.[44] The laws of Cnut encompassed legislation from the laws of Edgar and Æthelred, and the meeting of 1018 was instigated, in part, in order to smooth relations between the Danes and the English.[45] Wulfstan apparently made use of this meeting not only as an opportunity to preach to the assembled *witan* and to admonish them for their sins, but also to remind the various clerics and officials of their duties to the nation.[46] Lines 267/25–268/1 of Napier 50 contain the address to numerous officials:

> And we cyðað eac eorlan and heretogan, dêman and gerefan, þæt hig âgan þearfe, þæt hi georne unrihtes geswîcan and rihtwisnysse lufjan for gode and for worlde and nahwar þurh ûndom for feo ne for freondscipe forgyman heora wisdom, swa þæt hig wendan unriht to riht oððon undôm gedêman earmum to yrmðe…[47]

> And we proclaim also [to] earls and generals, judges and reeves that they need to go [and] that they zealously stop injustices and righteously for [the] love of God and the world nowhere neglect their wisdom through

41 Ibid., 180. I and II Cnut articulate the laws of good Christian kingship, laid out comprehensively.

42 Lionarons, *Homiletic Writings*, 7, 34. Lionarons argues that Napier 50, along with 51, was closely connected with the promulgation of Cnut's 1018 code. See also Wormald, *Making of English Law*, 355–60.

43 The homily focuses on the appropriate behavior of the clergy and the laity, and the need for the English to be prepared for the coming of the Antichrist and the end of the world. Lionarons, *Homiletic Writings*, 164, 171.

44 Kennedy, "Cnut's Law Code of 1018," 57–59.

45 Stafford, *Unification and Conquest*, 138–39; Wormald, *Making of English Law*, 129–33.

46 Lionarons, *Homiletic Writings*, 34, 173. Arthur S. Napier, ed., *Wulfstan: Sammlung der ihm zugeschriebenen Homilien nebst Untersuchungen über ihre Echtheit* (Berlin: Weidmann, 1883), 266–74 (no. L).

47 Napier, *Wulfstan*, 267–68 (no. L); my translation. See also Rabin, *Political Writings*, 145–53, esp. 146–47.

> unjust judgment, for money or for friendship, so that unright is turned to right, injustice into justice and the wretched from poverty.

This address bears similarities to elements of section nine of *Institutes of Polity* entitled "concerning earls." Wulfstan's emphasis on and repetition of this particular content may be an indicator of the importance he placed on it (though it must be remembered that Wulfstan often reused and recycled his own work). It is noteworthy that aside from the general exhortations to royal officials to judge justly and fairly and to avoid corruption, Wulfstan is instructing them to "nowhere neglect their wisdom." This may be reminiscent of the type of "wisdom" that Asser discusses in his *Life of King Alfred*, and that which Alfred himself famously ordered his officials to learn, lest they lose their positions.[48] Works generated in Alfred's circle had a lasting impact on political, social, and religious thought in the tenth and eleventh centuries. One of the apparent goals of Alfred's instruction was to educate the people as to how to live in the manner of good Christians.[49] Asser's *Life of King Alfred* contains a chapter (106) on reeves and ealdormen in their capacity as judges:

> Studebat <is> quoque in iudiciis etiam propter nobilium et ignobilium suorum utilitatem, qui saepissime in contionibus comitum et praepositorum pertinacissime inter se dissentiebant, ita ut pene nullus eorum, quicquid a comitibus et praepositis iudicatum fuisset, verum esse concederet.[50]
>
> King Alfred used to sit at judicial hearings for the benefit both of his nobles and of the common people, since they frequently disagreed amongst themselves at assemblies of ealdormen or reeves, to the point where virtually none of them could agree that any judgement reached by the ealdormen or reeves in question was just.

Furthermore, in order to improve his officials' ability to carry out their official duties, Alfred commanded them as follows:

48 *Life of King Alfred*, cap. 106: William Stevenson, ed., *Asser's Life of King Alfred* (Oxford: Clarendon, 1959), 92–95. Translation taken from Simon Keynes and Michael Lapidge, eds. and trans., *Alfred the Great: Asser's Life of King Alfred and Other Contemporary Sources* (London: Penguin, 1983), 109–10.

49 George Molyneaux, "The *Old English Bede*: English Ideology or Christian Instruction?" *English Historical Review* 124 (2009): 1310–12.

50 Stevenson, *Asser's Life of King Alfred*, 92. Translation taken from Keynes and Lapidge, *Alfred the Great*, 109.

> Nimium admiror vestram hanc insolentiam, eo quid, Dei dono et meo, sapientium ministerium et gradus usurpastis, sapientiae autem studium et operam neglexistis.[51]

> For that reason, I command you either to relinquish immediately the offices of worldly power that you possess, or else to apply yourselves much more attentively to the pursuit of wisdom.

For Alfred, it seems that wisdom, in the biblical sense discussed by Wormald, was indivisible from an official's ability to carry out his role and to judge fairly and wisely.[52] Alfred viewed the traditions of wisdom and good and just judgment as stretching through the ages from the time of Moses to his own *domboc*.[53] Solomonic wisdom was enacted through royal judgment and this was envisaged as a responsibility the king held toward his subjects, both ecclesiastic and secular.[54] The appointment of just judges, David Pratt contends, was an element of royal *ministerium*, and the importance of this is underlined in the Bible, with numerous Old Testament exemplars.[55] This in turn secured a place for Alfred's laws in a tradition of "divine law-giving," which would have lent his law the same authority as that of his biblical sources.[56] Alfred was preoccupied with the concept/notion of good Christian kingship – he consciously worked to present himself as a "thoughtful and learned king."[57] It is important to remember that early medieval kings viewed the Old Testament as a prescriptive guide for kingship.[58]

This idea was taken further during the ninth century, when kingship became viewed as "a ministry (*ministerium*), as an office (*officium*) which was charged with responsibility for the spiritual and material well-being of the people within its care (*cura*)."[59] Solomon was viewed as the ultimate example of such kingship, and Alfred embraced this Old Testament model and took it to heart, evidenced in the combination of God's law and

51 Stevenson, *Asser's Life of King Alfred*, 93. Translation taken from Keynes and Lapidge, *Alfred the Great*, 110.

52 Wormald, *Making of English Law*, 121–22.

53 David Pratt, *The Political Thought of King Alfred the Great* (Cambridge: Cambridge University Press, 2007), 222–23.

54 Ibid., 162.

55 Ibid., 163.

56 Ibid., 222–23.

57 Powell, "'Three Orders' of Society," 105.

58 Matthew Kempshall, "No Bishop, No King: The Ministerial Ideology of Kingship and Asser's *Res Gestae Aelfredi*," in *Belief and Culture in the Middle Ages: Studies Presented to Henry Mayr-Harting*, ed. Richard Gameson and Henrietta Leyser (Oxford: Oxford University Press, 2001), 109.

59 Ibid., 108.

secular law in his *domboc*.[60] Significantly, Matthew Kempshall highlights Alfred's acknowledgment of Gregory the Great's *Regula Pastoralis*, with its heavy emphasis on the importance of wisdom – Gregory presented Ezekiel as a model "for all those in authority (*praepositi*)."[61] Kempshall argues that Alfred viewed Gregory's *Regula Pastoralis* as the medium through which one could achieve reform of both "ecclesiastical and secular mores," and thus assuage God's anger and alleviate divine punishment; Kempshall equates Alfred's translation of Gregory's text into English in the 890s as a type of pastoral care.[62] Gregory's text highlights the necessity of wisdom in those in power, and their ability to provide advice and correction as a key feature of their office; indeed, Alfred is shown doing just that with the judgments of his ealdormen and reeves in the end of Asser's *Life*.[63]

Napier 50 seems to incorporate a deliberate echo from Asser's *Life of King Alfred* in its directive to royal officials. Pratt argues that regular contact between the king and bishops, ealdormen and reeves "sustained the active force of royal leadership."[64] *Institutes of Polity* also includes "scholars and lawyers" in its section on the nation's councilors;[65] possibly hearkening back to "better times," such as those enjoyed under Alfred's famed program of education. Wulfstan, in his exhortations to the royal officials – perhaps specifically those to reeves, to whom he dedicates a chapter in *Institutes of Polity* – may have been reaching back to the reign of Alfred: a king who not only was dedicated to learning and the pursuit of wisdom, but who was also able to successfully hold off the Viking onslaught of his day.

A major thread running through much of Wulfstan's works is the need to combat injustice in all matters; he details the failings of particular groups in both his homilies and *Institutes of Polity*. Wulfstan's famous *Sermo lupi ad Anglos* reinforces this concept by entreating the English people to not only recognize their past sins, but to repent for them as well:

> ⁊ þy us is þearf micel þæt we us beþencan ⁊ wið God sylfne þingian georne. ⁊ utan don swa us þearf is, gebugan to rihte, ⁊ be suman dæle unriht forlætan, ⁊ betan swyþe georne þæt we ær bræcan;[66]

60 Ibid., 110.
61 Ibid., 111.
62 Ibid., 112. As a result of this translation, along with Alfred's program of education, Gregory's text would be (in theory) more widely available.
63 Kempshall, "No Bishop, No King," 113.
64 Pratt, *Political Thought*, 122.
65 Jost, *Institutes of Polity*, 62–66.
66 Whitelock, *Sermo Lupi ad Anglos*, 52; translated in Swanton, *Anglo-Saxon Prose*, 184. Keynes highlights this in "An Abbot," 204.

> And therefore it is very necessary that we reflect about ourselves and earnestly plead with God himself. And let us do as is necessary for us – bow to justice and in some part to leave off injustice, and to compensate very carefully for what we previously broke.

From this sermon, as well as the legislation of Æthelred and Cnut, it is clear that Wulfstan wished to impress upon the English people that their past failures to properly observe the laws of God and the king was what caused the country's great misfortune of the past decades. Wulfstan also works in these texts to closely connect the aims of the laws of God and those of the king: he refers to the king in one of Æthelred's codes as "Christ's deputy," and as being ready to "avenge God's anger very eagerly."[67] The king is also cast in the role of shepherd in Napier 50 and in *Institutes of Polity*.[68] Wormald notes that the primary aim of Æthelred's laws was to imbue God's law with the same force as secular law.[69] Secular law and God's law were both, in essence, striving toward the same goal: a good Christian society. In this sentiment, Wulfstan was operating to some degree under Carolingian precedent,[70] wherein the ecclesiastics of the realm (particularly the bishops) were considered to be the king's servants, as well as those of God.[71] The importance and centrality of the bishop is evident in texts dating to early in Wulfstan's tenure as archbishop, such as Edward-Guthrum. Here, Gates argues, the bishop enjoys the ultimate authority, with the role of the king centered on the execution of sacred and secular law.[72] Writings dating from around the end of the archbishop's career, such as his additions to Cnut's Proclamation of 1020, take the further step to underline that the laws of the king were secondary to the laws of God.[73]

The necessity of both Christian faith and worldly justice to support the throne is emphasized in *Institutes of Polity*: if either of these breaks down, so too will the throne.[74] This text also highlights the noblemen – nobles, generals, secular judges, and reeves (*eorlas and heretogan and þas worlddeman and eac swa gerefan*) – who are charged with the responsibil-

67 Wormald, "Æthelred the Lawmaker," 76. This was perhaps a conscious echo of the term Æthelred's father Edgar used to describe himself: "vicar of Christ" (Wormald, "Æthelred the Lawmaker," 76).

68 Rabin, *Political Writings*, 145; and Rabin, *Wulfstan: Old English Legal Writings*, 61.

69 Wormald, "Æthelred the Lawmaker," 75.

70 To which he would have been exposed, especially though the works of Alcuin (Keynes, "An Abbot," 184).

71 Wormald, "Archbishop Wulfstan: Eleventh-Century State-Builder," 21.

72 Gates, "Preaching, Politics and Episcopal Reform," 115.

73 Rabin, *Wulfstan: Old English Legal Writings*, xxx–xxxi.

74 Ibid., 67.

ity of protecting the Church.[75] Wulfstan's writings demonstrate that he interpreted this responsibility in several ways. In the text *Episcopus* (or *On Episcopal Duties*, 1002 × 1008), extant in Oxford, Bodleian Library, MS Junius 121, it is clear that bishops were charged with providing guidance in both religious and secular matters, and that they should work together with secular judges in resolving disputes.[76] Wulfstan clearly expected cooperation between ecclesiastical and secular entities, while placing those of the Church in a more elevated position. Along these lines, VIII Æthelred 32 commands the king's reeves "to assist the abbots in all their worldly needs..."[77] Furthermore, Cnut's Proclamation of 1020 charges ealdormen with supporting the bishops in advancing the rights of the Church and royal authority.[78] Earl Thurkil is vested with the responsibility of bringing to justice anyone who violates God's law or secular law, and if this is not possible, the offender should be either killed or exiled, depending on his status.[79] The Proclamation commands reeves more gen-

[75] Ibid., 46–47 and 72–73. *I Polity*, "Concerning nobles": *Ac a hi sculon circan ofer ealle oðre þingc weorðian and werian; II Polity*, "Concerning nobles": *Ac a hy sculan cyrican ofer ealle oðre þing wyrðian and werian* (both translated as: "But they must venerate and protect the Church over all other things").

[76] Rabin, *Wulfstan: Old English Legal Writings*, xxi and 102–03. *[Item 1.] Bisceope gebyreð ælc rihting, ge on godcundan þingan ge on woruldcundan* ("It is proper for a bishop to offer guidance in all things, both in religious and secular matters"). *[Item 4.] He sceall georne saca sehtan and frið wyrcan mid þam woruldдеman þe riht lufian* ("He must readily resolve disputes and make peace along with those secular judges who love justice").

[77] Rabin, *Wulfstan: Old English Legal Writings, 201. [Item 32.] And se cyngc beodeð eallum his gerefan on æghwilcere stowe þæt ge þam abbodan æt eallum worldneodum beorgan swa ge betst magon, and be þam þe ge willan Godes oððe minne freondscipe habban, filstan heora wicneran æghwar to rihte, þæt heo sylfe magan þe oftor on mynstrum fæste gewunian and regollice libban* ("And the king commands all of his reeves in every community to assist the abbots in all their worldly needs as best you can, and if you seek to obtain God's friendship and mine, support their representatives everywhere in their legal interests, so that they themselves may, more often, remain secure in their monasteries and live by their rule").

[78] Rabin, *Wulfstan: Old English Legal Writings*, 229.

[79] Ibid., 228–29: ... *and eac minum ealdormannum ic beode þæt hy fylstan þam biscopum to Godes gerihtum and to minum kynescype and to ealles folces þearfe. Gif hwa swa dyrstig sy—gehadod oððe læwede, Denisc oððe Englisc—þæt he ongean Godes lage ga and ongean minne cynescype oððe ongean woroldriht, and nelle betan and geswican æfter minra biscopa tæcinge, þonne bidde ic Þurcyl eorl and eac beode þæt he ðæne unrihtwisan to rihte gebige, gyf he mæge. Gyf he ne mæge, þonne wille ic, mid uncer begra cræfte þæt he hine on earde adwæsce oððe ut of earde adræfe, sy he betera sy he wyrsa* ("... I also command my ealdormen to support the bishops in advancing the rights of the Church and my royal authority and the welfare of the whole people. If anyone – either cleric or lay, Danish or English – is so bold as to act in opposition to the law of God and in opposition to my royal authority or in

erally to govern with righteousness everywhere, with their rulings supervised by the bishops.[80] The command of ealdormen to support the bishops, the reeves to support the abbots, and the oversight of the reeves' work by bishops demonstrates both clear ecclesiastical precedent over secular law in Wulfstan's work, as well as the role of secular authorities in supporting the Church. This emphasis on secular support for the Church fits with Wulfstan's vision of a holy society, especially when set against the backdrop of the archbishop's interest in an ordered Christian society wherein the throne is supported by the work of the groups in the Three Pillars.

The payment of tithes and church dues was another area in which civil and ecclesiastical authorities were expected to work together and, ultimately, provide support to the Church. The laws of Æthelred call for reeves,[81] working alongside local priests, to ensure participation in mandated fasting and almsgiving.[82] In the event that tithes are not paid, VIII Æthelred 8 states that the king's reeve and the priest of the church or the reeves of the landlord and the bishop are to seize without consent

---

opposition to secular law, and he refuses to repent and refrain in keeping with the teachings of my bishops, then I ask, and indeed command, Earl Thurkil to bring the offender to justice, if he can. If he cannot, then I desire him to wipe him from the earth or drive him from the land with our combined strength, whether he is of higher or lower status").

80 Rabin, *Wulfstan: Old English Legal Writings*, 228–29: *And eac ic beode eallum minum gerefum, be minum freondscype and be eallum þam þe agon and be heora agenum life, þæt hy æghwær min folc rihtlice healdan and rihte domas deman be ðæra scira biscopa gewitnesse and swylce mildheortnesse þæron don, swylce þære scire biscope riht þince and þe man acuman mæge.* ("And further, I command all my reeves, for the sake of my friendship and all that they possess and their very lives, to govern my people with righteousness everywhere and to hand down just rulings with the oversight of the bishops of their shires, and to act with such mercy thereby that the bishop deems it just and the subject can abide by it.")

81 The terms used to denote "reeve" are *tungravius* and *tunes gerefan*, both of which appear only rarely in pre-Conquest texts. The OE term "tun" developed from "enclosed space" to indicate "an enclosure with a dwelling," to a farm, and then to mean "village." A. H. Smith, *English Place-Name Elements, Part II: The Elements Jafn–Ytri, Index and Maps* (Cambridge: Cambridge University Press, 1956), 189. Due to the use of this element in these compounds, the terms are likely meant to denote "village reeve" or "town reeve."

82 Rabin, *Wulfstan: Old English Legal Writings*, 182–83 and 186–87. VII Æthelred 2.5: *Et sciat omnis presbyter et tungravius et decimales homines, ut haec elemosina et ieiunium proveniat, sicut in sanctis iurare poterunt* ("And let every priest, town reeve, and tithingman oversee the almsgiving and fasting, so that they can swear to it on holy relics"). VIIa Æthelred 2.3: *And bringe man þæt to cirican and siððan on þreo dæle be scriftes and be tunes gerefan gewitnesse* ("And it is to be brought to church and subsequently divided in three with the confessor and town reeve acting as witnesses").

that which is owed the church.[83] In these clauses, a secular official is charged with providing active support to the Church. These agents arguably worked as "enforcers" of a sort: the muscle backed by royal power that ensured the Church received its proper tithes and dues. This not only served to fulfill the royal prerogative of supporting and protecting the Church, but it also ensured the correct payment of dues and tithes. While payment of tithes has a clear biblical precedent, tithes only first appear in England in King Æthelstan's Ordinance (926 × *c.* 930).[84] The "legal basis of church finance" was then later "overhauled" in the laws of Edgar (959 × 972), and this included enforcement of tithe payments by reeves.[85] According to Wormald, "the object of Edgar's laws, as of others in the Anglo-Saxon series, was to put the weight of royal power behind the Church's dues."[86]

Institutes of Polity and the Role of the Reeve

The culmination of all Wulfstan's efforts to return the English to a good Christian society was his *Institutes of Polity*. This text offers a mode of governance for what it envisages to be a Christian nation, and would have been the embodiment of what Wulfstan believed was the ecclesiastical role "to admonish and guide kings."[87] Stafford argues that the turmoil of the years 1014–1020 would have prepared and educated Wulfstan in what elements were necessary for good Christian kingship.[88] As a legislator for both Æthelred and Cnut, Wulfstan was able to articulate for the English a program to regain God's favor not just through a spiritual position, but also from a viewpoint born out of a deep understanding of

83 Rabin, *Wulfstan: Old English Legal Writings*, 194–95. VIII Æthelred 8: *Ðæt is: gif hwa teoþunge rihtlice gelæstan nelle, þonne fare to þæs cyninges gerefa and þæs mynstres mæssepreost–oððe þæs landrican and þæs biscopes gerefa–and niman unþances ðone teoðan dæl to ðam mynstre þe hit to gebirige, and tæcan him to ðam nigoðan dæle, and todæle man ða eahta dælas on twa and fo se landhlaford to healfum, to healfum se biscop, si hit cyninges man, sy hit þegnes* ("That is: if anyone refuses to offer up his tithes properly, then the king's reeve and the priest of the church – or the reeves of the landlord and bishop – are to go and seize without consent a one-tenth portion for the church to which it belongs, and the next tenth is to be left for the recreant, and the remaining eight-tenths are to be divided in two and the landlord shall receive half and the bishop the other half, whether he is a king's man or a thane's").

84 John Blair, *The Church in Anglo-Saxon Society* (Oxford: Oxford University Press, 2005), 435–36 and 440.

85 Blair, *Church in Anglo-Saxon Society*, 442.

86 Wormald, *Making of English Law*, 212.

87 Stafford, "Laws of Cnut," 188.

88 Ibid.

the workings of the pre-Conquest administrative framework. *Institutes of Polity* is heavily moralizing, and it focuses (primarily) upon the roles of the bishops, ealdormen, and administrative officials in establishing and maintaining an ordered Christian kingdom. Based on the manuscript transmission history, it is plausible that this text was unfinished at the time of Wulfstan's death in 1023.[89] This text has a complicated textual background. Parts are transmitted in Cambridge, Corpus Christi College 201, London, British Library, Cotton Nero A.i and Oxford, Bodleian Library, Junius 121, manuscripts which themselves have complex relationships.[90] What makes matters difficult is that there is no extant "complete" version of the text.[91] The early twentieth-century editor of *Institutes of Polity*, Karl Jost, published the text as two versions, *I Polity* and *II Polity*, collating the scattered material and wading through various elements of Wulfstan's editorial work.[92] *I Polity* is the shorter text and is thought to represent an earlier version, while *II Polity* has been deemed the "final" rendition of the text, compiled from material in Junius 121 and Nero A.i.[93] Rabin suggests a date of 1008 × 1010 for *I Polity* and 1018 × 1023 for *II Polity*.[94]

In *Institutes of Polity*, a number of Wulfstan's concerns canvassed above come together: the central importance of maintaining a well-ordered Christian society; the role of just laws in promoting the proper ordering of God's church (the centerpiece of a moral society); and the connection of peace with appropriate social regulation. Royal officials not only fit into and were important supports within this moral framework envisaged by Wulfstan (born out of his earlier meditations on status and the law), but the figure of the reeve in particular was allocated a new and important position as a "shepherd" working on behalf of the people.

89 Trilling, "Sovereignty and Social Order," 64.

90 Lionarons, *Homiletic Writings*, 13, 15, and 17. See also Ben Reinhard, "Cotton Nero A.i and the Origins of Wulfstan's *Polity*," *JEGP* 119 (2020): 175–89. Reinhard contends that based on the complicated relationships between the extant manuscripts, it would be best to do away with the distinction between *I* and *II Polity*. Rabin also points to the difficulty in determining the intended audience for the text and what the finished product (if indeed there was one) would have looked like (*Political Writings*, 101). Finally, in his "The Doubtful Evidence for Wulfstan's *Institutes of Polity* as 'a Text'" (forthcoming), Jay Paul Gates argues that *Polity* was not intended to take the form of a unified text but was instead a series of chapters "intended to function in a range of [textual] genres—whether as political theory, legal commentary, or sermon…"

91 Trilling, "Sovereignty and Social Order," 62.

92 Ibid., 63; and Jost, *Institutes of Polity*, 8–38. See also the recent editions by Rabin: *Political Writings* and *Wulfstan: Old English Legal Writings*.

93 Trilling, "Sovereignty and Social Order," 63.

94 Rabin, *Wulfstan: Old English Legal Writings*, xix.

Renée Trilling refers to *Polity* as a text compiling a collection of related ideas, concerned with the linked wellbeing of the Church and the Christian community.[95] The text imbues bishops and royal officials with a sort of social responsibility – bishops, priests, and reeves are all referred to in the context of shepherds here. The place of the bishops at the head of the nation's councilors (*ðeodwitan*) is underlined,[96] with emphasis that the "justice" which concerned the nation's councilors was that of the king's law *and* God's law – Trilling argues that *Institutes of Polity* places royal power below that of God.[97] The text would thus have been the embodiment of what Wulfstan believed was the ecclesiastical role to "admonish and guide kings."[98]

Two major strands in Wulfstan's campaign to reform English society were tracts on status, such as *Geþyncðu*, which were ringing reminders of the correct social stratifications, as well as moralizing texts, exhorting those in power – bishops, ealdormen, and administrative officials – to be just, virtuous, and obedient to God's law and thus do right by the English people and nation. One reason for reeves' prominence in this period would have been their role as royal officials. These were the royal agents "on the ground" who would have had the most contact with the people in the localities, active in the hundred and shire courts, collecting dues and tithes and, in the eleventh century, ensuring that the people participated in the mandated fasting.[99] Royal reeves begin to feature more prominently in the diplomatic during the reign of Æthelred, some of whom are referenced in the charters as not necessarily acting in accordance with law and custom, or in the state's (that is, the king's) best interest.[100] Stafford makes the important point that in the tenth and eleventh centuries, royal power and the exercise of *cynerihta* was very much in the hands of royal officials, and this power was "only as effective as the men on the ground were prepared to make it."[101] This underlines the importance of royal

95 Trilling, "Sovereignty and Social Order," 65 and 70–71.

96 Jost, *Institutes of Polity*, 62–77.

97 Trilling, "Sovereignty and Social Order," 76–77.

98 Stafford, "Laws of Cnut," 188.

99 For example: VII Æthelred 2.5: *Et sciat omnis presbiter et tungravius et decimales homines, ut haec elemosina et ieiunium proveniat, sicut in sanctis iurare poterunt* ("And every priest and the reeve of every village and the heads of the tithings shall be witnesses that this alms-giving and fasting is carried out, and shall be able to swear to it on the holy relics"). Liebermann, *Gesetze*, 1:261; Robertson, *Laws of the Kings of England*, 110, 111.

100 *Rectitudines Singularum Personarum* and *Gerefa* appear to be reminders to the reeve of his duties and responsibilities (with *Gerefa* having a decidedly moralizing tone), albeit on an estate, as opposed to the environs of the royal official.

101 Pauline Stafford, "King and Kin, Lord and Community: England in the Tenth and Eleventh Centuries," in *Gender, Family and the Legitimation of Power: England from the Ninth to Early Twelfth Century* (Aldershot: Ashgate, 2006), 6.

officials in the localities, particularly as the agents of royal power and influence. These are the men who dealt and interacted with the people on a personal level.[102]

Bearing this in mind, Wulfstan's heavy emphasis in his moral discourse on royal officials seems almost natural. These are the men who on a daily basis took the administration of justice into their hands, as is indicated by the law codes and the diplomatic evidence. Wulfstan, as a lawmaker, astute politician, and one of the leading ecclesiastics in pre-Conquest England, would have been well aware of royal officials' prescribed role in the localities, and thus it makes sense that he targeted them in his moral discourse in his effort to save the English nation from God's wrath and the Viking onslaught. Looking back to Bede, bishops were long viewed as bearing responsibilities toward the pastoral care of the people in their localities. In fact, in Bede's letter to Ecgberht, he complains bitterly about the Northumbrian bishops' neglect of their flocks, despite their continued collection of the people's tribute money.[103] Indeed, Blair argues that bishops and priests were envisaged to have not only the responsibility of pastoral care toward their flocks, but also to monitor the moral conduct of the people, enforcing just behavior, and even regulating weights and measurements.[104] This suggests that, whether it was always carried out or not, priests and bishops were viewed as bearing the burden of the moral and spiritual wellbeing of the people in their territories.

Wulfstan, in his multifaceted attempt to retrieve the English from what he may have perceived as the brink of destruction, took the view that some royal officials – particularly reeves – were in a sense "shepherds" of the people and responsible for "pastoral care" in a secular sense. Reeves were perhaps targeted for this particular role as a result of their operation at many levels of society in early England. These officials were found not only at the royal court, directly under the king, but also in villages, towns, and shires. They were associated with justice and the local courts, and also taxes and tithes, and as such they could wield considerable influence.

102 Stephen Baxter and John Blair argue convincingly for the existence of "ministerial land," or estates held by royal officials as a function of their royal office. "Land Tenure and Royal Patronage in the Early English Kingdom: A Model and a Case Study," *Anglo-Norman Studies* 28 (2005): 19–46. Possession of these lands would have been a benefit of holding a royal office; furthermore, Baxter and Blair view it as an enticement to help to vest a royal official's interests in justice and secular administration in his locality (of course, much of this applies primarily to earls, though Baxter and Blair have shown that other royal officials enjoyed this perquisite as well, often in the form of royal *lænland*).

103 Blair, *Church in Anglo-Saxon Society*, 155. For Bede's letter, see Dorothy Whitelock, *English Historical Documents, 500–1042*, 2nd ed. (London: Routledge, 1979), 735–45 (no. 170).

104 Blair, *Church in Anglo-Saxon Society*, 497.

Wulfstan must have viewed reeves as the ideal vehicle for enacting the secular element of his efforts to reform the English, which earned them a significant amount of attention in his writing. Furthermore, the laws demonstrate that reeves often worked alongside bishops and priests in the localities (or were expected to do so). Non-legal texts support this picture also: the Old English *Legend of the Seven Sleepers* depicts the *portgerefa* and the bishop together questioning in an official capacity a man suspected of a crime.[105] Reeves' work on the ground enforcing secular law and ecclesiastical decrees would have been an additional factor making them more attractive as the natural secular counterpart to the bishops, who appear from *Institutes of Polity* to be spearheading the ecclesiastical efforts to redeem the English people.

The section of *Institutes of Polity* dedicated to reeves is heavily moralizing and admonishes them for many types of rapacious behavior.[106] It is noteworthy that the section on reeves was not included in the text of *I Polity*. Gates regards the changes implemented to Wulfstan's text in order to generate *II Polity* as a reflection of the changes to the perceived role of the king and whom he should correct; that is, in *II Polity* the king's roles and responsibilities became more specific and expanded.[107] Therefore, the addition of the section on reeves to *Institutes of Polity* may well exemplify the results of Wulfstan's thinking and his changing views on the reeve and how the reeve's role fit into his picture of Christian kingship. Wulfstan accuses the reeves outright of robbery, and blames them for the rise of unjust laws and their negligence and betrayal of the flock they are supposed to guard:

> Ac nu hit is geworden ealles to swyðe, syððan Eadgar geendode, swa swa God wolde, þæt ma is þæra rypera þonne rihtwisra, and is earmlic ðing, þæt ða syndon ryperas, þe sceoldan beon hyrdas cristenes folces. Hy rypað þa earman butan ælcere scylde oðre hwile and hynað þa heorde, þe hi sceoldan healden, // and mid yfelan holan earme men beswicað and unlaga ræрað on æghwylce wisan earmum to hynþe and wydewan bestrypað oft and gelome.[108]
>
> But now it has happened all too greatly that since Edgar died, even as God willed, there are more robbers than righteous men; and it is a wretched thing that those who should be shepherds of the Christian

[105] Catherine Cubitt, "'As the Lawbook Teaches': Reeves, Lawbooks and Urban Life in the Anonymous Old English Legend of the Seven Sleepers," *English Historical Review* 124 (2009): 1028.

[106] Jost, *Institutes of Polity*, 81–82.

[107] Jay Paul Gates, "The Politics of Building the Holy Society: Wulfstan's Later Writings," (Colloquium presentation, Anglo-Saxon Studies Colloquium, Columbia University, New York, October 2012).

[108] Jost, *Institutes of Polity*, 81–82; Swanton, *Anglo-Saxon Prose*, 193.

> people are robbers. At times they rob the blameless poor and abuse the flock they should guard, and betray poor men with evil slanders, and give rise to unjust laws in all sorts of ways to the injury of the poor, and rob widows over and over again.

This text points to the reeves' deviation from their official roles as royal agents into avaricious figures grasping and jostling for money and position under Æthelred. Wulfstan proceeds to reminisce about the days when reeves respected and observed God's law, devoid of deceit and foul behavior.[109] Here the "golden era" of Edgar's reign is again evoked,[110] reminding the audience of the successful Christian rule demonstrated in the past, which had walked hand-in-hand with prosperity and God's favor. He then returns to the present, bemoaning the descent of the reeves into treachery and greed for riches; his distaste is almost palpable here. The success of the past is contrasted sharply with the apparent moral degradation of the present, with the familiar figure of the reeve standing as an example of such failings. The section ends with the emphasis that the reeves have angered God repeatedly and that atonement "for God and for the state" was necessary in order to fully repent.[111] This passage concerning reeves paints a picture of a group of thuggish, rapacious officials, combing the localities for opportunities to lie and cheat innocents out of their money, and jostling for riches and status. This is juxtaposed against the expectation that the reeve is to be a "shepherd" of the Christian people, helping to guide the people toward a holy society, committed to justice, right, and God's law.[112] The figure of the reeve is deployed here to two ends: first as a local, recognizable official described in vivid language to demonstrate and emphasize what was in Wulfstan's view the deeply problematic nature of English society in the present, and secondly to draw a sharp contrast between the good law and Christian mores of the past and the claimed moral decay of the present. In his homiletic rhetoric, Wulfstan seems to be aiming for an element of shock value – emotional, desperate descriptions of England's apparent dire circumstances intended to motivate the English people – and perhaps especially royal officials – to return to the morally correct behavior and good law of the past.

109 Jost, *Institutes of Polity*, 82.

110 Wulfstan's sense of a "golden era" under Edgar has been frequently observed in his writings. See, e.g., (in reference to Napier 50) Rabin, *Political Writings*, 112n50.

111 Jost, *Institutes of Polity*, 82.

112 There is an interesting correlation here between Wulfstan's passionate discourse against "bad" reeves and the literary convention of the "corrupt judge." It is perhaps possible that Wulfstan intended to underline a familiar tradition in order to strike a chord with the Anglo-Saxon people.

It is significant that Wulfstan uses the term *hyrdas*, or "shepherd," with its biblical and homiletic connotations of Christ,[113] to describe the role which the reeve ought to fulfill on behalf of the people. This analogy is used not once but twice (the second time referencing the people as the "flock" – *heorde*), emphasizing the importance Wulfstan attributed to this facet of the reeve's role. We can also see that bishops and priests are referred to as shepherds, with a responsibility toward the people, but no other secular officials are referenced in this manner. It is instructive in this context to turn to the organization of the chapters of *Institutes of Polity* in BL, Cotton MS Nero A.i.[114] In his study of the composition of Nero A.i, Gates states that the *Institutes of Polity* chapters in Section II represent a coherent collection of texts, all dealing with clergy and ecclesiastical authority – with the exception of the chapter *Be gerefan* ("On Reeves").[115] While *Be gerefan* concerns secular officials as opposed to those of the church, Gates observes that the section is nonetheless coherent, with *Be gerefan* following "the same pattern as those chapters for clergy."[116] This juxtaposition in the manuscript is striking – perhaps especially so as it is the only manuscript witness to *Institutes of Polity* that contains the archbishop's own hand[117] – considering Wulfstan's positioning of the reeve as a secular "shepherd" and counterpart to the bishop, the ecclesiastical figure that was central to the realization of Wulfstan's holy society.

Why are reeves analogized in the same language as ecclesiastics? It seems that Wulfstan believed that the reeve was responsible for a secular "pastoral care" of sorts, for the people in his local district. The reeve, as a powerful (in some instances) royal official, was active and recognizable in the localities – often in a judicial capacity alongside the bishop – and as such may have been an ideal "secular counterpart" to the spiritual and moral guidance provided by the bishops. Wulfstan emphasizes the reeve's role in judicial proceedings, not only in this section of *Institutes of Polity*, but also in the homily Napier 50, and in a more general sense, in the laws of Æthelred and Cnut, wherein the reeve is responsible for ensuring the correct collection of tithes and that minting is done fairly and honestly.[118] Furthermore, significantly, VII Æthelred 6.3 states that the penalty for a reeve's theft would be double that of any other person, which indicates that as the protectors and enforcers of the law and people under it, the reeves' transgressions would be far more grievous and less tolerated than

[113] Bosworth-Toller, s.v. *hirde*; DOE, s.v. *hyrde*.
[114] Gates, "Doubtful Evidence," 10–11.
[115] Ibid., 11.
[116] Ibid.
[117] Ibid., 8.
[118] VIII Æthelred 8; I Cnut 8.2 and II Cnut 8.2.

that of ordinary individuals.[119] Finally, II Cnut 69[120] states that the king's reeves are to supply him solely from his own property, and that no one is required to give the reeve "anything as purveyance,"[121] which strongly suggests that reeves had been guilty of rapacious and greedy behavior in the past – under Æthelred. The role outlined for reeves in *Institutes of Polity* provides a sharp contrast to this past behavior and activity, placing the reeve in an important position in the localities, providing for the secular welfare of the people in the same manner in which the bishops and priests attended to the people's moral and spiritual wellbeing.

Despite the relative frequency with which the reeve begins to appear in tenth- and eleventh-century English religious discourse, the image of the reeve as a "shepherd" (*hyrdas*) of the Christian people appears to have been solely Wulfstan's creation. Therefore, although Wulfstan's negative railings against reeves are perhaps not out of place in the context of tenth- and eleventh-century English religious writings, what is new is Wulfstan's particularly weighty focus on the reeve, as well as his view of the reeve as bearing the responsibility as a shepherd to the Christian people. Wulfstan utilized *Institutes of Polity* to give full expression to the new niche he had carved out for the reeve, building the official into an integral position in his mission to create and uphold the Christian kingdom he envisaged for the English. The work of this royal official was a significant element in Wulfstan's program to reform English society. Through his homilies, political tracts, tracts on ecclesiastical governance, and the legislation drafted for Æthelred II and Cnut, the archbishop built a program geared toward the establishment of an ordered, holy society. This was one in which the status of the church, the clergy, and church law were elevated above secular authority, and where royal officials such as ealdormen, judges, and reeves were charged with supporting the church. The work of these officials, especially reeves, provided the church and its clergy with

[119] *Et si quis praepositus eam fecerit duppliciter emendet quod alii iudicaretur.* ("And if any reeve has committed theft, the compensation paid by him shall be double that prescribed to any other person.") Liebermann, *Gesetze,* 1:261; Robertson, *Laws of the Kings of England,* 113. See also II Cnut 8.2, Liebermann, *Gesetze,* 1:314; Robertson, *Laws of the Kings of England,* 165.

[120] *[1.] Ðæt is ðonne ærost, þæt ic bebeode eallum minan gerefan þæt hig on minon agenan rihtlice tilian 7 me mid ðam feormian, 7 þæt him nan man ne ðearf to feormfultume nan ðingc syllan, butan he sylf wille. [2.] And gyf hwá æfter ðam wite crauian [wille], beo he his weres scyldig wið ðone cyningc.* ("[1.] The first provision is: I command all my reeves to provide for me in accordance with the law from my own property and support me thereby, and [declare] that no man need give them anything as purveyance, unless he himself is willing to do so. [2.] And if anyone [of my reeves] shall demand a fine [in such a case], he shall forfeit his wergeld to the king.") Liebermann, *Gesetze,* 1:356; Robertson, *Laws of the Kings of England,* 209.

[121] Robertson, *Laws of the Kings of England,* 209.

the powerful arm of secular authority. This work thus helped to fulfill Wulfstan's ideal of the good Christian king by providing material support and protection to the Church, as well as helping to realize his vision of an ordered, Christian, holy society. This was almost certainly driven by Wulfstan's deep interest in social structure and the strata of society, and accordingly, what he saw as the foundation of a good Christian nation.

Wulfstan utilized a range of approaches – legal, homiletic, and political – to give expression to his program for a holy society. In so doing, he centers the figure of the reeve: a royal official present at all levels of society, and one therefore ideally placed to support the realization of Wulfstan's multifaceted program. Tracing Wulfstan's reeve through the archbishop's texts offers insight into how the reeve fit into this program as well as how Wulfstan deployed a range of textual approaches in his efforts to bring his social project of reform to fruition. Wulfstan's laws showcase a royal official who was to bring the strong arm of secular power to the aid of the Church. This support was particularly instrumental in Wulfstan's program as it was to ensure the correct rendering and collection of church dues and tithes. The powerful oratory echoing through Wulfstan's homilies and at times in *Institutes of Polity* casts the reeves as servants of God and the English people, offering ringing reminders to blister the ears of the deviant that the English people are akin to a defenseless flock and the reeves the shepherds, with not just a legal but a moral duty to act rightly. Wulfstan's laws create the legislative framework for the holy society, but it is the impassioned homiletic material that helps to give it force.

10

Laying Down the Law? Bishop Headda's Visit to Saint Guthlac

Stefan Jurasinski

Among those who sought the help of Saint Guthlac (*c.* 674–714) in his fenland hermitage were, according to his biographer Felix, the parents of a young man named Hwætred. "Vexed for four years by an evil spirit" (*per quadrennium a maligno spiritu vexatum*), emaciated and devoid of strength, the boy had previously been brought by his mother and father to "the holy places of the saints so that he might be washed in holy water by priests and bishops" (*ad sacratas sedes sanctorum adductus est, ut a sacerdotibus episcopisque sacratis fontibus lavaretur*).[1] Without exception, these remedies had afforded no relief, and the parents nearly despaired until word reached them of the miracles wrought by "a certain hermit who dwelt in the midst of the fen on an island called Crowland."[2] And so they undertook the journey to Crowland where, after receiving his guests warmly, Guthlac immediately led the afflicted boy by the hand to his oratory. Three days of fasting and prayer followed. Then, at sunrise on the third day, Guthlac "washed him in the water of the sacred font and, breathing into his face the breath of healing, he drove away from him all the power of the evil spirit" (*tertia vero die, orto sole, sacrati fontis undis abluit, et, inflans in faciem*

1 Bertram Colgrave, ed. and trans., *Felix's Life of Saint Guthlac* (Cambridge: Cambridge University Press, 1956), 129. Like many earlier works of hagiography, Felix's account of Guthlac's life and miracles relies in part on prior models, the Latin version of Athanasius' *Life of Saint Anthony* not least among them: see Benjamin P. Kurtz, *From St. Antony to St. Guthlac: A Study in Biography* (Berkeley: University of California Press, 1926): 103–46; W. F. Bolton, "The Latin Revisions of Felix's 'Vita Sancti Guthlaci,'" *Mediaeval Studies* 21 (1959): 36–37; Catherine Cubitt, "Memory and Narrative in the Cult of Early Anglo-Saxon Saints," in *The Uses of the Past in the Early Middle Ages*, ed. Yitzhak Hen and Matthew Innes (Cambridge: Cambridge University Press, 2000), 50–57 ("Indeed, Felix's Life of Guthlac is almost entirely a textual confection, created from a modicum of personal recollection and much hagiographical borrowing" [50]); Audrey Meaney, "Felix's Life of St. Guthlac: Hagiography and/or Truth," *Proceedings of the Cambridge Antiquarian Society* 90 (2001): 29–48.

2 Colgrave, *Felix's Life of Saint Guthlac*, 129.

eius spiritum salutis, omnem valitudinem maligni spiritus de illo reppulit).[3] Not again for the rest of his life would Hwætred be so afflicted.

Accounts of saints' healings of demoniacs are, of course, very much to be expected in works of hagiography, demonstrating as they do how the heroes of these narratives shared in the "power over unclean spirits" Christ granted his apostles (Matthew 10:1). But it has not gone unnoticed that the cure just described is not wholly in keeping with the conventions of this tradition. Felix's divergences from prior examples, the present essay will suggest, indicate not only his occasional independence from them, but also something of the tensions between secular and regular clergy manifest in the conciliar legislation of this period; tensions that Felix does not manage wholly to conceal in his accounts of Guthlac's meeting with Bishop Headda and subsequent ordination. (It is notable, as we will see, that a later recasting of Felix's *Vita* removes outright the details that Felix had narrated with seeming evasiveness.) Before these aspects of the *Vita Sancti Guthlaci* may be considered, however, it will be necessary to clarify what is done on behalf of Hwætred by the priests and bishops and ultimately by Guthlac that releases him from the demon's power. As will be seen, there is much about Guthlac's cure that would have invited the scrutiny of a bishop, and these aspects of his ministry appear to go unremarked in commentary published so far.

The Nature of the Cure

The character both of the remedies earlier administered to the boy and of the rite later performed by Guthlac in his oratory are considered at length in Bertram Colgrave's remarks on the healing of Hwætred, the only ones of which I am aware that go much beyond merely paraphrasing Felix's account of the events in question. Of the parents' earlier visits to the *sacratas sedes sanctorum*, Colgrave suggests a connection to "the widespread type of miracle found in the lives of saints, in which when other relics are unsuccessful, those of a particular saint prove successful."[4] The sole example of such a "type" adduced by Colgrave, drawn from Gregory the Great's life of Saint Benedict (*Dialogi* II, cap. 16), seems of genuine but ultimately limited relevance. Much less is said in Pope Gregory's narrative of the remedies sought before the visit to Benedict: we are told only that the afflicted man "had been sent" by his bishop "to many places of the martyrs" (*per multa fuerat martyrum loca transmissus*) and that these "holy martyrs of God did not wish to grant him the gift of

[3] Ibid., 131.
[4] Ibid., 188.

health, so that they might show how much grace there was in Benedict" (*Sed sancti Dei martyres noluerunt ei sanitatis donum tribuere, ut quanta esset in Benedicto gratia demonstrarent*).[5] Once given through Benedict's prayers, the cure depends on the demoniac's no longer eating flesh or ever again attempting to live under a rule.[6] While affording some sense of the reason why Hwætred's visits to the *sacratas sedes sanctorum* are of no help, the analogue is ultimately an oblique one, not quite paralleling what few details Felix does provide about the manner in which the unnamed priests and bishops attempt to cure him.

Colgrave has more to say on Guthlac's means of healing the boy, and his remarks are worth quoting in full:[7]

> The ancient custom of *exsufflatio* to drive out the devil is still practised in the Roman rite of Baptism (cf. Cath. Enc. V, p. 711, s.v. 'exorcism'). The account seems to suggest that Guthlac did in fact baptize the boy in order to drive out the evil spirit. The story implies that the boy had already been baptized before on several occasions. But as the evil spirit had not been driven out, presumably the baptism was not considered valid. His parents may well have been heathen, or recent converts, who still looked upon the rite of baptism as a form of magic.

Colgrave's remarks appear to leave one aspect of Hwætred's cure – seemingly an important one – wholly unremarked. If the rite administered by Guthlac was indeed a baptism, as Colgrave suggests, was Guthlac authorized to perform it? Celebrated holy man that he was, Guthlac was not at this point ordained to the priesthood or even to the diaconate.[8] Whether

[5] J.-P. Migne, ed., *Vita S. Benedicti (ex libro II Dialogorum S. Gregorii Magni excerpta)*, PL 66 (Paris: Garnier Frères, 1866), 164.

[6] "Cui sanato præcipit, dicens: 'Vade, et posthac carnem non comedas; et ad sacrum ordinem nunquam accedere præsumas.'" ibid., 164.

[7] Colgrave, *Felix's Life of Saint Guthlac*, 188.

[8] Sarah Foot notes Bede's view that "the sacrament [of baptism] could not be administered by *any* member of a religious community." "'By Water in the Spirit': Baptism in Early Anglo-Saxon England," in *Pastoral Care before the Parish*, ed. John Blair and Richard Sharpe (Leicester: Leicester University Press, 1992), 185. That the administration of sacraments belonged uniquely to priests and bishops had been long established: cf. W. M. Lindsay, ed., *Isidori hispalensis episcopi: Etymologiarum sive originum, libri xx*, 2 vols. (Oxford: Oxford University Press, 1911 [repr. 2008]), 1:200 (VIII.xii); translated in Stephen A. Barney, et al., eds. and trans., *The Etymologies of Isidore of Seville* (Cambridge: Cambridge University Press, 2006), 171: "A priest (*sacerdos*) has a name compounded of Greek and Latin, as it were 'one who gives a holy thing' (*sacrum dans*), for as king (*rex*) is named from 'ruling' (*regere*), so priest from 'making sacrifice' (*sacrificare*)—for he consecrates (*consecrare*) and sanctifies (*sanctificare*)." See also Julia Barrow, *The Clergy in the Medieval World* (Cambridge: Cambridge University

Guthlac was in fact permitted to offer the rite of baptism is, as will be seen in later sections, a question of great and overlooked significance to his later dealings with Bishop Headda, which lead ultimately to his brief re-entry into worldly affairs as a priest and royal counselor. Though the passage that suggested the *exsufflatio* of the Roman rite of baptism to Colgrave – *inflans in faciem eius spiritum salutis* – seems to have been rendered differently in various witnesses, with the version of Felix's *Vita* in Cambridge, Corpus Christi College 307 giving the finite form *inflavit* and three others giving *insufflans*, the likeness of what Guthlac is doing to baptism (more accurately, the "catechesis" that came at this time to be appended to the baptismal rite) probably did not escape those who copied the text.[9] That Orderic Vitalis, in his abridgment of Felix's *Vita*, attributes the cure of the boy to fasting and prayer alone, omitting the matter of the exsufflation, was perhaps motivated by his own sense that reproducing Felix's wording here would imply presumption on Guthlac's part.[10]

Press, 2015), 51. "The priesthood was the top grade and only priests were able to celebrate Mass."

9 Not all commentators have attached such significance to this gesture: Audrey Meaney ("Felix's Life," 41) regards it as a simple instance of "wonder-working breath" probably derived from Felix's sources. It is surely more than that, however. Evident in most sacramentaries of this period is the intermingling of the "catechesis" (originally, a distinct rite in which the catechumen would renounce the devil) and the baptism itself. In the Gelasian Sacramentary, where these rites remain distinct, the priest begins the "catechesis" by addressing Satan with his hand above the heads of the catechumens: "Therefore, condemned one, give honor to the living and true God, give honor to Jesus Christ his son, and to the Holy Spirit, in whose name and in whose power I order you to leave and depart from this servant of God, whom today the Lord our God Jesus Christ by his gift has deigned to call to his holy grace and benediction and to the baptismal font" (*Proinde, damnate, da honorem Deo vivo et vero, da honorem Iesu Christo Filio eius, et Spiritui sancto, in cuius nomine atque virtute praecipio tibi ut exeas et recedes ab hoc famulo Dei, quem hodie Dominus Deus noster Iesus Christus ad suam sanctam gratiam et benedictionem fontemque baptismatis dono vocare dignatus est*). The renunciation of Satan and all his pomps follows immediately thereafter. H. A. Wilson, ed., *The Gelasian Sacramentary. Liber Sacramentorum Romanae Ecclesiae* (Oxford: Clarendon, 1894), 79. On the separation sometimes observed between the "catechesis" (which at this time lost the meaning "instruction" only to regain it in later centuries) and the baptism itself, see J. D. C. Fisher, *Christian Initiation: Baptism in the Medieval West* (London: S.P.C.K., 1965), 7.

10 "After four years of madness he [Hwætred] was taken to Crowland, where the man of God took him by the hand and led him into his cell: and after three days of continual prayer and fasting he was entirely delivered from the evil spirit" (*Post quattuor annos Crolandiam adductus est quem uir Dei manu arripiens intra oratorium suum duxit, et illic continuis tribus diebus ieiunans et orans ab omni inquietudine maligni spiritus curauit*). Marjorie Chibnall, ed. and trans., *The Ecclesiastical History of Orderic Vitalis*, vol. 2 (Books III and IV), (Oxford: Clarendon, 1969),

Not only was exsufflation a standard element of the baptismal rite, but it is fair to say that the entirety of the rite was directed at no other end than expelling from the baptismal candidate the influence of malignant spirits, as is plain from the relevant portions of liturgical books of this period.[11] In the early ninth-century Stowe Missal, for example, the rite of baptism (not, significantly, the "catechesis," as the passage in question falls under the rubric "ordo babtismi" [*sic*]) commences with a prayer to be intoned by the priest asking that God expel the devil and all vestiges of paganism from the baptismal candidate (*Domine sanctæ pater omnipotens æterne deus expelle diabulum et gentilitatem ab homine isto*); the exsufflation occurs immediately before the candidate is asked to renounce the devil and all his works.[12]

The uncertain distinction between baptism and analogous sacramental and exorcismal rites figures in other texts of the early Middle Ages. Attempts to remedy such confusion may be found in a text of ecclesiastical law perhaps contemporary with Felix's *Vita Sancti Guthlaci*, the early eighth-century *Pœnitentiale Theodori*. The *Pœnitentiale*, which was assembled at least in part from judgments issued by the late seventh-century archbishop of Canterbury, contains a series of canons (I, x, 1–2) dealing with what should be done with those who have been baptized more than once.[13] For those who have received a second baptism *ignorantes*, no penance is necessary, though they are to be excluded from ordination "unless some great necessity require it" (*nisi magna aliqua necessitas*

330–31. Orderic Vitalis' account of the cure of Hwætred otherwise depends fairly closely upon Felix's. The Old English version of Felix's text (Paul Gonser, ed., *Das angelsächsische Prosa-Leben des hl. Guthlac* [Heidelberg: Carl Winter, 1909]) does little to shed light on the questions considered in the present essay, and the same may be said of the two Old English poems, neither of which touches on the episodes under consideration.

11 See, e.g., Wilhelm Braune, ed., "Niederdeutsche Taufelgelöbnisse," in *Althochdeutsches Lesebuch*, 17th ed. (Tübingen: Max Niemeyer, 1994), 39, where, after a recitation of the Creed in the vernacular, the priest is instructed: "Breathe in his face and say this prayer: 'Go out from him, unclean spirit, and give honor to the true and living God" (*Suffla in faciem et dic hanc orationem: Exi ab eo immunde spiritus et redde honorem deo vivo et vero*). On the fundamentally exorcismal character of the baptismal rite, see Fisher, *Christian Initiation*, 8.

12 Sir George F. Warner, ed., *The Stowe Missal*, vol. 2 (London: Harrison and Sons, 1915), 24–25. On the background and nature of the Stowe Missal, see, e.g., Brendan Coffey, "The Stowe Enigma: Decoding the Mystery," *Irish Theological Quarterly* 75 (2010): 75–91.

13 On the background of the *Pœnitentiale Theodori*, see John T. McNeill and Helena M. Gamer, *Medieval Handbooks of Penance* (New York: Columbia University Press, 1938), 179–82; Cyrille Vogel, *Les 'Libri Paenitentiales'* (Turnhout: Brepols, 1968), 69–70; Allen J. Frantzen, *The Literature of Penance in Anglo-Saxon England* (New Brunswick: Rutgers University Press, 1980), 68.

cogat).[14] But of those who do so deliberately "as if they again crucified Christ" (*quasi iterum Christum crucifixerunt*), seven years of fasting are required. Subsequently, however, the text appears to drift into the same obscurity it was intended to remedy. Qualifying language appended to the canon concerning those knowingly baptized twice suggests that the penitential remedy is to be applied only to those who hoped thereby to expiate a particular vice (*si pro vitio aliquo fuerit*); if they thought it permissible for the sake of their purity (*pro munditia*) they may do penance for three years.[15] The difference between the two cases is far from obvious.[16] If the parents of Hwætred were indeed, as Colgrave suggests, deliberately having their son baptized on multiple occasions in the hope that one of them might "work," it is hard to see how they would not have fallen into one of these categories, though their being either unbaptized themselves or newly converted might render their actions (though probably not Guthlac's) more or less excusable.

"Catechesis," Validity, and Episcopal Authority over Priests

The problem of multiple baptisms also figures in an analogue for the cure of Hwætred perhaps more illuminating than the episode in Gregory's *Dialogi* mentioned by Colgrave. The text in question is a miracle attributed to John of Beverly, bishop of Hexham (and subsequently of York), one of several narrated in the final book of Bede's *Historia Ecclesiastica.* As far as I know, it has not yet been discussed in connection with the chapter of Felix's *Vita Sancti Guthlaci* considered above. The miracle related by Bede, made all the more relevant to the cure of Hwætred by its resting upon exsufflation (here notably occurring within the detached "catechesis" rite), is narrated by an abbot named Herebald who, when serving as "one of the bishop's clergy" (*in clero illius conversatus*), suffers an injury to his head in a riding accident.[17] Hovering between life and death, Herebald has a series of brief exchanges with the bishop, who ultimately asks him if he is sure he has been baptized. Herebald replies by asserting the certainty of his knowledge and gives the name of the priest who baptized him. At this point, John feels he has hit upon the problem:

14 Paul Willem Finsterwalder, ed., *Die Canones Theodori Cantuariensis und ihre Überlieferungsformen* (Weimar: Hermann Böhlaus Nachfolger, 1929), 303.

15 Finsterwalder, *Die Canones Theodori Cantuariensis,* 303.

16 The distinction is not much clarified by McNeill and Gamer's translation (*Medieval Handbooks of Penance,* 194), which suggests that the confusion is inherent in the text itself.

17 Bertram Colgrave and R. A. B. Mynors, eds., *Bede's Ecclesiastical History of the English People* (Oxford: Oxford University Press, 1969), 466–67 (v.6).

> "If you were baptized by that priest you were not perfectly baptized, for I know that, when he was ordained priest, he was so slow-witted that he was unable to learn the office of catechism or baptism; and for this reason I ordered him not to presume to exercise this ministry because he could not perform it properly."[18]

Having said this, Bishop John proceeds to catechize (*cathecizare*) Herebald; "As he did so and breathed upon my face," Herebald relates, "I immediately felt better" (*factumque est ut, exsufflante illo in faciem meam, confestim me melius habere sentirem*).[19] Only after his fractured skull has begun to heal does Herebald approach the baptismal font.

Though unrelated to events in the life of John of Beverly, the very next chapter of Bede's *Historia* concerns the abdication and baptism of the West Saxon king Cædwalla, who, as did Constantine and Theodosius II (though his knowledge of these examples seems improbable), delays his own baptism until the end of his life in the hope that, "soon after his baptism, he might be loosed from the bonds of the flesh and pass, cleansed as he was, to eternal joy" (*sperans quia, mox baptizatus, carne solutus ad aeterna gaudia iam mundus transiret*).[20] Though this is not a baptism performed twice and is therefore wholly licit, Caedwalla's might well be considered a baptism *pro munditia* all the same; at the very least, it offers a sense of the constraints under which the English Church labored during the lifetime of Guthlac. Here the relative normalcy of an adult catechumenate made possible gambits such as the strategic "clinical baptism" of Cædwalla.[21] (Even

18 *At ille 'Si ab hoc' inquit 'sacerdote baptizatus es, non es perfecte baptizatus; noui namque eum, et quia cum esset presbyter ordinatus, nullatenus propter ingenii tarditatem potuit cathecizandi uel baptizandi ministerium discere, propter quod et ipse illum ab huius praesumtione ministerii, quod regulariter implere nequibat, omnimodis cessare praecepi.* Colgrave and Mynors, *Ecclesiastical History*, 468–69.

19 Ibid.

20 Ibid., 470–71.

21 It should be said that, strictly speaking, to be baptized twice was not entirely forbidden even by the *Pœnitentiale Theodori*. In a clause that, given its interest in the distinction between "Greek" and "Roman" practice, probably rests on authentically Theodorean teaching, the *Pœnitentiale* asserts that the ordination rite observed for monks "is a second baptism according to the judgment of the fathers in which all sins are taken away as in baptism" (*secundum baptismum est iuxta iudicium partum in quo omnia peccata dimittuntur sicut in baptismo*). Finsterwalder, *Die Canones Theodori Cantuariensis*, 315 (II, iii, 3); trans. (with minor modifications) McNeill and Gamer, *Medieval Handbooks of Penance*, 201. "Clinical" baptism was a practice that could not at this time be prohibited outright but was nonetheless probably disfavored: see, e.g., B. Dombart and A. Kalb, eds., *Sancti Aurelii Augustini De civitate Dei*, Corpus Christianorum Series Latina 48 (Turnhout: Brepols, 1955), 390 (XIII, 7).

Guthlac's successor at Crowland was only baptized in adulthood.)[22] It is thus not hard to see how the sacrament might suffer abuse from perfectly innocent motives such as those of Hwætred's parents. English Britain in the seventh and eighth centuries was a place in which instruction in the rudiments of the faith was often sufficient in itself to occupy priests and bishops. As the episode concerning Herebald's ignorant priest suggests, having to rely on the recently and imperfectly converted to make up the ranks of the ordained sometimes caused acute problems of ecclesiastical governance, exposing the Church to the risks posed by the poorly trained as well as charismatic loners and charlatans.

The Arrival of Headda

As stories of Guthlac's miracles reach the ears of the ordained clergy, processes are set in motion that will permanently disturb the peace of Guthlac's hermitage. After Headda (identified by Colgrave as bishop of Lichfield and Leicester) arranges a visitation with Guthlac for reasons Felix does not explain, disagreement emerges within the bishop's retinue between those full of admiration for the hermit and those suspecting him of a counterfeit holiness.[23] Headda's secretary, Wigfrith, appears to figure among the latter group, and hopes to learn from the encounter with Guthlac "whether he was a follower of the divine religion or a pretender to false sanctity" (*utrum divinae religionis cultor esset aut pseudo-sanctitatis simulator*).[24] Wigfrith avers he will be able to draw on his experience among the Irish (*inter Scottorum*) in ferreting out signs of *pseudo-sanctitas* at Crowland, for in his travels there he had seen enough "false hermits and pretenders of various religions" (*pseudo-anchoritas diversarum religionum simulatores*) to judge the difference between authentic and pretended religion.[25]

About Bishop Headda's thoughts on the subject the text is silent. Nonetheless, it is not long after his encounter with Guthlac that the bishop "beg[ins] to beg and adjure Guthlac to receive priest's orders at his hand" (*supplex adiurare coepit illum, ut sacerdotale officium per eum suspiceret*).[26] Guthlac at once prostrates himself before the bishop and

[22] Colgrave, *Felix's Life of Saint Guthlac*, 148; John Blair, *The Church in Anglo-Saxon Society* (Oxford: Oxford University Press, 2005), 168n139.

[23] Colgrave, *Felix's Life of Saint Guthlac*, 190n. Felix explains the bishop's desire for a meeting with Guthlac with the assertion that the former did so "as if imbued with heavenly counsel" (*quasi caelesti consilio inbutus*): 142–43.

[24] Ibid.

[25] Ibid.

[26] Ibid., 144–45.

"promise[s] to be obedient to his wishes" (*volentiae illius se oboediturum esse promittit*).[27] Immediately after Guthlac is ordained, Bishop Headda consecrates the church in which Guthlac had already administered at least one baptism.

Colgrave has little to say about this episode beyond mentioning that the consecration of a church when its priest was ordained was a matter of course at this time.[28] Nor has the passage attracted much interest in the years since.[29] Nonetheless, one senses here, as in the episode concerning the cure of Hwætred, the pressure of a subtext upon Felix's narrative whose influence is not wholly effaced. Felix tells us nothing of the substance of the conversation between Headda and Guthlac other than that the former found the latter's teachings "sweeter than honey" (*melle dulciora*).[30] They were not so sweet, however, as to prevent Headda from interrupting Guthlac in the midst of his discourses to insist on ordaining him. The language with which he does so is significant. Much as an oath is the gravest form of asseveration or promise, an adjuration is the gravest form of demand, and for much the same reason: both attach to a proposed obligation an appeal that divine wrath follow any refusal.[31] The *Anonymous Life of Saint Cuthbert*, composed "between 699 and 705," features a gesture not unlike the one employed by Headda, but described at greater length.[32] When Alfflaed, a vowed virgin and member of the Northumbrian royal household, arranges for Cuthbert to meet with her,

> [t]he handmaiden of God on bended knees began to ask him many things and finally she adjured him boldly by the name of our Lord Jesus Christ and by the nine orders of angels and the persons of all the saints, and asked him concerning the length of life of her brother King Ecgfrith.[33]

27 Ibid.

28 Ibid., 191.

29 Meaney says that the bishop is "impressed" and implies that this is why he is ordained: "Felix's Life," 43.

30 Colgrave, *Felix's Life of Saint Guthlac*, 144–45.

31 On the nature of adjurations, see Saint Thomas Aquinas, *Summa Theologica*, q. XC, which offers a short summary of patristic thought on the gesture (oaths are considered at much greater length in the preceding section): *The "Summa Theologica" of St. Thomas Aquinas, part II (qq. LXXX–C)*, trans. "Fathers of the English Dominican Province" (London: Burns, Oates and Washbourne, 1922), 156–61.

32 Bertram Colgrave, ed. and trans., *Two Lives of Saint Cuthbert* (Cambridge: Cambridge University Press, 1940), 13.

33 *Cui ancilla Dei flectens genua, multa interrogare cepit. Postremo autem per nomen Domini nostri Iesu Christi et per nouem ordines angelorum, et omnium sanctorum personas, fiducialiter adiurauit, interrogans de longitudine vitae fratris sui regis Egfridi.* Colgrave, *Two Lives of Saint Cuthbert*, 102–03.

The anonymous *Life*'s *flectens genua* is not far from Felix's *supplex*, and the former passage suggests that Bishop Headda is not begging on his knees *to Guthlac* (as some commentators imply) but rather assuming the posture appropriate to someone imploring all the powers of heaven.[34] It is significant that adjuration is a gesture reserved for compelling a reluctant or even wholly unwilling person to undertake a particular action; in narrative sources of this period, it almost always has the desired effect.[35]

There is little reason to think that Headda arrived at Crowland for any other reason than to address the irregularities of Guthlac's ministry by requiring his submission.[36] The ordination itself seems to add little

[34] Colgrave's "beg and adjure" may therefore be somewhat misleading, though the vagueness may ultimately be attributed to Felix himself.

[35] Though a late example, the adjuration of Flosi by Hildiguðr in *Brennu-Njálssaga* (Chapter CXVI) has all the attributes of those just described. See Finnur Jónsson, ed., *Brennu-Njálssaga (Njála)* (Halle: Max Niemeyer, 1908), 265. Extreme reluctance to assume secular responsibilities, sometimes overcome only by compulsion and "adjuration," was (and remained) a feature of hagiographies of this period: see, e.g., *The Anonymous Life of Saint Cuthbert*'s narrative of Cuthbert's election to the bishopric of Lindisfarne (IV.i): "So he was led away unwillingly and under compulsion, weeping and wailing, while the council together with Archbishop Theodore still awaited him" ([...] *inuitus et coactus lacrimans et flens, abstractus est expectante etiam adhuc senatu, cum archiepiscopo Thedoro*). Colgrave, *Two Lives of Saint Cuthbert*, 110–11. In the corresponding note (p. 330), Colgrave offers other instances of "saints who were made bishops under protest," "the most extraordinary example" being "that of Ammonius who cut off part of his own ear to avoid being made a bishop, and even threatened to cut out his own tongue, so they left him to his life of contemplation." Seen in light of these examples, the most noticeable feature of Guthlac's ordination is his *lack* of resistance once a secular state is required of him.

[36] The view of Headda's interactions with Guthlac argued for here differs from those of other commentators. Stephanie Hollis, *Anglo-Saxon Women and the Church* (Woodbridge: Boydell, 1992), 123, attributes Guthlac's ordination to "much coaxing" on Headda's part, and conjectures that "Bishop Headda's insistence on ordaining Guthlac may well represent a movement, in the early 8th century, to put a stop to the informal pastoral ministries of the men – and women – whose influence on the laity derived solely from their personal sanctity, and to make their practitioners, where it was possible, part of the official church hierarchy." N. J. Higham, "Guthlac's *Vita*, Mercia and East Anglia in the First Half of the Eighth Century," in *Æthelbald and Offa: Two Eighth-Century Kings of Mercia*, ed. David Hill and Margaret Worthington (Oxford: Basingstoke Press, 2005), 87, sees mainly political machinations at work in Headda's arrival at Crowland, with Guthlac's "acceptance of ordination impl[ying] some level of recognition of the Mercian establishment." Helen Gittos sees Guthlac as initiating a "process" of domesticating the fenland wilderness that is "only completed, and institutionally recognized, when Bishop Headda ordained Guthlac a priest and then consecrated the church." *Liturgy, Architecture, and Sacred Places in Anglo-Saxon England* (Oxford: Oxford University Press, 2013),

that was previously wanting from the ministry of Guthlac, his actions as priest after Headda's departure being limited to two celebrations of Mass in his oratory as he senses the approach of his own death (cap. L). Had Guthlac done anything other than immediately yield to Headda's entreaty, he would have shown himself to be like the *peregrini* his secretary had observed among the Irish and thus a menace to those under the bishop's care. While Headda may well have looked favorably on Guthlac, the latter's having violated the requirement that baptisms be administered by the ordained (and not performed on those already baptized by someone else) seems probable.[37] That Felix contrasts Guthlac's baptism of Hwætred with the ineffectual earlier attempts of priests and bishops shows what was at stake for Headda and his clergy. The threat was not solely to their monopoly on pastoral care, as some commentators seem to imply. The disquieting iterations of Hwætred's baptisms aside, having the validity of sacraments depend upon the sanctity of the persons administering them (an implication Gregory's life of Saint Benedict is careful to avoid) brings Felix's text close to inadvertently reawakening the Donatist heresy.[38]

The Coyness of Felix

We may conclude by noting something about Felix's style. Its prolixity was first pointed out by Orderic Vitalis, and Felix has accordingly (with justification) been classified by present-day scholars as one of the chief

33. To Stefany J. Wragg, "The saint's interaction with the bishop clearly indicates both the saint's superiority and his humility; Headda begs to consecrate Guthlac, in recognition of his holiness (ch. XLVII), and in a demonstration of humility, Guthlac obeys the Mercian bishop." "The Early Texts of the Cult of St. Guthlac," *English Studies* 100 (2019): 256–57.

37 Cf. *Pœnitentiale Theodori* I, ix, 11: "If anyone who is not ordained performs baptism through temerity, he is cut off from the Church and shall never be ordained" (*Si quis baptizat per temeritatem non ordinatus abiciendus est ab ecclesia et nunquam ordinetur*): Finsterwalder, *Die Canones Theodori Cantuariensis*, 303; trans. McNeill and Gamer, *Medieval Handbooks of Penance*, 193. See also Foot, "By Water in the Spirit," 185.

38 Against the Donatists (a "schismatic body" of the early fourth century), "the Church maintained that the unworthiness of the minister did not affect the validity of sacraments, since, as Augustine insisted, their true minister was Christ." F. L. Cross, "Donatism," in *The Oxford Dictionary of the Christian Church*, ed. F. L. Cross and E. A. Livingstone, 2nd ed. (Oxford: Oxford University Press, 1985), 419. The same point is stressed by Bede with respect to the sacrament of baptism, though without mentioning the Donatist heresy by name: see M. L. W. Laistner, ed., *Bedae Venerabilis expositio actuum apostolorum et rectractatio* (Cambridge, MA: The Mediaeval Academy of America, 1939), 7.

exemplars of the bombastic Latin prose that emerged early in the Anglo-Saxon period.[39] But what has been observed about Felix's approach to his subject in the present essay is something rather different: a tendency to mumble or resort to strange contradictions when describing events that might give an unfavorable impression of Guthlac. A rite has all the attributes of baptism but is not a baptism; a bishop is so awed by a revered hermit's insights (about which we are told nothing) that he interrupts him to demand his immediate ordination to the priesthood; the hermit responds by "at once prostrat[ing] himself upon the ground and promis[ing] to be obedient to his wishes." Incidents and gestures of a seemingly straightforward nature are described in ways that require us to assign them more than one possible meaning, and not for reasons of rhetorical embellishment alone. Such is even the case for Guthlac's response to Headda's adjuration. While prostration was at this time an element of the ordination rite, it is notable that prostration in these contexts takes place before the altar, betokening absolute submission to the divine will (as well as one's own insufficiency unaided by grace). But it was also an element at this time of the rite of penance.[40] Given Guthlac's likely indifference to questions of Headda's authority, deliberate or not, before the bishop's arrival, his prostration before the bishop may not be without some penitential aspect. Does Guthlac's promise to be obedient to Headda's wishes come with an implied "from henceforth," acknowledging the error of having administered the sacrament of baptism for a second time to the same person, and without ordination? Here it is significant that Orderic Vitalis, in his epitome of

[39] See Chibnall, *Ecclesiastical History of Orderic Vitalis*, 322–23; Bolton, "The Latin Revisions," 38.

[40] Cf. the instructions attributed to Saint Boniface that conclude the penitential of Ecgberht: F. W. H. Wasserschleben, ed., *Die Bußordnungen der ablendländischen Kirche* (Halle: Verlag Graeger, 1851), 246; also the *ordo* given at the outset of the "Handbook for the Use of a Confessor," attributed to Jerome but of doubtful origins: "When someone wishes to make a confession of his sins, let him first prostrate himself upon the earth humbly in the sight of God" (*Quando aliquis uoluerit confessionem facere peccatorum suorum* [...] [*i*]*nprimis igitur prosternat se humiliter in conspectu Dei super terram*); see Roger Fowler, "A Late Old English Handbook for the Use of a Confessor," *Anglia* 83 (1965): 16. It should be said, however, that it would be a mistake to see the prostrations of the rite of ordination and those of penance as *fundamentally* distinct in motivation. Even in the prostration of the king prescribed in the tenth-century Coronation Order of Mainz, Ernst H. Kantorowicz discerned "a gesture of deepest humiliation and contrition"; see Kantorowicz, *Laudes Regiae: A Study in Liturgical Acclamations and Mediaeval Ruler Worship* (Berkeley: University of California Press, 1958), 91. In most *ordines* the prostration of the king took place before the altar in imitation of the ordination rite of priests: see, e.g., "Claudius Pontifical II," in D. H. Turner, ed., *The Claudius Pontificals* (Chichester: Moore and Tillyer, 1971), 89 (*perueniens rex ad aecclesiam, prosternat se coram altare, et ymnizetur*).

Felix's *Vita*, simply has Headda "compelling" Guthlac to become a priest.[41] It seems impossible that Felix was not himself alert to the subtext of the exchange between Headda and Guthlac given his own acknowledgment of the mischief of Irish *peregrini*. In the background of this encounter between the hermit and the bishop lay the long-fought submission of monastic establishments to episcopal authority, a development that was working its way toward becoming a settled matter of ecclesiastical law in England during the lifetimes of Guthlac and of Felix himself.[42]

Felix's style grows taciturn when it seems necessary to hide from view, presumably out of devotion to and even genuine affection for his subject, those instances in which Guthlac did indeed act without appropriate concern for ecclesiastical law in administering baptism. (Affection itself may not be ruled out among Felix's motives, as the text was composed not long – around sixteen years – after Guthlac's death.)[43] Felix may feel licensed to muddle his account of Guthlac's actions because they are somewhat excusable by the standards of Guthlac's and perhaps even Felix's own time. Guthlac's baptism of Hwætred was prompted by no other desire than easing the suffering of Hwætred and his desperate parents; ignorance on the hermit's part of a question of ecclesiastical law that was itself unsettled perhaps mitigates any guilt even more.[44] Guthlac's cure of Hwætred was thus not a baptism done *per temeritatem* of the sort condemned in the *Pœnitentiale Theodori*.[45] But to place Guthlac's error in full view and excuse it overtly might have tempted some readers to make allowances for less innocent forms of disobedience. As we saw in the miracle of John of Beverly and in the clauses of the *Pœnitentiale Theodori* earlier discussed, confusion reigned even among leading clerics as to the

41 "But the bishop [Headda] found in the holy man such a store of wisdom in expounding the Holy Scriptures that after he had dedicated the church of Crowland on 21 August he compelled the servant of God by virtue of his vow of obedience to receive the dignity of priesthood" (*eundem seruum Dei suscipere sacerdotii stemma inuiolabili obœdientiæ præcepto coegit*). Chibnall, *Ecclesiastical History of Orderic Vitalis*, 332–33.

42 While the council of Hertford (672–73) had prohibited bishops' interference in the affairs of minsters, the council of Clofesho (747) made allowances for episcopal governance, and "monastic independence from episcopal interference was not restored after 747; indeed, the later councils did much to increase the power of the bishops still further"; see Sarah Foot, *Monastic Life in Anglo-Saxon England, c.600–900* (Cambridge: Cambridge University Press, 2006), 130–32.

43 See Bolton, "Latin Revisions," 38.

44 The extent of confusion on whether rebaptisms were sometimes appropriate may be evident from the fact that Pope Zacharias admonished Boniface *not* to do precisely what John of Beverly did upon learning that his cleric had been baptized by an ignorant priest (Foot, "By Water in the Spirit," 189).

45 See above, note 37.

permissibility of second baptisms; to make things worse was probably all too easy. And so Felix does his best to camouflage Guthlac's contraventions of ecclesiastical law and conceal behind ungainly contradictions the true nature of the bishop's visitation. Hints of what really went on are unavoidable in the telling (despite Felix's evasions) and become fully apparent when viewed in light of the *Vita*'s legal and spiritual setting.

11

The Terms of Hypocrisy in Early English Law and Literature: Ælfric and Wulfstan

Sherif Abdelkarim

Scholars who periodize hypocrisy tend to associate it with early modern Europe;[1] however, by examining homiletic, legal, and hagiographic representations of hypocrisy across the early English corpus, this chapter will explore how discourses on the vice underpin their authors' visions of moral and legal behavior in public life.[2] The nature of hypocrisy as both a moral and political ill make it a useful vehicle for covering this legal and spiritual terrain. As a social disruption, the vice forces creative reflections on the ramifications of a society's legal breaches at the essential levels of trust and truth. As the authors examined here present it, moreover, hypocrisy reveals the institutional interplay of the early English literary, legal, and homiletic traditions. Texts from each genre concern

1 Unless otherwise indicated, translations are my own. For early modern scholarship on hypocrisy, see for instance Emily Butterworth, "Necessary Leaven: Hypocrisy and the *Heptaméron*," *Renaissance and Reformation* 43 (2020): 135–66, and *The Unbridled Tongue: Babble and Gossip in Renaissance France* (Oxford: Oxford University Press, 2016); Miriam Eliav-Feldon and Tamar Herzig, eds., *Dissimulation and Deceit in Early Modern Europe* (Houndmills, UK: Palgrave Macmillan, 2015); Ruth Weissbourd Grant, *Hypocrisy and Integrity: Machiavelli, Rousseau, and the Ethics of Politics* (Chicago: University of Chicago Press, 1997); Lucia Nigri and Naya Tsentourou, eds., *Forms of Hypocrisy in Early Modern England* (New York: Routledge, 2019); Jon R. Snyder, *Dissimulation and the Culture of Secrecy in Early Modern Europe* (Berkeley: University of California Press, 2009); Perez Zagorin, *Ways of Lying: Dissimulation, Persecution, and Conformity in Early Modern Europe* (Cambridge, MA: Harvard University Press, 2009).

2 It is not difficult to notice the sacred in secular law. Consider the divine invocation with which Justinian – and many lawmakers to follow – opens his code, or the premises of the early English oath and the ordeal, which Jurasinski and Oliver helpfully explain "involve the same process of calling God to witness to the truth of an assertion, with the implication that the person doing so mendaciously should expect divine retribution sooner or later." Stefan Jurasinski and Lisi Oliver, eds., *The Laws of Alfred: The Domboc and the Making of Anglo-Saxon Law* (Cambridge: Cambridge University Press, 2021), 89.

themselves (each with respect to their particular sphere of interest) with individuals' failure to consistently align their thoughts, intentions, and actions; what emerges is a vision of the world in which the integrity of the laity depends on that of the Church, and in which both seek to establish order and achieve resolution through legal prescriptions. I leave open the extent to which the exhortations and examples found in these textual traditions translated into actual social practice, even in the case of written law. Although pre-Conquest legislators from Alfred onward prescribed how local people should behave, sheriffs, reeves, and other authorities would not necessarily have enforced these prescriptions consistently or efficiently.[3] And one imagines that the vaguely-phrased moral crimes of the later law codes would have posed considerably greater problems for practical detection and enforcement than the usual run of local crimes.

To tease out the practicability of legislating a moral idea, I turn to two ecclesiastics whose rhetorically-rich spiritual writings envisioned a society standing on divinely-sanctioned legal ground: Ælfric (d. *c.* 1010) and Wulfstan (d. 1023).[4] My focus on these figures is not intended to delineate the peculiarities of their several approaches to the moral issue here examined; rather, my interest lies more broadly in the textual channels of the tenth and eleventh centuries. The eclectic flow of sermons, sacred histories, and saints' lives to which these men were significant and influential contributors mixed legal, spiritual, and poetic languages, and addressed a range of audiences, from royal patrons, to church masters and students, to lay audiences.[5] On the whole, then, I present their writ-

3 See, e.g., the chapter by Chelsea Shields-Más in this volume.

4 For the alliance between the legal and spiritual realms in early English law, see Andrew Rabin, *Crime and Punishment in Anglo-Saxon England* (Cambridge: Cambridge University Press, 2020), 10–14, 19–20, 33. For Ælfric's alliterative prose, see Mary Clayton and Juliet Mullins, *Ælfric: Old English Lives of the Saints*, vol. 1 (Cambridge, MA: Harvard University Press, 2019), xxv–xxvi; Helmut Gneuss, *Ælfric of Eynsham: His Life, Times, and Writings* (Kalamazoo: Medieval Institute Publications, 2009), 17–21. For Wulfstan's style and rhetoric, see Andrew Rabin, ed. and trans., *The Political Writings of Archbishop Wulfstan of York* (Manchester: Manchester University Press, 2015), 16–20, 31–38; Andrew Rabin, ed. and trans., *Wulfstan: Old English Legal Writings* (Cambridge, MA: Harvard University Press, 2020), xiii–xix.

5 For the literary language of the Reformist homily, see Dorothy Bethurum, "Style," in *The Homilies of Wulfstan* (Oxford: Clarendon, 1957), 87–98; D. R. Letson, "The Poetic Content of the Revival Homily," in *The Old English Homily and its Backgrounds*, ed. Paul E. Szarmach and Bernard F. Huppé (Albany: State University of New York Press, 1978), 139–56; Donald Scragg, "Dating and Style in Old English Composite Homilies," *H. M. Chadwick Memorial Lectures* 9 (1998): 1–24; Gabriella Corona, "Ælfric's Schemes and Tropes: *Amplificatio* and the Portrayal of Persecutors," in *A Companion to Ælfric*, ed. Hugh Magennis and Mary Swan (Leiden: Brill, 2009), 297–320; and see Kathleen Davis, "Boredom,

ings as similarly sourced if contextually discrete manifestations of church concerns at the turn of the eleventh century. As churchmen moving in different but overlapping spheres of the church (Ælfric in the realm of pedagogy, and Wulfstan the realm of the law), both ecclesiasts expressed in their writings the imperfect and perhaps tenuous nature of England's theocratic order. After the death of King Edgar (d. 975), the ideals of the Benedictine Revival received less royal (and thus legislative) support.[6] Royal protection and the promotion of Church interests were no longer guaranteed. In the wake of this royal-clerical rupture arose "a new ambivalence toward the exercise of royal authority," with reformists voicing these ambivalences in many ways, including critiques of royal and monastic governance, and a general alertness to the limits of royal affiliation.[7] For Ælfric and Wulfstan (and doubtless others working at the intersection of the clerical, royal, and lay communities) this ambivalence was a significant stimulus to complicated reflections on hypocrisy and its social implications. As these writers attempted to imagine into existence a society that fulfilled God's work through the rule of law, they strove to indoctrinate and reform their society as spiritual legislators. The sample of Ælfric and Wulfstan's writings (as well as certain anonymous texts) examined below reveals how the concept of hypocrisy was expressed and regulated in and beyond the written law, and conversely, how the legal articulation of crimes involving deception made use of literary expressions and ideas. To explicate the tenth- and eleventh-century ambition to order word and deed, I first turn to the Old English scriptural tradition, from whose cultural translations of hypocrisy Ælfric, Wulfstan, and their contemporaries proceed.

Scripture

Interpreting the Pharisees of the Gospels as hypocrites par excellence, patristic writers focus exclusively on the moral consequences of their deception. According to the ancient Greek dialect in which it appeared,

---

Brevity, and Last Things: Ælfric's Style and the Politics of Time," in *A Companion to Ælfric*, ed. Hugh Magennis and Mary Swan (Leiden: Brill, 2009), 321–44.

6 See Pauline Stafford, "Church and Society in the Age of Ælfric," in *The Old English Homily and its Backgrounds*, ed. Paul E. Szarmach and Bernard F. Huppé (Albany: State University of New York Press, 1978), 17–18; and see Christopher A. Jones, "Ælfric and the Limits of 'Benedictine Reform,'" in *A Companion to Ælfric*, ed. Hugh Magennis and Mary Swan (Leiden: Brill, 2009), 67–108.

7 Andrew Rabin, "Holy Bodies, Legal Matters: Reaction and Reform in Ælfric's *Eugenia* and the Ely Privilege," *Studies in Philology* 110 (2013): 231; and see also 224–25.

hypocrite could have meant *interpreter* (Homeric), *answerer* (Homeric; Ionic), *expounder, deliverer, reciter,* or *declaimer* (of an orator or choir); in the Attic and Koine Greek of Aristophanes, Plutarch, and the authors of the New Testament, it was associated closely with playing a part on the stage or skillfully delivering lines.[8] Alive to this late classical heritage, the archbishop Isidore (d. 636) explicates the morally neutral, performative roots of the "hypocrite" – but emphasizes a more narrow definition of hypocrisy as a Christian vice. After defining *hypocrite* as one who appears outwardly good while being evil within (*dum intus malus sit*),[9] Isidore registers its original theatrical content:

> Nomen autem hypocritae tractum est ab specie eorum qui in spectaculis contecta facie incedunt, distinguentes vultum caeruleo minioque colore et ceteris pigmentis, habentes simulacra oris lintea gipsata et vario colore distincta, nonnumquam et colla et manus creta perungentes, ut ad personae colorem pervenirent et populum, dum [in] ludis agerent, fallerent; modo in specie viri, modo in feminae, modo tonsi, modo criniti, anuli et viriginali ceteraque specie, aetate sexuque diverso, ut fallant populum, dum in ludis agunt.[10]

> Moreover, the name of *hypocrita* derives from the appearance of those who go in theatrical spectacles with countenance concealed, marking their face with blue and red and other pigments, holding masks of linen and plaster of Paris decorated with various colors, sometimes also smearing their necks and hands with white clay, in order to arrive at the coloring of the character they portray and to deceive the public while they act in plays. Now they look like a man, now a woman, now a man with barbered hair, now with long, now a woman with an old crone's, a maiden's, or some other appearance, with age and sex varied, to deceive the people while they act in plays.[11]

While Isidore underscores the moral opprobrium of *hypocrisy,* he does acknowledge the theatrical power of the term, a dimension of meaning that first-millennium England generally did not inherit. Though he insists

[8] Henry George Liddell and Robert Scott, *A Greek-English Lexicon,* rev. Henry Stuart Jones et al. (Oxford: Oxford University Press, 1968 [orig. publ. 1843]), s.v. ὑποκρισία; Robert Beekes, *Etymological Dictionary of Greek: Volume 1* (Leiden: Brill, 2010), s.v. *κρινω*; Frederic Amory, "Whited Sepulchres: The Semantic History of Hypocrisy to the High Middle Ages," *Recherches de théologie ancienne et médiévale* 53 (1986): 5–6.

[9] W. M. Lindsay, ed., *Isidori hispalensis episcopi: Etymologiarum sive originum, libri xx,* vol. 2 (Oxford: Oxford University Press, 1911), X.118.

[10] Ibid., X.119.

[11] Stephen A. Barney et al., eds. and trans., *The Etymologies of Isidore of Seville* (Cambridge: Cambridge University Press, 2006), s.v. *Hypocrite.*

that his explanation now survives as a dead metaphor that refers to those who with a false face go forth and dissemble (*qui falso vultu incedunt et simulant quod non sunt*),[12] Isidore momentarily captures dissimulation's uses beyond the moral frame. Theologians would characterize the late-antique theater as a site of debauchery and paganism, the inherited connotations of performance therefore tended to be overwhelmingly negative.[13]

Early English authors found it easy to equate hypocrisy with godlessness, impurity, and disguise as a form of deceit. There, we find several Hebrew terms for hypocrisy's traits of deception and dissimulation, such as *ḥanef* (חָנֵף), "*to be polluted, profane,*" construed in later Aramaic as "*to act falsely toward, flatter,*" hence *hypocrisy, ḥanufáh* (חֲנוּפָּה).[14] As it is used in Isaiah 24:5, the term connotes defilement as a consequence of transgressing the law; in the Book of Job, a text Ælfric references on multiple occasions, it maintains senses of godlessness and false flattery, associated especially with the concealment of wickedness out of fear or contempt of others.[15]

12 Lindsay, *Isidori*, X.120.

13 See Tertullian, "De Spectaculis," in *Tertullian: Apology. De Spectaculis. Minucius Felix: Octavius*, ed. and trans. T. R. Glover and Gerald H. Rendall (Cambridge, MA: Harvard University Press, 1977 [orig. publ. 1931]); Augustine, *De Sermone Domini in Monte: Libros Duos*, ed. Almut Mutzenbecher (Turnhout: Brepols, 1967), II.2.5.89–98; Donnalee Dox, *The Idea of Theater in Christian Thought: Augustine to the Fourteenth Century* (Ann Arbor: University of Michigan Press, 2004), 11–42. The Old English adaptation of Orosius' fifth-century *History* upholds Isidore's sentiments when it sneers at its readers for taking to the theater: *Nu mæg þa cristenan gescomian þe swylc deofolgyld lufiað and begongað, þa se þe cristen næs hit swa swið forseah, se þe hit fyrðian sceolde æfter heora agnum gewunan* ("Now Christians who like such devilries and engage in them can be ashamed, when one who wasn't a Christian [Scipio] and who ought to have promoted the theater according to their own customs so strongly denounced it"). Malcolm R. Godden, ed. and trans., *The Old English History of the World: An Anglo-Saxon Rewriting of Orosius* (Cambridge, MA: Harvard University Press, 2016), 294–95.

14 Francis Brown, S. R. Driver and Charles A. Briggs, *The Brown-Driver-Briggs Hebrew and English Lexicon with an Appendix Containing Biblical Aramaic* (Peabody, MA: Hendrickson, 2020 [orig. publ. 1906]), s.v. חָנֵף (*ḥanef*). Compare the terms בגד (*bâgad*) and מְעִיל (*me'íl*), which each connote *garment* and *traitor* or *deception*; presumably, the shared element lies in the act of concealment. Matityahu Clark, *Etymological Dictionary of Biblical Hebrew: Based on the Commentaries of Samson Raphael Hirsch* (New York: Feldheim, 1999), x.

15 Bernard Ehrlich, "The Book of Job as a Book of Morality," *Jewish Bible Quarterly*, 34 (2006): 36–37; Amory, "Whited Sepulchres," 6–8. See Job 8:13, 13:16, 31:33–34; 36:13. In his writings on Job, Ælfric does not appear to expand on insincere or faithless friends, but rather focuses on the Devil's deception and Job's faith. See Martin Chase, "The Book of Job and the Figure of Job in Old English Literature," in *A Companion to Job in the Middle Ages*, ed. Franklin Harkins and Aaron Canty

The Pharisees of the Gospels effectively embody these meanings. Their show of holiness carries the stigma of dissimulating performance; any association of this performance with cleverness, entertainment, and instruction, is negated by Jesus' simile of the whited sepulcher (Matthew 23:27): *Wa eow hiwerum. ge sind gelice. gemettum ofergeweorcum. þe beoð wiðutan wlitige mannum æteowode. and seo byrgen ðeah bið afylled mid deadum banum*[16] ("Woe you hypocrites. You are like painted tombs; you are shown outwardly fair to men, and yet the sepulcher is filled with dead bones"). As it is used by Ælfric, the term *hiwere* carries only morally negative senses. The *Dictionary of Old English* defines the agent noun as "one who fabricates falsehoods," "one who pretends or dissembles; hypocrite," with the concept noun *hiwung* denoting "forming, shaping ... feigning ... dissimulation" as well as "hypocrisy."[17] These terms provide a sense of how fakers were understood in Ælfric's day: not as actors but as illusionists, effective but false imaginers. In elaborating the biblical verse above, Ælfric employs another major term by which to identify false prophets: *liccetere*.[18] Though it stands consistently for *hypocrite* and its forms in the Old English Gospels, the term lacks any cultural history to connect it with theatrical performance.[19] *Licettere* and *licettung* ("hypocrisy") thus denote feigning and simulation at a still greater remove from any originary sense of valid artistic performance.[20]

(Leiden: Brill, 2016), 364, 371–74; Robert E. Bjork, "The Symbolic Use of Job in Ælfric's Homily on Job, *Christ II*, and the *Phoenix*," in *Latin Learning and English Lore, Volume II: Studies in Anglo-Saxon Literature for Michael Lapidge*, ed. Katherine O'Brien O'Keeffe, et al. (Toronto: University of Toronto Press, 2005), 316. Ælfric does, however, interpose his remarks on Job alongside reflections on the wickedness of the last days, when Antichrist reigns, as well as his own day's false priests. See John C. Pope, *Homilies of Ælfric: A Supplementary Collection*, 2 vols., EETS, o.s. 259 and 260 (Oxford: Oxford University Press, 1967), vol. 2, no. XVIII, esp. lines 75–140 and 376–99.

16 Malcolm R. Godden, ed., *Ælfric's Catholic Homilies: The Second Series, Text*, EETS, s.s. 5 (London: Oxford University Press, 1979), no. XXVI.24–26; see also lines 30–41, 133–39.

17 *DOE*, s.v. *hiwere* (1–2), *hiwung*[1].

18 Godden, *Ælfric's Catholic Homilies*, no. XXVI.31.

19 Bosworth-Toller simply defines *licettere* as "One who feigns, a hypocrite." See Roy Liuzza, *The Old English Versions of the Gospels*, EETS, o.s. 304 (Oxford: Oxford University Press, 1994); Matthew 6:2, 5, 16; 7:5; 23:13, 15, 25, 27, 28; Mark 7:6; Luke 6:42, 12:1, 56. Less exact synonyms for hypocrisy are also used throughout the New Testament, such as *deceit*, from the Greek δόλος (Lat. *fraus*), translated as *facn* and its forms. See for instance John 1:47; Matthew 22:18, 26:5; Luke 20:23; Mark 14:1, 7:22.

20 Whether *licettung* derives from some hybrid intended to reconstruct *hypocrisy*'s false performance (*lican* [to please], or *lycce* [lying, mendacious], and *tung* [tongue]? [compare *lyffetung, flattery*]), or comes from another etymology

More broadly, Old English authors who name hypocrisy do so with the Gospels' cultural context in mind.[21]

Ælfric's *Colloquy* is a case in point. This text is a children's manual on vocabulary-building that describes (and prescribes) the proper roles of society's members, especially monks or affiliates of a monastic community. According to Katherine O'Brien O'Keeffe, it promotes a Benedictine reformist conception of personal freedom as sacrifice and, conversely, obedience to divine law as the willful choice of what is morally good.[22] For Ælfric, it is the act of choosing (*cyre*) that makes moral accountability possible.[23] Within the framework of this focus on agency, sincerity can only be achieved insofar as one chooses to align one's will with God's (and conversely, of course, against the sinful will of the Devil). By ordering their words and deeds according to the will of God (as prescribed by the sacred lawgivers, namely Ælfric, Wulfstan, and others of their milieu), readers of the *Colloquy* – whom O'Brien O'Keeffe imagines to have been "oblates in a post-Reform Benedictine monastery" – would have sought in the text direction for aligning their actions and intentions in ways consonant with divine law.[24] Paradoxically, such sincerity entailed a strong performative element, both initially, as pupils learned how to properly assume their various social roles, and subsequently, since obedience stood in constant need of strengthening and withstanding from ungodly whims. Completely aligning one's will with God's would not have been possible. Sincerity on these terms meant making one's best efforts to maintain a proper role in a moral society.[25]

Embedded in the *Colloquy*'s morally prescriptive exhortation for its pupils is a strong sense of defined social identity. In the immediate reader's case, this identity is a monastic one, meant to mimic God's will as defined and interpreted by the lawgiving theologian.[26] In this context, the teacher's question to his students on the matter of hypocrisy aims to test

entirely, obscured by Christianity's literary influence, I do not know. For a discussion of borrowings and substitutes in Old English, see Helmut Gneuss, *Lehnbildungen und Lehnbedeutungen im Altenglischen* (Berlin: E. Schmidt, 1955), chapters 1–2; Philip Durkin, *Borrowed Words: A History of Loanwords in English* (Oxford: Oxford University Press, 2014), 161–67.

21 Descriptions of word-deed disconnects, such as the many that appear in Old English poetry, do not appear inevitably indebted to this Christian context.

22 Katherine O'Brien O'Keeffe, *Stealing Obedience: Narratives of Agency and Identity in Later Anglo-Saxon England* (Toronto: University of Toronto Press, 2012), 14–16.

23 Ibid., 18–26.

24 Ibid., 94. Oblates were "children given to a monastery by their parents as gifts to God" (ibid.).

25 Ibid., 93, 52–53.

26 Ibid., 95–96, 104–05.

scriptural literacy, as O'Brien O'Keeffe has argued. Yet at the same time, it sheds light on Ælfric's definition and evaluation of hypocrisy as it pertains to the community at large.[27] Upon his students' expressing a wish to be wise, the Teacher asks:

> On hwilcon wisdome? Wille ge beon prættige oþþe þusenthiwe on leasungum, lytige on spræcum, onglæwlice, hindergepe, wel sprecende 7 yfele þencende, swæsum wordum underþeodde, facn wiðinnan tyddriende, swa swa bergyls metton ofergeweorke, wiþinnan full stence?[28]

> In which kind of wisdom? Will you be plastic or multifarious in your pretense, deceitful in speech, illogical, sneaky, speaking well and thinking evil, subjugated by charming words, weakened by guile within, just as tombs are decorated on their exteriors, but full of stench within?[29]

This unusually verbose response departs from the teacher's typically spare dialogue; perhaps Ælfric introduces his own voice into the fiction of the *Colloquy* to underline the socio-moral import of the question. Given the length and scriptural density of the question, it comes as no surprise that the students respond just as volubly:

> We nellaþ swa wesan wise, forþam he nys wis, þe mid dydrunge hyne sylfne beswicð. [...] We wyllaþ beon bylewite butan licetunge,[30] 7 wise þæt we bugon fram yfele 7 don goda.[31]

> We don't want to be wise in that way, since he is not wise who seduces himself with deception. [...] We would like to be sincere without hypocrisy, and wise so that we turn away from evil and do good.[32]

This dialogue conveys the pupils' sound knowledge of hypocrisy as defined by Scripture (insincere piety, ostentation, and self-deception). At the same time, it also demonstrates the importance of avoiding hypocrisy for religious leaders – and does so in social terms. The implied expectation

27 Ibid., 124.

28 George Garmonsway, *Ælfric's Colloquy* (Liverpool: Liverpool University Press, 2003 [orig. publ. 1939]), cap. 43.254–58. *Wynn* and *yogh* in this and other editions are silently rendered "w" and "g" throughout.

29 Stephen J. Harris, "Ælfric's *Colloquy*," in *Medieval Literature for Children*, ed. Daniel T. Kline (New York: Routledge, 2003), 125.

30 Compare with Ælfric's Latin version of the *Colloquy*, which renders *butan licetunge* "sine hipocrisi." Joyce M. Hill, "Ælfric's *Colloquy*: The Antwerp/London Version," in *Latin Learning and English Lore: Studies in Anglo-Saxon Literature for Michael Lapidge, Volume II*, ed. Katherine O'Brien O'Keeffe and Andy Orchard (Toronto: University of Toronto Press, 2005), 345.

31 Garmonsway, *Ælfric's Colloquy*, cap. 43.259–63.

32 Harris, "Ælfric's *Colloquy*," 125.

is that those holding other roles in society should be similarly morally aware. It is significant to note that the performative aspect of hypocritical behavior alone does not render it evil (*yfel*), but rather the plastic (*prættig*) and multiform (*þusenthiwe*) nature of the performance. These are significant terms, and their implications underpin Ælfric's articulation of hypocrisy across his works. For Old English *prættig* ("wily, crafty, astute") Ælfric's Latin version has *versipelles* – literally "able to change one's skin," and thus figuratively "skilled in dissimulation." Stephen J. Harris's translation here ("plastic") catches the anxiety expressed by the teacher's rhetoric: that the craft of the would-be wise embody itself in slippery shifts of self-presentation. *Þusenthiwe* ("of a thousand shapes"; in Ælfric's Latin, *milleformes*) articulates the same shape-shifting destabilization of identity that characterizes the *leasung* ("lying") and reveals hypocrisy in the fullness of its social danger.[33] Other, more dutiful forms of performance are thus readily distinguished from hypocrisy. Obedience – to one's social station, and to the law of God – certainly entails the active process of shaping one's will to accord with righteous dictates, but this virtuous performance of duty carries no connotation of wily disguise: intention and action are not out of joint. Thus the *Colloquy* at once prescribes roles for monastic and other socially-specific identities (and requires each such proper role to be played well) and renounces those insincere performances that enact an exterior at odds with interior identity.

Elsewhere in Ælfric's works, his versions of the seven or eight deadly sins inevitably cast hypocrisy in a central role; it regularly appears as an element in accounts of these sins, and always defines the seventh, vainglory, or *idel gylp*, that is, *þonne se man bið lofgeorn and mid licetunge færð* ("when a person is eager for praise and behaves with hypocrisy").[34] Elsewhere, Ælfric frames hypocrisy as a social breach by positioning it as an offense amidst other crimes. He explains avarice, *gitsung*, as made up of lies, envy, fraud, rapine, theft, perjury, false witness, and excessive

[33] See Bosworth-Toller, s.v. *prættig*; *þusend-hiwe*. And see Harris, "Ælfric's *Colloquy*," 129n46.

[34] Mary Clayton, ed. and trans., *Two Ælfric Texts: The Twelve Abuses and the Vices and Virtues* (Cambridge: D. S. Brewer, 2013), 146–47. See Pope, *Homilies of Ælfric*, vol. 1, no. IV.239–51, where the deadly sins are introduced as characteristics of the Devil, model hypocrite and sinner. Vainglory is further elaborated in hypocritical terms in Godden, *Ælfric's Catholic Homilies*, no. XII.524–31, and Clayton and Mullins, *Ælfric*, 106–12. More generally, forswearing is condemned as a common sin. See Peter Clemoes, ed., *Ælfric's Catholic Homilies: The First Series, Text*, EETS, s.s. 17 (Oxford: Oxford University Press, 1997), no. VIII.181–99.

violence.[35] vainglory, or doing good for worldly compensation,[36] carried as much moral opprobium as pride for Ælfric, who attributes both to the corruption of reason.[37] In his *Grammar and Glossary*, the homilist classifies hypocrisy among social and legal terms of betrayal. Notice the semantic field in which he lodges the *licettere* (Table 11.1).

Table 11.1. Context of "hypocrite" in Ælfric's *Grammar and Glossary*.

Latin	**Old English**	**Modern English**
profanus	mānful	wicked/unholy/impious
exosus *or* perosus	andsǣte	hateful/detesting
callidus	gēap	shrewd/clever
simulator	hiwere	dissembler
Hipochrita	līccettere	deceiver/hypocrite
adulator	lyffetere	flatterer/sycophant
adulatio	lyffetung	adulation/fawning
deceptor *or* seductor	bepǣcend	deceiver/impostor
proditor *or* traditor	lǣwa	betrayer/traitor
homicida	manslaga	murderer
patricida	fæderslaga	father-slayer
matricida	mōderslaga	mother-slayer
fratricida	broðerslaga	brother-slayer
parricidia	mǣgslaga	slayer of a relative[38]

In this classification, Ælfric's hypocrites move away from the explicitly religious context of the Pharisees and fall among a wider social circle of parasites and criminals, from flatterers and impostors to traitors and familicides. In this broader social world, the hypocrite's insincerity is associated with any task that can be performed dishonestly. Thus, though it remains fundamentally a Christian vice, hypocrisy finds ample expres-

35 *Of ðisum leahtre beoð acennede leasunga. and andan. facn. and reaflac. stala. and forsworennys. leas gewitnyss. and unmæðlic neadung* (Godden, *Ælfric's Catholic Homilies*, no. XII.507–10). Compare Godden, *Ælfric's Catholic Homilies*, nos. XXV.46–52 and XL.279–82, where bearing false witness is likewise listed among the capital offenses (*heafodleahtras*).

36 Clemoes, *Ælfric's Catholic Homilies*, no. VIII.56–60.

37 Clayton and Mullins, *Ælfric*, 29.

38 Priscilla Throop, trans., *Ælfric's Grammar and Glossary: The Complete English Translation* (Charlotte, VT: MedievalMS, 2008), 257–58.

sion in the Old English corpus as a crafty betrayal of truth, in which thoughts, intentions and deeds deceitfully fail to align.

This extension of the Pharisaical sense of the hypocrite is seen in many tenth- and eleventh-century homilies – those of Wulfstan and others as well as Ælfric. Homilists regularly apply the label of hypocrisy to an array of social and moral offenses beyond those of the prophet-priest. One major mode by which hypocrisy is evoked entails the deployment of a cast of hypocritical characters – most appearing in passing descriptions, some in brief dramatizations. These stock icons of the early Christian era personify Hypocrisy in all its social and spiritual harms, including its self-deceptions. Those who betray Christ are exemplary hypocrites; they deny his divinity upon his birth and during his life with a fraudulent mind (*mid facenfullum mode*); after his Ascension, Christ continues to endure the calumnies and curses from these lying hypocrites (*leasum licceterum*).[39] Other types of hypocrites are specified in terms of their social or vocational function or else by name; these include false prophets, the Pharisees (sometimes expanded to encompass, vaguely, "the Jews"), wicked wives, magicians, Simon Magus, Julian the Apostate, Gehazi, Ananias and Sapphira, Judas, and Herod.[40] Wulfstan's Antichrist stands out among these homiletic types for his special title of *se þeodlicetere*, the arch-hypocrite who teaches humanity – his servants – to sin.[41] Analyzing Wulfstan's description of Antichrist here, Joyce Lionarons explains that as the prime hypocrite, Antichrist (the Devil's emissary in end times) achieves this title by virtue of his world-wisdom: *ne weorþeð on worulde ænig woruldsnotera ne on wordum getingra ne on heortan wyrsa and lytelice swicolra þonne he wyrðeþ* ("There will never be anyone in the world more worldly-wise nor more fluent in words nor worse in heart and more deceptively deceitful than he").[42] Not surprisingly, then, the Devil operates as the principal *licetere*, the father of falsehood (*fæder ælcere leasunge*), whose dissembling leads humanity astray.[43] He is *yfeltihtend 7 leaswyrcend. synna ordfruma 7 sawla*

39 Clemoes, *Ælfric's Catholic Homilies*, nos. VII.258–61, XXXVI.258–59.

40 Ibid., Praefatio, nos. III.81–105, IV.14, 74, 227, VII.79–101 and 202–18, XIV.121, XXIX, XXI, XXVI, XXXII.172–88; Pope, *Homilies of Ælfric*, vol. 2, nos. VIII, X.113–26; Pope, *Homilies of Ælfric*, vol. 1, nos. XIII, XIV, XVIII.100–09; Dorothy Bethurum, ed., *The Homilies of Wulfstan* (Oxford: Clarendon, 1957), passim, esp. "I. Eschatological Homilies," "4. Evil Days."

41 Bethurum, *Homilies*, no. IX (VII) "Gifts of the Holy Spirit," p. 189, line 116.

42 Joyce Tally Lionarons, "Napier Homily L: Wulfstan's Eschatology at the Close of his Career," in *Wulfstan, Archbishop of York: The Proceedings of the Second Alcuin Conference*, ed. Matthew Townend (Turnhout: Brepols, 2004), 423, citing and translating Bethurum, *Homilies*, no. IX, p. 189, lines 117–20.

43 Clemoes, *Ælfric's Catholic Homilies*, no. XI.64. Fittingly, *devil* literally means *accuser* or *slanderer* – the essence of underhanded deceit and betrayal. OED, s.v. devil (n.).

bepæcend ("the igniter of evil, worker of lies, source of sins, and deceiver of souls").[44] Ultimately, it is the Devil's interested involvement in the production of hypocrisy on earth that renders it the worst evil to humanity at large, for *deofol sylf hit gefadað and gehywað to þam* ("the Devil himself guides and forms it").[45]

The offenses committed by these varied characters are equally varied in their degrees of deception, from lying to bearing false witness (*leasgewitan*), and may or may not include such greater betrayals as murder or idolatry.[46] Reading Ælfric's homilies in particular, one meets an array of oathbreakers and traitors, glimpsing as well their performative potentials. Though Satan and his troupe are associated with ill-willed, antisocial tricks, they deceive also with seductive words, fabulous disguises, and by *deofles searocræftum*, that signature skill of the Devil's treacherous artifice.[47] Among hypocrisy's chief dangers is the attractive mantle with which it cloaks corrupt intention. More intriguing is these figures' *desire* to deceive: of Satan's plans for Adam, for example, readers are told that *mid leasunge he* wile *beswican* ("with deceit he *wills* to deceive").[48] Stylistically, Ælfric and Wulfstan in their homilies tend to offer neutral descriptions of these colorful deceivers. And in terms of content, they summarize rather than dramatize their antagonists' frauds, glossing over the acting talent that is showcased where these figures appear in the period's poetry.[49] With few exceptions, such as their respective sermons on the false gods of pre-Christian times,[50] the homilists deploy figures and episodes from the Bible in order to illustrate the import of the homily for its immediate audience. Ælfric's *temporale* homilies, for instance, regularly relate Satan's temptations and refer to the faithless among Jesus' believers. But the aim of these references is to alert current listeners (including the skeptics and

44 Clemoes, *Ælfric's Catholic Homilies,* no. VI.176–77. For the Devil as the source of deception, see for instance Clemoes, *Ælfric's Catholic Homilies,* nos. I.159–60, VI.175–76, VII.186–89, XIII.8–17, XIV.154–66, XIX.146–64.

45 Lionarons, "Napier Homily L," 423, citing and translating Bethurum, *Homilies,* no. IX, p. 189, lines 107–08.

46 See, for instance, Saint Stephen's passion: Clemoes, *Ælfric's Catholic Homilies,* no. III.

47 Clemoes, *Ælfric's Catholic Homilies,* no. XIII.13–14.

48 Ibid., no. I.120, my emphasis.

49 The Satan of *Genesis A/B* and the demons of *Guthlac* and *Juliana,* for example, all utilize an arsenal of subtle disguises and verbal sleights.

50 Both Ælfric (Pope, *Homilies of Ælfric,* vol. 2, no. XXI) and Wulfstan (Bethurum, *Homilies,* no. XII) condemn the misguided nature of past peoples in their worship of false gods, yet relegate them to pre-Christian times without cautioning against any present threats to society. Perhaps their condemnation of ongoing pagan practices, whether among the Danes or other populations in the British Isles, would have been assumed.

weak of faith) to the temptations of their own lives: a case in point is the homily known as "Dominica I in Qvadragessima," which sketches Jesus' forty days in the desert (Matthew 4:1–11) to commemorate the first Sunday in Lent. Ælfric first summarizes the temptations Jesus endured and overcame to remind audiences that only those who willfully embrace the Devil's temptation come under his control:

> Se lyþra man ana þonne he forsihð godes beboda; 7 fulgæð deofles willan. oððe þurh gitsunge. oððe þurh leasunge. oððe ðurh graman. oððe þurh oðrum leahtrum. þonne bið he deofles þeowa; þonne he deofle gecwemð; 7 þone forsihð þe hine geworhte;[51]
>
> The wicked man alone, when he hates God's commands and carries out the Devil's will, either through cupidity, or through falsehood, or through rage, or through other sins; he is then the Devil's servant; he then pleases the Devil, and hates [the one] who made him.

Interrupting his account of Jesus' resistance to the Devil's temptations, and punctuating his reassurance that all of creation belongs to God, this claim by Ælfric emphasizes the enduring danger of choosing sin. It also reinforces the idea that this danger has its roots in hypocritical dissembling – it happens through falsehood (*þurh leasunge*). Ælfric will conclude his paraphrase of Matthew 4:1–11 by addressing his audience more directly, encouraging them to guard against the earthly temptations of their present lives and explaining the function and etiquette of fasting and giving alms.

Society

If biblical narrative is one fruitful source of hypocrites to hold up as an example and a warning, homilists find another (and perhaps equally rich) source in local figures familiar to the lived experience of their audience. Homilists hammer home their prescriptions on social sincerity by pointing to the inconsistencies all around them, including those at the highest levels of secular and ecclesiastical legislation. Wulfstan especially uses this rhetorical method, taking aim at such representative figures as thieves, perjurers, murderers, and various other traitors among the flock. He also takes aim at potentially less anonymous (and higher ranking) figures – misguided priests who misguide their fold, or *eorlan and heretogan, deman and gerefan* ("nobles, generals, judges, and

[51] Clemoes, *Ælfric's Catholic Homilies*, no. XI.104–07.

reeves") who *wendan unriht to rihte* ("twist injustice into justice").[52] The verb *wendan* here ("move... turn... alter")[53] recalls that slipperiness of identity captured by Ælfric's language of hypocrisy in the *Colloquy*, and the passage is similarly concerned with the proper performance of mundane roles. In thus shifting attention to everyday crimes and their social cost, Wulfstan effectively prescribes a practical ethics for restoring faith within the community through adherence to the law. Seen in this light, obeying the law becomes the yardstick by which community members measure how sincerely or insincerely they enact their true natures as legal subjects and spiritual beings. The sincerity advocated by the homilists is addressed to the congregants' behavior across many domains of action, but the frequency with which Wulfstan calls on listeners to follow the law in particular makes clear his position that preparing for the next world entailed living honorably and without hypocrisy in this life – and that this required obedience to worldly laws. At the same time, his homilies warn that in failing to reflect on the consequences of hypocritical action, and failing to enact the appropriate and legally-required sincerity, the unrepentant also fail to serve themselves and their society in *this* world.[54]

Wulfstan spells out this formula most forcefully in his famous *Sermo lupi ad Anglos*. In keeping with his other homilies, the sermon blames the Devil and Antichrist for leading his people astray, but goes on to blame the people themselves for their *unlaga*, or lawlessness; *huru*, he explains, *unrihtlice mæst ælc oþerne æftan heaweþ mid sceandlican onscytan* ("here, nearly everyone wrongfully stabs the other in the back with disgraceful attack").[55] Consequently, England endures famines, disease, humiliation from Viking domination, and manifold social disorders, from familial strife to the widespread insubordination of lords by their servants, to murder (including the regicide of King Edward the Martyr [d. 978]), dispossession, sexual exploitation, and human trafficking.[56] Worse than these deeds, adds Wulfstan, are the flawed social values they reveal: *7 gyt hit is mare 7 eac mænigfældre þæt dereð þysse þeode:*

52 Arthur S. Napier, ed., *Wulfstan: Sammlung der ihm zugeschriebenen Homilien nebst Untersuchungen über ihre Echtheit* (Berlin: Weidmann, 1883), no. L, p. 267, line 29. The translation is Rabin, *Political Writings*, 146–47. See also Rabin, *Political Writings*, 142, 156–58, 160–61.

53 Bosworth-Toller, s.v. *wendan* (v.).

54 For a helpful discussion on the balance of upholding the law on one hand and preparing for imminent Judgment on the other, see Joyce Tally Lionarons, *The Homiletic Writings of Archbishop Wulfstan: A Critical Study* (Cambridge: D. S. Brewer, 2010), 164–75.

55 Dorothy Whitelock, ed., *Sermo Lupi ad Anglos* (London: Methuen & Company, 1952 [orig. publ. 1939]), 41, lines 70–71.

56 Ibid., 34, line 14.

mænige synd forsworene 7 swyþe ferlogene, 7 wed synd tobrocene oft 7 gelome[57] ("Yet it is more widespread what harms this people: many are forsworn and greatly belied, and pledges are broken continuously"). In breaking the law and sinning, the English people effectively perpetuate a vicious cycle: as long as the people disregard the need for sincerity in their words and deeds, Wulfstan warns, they will continue to suffer at their own hands *þurh swicdomas 7 þurh searacræftas, þurh lahbrycas 7 þurh æswicas, [...] þurh aðbricas 7 þurh wedbrycas 7 þurh mistlice leasunga forloren 7 forlogen ma þonne scolde* ("Through treacheries, wiles, legal breaches, frauds, [...] through oathbreaking, pledge-breaking, and various lies, more than should will be misled and belied").[58] As a first step toward redemption, Wulfstan urges his flock to cease lying. Once again, it is the renunciation of hypocrisy that underpins and makes possible a lawful and ordered society. Wulfstan prescribes: *7 utan God lufian 7 Godes lagum fylgean, [...] 7 utan word 7 weorc rihtlice fadian, 7 ure ingeþanc clænsian georne, 7 að 7 wed wærlice healdan, 7 sume getrywða habban us betweonan butan uncræftan*[59] ("Let us love God and carry out his laws, [...] let us rightly order word and work, earnestly cleanse our conscience, oath and pledge carefully hold, and have some truth between us without guile").

As they are invoked in the homilies, legal discussions arise naturally alongside the themes of community cohesion, protection, and growth. The *Blickling Homilies*' Fifth Sunday in Lent does just that, opening with King David's imagined prescriptions regarding how to act in a transient, treacherous world. The king advises against the seemingly innocent gesture of flattering one's neighbor:

> Se mon se þa soþfæstnesse mid his muþe sprecþ, & hie on his heortan georne geþencþ, & he hi fullice gelæsteþ, & he afylleþ þa inwitfullan word of his tungan, þæt beoþ þa men þa þe Godes rices geleafan habbað & healdaþ; forþon hi noldan heora nehstan beswican þurh þa facenfullan word.
>
> The man who speaketh truth with his mouth, and sincerely thinketh it in his heart, and truly performeth it, and puts down the deceitful words of his tongue – he is the man who hath and holdeth the belief of God's kingdom, because he would not deceive his neighbour through treacherous words.[60]

57 Ibid., 44, lines 97–100.

58 Ibid., 46–47, lines 140–45; and see lines 134–35.

59 Ibid., 52, lines 201–07.

60 R. Morris, ed. and trans., *The Blickling Homilies* (Millwood: Kraus Reprint, 1990 [orig. publ. 1874]), 54–55.

For the anonymous author of this homily, following the law once again involves aligning intentions and deeds. Community members reflect their belief in God's kingdom by living the law in their earthly one. By contrast, those who deny the law inevitably fail to align the *right* thoughts and actions:

> þeofas, & flyteras, & gitseras þe on mannum heora æhta on woh nimaþ, & þa oformodan men, & þa scinlæcan þa þe galdor-cræftas & gedwolan begangaþ, & mid þam unwære men beswicaþ & adwellaþ, & hi aweniaþ from Godes gemynde mid heora scinlacum, & gedwolcræftum; þær beoþ eac yfele gerefan þa þe nu on woh demaþ, & rihte domas soþfæstra manna onwendaþ, þa þe ær rihtlice gesette wæron.

> thieves, chiders, covetous men, who deprive men wrongfully of their property, proud men, and magicians who practise enchantments and deceptions, and deceive and mislead unwary men thereby, and wean them from the contemplation of God by means of their sleights and deceptions. There are also evil reeves (governors) who now give wrong judgments, and pervert the right laws of just men, which aforetime were rightly instituted.[61]

In a shift in subject reminiscent of Wulfstan, the anonymous author expands on everyday breaks of faith by those placed in earthly positions of authority, and charged to protect the law, in particular *yfela dema*, false judges: *Hi habbaþ demena naman, & sceaþena dæda; forþon hi beoþ betuh him sylfum slitende wulfas, þonne hie for feos lufan earmne fordemaþ buton scylde* ("They have the name of judges, but the actions of thieves; for they are, among themselves, ravenous wolves, when, for the sake of bribes, they condemn the innocent poor").[62] The metaphor here is perfectly adapted to the logic of hypocrisy that underpins this denunciation. The external identity of the judges is at odds with their behavior as thieves; and with the skin-changing skill of the deceivers in Ælfric's Latin *Colloquy*, they transform into wolves when among themselves. This shifting identity reveals the source of their evil to be hypocrisy. Alluding to the false prophets of the Gospels, this condemnation suggests once more the hypocrite's negative skills of subtlety. For all their charming exterior and pretense to justice, such false leaders harm far more community members than the ordinary flatterer. From the homilists' perspective, it is the most powerful whose hypocrisy does the most damage, and is thus most to be reviled, and it is perhaps the makers and enforcers of law whose perversions of truth present the most vivid examples of sin. In Wulfstan and the anonymous *Blickling* homilist, we find perhaps the most pointed examples of the hypocrite on earth: the

61 Ibid., 60–61.
62 Ibid., 61–63.

lawbreaking subject, and in particular, the law-perverting judge. Both figures risk not only their own souls, but the stability and cohesion of their society; the hypocritical judge, moreover, threatens the foundations of earthly order and law itself. It is little wonder, then, that the law codes should repeatedly invoke sincerity, trustworthiness, and loyalty to the law: from the perspective of the lawmakers, a lack of these qualities (the hallmark of the hypocrite) posed a substantial threat.[63]

Law

The stock biblical figure of the hypocrite (expressed by the term *licettere*) rarely appears in the law codes. Only Wulfstan appears to employ it in Cnut's laws, where this figure is condemned among magicians, prostitutes, murderers, perjurers, adulterers, various heathens, and counterfeiters: *Licceteras and leogeras, ryperas and reaferas Godes graman habban butan hig geswican and þe deoppar gebetan* ("Hypocrites and liars, thieves and looters will suffer God's wrath unless they cease and most sincerely repent").[64] Beyond this instance, hypocrisy appears indirectly in the laws insofar as its traits of secrecy, dishonest performance, deception, and betrayal inhere in several crimes, such as theft or perjury.[65] Among the lawgivers, Æthelstan (d. 939) stands out for his equation of crime – especially theft, the secrecy of which rendered it especially dangerous – with disloyalty to the king.[66] Under his broad rubric of loyalty and treachery, all subjects are expected to conduct their affairs in a manner that promotes the trust and peace of the kingdom; those who fail to live up to this ideal betray the royal trust, breaking their oath and ruining their character by

63 In this sense, *hypocrisy* contrasts neatly with the well-studied term (albeit in Chaucer's age) *treuth*, from OE *treowþ*. (*Not* to be confused with *truð*, "A player on a trumpet, an actor, buffoon" [Bosworth-Toller, s.v. *truð*]!)

64 Rabin, *Wulfstan: Old English Legal Writings*, II Cnut 7. See II Cnut 4–11.1. Compare Cnut's Oxford Legislation of 1018, 7–10.1.

65 Such indirect terms abound in the law codes. See, e.g., Felix Liebermann, ed., *Die Gesetze der Angelsachsen*, 3 vols. (Halle: Max Niemeyer, 1903–16), 2: s.v. *aleogan; belewedan; leas; leasgewitnesse; leasunga; l[ie]san; man[n]swica; man[n]þeof; manswara*. For an efficient survey of the enormity of perjury in early English law and its severe punishments, from ostracization to forfeiture of property, to excommunication, to treason, see Rabin, *Crime and Punishment*, 36, 45. For a sense of the centrality of oaths in early English law, see Liebermann, *Gesetze*, Ine 13–16, 21, 25, 30, 35, 46.

66 See Foot, *Æthelstan*, 143–48; Lambert, *Law and Order*, 89, 173–77, 203–04; Patrick Wormald, *Papers Preparatory to the Making of English Law: King Alfred to the Twelfth Century*, ed. Stephen Baxter and John Hudson (London: Early English Laws, 2014), 127–29, 138–41.

default.[67] Such breaches devalued the community's stock of trust in its members – the currency of interpersonal dealings. For this reason, "crimes of concealment," such as thieving, murdering, perjuring, harboring, or otherwise obstructing justice, were doubly detested, both for the deception they involved – which rendered them difficult to detect – and for the distrust they sowed among the people.[68] Functionally, corrupt business and administrative practices drew increasing ire by Wulfstan's time. Dishonest reeves, for instance, could undermine a district's economy by directly or indirectly aiding in the minting of forged coins, an offense punishable by amputation. Little wonder that reeves play so regular a role as stock villains.[69]

Other offenses entailing falsehood, such as slandering another member or otherwise damaging their reputation, were taken to defame king and community alike. The force of the culture's political honor manifests in its corporal punishments, with penalties including such bodily harm as the amputation of the tongue or hand.[70] In addition to serving as visible deterrents to specific crimes, bodily punishments rendered local participants witnesses to the enacted legal process, and through this participation, demonstrating their own sincere commitment to the law.[71] In the process of establishing the legal system as a reliable measure to counteract defamation and similar crimes against reputation, early English laws call for honest witnesses to give full and trustworthy testimony, *mid fulre gewitnesse 7 getreowre* – literally "unlying men" (*unlygnes monnes*)[72] – fit to uphold the law's standards of sincerity. Relatedly, the laws repeatedly

[67] For a helpful sample of decrees from Alfred to Cnut that verbalize the development of crimes that indirectly undermine the king, see Wormald, *Papers Preparatory*, 112–19. This development was an anticipation of the later medieval concept of the rights of the Crown (*corona*): see J. G. Bellamy, *The Law of Treason in England in the Later Middle Ages* (Cambridge: Cambridge University Press, 1970), 63–64.

[68] On this issue, see also Benjamin A. Saltzman, *Bonds of Secrecy: Law, Spirituality, and the Literature of Concealment in Early Medieval England* (Philadelphia: University of Pennsylvania Press, 2019), 19–44.

[69] See Rabin, *Wulfstan: Old English Legal Writings*, "Institutes of Polity (2)," and "*Be gerefan*" [Concerning Reeves]; Rabin, *Crime and Punishment*, 41–42.

[70] Daniel O'Gorman, "Mutilation and Spectacle in Anglo-Saxon Legislation," in *Capital and Corporal Punishment in Anglo-Saxon England*, ed. Jay Paul Gates and Nicole Marafioti (Woodbridge: Boydell, 2014), 150n7. Among other laws, O'Gorman cites Alfred 32, III Edgar 4, II Cnut 16, and II Cnut 36, which stipulate the amputation of the tongue or hand for slander or perjury.

[71] For the evidentiary nature of mutilation and its function in producing knowledge about the criminal, the value of the crime, and the social efficacy of its punishment, see Katherine O'Brien O'Keeffe, "Body and Law in Late Anglo-Saxon England," *Anglo-Saxon England* 27 (1998): 209–32.

[72] Liebermann, *Gesetze*, VI Æthelstan 10; II Æthelstan 12. Even evil men (*yfelra*

insist upon fidelity to the king. A code of King Edmund (d. 946) asks for such faith without any open or secret debate or deceit (*sine controuersia et seductione, in manifesto, in occulto*); with this fidelity, the king expects adherents to match their intentions with his, loving what he loves, loathing what he loathes (*amando quod amabit, nolendo quod nolet*), concealing nothing to anyone in the realm.[73] Wulfstan elaborates these sentiments in laws written for Æthelred (d. 1016):

> And word and weorc fadige mid rihte and að and wedd wærlice healde. [...] And swicollice dæda and laðlice unlaga ascunige man swyðe, þæt is: false gewihta and woge gemeta and lease gewitnessa and fracodlice ficunga; and egeslice manswara and deoflice dæda on morðweorcan and on manslihtan, on stalan and on strudungan, on gitsungan and on gifernessan, on oferfyllan, on swiccræftan and on mistlican lahbrycan, on hadbrycan and on æwbrican and on mæniges cynnes misdædan. Ac lufige man Godes riht heonan forð georne wordes and dæde; þonne wyrð þysse þeode sona God milde.

> And words and deeds are to be ordered properly, and oath and pledge carefully upheld. [...] And fraudulent deeds and hateful injustices are to be entirely rejected, that is: false weights and counterfeit measures and perjured testimony and shameful deceptions; and dreadful falsehoods and devilish deeds, such as murder and manslaughter, theft and robbery, avarice and cupidity, gluttony and overindulgence, treachery and countless violations of the law, of holy orders, of marriage vows, and misdeeds of many kinds. But God's law is to be willingly embraced henceforth in word and deed; then will God immediately show mercy to this people.[74]

Here as elsewhere, Wulfstan inscribes into law a signature code of conduct – a requirement for morally upright deeds that reflect transparent thoughts. Similarly, the archbishop draws a direct line between individuals' ethical characters and their kingdom's wellbeing. As observed in the above discussion of the homilies, failing to follow the law not only amounts to sin and a risk to the soul, but threatens social order (and here, precipitates divine anger) on earth. In the context of the depictions and denunciations of hypocrisy found across the textual output of the period, Wulfstan's extensive list of crimes suggests a common evil. His references to *swicollice dæda* ("fraudulent deeds") and his censure of things and actions that are *false* ("false"), *woge* ("counterfeit"), and *lease* ("lying")

---

manna) were expected to conduct themselves without fraud and deceit (*butan brede 7 bigswice*): I Edward 1.5.

73 Liebermann, *Gesetze*, III Edmund 1.

74 Rabin, *Wulfstan: Old English Legal Writings*, 154–55 (V Æthelred 22.2–26).

lead directly to his condemnation of the breach of marriage vows, religious duties – and law. The fundamental error is a failure to order (*fadian*) words and deeds properly, and the only remedy is to embrace God's law in both word and deed – that is, to embrace it with the sincerity that stands in opposition to hypocrisy.

Law and Order in Ælfric's Lives of Saints

Ælfric's hagiography offers unique insights into England's pre-Conquest legal culture on account of its generic hybridity. At the intersection of the literary and the theological, the legal representations in these texts impart attitudes toward the uses and abuses of the law in more nuanced ways than the law codes allow. Throughout Ælfric's saints' lives, antagonists wield the law as a weapon against their innocent victims while shielding themselves with it, a formulation that perfectly reverses Saint Sebastian's conception that *laga gesætte þæt menn rihtlice libban / and þæt þa rihtwisan beon geherode and þa unrihtwisan geynde* ("Laws are decreed in order that people may live justly and so that the just may be praised and the unjust humbled").[75] Though the law promises in theory to keep the peace through the corrections of the guilty, in the hands of the wicked, the legal process makes possible the oppression of the powerless. In this context, the spiritual and social dangers posed by the hypocrite are vividly laid out, and at the same time, the role of dissimulation becomes more complex. *Saint Eugenia* offers a particularly pertinent example. The whole narrative is driven by a series of deceptions and dissimulations; hypocrisy (especially as practiced by those in positions of authority) lies behind the array of false dealings that threaten the saint. At the same time, however, performance and disguise are not inevitably condemned. Hypocrisy and sincerity – and their role in earthly law – are here explored more subtly than in any text so far examined.

The early actions of the antagonists present hypocrisy in its familiar guise. When Eugenia heals an ailing aristocrat and widow, Melantia, the latter tries, but fails, to reward her with expensive gifts. She then decides to seduce Eugenia, whom she believes to be a man. With a deceiving mind (*mid leasum mode*) the widow pretended to be sick (*gebræd hi seoce*)[76] in order to attain her end. Recognizing the woman's flatteries as such, Eugenia rejects the worldly pleasures offered as false (*swicole*), prompting the rich widow to make a slanderous and deceitful (*facenfullan*) accusation against her. Melantia's false flatteries are the work of the hypocrite;

[75] Clayton and Mullins, *Ælfric*, 174, lines 282–83 and 175, lines 282–84.
[76] Ibid., 54, lines 146 and 152.

Eugenia's sincerity protects her from temptation. The saint's persecutors next make the law their weapon. Melantia seduces the corrupt reeve, Philip, who happens to be Eugenia's father, and claims that the saint, disguised as a doctor, attempted to seduce her.[77] Philip (here enacting precisely the duplicitous behavior condemned by the *Blickling* homilist) swears to protect this *leasan wudewan* ("false widow"), *ðeah þe heo gelignod wurðe* ("even if she were guilty of falsehood").[78] His own hypocrisy is compounded by his condoning of Melantia's. Apprehended and tried, Eugenia endures also the false testimonies of Melantia's servants:

> Ða sædon þa hyred-menn þæt hit soð wære
> and ealle mid aðe Eugenian forlugan.
> Þa wearð se geræfa þearle gebolgen
> and axude Eugenian hu heo ane mihte
> ealle þa gewyten awægan mid aðe
> oððe þurh ænige swutelunge hi sylfe aclænsian.

> Then the members of the household said that this was true and they all testified falsely against Eugenia under oath. Then the prefect was greatly enraged and asked Eugenia how she alone could repudiate all those witnesses with an oath or clear herself by any evidence.[79]

Eugenia is beset by hypocrites: the false dealings of Melantia precipitate those of Philip, and the lies of both are corroborated by the deceitful servants, whose testimony *mid aðe* ("under oath") enacts a hypocritical failure of accord between word and action, outward performance and inward reality. In the context of Wulfstan's homiletic and legislative denunciations of lawlessness, Philip's familial relation to Eugenia renders the scene's betrayal all the more flagrant – his hypocrisy leads him to a severe transgression of natural law. Altogether, the trial imagines human legislation at its most corrupted by hypocritical participants – figures of legal authority and ordinary witnesses collude to render it an institution for cultivating immorality and oppression under perfectly false pretenses.

Of course, Ælfric's saint benefits from divine intervention. The possibility of such divine involvement in earthly action is perhaps implied in the law codes through processes like the ordeal, and in such passages as Wulfstan's prediction (in V Æthelred) that God will show mercy to those who are true to their oaths. In *Saint Eugenia*, that intervention is literal and spectacular. Eugenia's trial prompts her confession that she disguised herself as a young man to protect her virginity – just one of many instances of saints disguising themselves for positive ends or as a matter

77 Ibid., 54, line 166, and 56, line 191.

78 Ibid., 58.

79 Ibid., 58, lines 222–27, and 59, lines 222–28.

of survival.[80] But it may be significant that it is the spectacular moment of revelation, when Eugenia exposes her true identity, that induces God's involvement in the plot. The implied threat to oathbreakers contained in V Æthelred (the withholding of God's mercy) is fully enacted in this narrative: despite Eugenia's intercessions for her father and patient-accuser, *Crist sylf asende swægende fyr / ufan of heofonum, þæt menn onhawoden, / to Melantian botle and hit mid ealle forbernde* ("Christ himself sent a roaring fire from the heavens above, that people could see, to Melantia's house and burned it all up").[81] Ælfric's literary representation of the law in *Saint Eugenia,* (and in *Saint Agnes, Saint Agatha, The Forty Soldiers,* and other lives) thus both reveals the vulnerability of earthly judicial processes to hypocritical reeves and judges, and offers the law's victims protection in the form of divine justice and the truth of God.

The world of divine interventions imagined in these saints' lives is one that (in a neat reversal) positions hypocritical anti-Christians as dupes within God's larger drama. Here, corruptible earthly laws are swept away in favor of divine justice; physical pain becomes spiritual pleasure; and the costumes of the oppressed – various chains, ropes, and other contraptions – are revealed to be the trappings of martyrdom, an homage to the crown of thorns.[82] Appearance and reality are tested according to God's touchstone, which can discern spiritual sincerity in earthly disguise, and which recognizes and punishes culpable hypocrisy in all its guises. These lives, particularly in their treatment of hypocrisy, showcase the inadequacies of royal legal systems divorced from a moral framework, thereby advertising an essential need for ecclesiastical and spiritual authority in local and royal legislation and legal processes. And they entertain the possibility for positive disruptions in the earthly legal process itself – disruptions made

80 Compare, for instance, Saint Sebastian, who conceals his Christianity to survive Diocletian's persecution. Clayton and Mullins, *Ælfric,* 157, lines 8–11. Andrew Rabin more broadly reads Eugenia's disruptive sexuality as an analogue to the struggles of royal authority in tenth-century England in response to the anti-monastic reaction ("Holy Bodies," esp. 243–48).

81 Clayon and Mullins, *Ælfric,* 60–61, lines 261–63. A similarly spectacular court scene is found in *Saint Agnes.* Upon being stripped naked and led to a brothel upon orders of a mad judge (*woda dema*) (Clayton and Mullins, *Ælfric,* 228, line 141), God reveals his hand, preserving the eponymous protagonist's modesty by having her hair cover her body; those who stared eagerly lost their sight. Meanwhile, the brothel morphs into a prayer house (228, lines 141–62).

82 For a helpful meditation on the invention of torture in medieval drama, which, like hagiography, negotiates the roles played by the law, rhetoric, and art in the mediation of a culture's "real" violence, see Jody Enders, *The Medieval Theater of Cruelty: Rhetoric, Memory, Violence* (Ithaca: Cornell University Press, 2002), esp. 160–229.

possible by God's perfect knowledge of truth and sincerity, and rendered necessary by humanity's sinful tendency toward untruth and hypocrisy.

Conclusion: Who's Afraid of Hypocrisy?

As it is articulated in Old English in the legal and homiletic writings of Ælfric and Wulfstan, the danger posed by hypocrites is especially acute in that it can pervert even the institutions of legitimate authority on earth. Spiritual purity, and ultimately God's omniscience, are offered as the most secure defense. But despite the repeated association of hypocrisy with punishment in the next life, the pastoral focus of Ælfric, Wulfstan, and their professional class meant that their writings also waged a cultural war in *this* life. If their listeners could only order their words and deeds and see life's treacherous traps (the homilists believe) the Christian community would establish God's law on earth – and would thus also progress more securely toward eternal life.

The homiletic and hagiographic writings of Wulfstan and Ælfric, however, ultimately leave their audiences without specific instruction as to the practicalities of living according to the perfect order, in the sense that precise prohibitions and sanctions are not offered. While they expect their audiences to apply the lessons of the past to their present lives, they do not (with respect to hypocrisy) prescribe the regulation of "Christian living" in legal terms. Despite this, both moralists insist on the paramount danger posed by the vice – it is a threat equally to the individual soul and the Christian community as a whole. Duplicitous behavior was behind the wicked actions of Christ's betrayers and provides the modus operandi for the Devil. In tenth- and eleventh-century England, it manifests in crimes from slander to secret murder, and threatens the operation of earthly law itself. Homilists and law-writers, therefore, unite in condemning it. For Wulfstan in particular, attacks on hypocrisy become a central means by which the perceived degeneration of the current age is exposed and excoriated. Hypocrisy may have carried a different conceptual weight in the early medieval period from that of the classical or early modern periods, but as the writings of Ælfric and Wulfstan demonstrate, its baggage was just as heavy, its drama just as piercing.

Bibliography

Abels, Richard. "Household Men, Mercenaries and Vikings in Anglo-Saxon England." In *Mercenaries and Paid Men*, ed. John France, 143–66. Leiden: Brill, 2008.

———. *Lordship and Military Obligation in Anglo-Saxon England*. Berkeley: University of California Press, 1988.

Abraham, Leonore McGaffey. "Cynewulf's *Juliana*: A Case at Law." *Allegorica* 3 (1978): 172–89.

Alcuin. *Epistolae*, ed. E. Dümmler. Monumenta Germaniae Historica, Epistolae 4. Berlin: Weidmann, 1895.

Ammon, Matthias. "'Ge mid wedde ge mid aðe': The Functions of Oath and Pledge in Anglo-Saxon Legal Culture." *Historical Research* 86 (2013): 515–35.

Amory, Frederic. "Whited Sepulchres: The Semantic History of Hypocrisy to the High Middle Ages." *Recherches de théologie ancienne et médiévale* 53 (1986): 5–39.

Anderson, Earl R. "Treasure Trove in Beowulf: A Legal View of the Dragon's Hoard." *Mediaevalia* 3 (1977): 141–64.

Andersson, Theodore M. "The Thief in Beowulf." *Speculum* 59 (1984): 493–508.

Andersson, Theodore M., and William Ian Miller. *Law and Literature in Medieval Iceland: Ljósvetninga saga and Valla-Ljósts saga.* Stanford: Stanford University Press, 1989.

Anlezark, Daniel. "Which Books are 'Most Necessary' to Know? The Old English *Pastoral Care* Preface and King Alfred's Educational Reform." *English Studies* 98 (2017): 759–80.

Appleton, Helen, and Francis Leneghan. "The Psalms in Anglo-Saxon and Anglo-Norman England." *English Studies* 98 (2017): 1–4.

Aquinas, Saint Thomas. *The "Summa Theologica" of St. Thomas Aquinas, part II (qq. LXXX–C)*. Translated by "Fathers of the English Dominican Province." London: Burns, Oates and Washbourne, 1922.

Attenborough, Frederick Levi. *The Laws of the Earliest English Kings.* Cambridge: Cambridge University Press, 1922.

Augustine, *De Sermone Domini in Monte: Libros Duos*, ed. Almut Mutzenbecher. Turnhout: Brepols, 1967.

Baird, Joseph L. "Grendel the Exile." *Neuphilologische Mitteilungen* 67 (1966): 375–81.

Baldwin, John W. "The Intellectual Preparation for the Canon of 1215 against Ordeals." *Speculum* 36 (1961): 613–36.

Bammesberger, Alfred. "Grendel's Death (Beowulf 850–852)." *Neophilologus* 86 (2002): 467–69.

Barlow, Frank. *The English Church 1000–1066: A Constitutional History.* New York: Longman, 1979.

——. *The English Church 1066–1154.* New York: Longman, 1979.

Barney, Stephen A., W. J. Lewis, J. A. Beach and Oliver Berghof, eds. and trans. *The Etymologies of Isidore of Seville.* Cambridge: Cambridge University Press, 2006.

Barnwell, P. S. "The Early Frankish *Mallus*: Its Nature, Participants, and Practices." In *Assembly Places and Practices in Medieval Europe,* ed. Aliki Pantos and Sarah Semple. Dublin: Four Courts Press, 2004.

Barrow, Julia. *The Clergy in the Medieval World.* Cambridge: Cambridge University Press, 2015.

——. "The Ideology of the Tenth-Century English Benedictine 'Reform.'" In *Challenging the Boundaries of Medieval History: The Legacy of Timothy Reuter,* ed. Patricia Skinner, 141–54. Turnhout: Brepols, 2009.

Bartlett, Robert. *Trial by Fire and Water: The Medieval Judicial Ordeal.* Oxford: Clarendon, 1986.

Bately, Janet. "Alfred as Author and Translator." In *A Companion to Alfred the Great,* ed. Nicole G. Discenza and Paul E. Szarmach, 111–42. Leiden: Brill, 2015.

——. "Did King Alfred Actually Translate Anything? The Integrity of the Alfredian Canon Revisited." *Medium Ævum* 78 (2009): 189–215.

——. "The Alfredian Canon Revisited: One Hundred Years On." In *Alfred the Great: Papers from the Eleventh-Centenary Conferences,* ed. Timothy Reuter, 107–20. Aldershot: Ashgate, 2003.

Baxter, Stephen. "Lordship and Justice in Late Anglo-Saxon England: The Judicial Functions of Soke and Commendation Revisited." In *Early Medieval Studies in Memory of Patrick Wormald,* ed. Stephen Baxter, Catherine E. Karkov, Janet Nelson and David Pelteret, 383–419. Farnham: Ashgate, 2009.

——. *The Earls of Mercia: Lordship and Power in Late Anglo-Saxon England.* Oxford: Oxford University Press, 2007.

——. "Archbishop Wulfstan and the Administration of God's Property." In *Wulfstan, Archbishop of York: The Proceedings of the Second Alcuin Conference,* ed. Matthew Townend, 161–205. Turnhout: Brepols, 2004.

Baxter, Stephen and John Blair. "Land Tenure and Royal Patronage in the Early English Kingdom: A Model and a Case Study." *Anglo-Norman Studies* 28 (2005): 19–46.

Bedingfield, M. Bradford. *The Dramatic Liturgy of Anglo-Saxon England.* Woodbridge: Boydell, 2002.

Beekes, Robert. *Etymological Dictionary of Greek: Volume 1*. Leiden: Brill, 2010.

Bellamy, J. G. *The Law of Treason in England in the Later Middle Ages*. Cambridge: Cambridge University Press, 1970.

Berghaus, Frank-Günter. *Die Verwandtschaftsverhältnisse der altenglischen Interlinearversionen des Psalters und der Cantica*. Göttingen: Vandenhoeck & Ruprecht, 1979.

Bethurum, Dorothy, ed. *The Homilies of Wulfstan*. Oxford: Clarendon, 1957.

Birch, Walter de Gray, ed. *Cartularium Saxonicum: A Collection of Charters Relating to Anglo-Saxon History, Vol. 2: A.D. 840–947*. London: Whiting, 1887.

Bjork, Robert E. "The Symbolic Use of Job in Ælfric's Homily on Job, *Christ II*, and the *Phoenix*." In *Latin Learning and English Lore, Volume II: Studies in Anglo-Saxon Literature for Michael Lapidge*, ed. Katherine O'Brien O'Keeffe, et al., 315–30. Toronto: University of Toronto Press, 2005.

——."Speech as Gift in *Beowulf*." *Speculum* 69 (1994): 993–1022.

Black, Henry Campbell. *Black's Law Dictionary*, ed. Bryan A. Garner. St. Paul, MN: Thomson Reuters, 2019.

Blair, John. *The Church in Anglo-Saxon Society*. Oxford: Oxford University Press, 2005.

Blake, E. O., ed. *Liber Eliensis*. London: The Royal Historical Society, 1962.

Bloomfield, Morton W. "Beowulf, Byrhtnoth, and the Judgment of God: Trial by Combat in Anglo-Saxon England." *Speculum* 44 (1969): 545–59.

Bolton, W. F. "The Latin Revisions of Felix's 'Vita Sancti Guthlaci.'" *Mediaeval Studies* 21 (1959): 36–52.

Bosworth, Joseph. *An Anglo-Saxon Dictionary Online*, ed. Thomas Northcote Toller, Sean Christ, and Ondřej Tichý. Prague: Charles University, 2014. <https://bosworthtoller.com>.

Bouwsma, William. *The Waning of the Renaissance, 1550–1640*. New Haven: Yale University Press, 2000.

Bowman, Jeffrey A. *Shifting Landmarks: Property, Proof, and Dispute in Catalonia around the Year 1000*. Ithaca: Cornell University Press, 2004.

Bracton, Henry de. *Bracton Online*. 2003. <https://amesfoundation.law.harvard.edu/Bracton>.

Brasington, Bruce C. *Order in the Court: Medieval Procedural Treatises in Translation*. Leiden: Brill, 2016.

Braune, Wilhelm, ed. *Althochdeutsches Lesebuch*. 17th ed. Tübingen: Max Niemeyer, 1994.

Bredehoft, Thomas A. *Textual Histories: Readings in the Anglo-Saxon Chronicle*. Toronto: University of Toronto Press, 2001.

Breen, Nathan. "The King's Closest Counselor: The Legal Basis of Wealhtheow's Comments to Hrothgar, *Beowulf* 1169–87." *The Heroic Age* 14 (2010): n.p.

Bremmer, Rolf H. "Proverbs in the Anglo-Saxon Laws." In *Languages of the Law in Early Medieval England: Essays in Memory of Lisi Oliver*, ed. Stefan Jurasinski and Andrew Rabin, 179–92. Leuven: Peeters, 2019.

——."The Final Countdown: Apocalyptic Expectations in Anglo-Saxon Charters." In *Time and Eternity: The Medieval Discourse*, ed. Gerhard Jaritz and Gerson Moreno-Riano, 501–14. Turnhout: Brepols, 2003.

——."Grendel's Arm and the Law." In *Doubt Wisely: Papers in Honour of E. G. Stanley*, ed. M. J. Toswell and E. M. Tyler, 121–32. London: Routledge, 1996.

Brooks, Nicholas P. "The Laws of King Æthelberht of Kent: Preservation, Content, and Composition." In *Textus Roffensis: Law, Language, and Libraries in Early Medieval England*, ed. Bruce O'Brien and Barbara Bombi, 105–36. Turnhout: Brepols, 2015.

——."The Fonthill Letter, Ealdorman Ordlaf, and Anglo-Saxon Law in Practice." In *Early Medieval Studies in Memory of Patrick Wormald*, ed. Stephen Baxter, Catherine E. Karkov, Janet Nelson and David Pelteret, 301–18. Farnham: Ashgate, 2009.

Brooks, Nicholas P., and S. E. Kelly. *Charters of Christ Church, Canterbury*. 2 vols. Oxford: Oxford University Press, 2013.

Brown, Francis, S. R. Driver and Charles A. Briggs. *The Brown-Driver-Briggs Hebrew and English Lexicon with an Appendix Containing Biblical Aramaic*. Peabody, MA: Hendrickson, 2020 [orig. publ. 1906].

Brown, George H. "The Psalms as the Foundation of Anglo-Saxon Learning." In *The Place of the Psalms in the Intellectual Culture of the Middle Ages*, ed. Nancy Van Deusen, 1–24. Albany: State University Press of New York, 1999.

Brown, Peter. "Society and the Supernatural: A Medieval Change." *Daedalus* 104 (1975): 133–51.

Brown, Warren. "Charters as Weapons: On the Role Played by Early Medieval Dispute Records in the Disputes They Record." *Journal of Medieval History* 28 (2002): 227–48.

——.*Unjust Seizure: Conflict, Interest, and Authority in an Early Medieval Society*. Ithaca: Cornell University Press, 2001.

Brundage, James A. *The Medieval Origins of the Legal Profession: Canonists, Civilians, and Courts*. Chicago: University of Chicago Press, 2008.

Brunner, Heinrich. *Deutsche Rechtsgeschichte*. 2 vols. Leipzig: Verlag von Duncker & Humblot, 1892.

Buck, Thomas Martin. *Admonitio und Praedicatio: Zur religiös-pastoralen Dimension von Kapitularien und kapitulariennahen Texten (507–814)*. Frankfurt am Main: Lang, 1997.

Bullough, D. A. *Alcuin: Achievement and Reputation*. Leiden: Brill, 2004.

——. "Alcuin and the Kingdom of Heaven: Liturgy, Theology, and the Carolingian Age." In *Carolingian Renewal*, ed. D. A. Bullough. Manchester: Manchester University Press, 1991.

Burnside, Jonathan. *God, Justice and Society: Aspects of Law and Legality in the Bible*. Oxford: Oxford University Press, 2011.

Butler, Emily. "The Role of the Compiler in the Paris Psalter." *English Studies* 98 (2017): 26–34.

Butler, Sara M. *Forensic Medicine and Death Investigation in Medieval England.* New York: Routledge, 2015.

——."Representing the Middle Ages: The Insanity Defense in Medieval England." In *The Treatment of Disabled Persons in Medieval Europe: Examining Disability in the Historical, Legal, Medical, and Religious Discourses of the Middle Ages,* ed. Wendy J. Turner and Tory Vandeventer Pearman, 117–33. Lewiston: Edwin Mellen Press, 2010.

Butterworth, Emily. "Necessary Leaven: Hypocrisy and the *Heptaméron.*" *Renaissance and Reformation* 43 (2020): 135–66.

——. *The Unbridled Tongue: Babble and Gossip in Renaissance France.* Oxford: Oxford University Press, 2016.

Cameron, Angus, Ashley Crandell Amos, Antonette diPaolo Healey et al., eds. *Dictionary of Old English: A to I Online.* Dictionary of Old English Project, 2016. <https://www.doe.utoronto.ca>.

Campbell, Alistair, ed. *Encomium Emmae Reginae.* London: Cambridge University Press, 1998 [orig. publ. 1949].

Campbell, James. "Some Agents and Agencies of the Late-Anglo-Saxon State." In *The Anglo-Saxon State,* 201–26. London: Hambledon, 2000.

Carella, Kristen. "Northumbrian Law before the Vikings: A Preliminary Assessment of the Evidence." In *Languages of the Law in Early Medieval England: Essays in Memory of Lisi Oliver,* ed. Stefan Jurasinski and Andrew Rabin, 45–58. Leuven: Peeters, 2019.

Carella, Bryan [who now publishes as Kristen Carella]. "Alcuin and the Legatine Capitulary of 786: The Evidence of Scriptural Citations." *Journal of Medieval Latin* 22 (2012): 221–56.

——. "The Earliest Expression for Outlawry in Anglo-Saxon Law." *Traditio* 70 (2015): 111–43.

——. "Alcuin and the Legatine Capitulary of 786: The Evidence of Scriptural Citations." *Journal of Medieval Latin* 22 (2012): 221–56.

——."Evidence for Hiberno-Latin Thought in the Prologue to the Laws of Alfred." *Studies in Philology* 108 (2011): 1–26.

——."Reconstructing a Lost Latin Homily on Ecclesiasticus (Sirach) 5:8." *Revue Bénédictine* 117 (2007): 261–93.

——."The Source of the Prologue to the Laws of Alfred." *Peritia* 19 (2005): 91–118.

Chase, Martin. "The Book of Job and the Figure of Job in Old English Literature." In *A Companion to Job in the Middle Ages,* ed. Franklin Harkins and Aaron Canty, 354–91. Leiden: Brill, 2016.

Chibnall, Marjorie, ed. and trans., *The Ecclesiastical History of Orderic Vitalis.* Vol. 2. Oxford: Clarendon, 1969.

Clanchy, Michael. "Literacy, Law, and the Power of the State." In *Culture et idéologie dans la genèse de l'état moderne*, 25–34. Rome: École Française de Rome, 1985.

Clark, Matityahu. *Etymological Dictionary of Biblical Hebrew: Based on the Commentaries of Samson Raphael Hirsch*. New York: Feldheim, 1999.

Clark, Stephanie. "A More Permanent Homeland: Land Tenure in *Guthlac A*." *Anglo-Saxon England* 40 (2012): 75–102.

Clarke, Catherine A. M. *Writing Power in Anglo-Saxon England: Texts, Hierarchies, Economies*. Cambridge: D. S. Brewer, 2012.

Clayton, Mary, ed. and trans. *Two Ælfric Texts: The Twelve Abuses and the Vices and Virtues*, Cambridge: D. S. Brewer, 2013.

——."The Old English *Promissio regis*." *Anglo-Saxon England* 37 (2008): 91–150.

Clayton, Mary, and Juliet Mullins. *Ælfric: Old English Lives of the Saints*. 3 vols. Cambridge, MA: Harvard University Press, 2019.

Clemoes, Peter, ed., *Ælfric's Catholic Homilies: The First Series, Text*. EETS, s.s. 17. Oxford: Oxford University Press, 1997.

Coffey, Brendan. "The Stowe Enigma: Decoding the Mystery." *Irish Theological Quarterly* 75 (2010): 75–91.

Colgrave, Bertram, ed. and trans. *Felix's Life of Saint Guthlac*. Cambridge: Cambridge University Press, 1956.

——, ed. and trans. *Two Lives of Saint Cuthbert*. Cambridge: Cambridge University Press, 1940.

Colgrave, Bertram, and R. A. B. Mynors, eds. *Bede's Ecclesiastical History of the English People*. Corrected reprint ed. Oxford: Clarendon, 1991 [orig. publ. 1969].

Colman, Rebecca V. "Reason and Unreason in Early Medieval Law." *The Journal of Interdisciplinary History* 4 (1974): 571–91.

Corona, Gabriella. "Ælfric's Schemes and Tropes: *Amplificatio* and the Portrayal of Persecutors." In *A Companion to Ælfric*, ed. Hugh Magennis and Mary Swan, 297–320. Leiden: Brill, 2009.

Cross, F. L. "Donatism." In *The Oxford Dictionary of the Christian Church*, ed. F. L. Cross and E. A. Livingstone, 2nd ed. Oxford: Oxford University Press, 1985.

Cubitt, Catherine."'As the Lawbook Teaches': Reeves, Lawbooks and Urban Life in the Anonymous Old English Legend of the Seven Sleepers." *English Historical Review* 124 (2009): 1021–49.

——."Memory and Narrative in the Cult of Early Anglo-Saxon Saints." In *The Uses of the Past in the Early Middle Ages*, ed. Yitzhak Hen and Matthew Innes, 29–66. Cambridge: Cambridge University Press, 2000.

——. *Anglo-Saxon Church Councils, c.650–c.850*. London: Leicester University Press, 1995.

Dance, Richard. "Sound, Fury, and Signifiers." In *Wulfstan, Archbishop of York: The Proceedings of the Second Alcuin Conference*, ed. Matthew

Townend, 29–61. Turnhout: Brepols, 2004.

Danet, Brenda, and Bryna Bogoch. "'Whoever Alters This, May God Turn His Face from Him on the Day of Judgement': Curses in Anglo-Saxon Legal Documents." *Journal of American Folklore* 105 (1992): 132–65.

Davies, Wendy, and Paul Fouracre. "Procedure and Practice in the Settlement of Disputes." In *The Settlement of Disputes in Early Medieval Europe*, ed. Wendy Davies and Paul Fouracre, 215–28. Cambridge: Cambridge University Press, 1986.

Davis, Kathleen. "Boredom, Brevity, and Last Things: Ælfric's Style and the Politics of Time." In *A Companion to Ælfric*, ed. Hugh Magennis and Mary Swan, 321–44. Leiden: Brill, 2009.

———. "National Writing in the Ninth Century: A Reminder for Postcolonial Thinking about the Nation." *Journal of Medieval and Early Modern Studies* 28 (1998): 611–37.

Davis-Secord, Jonathan. *Joinings: Compound Words in Old English Literature.* Toronto: University of Toronto Press, 2016.

Day, David D. "Hands across the Hall: The Legalities of Beowulf's Fight with Grendel." *JEGP* 98 (1999): 313–24.

Dempsey, George T. "Legal Terminology in Anglo-Saxon England: The Trimoda Necessitas Charter." *Speculum* 57 (1982): 843–49.

Dietrich, Eduard. "Abt Aelfrik. Zur Literatur-Geschichte der angelsächsischen Kirche." *Zeitschrift für historische* Theologie 25 (1855): 487–594, and 26 (1856): 163–256.

Dombart B., and A. Kalb, eds. *Sancti Aurelii Augustini De civitate Dei.* Corpus Christianorum Series Latina 48. Turnhout: Brepols, 1955.

Dox, Donnalee. *The Idea of Theater in Christian Thought: Augustine to the Fourteenth Century*. Ann Arbor: University of Michigan Press, 2004.

Doyle, Arthur Conan. "The Adventure of the Silver Blaze." In *The Strand Magazine*, ed. George Newnes, vol. 4, July to December, 645–60. London: George Newnes Ltd., 1892.

Durkin, Philip. *Borrowed Words: A History of Loanwords in English*. Oxford: Oxford University Press, 2014.

Edgar, Swift, ed. *The Vulgate Bible, Volume I: The Pentateuch*. Cambridge, MA: Harvard University Press, 2010.

Edgar, Swift, and Angela M. Kinney, eds. *The Vulgate Bible, Volume III: The Poetical Books*. Cambridge, MA: Harvard University Press, 2011.

Ehrlich, Bernard. "The Book of Job as a Book of Morality." *Jewish Bible Quarterly* 34 (2006): 30–38.

Ehwald, Rudolf, ed. *Aldhelmi opera*, Monumenta Germaniae Historica. Auctores antiquissimi Vol. 15. Berlin: Weidmann, 1919.

Eklund, Sten. "The Use and Abuse of Cursus in Textual Criticism." *Archivum Latinitatis Medii Aevi* 43 (1984): 27–56.

Eliav-Feldon, Miriam, and Tamar Herzig, eds. *Dissimulation and Deceit in Early Modern Europe*. Houndmills, UK: Palgrave Macmillan, 2015.

Enders, Jody. *The Medieval Theater of Cruelty: Rhetoric, Memory, Violence*. Ithaca: Cornell University Press, 2002.

Fairweather, Janet, trans. *Liber Eliensis: A History of the Isle of Ely from the Seventh Century to the Twelfth*. Woodbridge: Boydell, 2005.

Fehr, Bernard, ed. *Die Hirtenbriefe Ælfrics in altenglischer und lateinischer Fassung*. Hamburg: H. Grand, 1914.

Fisher, J. D. C. *Christian Initiation: Baptism in the Medieval West*. London: S.P.C.K., 1965.

Flechner, Roy. *The Hibernensis: A Study and Edition*. Vol. 1. Washington, D.C.: Catholic University of America Press, 2019.

Fleming, Robin. *Domesday Book and the Law: Society and Legal Custom in Early Medieval England*. Cambridge: Cambridge University Press, 1998.

——."Monastic Lands and England's Defence in the Viking Age." *English Historical Review* 100 (1985): 247–65.

Foot, Sarah. *Æthelstan: The First King of England*. New Haven: Yale University Press, 2011.

——. *Monastic Life in Anglo-Saxon England, c.600–900*. Cambridge: Cambridge University Press, 2006.

——. "Reading Anglo-Saxon Charters: Memory, Record, or Story?" In *Narrative and History in the Early Medieval West*, ed. Elizabeth M. Tyler and Ross Balzaretti, 39–65. Turnhout: Brepols, 2006.

——. "The Making of *Angelcynn*: English Identity Before the Norman Conquest." *TRHS*, 6th series, 6 (1996): 25–49.

——."'By Water in the Spirit': Baptism in early Anglo-Saxon England." In *Pastoral Care before the Parish*, ed. John Blair and Richard Sharpe, 171–92. Leicester: Leicester University Press, 1992.

Forbes, Helen Foxhall. "Making Manifest God's Judgement: Interpreting Ordeals in Anglo-Saxon England." In *Writing, Kingship, and Power in Anglo-Saxon England*, ed. Rory Naismith and David A. Woodman, 259–80. Cambridge: Cambridge University Press, 2018.

——.*Heaven and Earth in Anglo-Saxon England: Theology and Society in an Age of Faith*. Aldershot: Ashgate, 2013.

Fowler, Herbert. "Notes on the Pronunciation of Medieval Latin in England." *History*, n.s. 22 (1937–38): 97–109.

Fowler, Roger. "A Late Old English Handbook for the Use of a Confessor." *Anglia* 83 (1965): 1–34 .

Frantzen, Allen J. *The Literature of Penance in Anglo-Saxon England*. New Brunswick: Rutgers University Press, 1980.

Friedland, Paul. *Seeing Justice Done: The Age of Spectacular Capital Punishment in France*. Oxford: Oxford University Press, 2012.

Fruscione, Daniela. "*Riht* in Earlier Anglo-Saxon Legislation: A Semasiological Approach." *Historical Research* 86 (2013): 498–504.

Fulk, R. D., ed. *The Beowulf Manuscript: Complete Texts and the Fight at Finnsburg*. Cambridge, MA: Harvard University Press, 2010.

——. "Some Emendations and Non-Emendations in 'Beowulf' (Verses 600a, 976a, 1585b, 1663b, 1740a, 2525b, 2771a, and 3060a)," *Studies in Philology* 104 (2007): 159–74.

Fulk, R. D., Robert E. Bjork, and John D. Niles, eds. *Klaeber's Beowulf and the Fight at Finnsburg*, 4th ed. Toronto: University of Toronto Press, 2008.

Garmonsway, George. *Ælfric's Colloquy*. Liverpool: Liverpool University Press, 2003 [orig. publ. 1939].

Garnett, George. "The Third Recension of the English Coronation *Ordo*: The Manuscripts." *Haskins Society Journal* 11 (1998): 43–71.

Gates, Jay Paul. "Prologue to the Laws of King Alfred: An Edition and Translation for Students." *The Heroic Age* 18 (2018).

——. "Preaching, Politics and Episcopal Reform in Wulfstan's Early Writings." *Early Medieval Europe* 23 (2015): 93–116.

——. "The Politics of Building the Holy Society: Wulfstan's Later Writings." Paper presented at the Anglo-Saxon Studies Colloquium, Columbia University, October 2012.

Gates, Jay Paul, and Nicole Marafioti, eds. *Capital and Corporal Punishment in Anglo-Saxon England*. Woodbridge: Boydell, 2014.

Genette, Gérard. *Paratexts: Thresholds of Interpretation*. Translated by Jane E. Lewin. Cambridge: Cambridge University Press, 1997.

Giandrea, Mary Frances. *Episcopal Culture in Late Anglo-Saxon England*. Woodbridge, Boydell, 2007.

Gillingham, Susan. *Psalms Through the Centuries: Volume One*. Malden: Wiley-Blackwell, 2012.

Gillis, Matthew. "Legal Traditions, Manuscripts of Law, and Influences on King Alfred's *Domboc*." Presentation at the Books of Law in the Very Long Tenth Century conference, Vienna, Austria, September 5, 2019, to be published in *Books of Law in the Long Tenth Century*, ed. Thom Gobbitt (Binghamton: Gracchi Books).

Gittos, Helen. *Liturgy, Architecture, and Sacred Places in Anglo-Saxon England*. Oxford: Oxford University Press, 2013.

Glare, P. G. W., ed. *Oxford Latin Dictionary*. Oxford: Clarendon, 1982.

Gneuss, Helmut. *Ælfric of Eynsham: His Life, Times, and Writings*. Kalamazoo: Medieval Institute Publications, 2009.

——. "The Study of Language in Anglo-Saxon England." In *Language and History in Early England*, ed. Helmut Gneuss, 3–32. Aldershot: Variorum, 1996.

——. "The Origin of Standard Old English and Æthelwold's School at Winchester." *Anglo-Saxon England* 1 (1972): 63–85.

——. *Hymnar und Hymnen im englischen Mittelalter: Studien zur Überlieferung, Glossierung und Übersetzung lateinischer Hymnen in England*. Tübingen: Max Niemeyer, 1968.

——. *Lehnbildungen und Lehnbedeutungen im Altenglischen*. Berlin: E. Schmidt, 1955.

Gneuss, Helmut, and Michael Lapidge. *Anglo-Saxon Manuscripts: A Bibliographical Handlist of Manuscripts and Manuscript Fragments Written or Owned in England up to 1100*. Toronto: University of Toronto Press, 2014.

Godden, Malcolm R., ed. and trans., *The Old English History of the World: An Anglo-Saxon Rewriting of Orosius*. Cambridge, MA: Harvard University Press, 2016.

——."Did King Alfred Write Anything?" *Medium Ævum* 76 (2007): 1–23.

——."Ælfric and Anglo-Saxon Kingship." *English Historical Review* 102 (1987): 911–15.

——, ed., *Ælfric's Catholic Homilies: The Second Series, Text*. EETS, s.s. 5. London: Oxford University Press, 1979.

Godden, Malcolm R., and Susan Irvine, ed. *The Old English Boethius: An Edition of the Old English Versions of Boethius's De Consolatione Philosophiae*. Vol. 1. Oxford: Oxford University Press, 2009.

Goebel, Julius. *Felony and Misdemeanor: A Study in the History of Criminal Law*. Philadelphia: University of Pennsylvania Press, 1976 [orig. publ. 1937].

Goldbacher, Alois, ed. *Augustinus: Epistulae (Ep. 185–270)*. Vienna: Austrian Academy of Sciences, 1911.

Gonser, Paul, ed. *Das angelsächsische Prosa-Leben des hl. Guthlac*. Heidelberg: Carl Winter, 1909.

Goodrich, Peter. *Law in the Courts of Love: Literature and Other Minor Jurisprudences*. London: Routledge, 1996.

——. *Oedipus Lex: Psychoanalysis, History, Law*. Berkeley: University of California Press, 1995.

Gorman, Michael. "Commentaries from Isidore to Wigbod: A Guide to Manuscripts, Editions and Bibliography." <http://ccat.sas.upenn.edu/jod/genesis>.

——."Wigbod, Charlemagne's Commentator: the Quaestiunculae super Euangelium." *Revue Bénédictine* 114 (2004): 5–74.

——."Wigbod and Biblical Studies under Charlemagne." *Revue Bénédictine* 107 (1997): 40–76.

——."Wigbod and the Lectiones on the Hexateuch attributed to Bede in Paris, Lat. 2342." *Revue Bénédictine* 105 (1995): 310–47.

——. "The Encyclopedic Commentary on Genesis Prepared for Charlemagne by Wigbod." *Recherches Augustiniennes et Patristiques* 17 (1982): 173–201.

Grant, Ruth Weissbourd. *Hypocrisy and Integrity: Machiavelli, Rousseau, and the Ethics of Politics*. Chicago: University of Chicago Press, 1997.

Green, Richard Firth. *A Crisis of Truth: Literature and Law in Ricardian England*. Philadelphia: University of Pennsylvania Press, 1999.

——."Medieval Literature and Law." In *The Cambridge History of Middle English Literature*, ed. David Wallace, 407–31. Cambridge: Cambridge University Press, 1998.

Green, Thomas Andrew. *Verdict According to Conscience: Perspectives on the English Criminal Trial Jury, 1200–1800.* Chicago: University of Chicago Press, 1985.

Gretsch, Mechthild. "The Fonthill Letter: Language, Law and the Discourse of Disciplines." *Anglia* 123 (2006): 667–86.

——. *The Intellectual Foundations of the English Benedictine Reform.* Cambridge: Cambridge University Press, 1999.

——. "The Language of the 'Fonthill Letter.'" *Anglo-Saxon England* 23 (1994): 57–102.

Grimm, Jacob. *Deutsche Rechtsaltertümer.* 2 vols. Göttingen: Dieterichsche Buchhandlung, 1828.

——. "Von der Poesie im Recht." In *Zeitschrift für geschichtliche Rechtswissenschaft*, 25–99. Digitale Bibliothek des Max-Planck-Instituts für Europäische Rechtsgeschichte, 1816.

Grocock, Christopher, and I. N. Wood, ed. and trans. *Abbots of Wearmouth and Jarrow.* Oxford: Clarendon, 2013.

Gwara, Scott. "A Record of Anglo-Saxon Pedagogy: Aldhelm's 'Epistola ad Heahfridum' and its Gloss." *Journal of Medieval Latin* 6 (1996): 84–134.

Harding, Alan. *The Law Courts of Medieval England.* London: Allen & Unwin, 1973.

Harmer, Florence E., ed. *Anglo-Saxon Writs*, 2nd ed. Stamford: Paul Watkins, 1989.

Harris, Stephen J. "Ælfric's *Colloquy*." In *Medieval Literature for Children*, ed. Daniel T. Kline, 112–30. New York: Routledge, 2003.

——."Bede and Gregory's Allusive Angles." *Criticism* 44 (2002): 271–89.

Hart, Cyril. "Danelaw and Mercian Charters of the Mid Tenth Century." In *The Danelaw*, 431–53. London: Hambledon, 1992.

Harvey, Sally. *Domesday: Book of Judgment.* Oxford: Oxford University Press, 2014.

Helmholz, R. H. *The Ius Commune in England: Four Studies.* New York: Oxford University Press, 2001.

——. *The Spirit of Classical Canon Law.* Athens: University of Georgia Press, 1996.

Hermanson, Lars. "How to Legitimate Rebellion and Condemn Usurpation of the Crown: Discourses of Fidelity and Treason in the *Gesta Danorum* of Saxo Grammaticus." In *Disputing Strategies in Medieval Scandinavia*, ed. Kim Esmark, Lars Hermanson, Hans Jacob Orning and Helle Vogt, 107–42. Leiden: Brill, 2013.

Hexter, Ralph J. *Equivocal Oaths and Ordeals in Medieval Literature.* Cambridge, MA: Harvard University Press, 1975.

Higham, N. J. "Guthlac's *Vita*, Mercia and East Anglia in the First Half of the Eighth Century." In *Æthelbald and Offa: Two Eighth-Century Kings of Mercia*, ed. David Hill and Margaret Worthington, 85–90. Oxford: Basingstoke Press, 2005.

Hill, John. *The Cultural World in Beowulf*. Toronto: University of Toronto Press, 1995.

Hill, Joyce M. "Ælfric's *Colloquy*: The Antwerp/London Version." In *Latin Learning and English Lore: Studies in Anglo-Saxon Literature for Michael Lapidge, Volume II*, ed. Katherine O'Brien O'Keeffe and Andy Orchard, 331–48. Toronto: University of Toronto Press, 2005.

——."Archbishop Wulfstan: Reformer?" In *Wulfstan, Archbishop of York: The Proceedings of the Second Alcuin Conference*, ed. Matthew Townend, 309–24. Turnhout: Brepols, 2004.

——."Æfric's 'Silent Days.'" In *Sources and Relations: Studies in Honour of J. E. Cross*, ed. Marie Collins, Jocelyn Price, and Andrew Hamer, 118–31. Leeds Studies in English, n.s. 16, Leeds: University of Leeds, School of English, 1985.

Ho, H. L. "The Legitimacy of Medieval Proof." *Journal of Law and Religion* 19 (2004): 259–98.

Hofstetter, Walter. "Winchester and the Standardization of Old English Vocabulary." *Anglo-Saxon England* 17 (1988): 139–61.

——. *Winchester und der spätaltenglische Sprachgebrauch: Untersuchungen zur geographischen und zeitlichen Verbreitung altenglischer Synonyme*. Munich: W. Fink, 1987.

Hollis, Stephanie. "Old English 'Cattle-Theft Charms': Manuscript Contexts and Social Uses." *Anglia* 115 (1997): 139–64.

——.*Anglo-Saxon Women and the Church*. Woodbridge: Boydell, 1992.

Hollister, C. Warren. *Anglo-Saxon Military Institutions on the Eve of the Norman Conquest*. Oxford: Clarendon, 1962.

Holthausen, Ferdinand. *Altenglisches Etymologisches Wörterbuch*. Heidelberg: C. Winter, 1934.

Hooper, Nicholas J. "Some Observations on the Navy in Late Anglo-Saxon England." In *Anglo-Norman Warfare: Studies in Late Anglo-Saxon and Anglo-Norman Military Organization and Warfare*, ed. Matthew Strickland, 17–27. Woodbridge: Boydell, 1992.

Hough, Carole. "Cattle-Tracking in the Fonthill Letter." *English Historical Review* 115 (2000): 864–92.

Howe, Nicholas. *Migration and Mythmaking in Anglo-Saxon England*. Notre Dame: University of Notre Dame Press, 2001.

Hudson, John. *The Formation of the English Common Law: Law and Society in England from the Norman Conquest to Magna Carta*, 2nd ed. New York: Routledge, 2018.

——.*The Oxford History of the Laws of England, Volume II: 871–1216*. Oxford: Oxford University Press, 2012.

——. "Court Cases and Legal Arguments in England, *c.*1066–1166." *TRHS*, 6th series, 10 (2000): 91–115.

——.*Land, Law, and Lordship in Anglo-Norman England*. Oxford: Oxford University Press, 1994.

Hurnard, Naomi D. *The King's Pardon for Homicide before A.D. 1307.* Oxford: Clarendon, 1969.

Huscroft, Richard. *Making England, 796–1042.* New York: Routledge, 2019.

Hyams, Paul R. *Rancor and Reconciliation in Medieval England.* Ithaca: Cornell University Press, 2018.

——."Norms and Legal Argument before 1150." In *Law and History,* ed. Andrew Lewis and Michael Lobban, 41–61. Oxford: Oxford University Press, 2004.

——."The Charter as a Source for the Early Common Law." *The Journal of Legal History* 12 (1991): 173–89.

——."Trial by Ordeal: The Key to Proof in Early Common Law." In *On the Laws and Customs of England: Essays in Honor of Samuel E. Thorne,* ed. Morris S. Arnold, Thomas A. Green, Sally A. Scully, and Stephen D. White, 90–126. Chapel Hill: University of North Carolina Press, 1981.

Insley, Charles. "Collapse, Reconfiguration or Renegotiation? The Strange End of the Mercian Kingdom, 850–924." *Reti medievali rivista* 17 (2016): 231–49.

Irvine, Martin. *The Making of Textual Culture: "Grammatica" and Literary Theory, 350–1100.* Cambridge: Cambridge University Press, 1994.

Irvine, Susan. "Uncertain Beginnings: The Prefatory Tradition in Old English." *H. M. Chadwick Memorial Lectures* 27 (2017): 1–18.

——."The Alfredian Prefaces and Epilogues." In *A Companion to Alfred the Great,* ed. Nicole G. Discenza and Paul E. Szarmach, 143–70. Leiden: Brill, 2015.

Jackson, Richard A., ed. *Ordines Coronationis Franciae, Volume 1: Texts and Ordines for the Coronation of Frankish and French Kings and Queens in the Middle Ages*. Philadelphia: University of Pennsylvania Press, 1995.

Janson, Tore. *Prose Rhythm in Medieval Latin from the 9th to the 13th Century.* Stockholm: Almqvist & Wiksell, 1975.

Johansen, J. G. "Grendel the Brave? *Beowulf,* Line 834." *English Studies* 63 (1982): 193–97.

Jones, Christopher A. "Ælfric and the Limits of 'Benedictine Reform.'" In *A Companion to Ælfric,* ed. Hugh Magennis and Mary Swan, 67–108. Leiden: Brill, 2009.

——. *Ælfric's Letter to the Monks of Eynsham.* Cambridge: Cambridge University Press, 1998.

Jónsson, Finnur, ed., *Brennu-Njálssaga (Njála).* Halle: Max Niemeyer, 1908.

Jordan, William Chester. "A Fresh Look at Medieval Sanctuary." In *Law and the Illicit in Medieval Europe,* ed. Ruth Mazo Karras, Joel Kaye, and E. Ann Matter, 17–33. Philadelphia: University of Pennsylvania Press, 2008.

Jost, Karl, ed., *Die "Institutes of Polity, Civil and Ecclesiastical": Ein Werk Erzbischof Wulfstans von York.* Bern: Francke, 1959.

——.*Wulfstanstudien*. Bern: Francke, 1950.

Joy, Eileen. "The Old English Seven Sleepers, Eros, and the Unincorporable Infinite of the Human Person." In *Anonymous Interpolations in Ælfric's Lives of Saints*, ed. Robin Norris, 71–96. Kalamazoo: Medieval Institute Publications, 2011.

Jurasinski, Stefan. "English Law Before the Conquest." In *The Cambridge Companion to Medieval English Law and Literature*, ed. Candace Barrington and Sebastian Sobecki, 3–16. Cambridge: Cambridge University Press, 2019.

——. *The Old English Penitentials and Anglo-Saxon Law.* Cambridge: Cambridge University Press, 2015.

——.*Ancient Privileges: Beowulf, Law and the Making of Germanic Antiquity.* Morgantown: West Virginia University Press, 2006.

Jurasinski, Stefan, and Lisi Oliver, eds. *The Laws of Alfred: The Domboc and the Making of Anglo-Saxon Law.* Cambridge: Cambridge University Press, 2021.

Jurasinski, Stefan, Lisi Oliver, and Andrew Rabin, eds. *English Law Before Magna Carta: Felix Liebermann and Die Gesetze der Angelsachsen.* Leiden: Brill, 2010.

Kamali, Elizabeth Papp. *Felony and the Guilty Mind in Medieval England.* Cambridge: Cambridge University Press, 2019.

——."Trial by Ordeal by Jury in Medieval England, or Saints and Sinners in Literature and Law." In *Emotion, Violence, Vengeance and Law in the Middle Ages: Essays in Honor of William Ian Miller*, ed. Kate Gilbert and Stephen D. White, 49–79. Leiden: Brill, 2018

Kantorowicz, Ernst H. *Laudes Regiae: A Study in Liturgical Acclamations and Mediaeval Ruler Worship.* Berkeley: University of California Press, 1958.

Kantorowicz, Ernst H. *The King's Two Bodies: A Study in Medieval Political Theology.* Princeton: Princeton University Press, 1957.

Karn, Nicholas. *Kings, Lords, and Courts in Anglo-Norman England.* Woodbridge: Boydell, 2020.

Keefer, Sarah Larratt. "*Ðonne se cirlisce man ordales weddieð*: The Anglo-Saxon Lay Ordeal." In *Early Medieval Studies in Memory of Patrick Wormald*, ed. Stephen Baxter, Catherine E. Karkov, Janet Nelson, and David Pelteret, 353–68. Farnham: Ashgate, 2009.

——."Ut in Omnibus Honorificetur Deus: The *Corsnæd* Ordeal in Anglo-Saxon England." In *The Community, the Family and the Saint: Patterns of Power in Early Medieval Europe*, ed. Joyce M. Hill and Mary Swan, 237–64. Turnhout: Brepols, 1998.

Kelly, S. E., ed. *Charters of Glastonbury Abbey*. Oxford: Oxford University Press, 2012.

——, ed., *Charters of Abingdon Abbey*. 2 vols. Oxford: Oxford University Press, 2000.

Kempshall, Matthew. "No Bishop, No King: The Ministerial Ideology of Kingship and Asser's *Res Gestae Aelfredi*," in *Belief and Culture in the Middle Ages: Studies Presented to Henry Mayr-Harting*, ed. Richard Gameson and Henrietta Leyser, 106–27. Oxford: Oxford University Press, 2001.

Kendall, Calvin B., ed. *Bedae Venerabilis Opera, Pars I: Opera didascalica.* Corpus Christianorum Series Latina 123A. Turnhout: Brepols, 1975.

Kennedy, A. G. "Cnut's Law Code of 1018." *Anglo-Saxon England* 11 (1982): 57–81.

Ker, N. R. "The Handwriting of Archbishop Wulfstan." In *Books, Collectors and Libraries*, ed. A. Watson, 9–26. London: Hambledon, 1985.

Kern, Fritz. *Kingship and Law in the Middle Ages.* Translated by S. B. Chrimes. Oxford: Basil Blackwell, 1948.

Kerr, Margaret H., Richard D. Forsyth, and Michael J. Plyley. "Cold Water and Hot Iron: Trial by Ordeal in England." *The Journal of Interdisciplinary History* 22 (1992): 573–95.

Kershaw, Paul J. E. *Peaceful Kings: Peace, Power, and the Early Medieval Political Imagination*. Oxford: Oxford University Press, 2011.

Keynes, Simon. "The 'Cuckhamsley Chirograph.'" In *Languages of the Law in Early Medieval England: Essays in Memory of Lisi Oliver*, ed. Stefan Jurasinski and Andrew Rabin, 195–97. Leuven: Peeters, 2019.

——. "Church Councils, Royal Assemblies, and Anglo-Saxon Royal Diplomas." In *Kingship, Legislation and Power in Anglo-Saxon England*, ed. Gale R. Owen-Crocker and Brian W. Schneider, 17–182. Woodbridge: Boydell, 2013.

——."Edgar, Rex Admirabilis." In *Edgar, King of the English 959–975: New Interpretations*, ed. Donald Scragg, 3–59. Woodbridge: Boydell, 2008.

——."An Abbot, an Archbishop, and the Viking Raids of 1006–7 and 1009–12." *Anglo-Saxon England* 36 (2007): 151–220.

——."Apocalypse Then: England A.D. 1000." In *Europe Around the Year 1000*, ed. P. Urbańczyk, 247–70. Warsaw: Institute of Archaeology and Ethnology, Polish Academy of Sciences, 2001.

——."Edward, King of the Anglo-Saxons." In *Edward the Elder, 899–924*, ed. N. J. Higham and D. H. Hill, 40–66. London: Routledge, 2001.

——. *An Atlas of Attestations in Anglo-Saxon Charters, c.670–1066.* Department of Anglo-Saxon, Norse and Celtic, University of Cambridge, 1998.

——. "The Fonthill Letter." In *Words, Texts and Manuscripts: Studies in Anglo-Saxon Culture Presented to Helmut Gneuss on the Occasion of His Sixty-Fifth Birthday*, ed. Michael Korhammer, 53–97. Cambridge: D. S. Brewer, 1992.

– – – . "King Athelstan's Books." In *Learning and Literature in Anglo-Saxon England: Studies Presented to Peter Clemoes*, ed. Michael Lapidge and Helmut Gneuss, 143–201. Cambridge: Cambridge University Press, 1985.

Keynes, Simon and Michael Lapidge, eds. and trans., *Alfred the Great: Asser's Life of King Alfred and Other Contemporary Sources*. London: Penguin, 1983.

King, P. D., trans. *Charlemagne: Translated Sources*. Lambrigg: P.D. King, 1987.

Kinney, Angela M., ed. *The Vulgate Bible, Volume VI: The New Testament*. Cambridge, MA: Harvard University Press, 2013.

Kirschner, Josef. *Die Bezeichnungen für Kranz und Krone im Altenglischen*. Munich: Salzer, 1975.

Knowles, David. *The Monastic Order in England: A History of its Development from the Times of St. Dunstan to the Fourth Lateran Council, 940–1216*, 2nd reprint ed. Cambridge: Cambridge University Press, 1976.

Kornexl, Lucia. "Chapter 12: Standardization." In *The History of English*. Vol. 2, *Old English*, ed. Laurel Brinton and Alexander Bergs, 220–35. The Hague: De Gruyter Mouton, 2017.

Kurtz, Benjamin P. *From St. Antony to St. Guthlac: A Study in Biography*. Berkeley: University of California Press, 1926.

Laistner, M. L. W., ed. *Bedae Venerabilis expositio actuum apostolorum et rectractatio*. Cambridge, MA: The Mediaeval Academy of America, 1939.

Lambert, Tom. *Law and Order in Anglo-Saxon England*. Oxford: Oxford University Press, 2017.

Langbein, John H. *Torture and the Law of Proof: Europe and England in the Ancien Régime*, 2nd ed. Chicago: University of Chicago Press, 1976.

Lapidge, Michael, ed. and trans. *Byrhtferth of Ramsey: The Lives of St Oswald and St Ecgwine*. Oxford: Clarendon, 2009.

——.*The Cult of St Swithun*. Winchester Studies. Oxford: Clarendon, 2003.

Lapidge, Michael, and Michael Herren, trans. *Aldhelm: The Prose Works*. Cambridge: Cambridge University Press, 1979.

Laughlin, J. Laurence. "The Anglo-Saxon Legal Procedure." In *Essays in Anglo-Saxon Law*, ed. Henry Adams, 183–306. Boston: Little Brown, 1876.

Lawson, M. K. "Archbishop Wulfstan and the Homiletic Element in the Laws of Æthelred II and Cnut." *English Historical Review* 107 (1992): 565–86.

Lee, Stuart D., ed. *Ælfric's Homilies on 'Judith,' 'Esther' and 'The Maccabees'*. 1999. <http://users.ox.ac.uk/~stuart/kings>

Leeson, Peter T. "Ordeals." *The Journal of Law and Economics* 55 (2012): 691–714.

Lenker, Ursula. "The Monasteries of the Benedictine Reform and the 'Winchester School': Model Cases of Social Networks in Anglo-Saxon England?" *European Journal of English Studies* 4 (2000): 225–38.

Lerer, Seth. "Grendel's Glove." *English Literary History* 61 (1994): 721–51.

Letson, D. R. "The Poetic Content of the Revival Homily." In *The Old English Homily and its Backgrounds*, ed. Paul E. Szarmach and Bernard F. Huppé, 139–56.

Levison, Wilhelm. *England and the Continent in the Eighth Century*. Oxford: Clarendon, 1946.

Liddell, Henry George, and Robert Scott. *A Greek-English Lexicon*, revised by Henry Stuart Jones et al. Oxford: Oxford University Press, 1968 [orig. publ. 1843].

Liebermann, Felix, ed. *Die Gesetze der Angelsachsen*. 3 vols. Halle: Max Niemeyer, 1903–16.

——."King Alfred and Mosaic Law." *Transactions of the Jewish Historical Society of England* 6 (1908): 21–31.

Lindholm, Gudrun. *Studien zum mittellateinischen Prosarhythmus: seine Entwicklung und sein Abklingen in der Briefliteratur Italiens*. Stockholm: Almqvist & Wiksell, 1963.

Lindsay, W. M., ed. *Isidori hispalensis episcopi: Etymologiarum sive originum, libri xx*. 2 vols. Oxford: Oxford University Press, 1911.

Lionarons, Joyce Tally. *The Homiletic Writings of Archbishop Wulfstan: A Critical Study*. Cambridge: D. S. Brewer, 2010.

——."Napier Homily L: Wulfstan's Eschatology at the Close of his Career." In *Wulfstan, Archbishop of York: The Proceedings of the Second Alcuin Conference*, ed. Matthew Townend, 413–28. Turnhout: Brepols, 2004.

Liuzza, Roy. *The Old English Versions of the Gospels*. EETS, o.s. 304. Oxford: Oxford University Press, 1994.

Lockett, Leslie. "The Role of Grendel's Arm in Feud, Law, and the Narrative Strategy of *Beowulf*." In *Latin Learning and English Lore: Studies in Anglo-Saxon Literature for Michael Lapidge*, ed. Katherine O'Brien O'Keeffe and Andy Orchard, 368–88. Toronto: University of Toronto Press, 2016.

Loyn, H. R. *The English Church, 940–1154*. Harlow: Pearson, 1999.

——.*The Governance of Anglo-Saxon England, 500–1087*. Stanford: Stanford University Press, 1984.

Lund, Arendse. "Law as Literature in the Vernacular Codes of Early Medieval England." PhD diss., University College London, 2021.

Magennis, Hugh, ed. *The Anonymous Old English "Legend of the Seven Sleepers" and its Latin Source*. Durham Medieval Texts 7. Durham, UK: Department of English Studies, 1994.

——."The Anonymous Old English 'Legend of the Seven Sleepers' and its Latin Source." *Leeds Studies in English* 22 (1991): 43–56.

Maitland, Frederic William. "Outlines of English Legal History, 500–1600." In *The Collected Papers of Frederic William Maitland*, ed. H. A. L. Fisher, 417–96. Cambridge: Cambridge University Press, 1911.

——. *Select Pleas of the Crown, Vol. I: A.D. 1200–1225*. Selden Society. London: Bernard Quaritch, 1887.

Mangina, Elisa Miller. "Selfhood and the Psalms: The First-Person Voice in Old English Poetry." PhD diss., Cornell University, 2002.

Manson, Edward. "Truth in Judicial Proceedings." *The Juridical Review* 7 (1895): 367–83.

Marafioti, Nicole. "Crime and Sin in the Laws of Alfred." In *Languages of the Law in Early Medieval England: Essays in Memory of Lisi Oliver*, ed. Stefan Jurasinski and Andrew Rabin, 59–84. Leuven: Peeters, 2019.

——."The Legacy of King Edgar in the Laws of Archbishop Wulfstan." In *Remembering the Medieval Present: Generative Uses of England's Pre-Conquest Past, 10th to 15th Centuries*, ed. Jay Paul Gates and Brian T. O'Camb, 21–50. Leiden: Brill, 2019.

——. "Unconsecrated Burial and Excommunication in Anglo-Saxon England: A Reassessment." *Traditio* 74 (2019): 55–123.

——."Seeking Alfred's Body: Royal Tomb as Political Object in the Reign of Edward the Elder." *Early Medieval Europe* 23 (2015): 202–28.

——.*The King's Body: Burial and Succession in Late Anglo-Saxon England.* Toronto: University of Toronto Press, 2014.

——. "Punishing Bodies and Saving Souls: Capital and Corporal Punishment in Anglo-Saxon England." *Haskins Society Journal* 20 (2008): 39–57.

Marsden, Richard. "The Will of Ælfgifu." In *The Old English Reader*, ed. Richard Marsden, 128–31, 2nd ed. Cambridge: Cambridge University Press, 2015.

Masschaele, James. *Jury, State, and Society in Medieval England.* New York: Palgrave Macmillan, 2008.

McAuley, Finbarr. "Canon Law and the End of the Ordeal." *Oxford Journal of Legal Studies* 26 (2006): 473–513.

McKitterick, Rosamond. *The Frankish Church and the Carolingian Reforms 789–895*. London: Royal Historical Society, 1977.

McNeill, John T., and Helena M. Gamer. *Medieval Handbooks of Penance.* New York: Columbia University Press, 1938.

Meaney, Audrey. "Felix's Life of St. Guthlac: Hagiography and/or Truth." *Proceedings of the Cambridge Antiquarian Society* 90 (2001): 29–48.

Migne, J.-P., ed. *Vita S. Benedicti (ex libro II Dialogorum S. Gregorii Magni excerpta)*. PL 66. Paris: Garnier Frères, 1866.

Miles, Brent. "The *Carmina Rhythmica* of Æthilwald: Edition, Translation, and Commentary." *Journal of Medieval Latin* 14 (2004): 73–117.

Miller, William Ian. *Eye for an Eye.* Cambridge: Cambridge University Press, 2006.

——.*Bloodtaking and Peacemaking: Feud, Law, and Society in Saga Iceland.* Chicago: University of Chicago Press, 1990.

——."Ordeal in Iceland." *Scandinavian Studies* 60 (1988): 189–218.

Milsom, S. F. C. *A Natural History of the Common Law.* New York: Columbia University Press, 2003.

Mitchell, Bruce, and Fred C. Robinson, eds. *Beowulf: An Edition with Relevant Shorter Texts*. Oxford: Blackwell, 1998.

Molyneaux, George. *The Formation of the English Kingdom in the Tenth Century*. Oxford: Oxford University Press, 2015.

——. "The *Old English Bede*: English Ideology of Christian Instruction?" *English Historical Review* 124 (2009): 1289–323.

Mordek, Hubert. "Karolingische Kapitularien." In *Überlieferung und Geltung normativer Texte des frühen und hohen Mittelalters*, ed. Hubert Mordek, 55–80. Sigmaringen: Thorbecke, 1986.

Mordek, Hubert, Klaus Zechiel-Eckes, and Michael Glattaar, eds. and trans. *Die Admonitio generalis Karls des Großen*. Hannover: Hahnsche Buchhandlung, 2012.

Morris, John, et al., eds. *Domesday Book*. 35 vols. [in 40 pts]. Chichester: Phillimore, 1975–86.

Morris, R., ed. and trans. *The Blickling Homilies*. Millwood: Kraus Reprint, 1990 [orig. publ. 1874].

Müller, Wolfgang. *The Criminalization of Abortion in the West*. Ithaca: Cornell University Press, 2012.

Musson, Anthony. *Medieval Law in Context: The Growth of Legal Consciousness from Magna Carta to the Peasants' Revolt*. New York: Manchester University Press, 2001.

Napier, Arthur S., ed. *Wulfstan: Sammlung der ihm zugeschriebenen Homilien nebst Untersuchungen über ihre Echtheit*. Berlin: Weidmann, 1883.

Neff, Charlotte. "Scandinavian Elements in the Wantage Code of Æthelred II." *The Journal of Legal History* 10 (1989): 285–316.

Nelson, Janet L. "Liturgy or Law: Misconceived Alternatives?" In *Early Medieval Studies in Memory of Patrick Wormald*, ed. Stephen Baxter, Catherine E. Karkov, Janet Nelson and David Pelteret, 433–47. Farnham: Ashgate, 2009.

——. "The First Use of the Second Anglo-Saxon *Ordo*." In *Myth, Rulership, Church and Charters: Essays in Honour of Nicholas Brooks*, ed. Julia Barrow and Andrew Wareham, 117–26. Aldershot: Ashgate, 2008.

——. *Politics and Ritual in Early Medieval Europe*. London: Hambledon, 1986.

Nigri, Lucia, and Naya Tsentourou, eds. *Forms of Hypocrisy in Early Modern England*. New York: Routledge, 2019.

Niles, John D. "The Myth of the Feud in Anglo-Saxon England." *JEGP* 114 (2015): 163–200.

——. "The Fonthill Ghost Word, the Fonthill Thief, and Early West Saxon Scribal Culture." In *The Genesis of Books: Studies in the Scribal Culture of Medieval England in Honour of A. N. Doane*, ed. Matthew T. Hussey and John D. Niles, 69–95. Turnhout: Brepols, 2012.

Norberg, Dag. *An Introduction to the Study of Medieval Latin Versification*. Translated by Grant C. Roti and Jacqueline de La Chapelle Skubly. Washington, D.C.: Catholic University of America Press, 2004.

——. *Manuel pratique de latin médiéval*. Paris: Picard, 1968.

O'Brien O'Keeffe, Katherine. *Stealing Obedience: Narratives of Agency and Identity in Later Anglo-Saxon England*. Toronto: University of Toronto Press, 2012.

——. *The Anglo-Saxon Chronicle: A Collaborative Edition, Volume 5: MS. C.* Cambridge: D. S. Brewer, 2001.

——. "Body and Law in Late Anglo-Saxon England." *Anglo-Saxon England* 27 (1998): 209–32.

——. "Beowulf, Lines 702b–836: Transformations and the Limits of the Human." *Texas Studies in Literature and Language* 23 (1981): 484–94.

O'Gorman, Daniel. "Mutilation and Spectacle in Anglo-Saxon Legislation." In *Capital and Corporal Punishment in Anglo-Saxon England*, ed. Jay Paul Gates and Nicole Marafioti, 149–64. Woodbridge: Boydell, 2014.

O'Neill, Patrick P., ed. and trans. *Old English Psalms*. Cambridge, MA: Harvard University Press, 2016.

——. *King Alfred's Old English Prose Translation of the First Fifty Psalms*. Cambridge, MA: Medieval Academy of America, 2001.

Oberhelman, Steven M. *Rhetoric and Homiletics in Fourth-Century Christian Literature: Prose Rhythm, Oratorical Style, and Preaching in the Works of Ambrose, Jerome, and Augustine*. Atlanta, GA: Scholars Press, 1991.

Oliver, Lisi, ed. *The Beginnings of English Law*. Toronto: University of Toronto Press, 2002.

——. *The Body Legal in Barbarian Law*. Toronto: University of Toronto Press, 2011.

Orchard, Andy. "Wulfstan as Reader, Writer, Rewriter." In *The Old English Homily: Precedent, Practice, and Appropriation*, ed. Aaron J. Kleist, 311–41. Turnhout: Brepols, 2007.

——. "Artful Alliteration in Anglo-Saxon Song and Story." *Anglia* 113 (1995): 429–63.

——. *The Poetic Art of Aldhelm*. Cambridge: Cambridge University Press, 1994.

Orchard, Nicholas, ed. *The Sacramentary of Ratoldus (Paris, Bibliothèque nationale de France, lat. 12052)*. London, Boydell, 2005.

——, ed. *The Leofric Missal*. 2 vols. London: Boydell, 2002.

Orlandi, Giovanni. "Metrical and Rhythmical Clausulae in Medieval Latin Prose: Some Aspects and Problems." In *Aspects of the Language of Latin Prose*, ed. Tobias Reinhardt, Michael Lapidge, and J. N. Adams, 395–412. Oxford: Oxford University Press, 2005.

Pelteret, David. *Slavery in Early Mediaeval England*. Woodbridge: Boydell, 1995.

Pilarczyk, Ian C. "Between a Rock and a Hot Place: The Role of Subjectivity and Rationality in the Medieval Ordeal by Hot Iron." *Anglo-American Law Review* 25 (1996): 87–112.

Plucknett, T. F. T. *Edward I and Criminal Law*. Cambridge: Cambridge University Press, 1960.

Pollock, Frederick, and Frederic William Maitland. *The History of English Law before the Time of Edward I*, 2nd ed. 2 vols. Cambridge: Cambridge University Press, 1911.

Pope, John C., ed. *Homilies of Ælfric: A Supplementary Collection*. 2 vols. EETS, o.s. 259, 260. Oxford: Oxford University Press, 1967–68.

Powell, T. E. "The 'Three Orders' of Society in Anglo-Saxon England." *Anglo-Saxon England* 23 (1994): 103–32.

Pratt, David. "The Making of the Second English Coronation *Ordo*." *Anglo-Saxon England* 46 (2017): 147–258.

——. *The Political Thought of King Alfred the Great*. Cambridge: Cambridge University Press, 2007.

Preston, Todd. *King Alfred's Book of Laws: A Study of the Domboc and its Influence on English Identity, with a Complete Translation*. Jefferson, NC: McFarland, 2012.

Pryce, Huw. *Native Law and the Welsh Church*. Oxford: Oxford University Press, 1993.

Rabb, Intisar A. *Doubt in Islamic Law: A History of Legal Maxims, Interpretation, and Islamic Criminal Law*. Cambridge: Cambridge University Press, 2015.

Rabin, Andrew. "The Oldest English Lawyer Joke? *Guthlac A*, l.265a and *Christ II*, l.733a." *Notes and Queries* 28 (2021): 156–57.

——. *Crime and Punishment in Anglo-Saxon England*. Cambridge: Cambridge University Press, 2020.

——. "The Mound, the Altar, and the Tomb: Sanctuary, Jurisdiction, and Punishment in Early Medieval Hagiography." *Studies in Philology* 117 (2020): 439–68.

——, ed. and trans., *Wulfstan: Old English Legal Writings*. Cambridge, MA: Harvard University Press, 2020.

——. "The Reception of Kentish Law in the Eleventh Century: Archbishop Wulfstan as Legal Historian." In *Languages of the Law in Early Medieval England*, ed. Stefan Jurasinski and Andrew Rabin, 225–40. Leuven: Peeters, 2019.

——. "'Sharper Than a Serpent's Tooth': Parent-Child Litigation in Anglo-Saxon England." In *Childhood and Adolescence in Anglo-Saxon Literary Culture*, ed. Susan Irvine and Winfried Rudolph, 270–90. Toronto: University of Toronto Press, 2018.

——, ed. and trans. *The Political Writings of Archbishop Wulfstan of York*. Manchester: Manchester University Press, 2015.

——. "Capital Punishment and the Anglo-Saxon Judicial Apparatus: A Maximum View?" In *Capital and Corporal Punishment in Anglo-Saxon England*, ed. Jay Paul Gates and Nicole Marafioti, 181–200. Woodbridge: Boydell, 2014.

——. "Holy Bodies, Legal Matters: Reaction and Reform in Ælfric's *Eugenia* and the Ely Privilege." *Studies in Philology* 110 (2013): 220–65.

——. "Witnessing Kingship: Royal Power and the Legal Subject in the Old English Laws." In *Kingship, Legislation and Power in Anglo-Saxon England*, ed. Gale R. Owen-Crocker and Brian Schneider, 219–36. Woodbridge: Boydell, 2013.

——."Testimony and Authority in Old English Law: Writing the Subject in the 'Fonthill Letter.'" In *Law and Sovereignty in the Middle Ages and the Renaissance*, ed. Robert S. Sturges, 147–71. Tempe: Arizona Center for Medieval and Renaissance Studies, 2011.

——. "Ritual Magic or Legal Performance? Reconsidering an Old English Charm against Theft." In *English Law Before Magna Carta: Felix Liebermann and Die Gesetze der Angelsachsen*, ed. Stefan Jurasinski, Lisi Oliver and Andrew Rabin, 177–96. Leiden: Brill, 2010.

——."Female Advocacy and Royal Protection in Tenth-Century England: The Legal Career of Queen Ælfthryth." *Speculum* 84 (2009): 261–88.

——."The Wolf's Testimony to the English: Law and the Witness in the *Sermo Lupi ad Anglos*." *JEGP* 105 (2006): 388–414.

Radding, Charles M. "Superstition to Science: Nature, Fortune, and the Passing of the Medieval Ordeal." *The American Historical Review* 84 (1979): 945–69.

Reinhard, Ben. "Cotton Nero A.i and the Origins of Wulfstan's *Polity*." *JEGP* 119 (2020): 175–89.

Reynolds, Andrew. *Anglo-Saxon Deviant Burial Practices.* Oxford: Oxford University Press, 2009.

Reynolds, Susan. "What Do We Mean by 'Anglo-Saxon' and 'Anglo-Saxons'?" *Journal of British Studies* 4 (1985): 395–414.

Richards, Mary P. "The Body as Text in Early Anglo-Saxon Law." In *Naked before God: Uncovering the Body in Anglo-Saxon England*, ed. Benjamin C. Withers and Jonathan Wilcox, 97–116. Morgantown: West Virginia University Press, 2003.

——."The Dictionary of Old English and Old English Legal Terminology." In *The Dictionary of Old English: Retrospects and Prospects*, ed. M. J. Toswell, 57–61. Kalamazoo: Medieval Institute Publications, 1998.

——."Anglo-Saxonism in the Old English Laws." In *Anglo-Saxonism and the Construction of Social Identity*, ed. Allen J. Frantzen and John D. Niles, 40–59. Gainesville: The University Press of Florida, 1997.

——. "Elements of a Written Standard in the Old English Laws." In *Standardizing English: Essays in the History of Language Change*, ed. Joseph B. Trahern, 1–22. Knoxville: University of Tennessee Press, 1989.

Richardson, William Payson, and Jerome Prince. *The Law of Evidence*, 7th ed. New York: Brooklyn Law School, 1948.

Roach, Levi. *Æthelred the Unready*. New Haven: Yale University Press, 2016.

——.*Kingship and Consent in Anglo-Saxon England, 871–978: Assemblies and the State in the Early Middle Ages*. Cambridge: Cambridge University Press, 2013.

——. "Law Codes and Legal Norms in Later Anglo-Saxon England." *Historical Research* 86 (2013): 465–86.

——."Penance, Submission and *Deditio*: Religious Influences on Dispute

Settlement in Later Anglo-Saxon England (871–1066)." *Anglo-Saxon England* 41 (2012): 343–71.

Roberts, Jane, ed. *The Guthlac Poems of the Exeter Book.* Oxford: Oxford University Press, 1979.

Robertson, A. J., ed. and trans. *Anglo-Saxon Charters*, 2nd ed. Cambridge: Cambridge University Press, 1956.

——, ed. and trans. *The Laws of the Kings of England from Edmund to Henry I.* Cambridge: Cambridge University Press, 1925.

Robinson, J. Armitage. "The Coronation Order in the Tenth Century." *Journal of Theological Studies* 19 (1917): 56–72.

Rollason, David. *Saints and Relics in Anglo-Saxon England.* Oxford: Basil Blackwell, 1989.

——. *Two Anglo-Saxon Rituals: The Dedication of a Church and the Judicial Ordeal.* Fifth Brixworth Lecture. Brixworth: Friends of All Saints Church, Brixworth, 1988.

Rosenwein, Barbara. *Negotiating Space: Power, Restraint, and Privileges of Immunity in Early Medieval Europe.* Ithaca: Cornell University Press, 1999.

Rule, Martin. *Eadmeri historia novorum in Anglia, et opuscula duo de vita Sancti Anselmi et quibusdam miraculis ejus.* Rolls Series. London: Longman, 1884.

Saltzman, Benjamin A. *Bonds of Secrecy: Law, Spirituality, and the Literature of Concealment in Early Medieval England.* Philadelphia: University of Pennsylvania Press, 2019.

Sawyer, P. H., ed. *Charters of Burton Abbey.* Oxford: Oxford University Press, 1979.

——. *Anglo-Saxon Charters: An Annotated List and Bibliography.* London: Royal Historical Society, 1968.

Schaefer, Ursula. "On the Linguistic and Social Development of a Binomial: The Example of to Have and to Hold." In *Binomials in the History of English: Fixed and Flexible*, ed. Hans Sauer and Joanna Kopaczyk, 322–43. Cambridge: Cambridge University Press, 2017.

Scharer, Anton. "A New Second 'English' *Ordo*?" In *Changing Perspectives on England and the Continent in the Early Middle Ages.* Farnham: Ashgate, 2014.

Scheibe, F.-C. "Alcuin und die Briefe Karls des Grosen." *Deutsches Archiv für Erforschung des Mittelalters* 15 (1959): 181–93.

——."Alcuin und die *Admonitio Generalis.*" *Deutsches Archiv für Erforschung des Mittelalters* 14 (1958): 221–29.

Scragg, Donald. "Dating and Style in Old English Composite Homilies." *H. M. Chadwick Memorial Lectures* 9 (1998): 1–24.

Sigfússon, Björn. *Ljósvetninga saga.* Íslenzk fornrit. Reykjavík: Hið Íslenzka Fornritafélag, 1940.

Sisam, Celia, and Kenneth Sisam, eds. *The Salisbury Psalter.* EETS, o.s. 242. Oxford: Oxford University Press, 1959.

Sisam, Kenneth. "The West Saxon Royal Genealogies." *Proceedings of the British Academy* 39 (1953): 287–348.

Skeat, W. W., ed. *Ælfric's Lives of Saints*. London: N. Trübner, 1881.

Smith, A. H. *English Place-Name Elements, Part II: The Elements Jafn–Ytri, Index and Maps*. Cambridge: Cambridge University Press, 1956.

Smith, Scott T. *Land and Book: Literature and Land Tenure in Anglo-Saxon England*. Toronto: University of Toronto Press, 2012.

——."Of Kings and Cattle Thieves: The Rhetorical Work of the Fonthill Letter." *JEGP* 106 (2007): 447–67.

Snook, Ben. *The Anglo-Saxon Chancery: The History, Language and Production of Anglo-Saxon Charters from Alfred to Edgar*. Woodbridge: Boydell, 2015.

Snyder, Jon R. *Dissimulation and the Culture of Secrecy in Early Modern Europe*. Berkeley: University of California Press, 2009.

Stacey, Robin Chapman. *Law and the Imagination in Medieval Wales*. Philadelphia: University of Pennsylvania Press, 2018.

——.*The Road to Judgment: From Custom to Court in Medieval Ireland and Wales*. Philadelphia: University of Pennsylvania Press, 1994.

Stafford, Pauline. "King and Kin, Lord and Community: England in the Tenth and Eleventh Centuries." In *Gender, Family and the Legitimation of Power: England from the Ninth to Early Twelfth Century*. Aldershot: Ashgate 2006.

——.*Unification and Conquest: A Political and Social History of England in the Tenth and Eleventh Centuries*. London: E. Arnold, 1989.

——."The Laws of Cnut and the History of Anglo-Saxon Royal Promises." *Anglo-Saxon England* 10 (1981): 173–90.

——."Church and Society in the Age of Ælfric." In *The Old English Homily and its Backgrounds*, ed. Paul E. Szarmach and Bernard F. Huppé, 11–42. Albany: State University of New York Press, 1978.

Stanley, Eric G. "Wulfstan and Ælfric: 'The True Difference between the Law and the Gospel.'" In *Wulfstan, Archbishop of York: The Proceedings of the Second Alcuin Conference*, ed. Matthew Townend, 429–41. Turnhout: Brepols, 2004.

——. "On the Laws of King Alfred: The End of the Preface and the Beginning of the Laws." In *Alfred the Wise: Studies in Honor of Janet Bately on the Occasion of her Sixty-Fifth Birthday*, ed. Jane Roberts, Janet Nelson, and Malcolm R. Godden, 211–21. Cambridge: D. S. Brewer, 1997.

Steiner, Emily, and Candace Barrington, eds. *The Letter of the Law: Legal Practice and Literary Production in Medieval England*. Ithaca: Cornell University Press, 2002.

Stephenson, Rebecca, and Emily V. Thornbury, eds. *Latinity and Identity in Anglo-Saxon Literature*. Toronto: University of Toronto Press, 2016.

Stevenson, William Henry, ed. *Asser's Life of King Alfred*. Oxford: Clarendon, 1959.

Swain, Larry J. "Of Hands, Halls, and Heroes: Grendel's Hand, Hroþgar's

Power, and the Problem of *Stapol* in *Beowulf*." *Anglia* 134 (2016): 260–84.

Swanton, Michael, trans. *Anglo-Saxon Prose*. London: Dent, 1993 [orig. publ. 1975].

Sweet, Henry, ed. *King Alfred's West-Saxon Version of Gregory's Pastoral Care, Part I*. EETS, o.s. 45. London: Oxford University Press, 1871.

Symons, Thomas, ed. *Regularis concordia Anglicae nationis monachorum sanctimonialiumque / The Monastic Agreement of the Monks and Nuns of the English Nation*. London: Thomas Nelson, 1953.

Tanner, Norman P., ed. *Decrees of the Ecumenical Councils*. 2 vols. London: Sheed & Ward, 1990.

Taylor, Alice. "*Lex Scripta* and the Problem of Enforcement: Anglo-Saxon, Welsh, and Scottish Law Compared." In *Legalism: Community and Justice*, ed. Fernanda Pirie and Judith Scheele, 47–75. Oxford: Oxford University Press, 2014.

Terasawa, Jun. "*Beowulf* 128: *æfter wiste*." In *"And Gladly Wolde He Lerne and Gladly Teche": Essays on Medieval English Presented to Professor Matsuji Tajima on his Sixtieth Birthday*, ed. Yoko Iyeiri and Margaret Connolly, 147–54. Tokyo: Kaibunsha, 2002.

Tertullian, "De Spectaculis." In *Tertullian: Apology. De Spectaculis. Minucius Felix: Octavius*, ed. and trans. T. R. Glover and Gerald H. Rendall. Cambridge, MA: Harvard University Press, 1977 [orig. publ. 1931].

Thomas, Daniel. "Incarceration as Judicial Punishment in Anglo-Saxon England." In *Capital and Corporal Punishment in Anglo-Saxon England*, ed. Jay Paul Gates and Nicole Marafioti, 92–112. Woodbridge: Boydell, 2014.

Thomas, P. G. "Further Notes on 'Beowulf.'" *The Modern Language Review* 22 (1927): 70–73.

Thoreau, Henry David. "Journal, 11 Nov. 1850." In *The Journal of Henry D. Thoreau*, ed. Bradford Torrey and Francis H. Allen, 94. New York: Dover, 1962.

Throop, Priscilla, trans., *Ælfric's Grammar and Glossary: The Complete English Translation*. Charlotte, VT: MedievalMS, 2008.

Tinkler, John D. *Vocabulary and Syntax of the Old English Version in the Paris Psalter: A Critical Commentary*. The Hague: Mouton, 1971.

Toswell, M. J. *The Anglo-Saxon Psalter*. Turnhout: Brepols, 2014.

Treschow, Michael. "The Prologue to Alfred's Law Code: Instruction in the Spirit of Mercy." *Florilegium* 13 (1994): 79–110.

Trilling, Renée. "Sovereignty and Social Order: Archbishop Wulfstan and the *Institutes of Polity*." In *The Bishop Reformed: Studies in Episcopal Power and Culture in the Central Middle Ages*, ed. Anna T. Jones and John S. Ott, 58–85. Aldershot: Ashgate, 2007.

Trips, Carola. *Lexical Semantics and Diachronic Morphology: The Development of -hood, -dom and -ship in the History of English*. Berlin: Walter de Gruyter, 2009.

Trousdale, Alaric A. "Being Everywhere at Once: Delegation and Royal Authority in Late Anglo-Saxon England." In *Languages of the Law in Early Medieval England: Essays in Memory of Lisi Oliver*, ed. Stefan Jurasinski and Andrew Rabin, 275–96. Leuven: Peeters, 2019.

Tunberg, Terence O. "Prose Styles and *Cursus*." In *Medieval Latin: An Introduction and Bibliographical Guide*, ed. F. A. C. Mantello and A. G. Rigg, 111–21. Washington, D.C.: Catholic University of America Press, 1996.

Turk, Milton Haight. *The Legal Code of Ælfred the Great*. Halle: Max Niemeyer, 1893.

Turner, D. H., ed. *The Claudius Pontificals*. Chichester: Moore and Tillyer, 1971.

Upchurch, Robert K. "A Big Dog Barks: Ælfric of Eynsham's Indictment of the English Pastorate and Witan." *Speculum* 85 (2010): 505–33.

Van Caenegem, R. C. "Methods of Proof in Western Medieval Law." In *Legal History: A European Perspective*, 71–113. London: Hambledon, 1991.

——.*The Birth of the English Common Law*, 2nd ed. Cambridge: Cambridge University Press, 1988.

Vogel, Cyrille. *Les 'Libri Paenitentiales.'* Turnhout: Brepols, 1968.

Wallace-Hadrill, J. M. *Bede's Ecclesiastical History of the English People: A Historical Commentary*. London: Oxford University Press, 1988.

Wallach, Luitpold. *Alcuin and Charlemagne: Studies in Carolingian History and Literature*. Ithaca: Cornell University Press, 1959.

Ward, Ian. *Law and Literature: Possibilities and Perspectives.* Cambridge: Cambridge University Press, 1995.

Warner, Sir George F., ed. *The Stowe Missal*. Vol. 2. London: Harrison and Sons, 1915.

Wassenhoven, Dominik. "The Role of the Bishop in Anglo-Saxon Succession Struggles." In *Leaders of the Anglo-Saxon Church: From Bede to Stigand*, ed. Alexander R. Rumble, 97–107. Woodbridge: Boydell, 2012.

Wasserschleben, F. W. H., ed. *Die Bußordnungen der ablendländischen Kirche*. Halle: Verlag Graeger, 1851.

White, Stephen D. "Proposing the Ordeal and Avoiding It: Strategy and Power in Western French Litigation, 1050–1110." In *Cultures of Power: Lordship, Status, and Process in Twelfth-Century Europe*, ed. Thomas N. Bisson, 89–123. Philadelphia: University of Pennsylvania Press, 1995.

Whitelock, Dorothy, ed. and trans. *English Historical Documents. Volume I: c.500–1042*, 2nd ed. London: Oxford University Press, 1979.

——, ed. and trans. *Anglo-Saxon Wills*. Cambridge, Cambridge University Press, 1930.

——."Archbishop Wulfstan, Homilist and Statesman." *TRHS*, 4th series, 24 (1942): 25–46.

——, ed., *Sermo Lupi ad Anglos*, 3rd ed. Exeter: University of Exeter Press, 1980 [orig. publ. 1939].

——."Beowulf 2444–2471." *Medium Ævum* 8 (1939): 198–204.

Whitelock, Dorothy, Susie I. Tucker and David C. Douglas, ed. and trans. *The Anglo-Saxon Chronicle: A Revised Translation*. London: Eyre & Spottiswoode, 1961.

Whitelock, Dorothy, M. Brett, and C. N. L. Brooke, eds. *Councils and Synods, with Other Documents Relating to the English Church, 871–1204*. 2 vols. Oxford: Clarendon, 1981.

Whitman, James Q. *The Origins of Reasonable Doubt: Theological Roots of the Criminal Trial.* New Haven: Yale University Press, 2008.

Wilcox, Jonathan. "The Wolf on Shepherds: Wulfstan, Bishops, and the Context of the *Sermo Lupi ad Anglos*." In *Old English Prose: Basic Readings*, ed. Paul E. Szarmach, with the assistance of Deborah A. Oosterhouse, 395–418. New York: Garland Publishing, 2000.

——, ed. *Ælfric's Prefaces*. Durham Medieval Texts 9. Durham, UK: Department of English Studies, 1995.

——."The Dissemination of Wulfstan's Homilies: The Wulfstan Tradition in Eleventh-Century Vernacular Preaching." In *England in the Eleventh Century: Proceedings of the 1990 Harlaxton Symposium*, ed. Carola Hicks, 199–217. Stamford: Paul Watkins, 1992.

Wilkins, Katrina M. "On Esther." *Journal of Languages, Texts, and Society* 2 (2018): 130–53.

Williams, Ann. *Kingship and Government in Pre-Conquest England, c.500–1066*. London: MacMillan, 1999.

——. "An Introduction to the Worcestershire Domesday." In *The Worcestershire Domesday*, ed. Ann Williams and R. W. H. Erskine, 1–39. London: Alecto Historical Editions, 1988.

Wilson, H. A., ed. *The Benedictional of Archbishop Robert*. London: Henry Bradshaw Society, 1903.

——, ed. *The Gelasian Sacramentary. Liber Sacramentorum Romanae Ecclesiae.* Oxford: Clarendon, 1894.

Winterbottom, Michael. *Three Lives of English Saints*. Toronto: Pontifical Institute of Mediaeval Studies, 1972.

Wisenekker, Evert. *Word be worde, andgit of andgite: Translation Performance in the Old English Interlinear Glosses of the Vespasian, Regius and Lambeth Psalters*. Huizen: Drukkerij J. Bout & Zn., 1991.

Wolfram, Herwig. "Political Theory and Narrative in Charters." *Viator* 26 (1995): 39–51.

Woodman, D. A. "'Æthelstan A' and the Rhetoric of Rule." *Anglo-Saxon England* 42 (2013): 217–48.

Woolf, Alex. "Community, Identity and Kingship in Early England." In *Social Identity in Early Medieval Britain*, ed. William O. Frazer and Andrew Tyrrell, 91–109. London: Bloomsbury, 2000.

Wormald, Patrick. *Papers Preparatory to the Making of English Law: King Alfred to the Twelfth Century, Vol. II: From God's Law to Common Law*, ed.

Stephen Baxter and John Hudson. University of London: Early English Laws, 2014.

——."Bede, the *Bretwaldas* and the Origins of the *Gens Anglorum*." In *The Times of Bede: Studies in Early English Christian Society and its Historian*, 106–34. Malden: Blackwell, 2006.

——. "Archbishop Wulfstan: Eleventh-Century State-Builder." In *Wulfstan, Archbishop of York: The Proceedings of the Second Alcuin Conference*, ed. Matthew Townend, 9–27. Turnhout: Brepols, 2004.

——. *Legal Culture in the Early Medieval West: Law as Text, Image, and Experience.* London: Hambledon, 1999.

——."Archbishop Wulfstan and the Holiness of Society." In *Legal Culture in the Early Medieval West: Law as Text, Image, and Experience*, 225–52. London: Hambledon, 1999.

——. "Charters, Law and the Settlement of Disputes in Anglo-Saxon England." In *Legal Culture in the Early Medieval West: Law as Text, Image and Experience*, 289–312. London: Hambledon, 1999.

——."Giving God and King Their Due: Conflict and its Regulation in the Early English State." In *Legal Culture in the Early Medieval West: Law as Text, Image, and Experience*, 333–57. London: Hambledon, 1999.

——."*Lex scripta* and *verbum regis*: Legislation and Germanic Kingship, from Euric to Cnut." In *Legal Culture in the Early Medieval West: Law as Text, Image, and Experience*, 1–43. London: Hambledon, 1999.

——."Lordship and Justice in the Early English Kingdom: Oswaldslow Revisited." In *Legal Culture in the Early Medieval West: Law as Text, Image, and Experience*, 313–32. London: Hambledon, 1999.

——.*The Making of English Law: King Alfred to the Twelfth Century*. Malden: Blackwell, 1999.

——. "*Engla Lond*: The Making of an Allegiance." *Journal of Historical Sociology* 7 (1994): 1–24.

——. "Æthelred the Lawmaker." In *Ethelred the Unready: Papers from the Millenary Conference*, ed. David Hill, 47–80. Oxford: British Archaeological Reports, 1978.

Wragg, Stefany J. "The Early Texts of the Cult of St. Guthlac." *English Studies* 100 (2019): 253–72.

Wright, Roger. "Abbo of Fleury in Ramsey (985–987)." In *Conceptualizing Multilingualism in England, c.800–c.1250*, ed. Elizabeth M. Tyler, 105–20. Turnhout: Brepols, 2011.

Wulfstan of Winchester, *The Life of St Æthelwold*, ed. and trans. Michael Lapidge and Michael Winterbottom. Oxford: Clarendon, 1991.

Yorke, Barbara. "The Representation of Early West Saxon History in the Anglo-Saxon Chronicle." In *Reading the Anglo-Saxon Chronicle: Language, Literature, History*, ed. Alice Jorgensen, 141–59. Turnhout: Brepols, 2010.

——. "Æthelwold [St Æthelwold, Ethelwold] (904x9–984), Abbot of Abingdon and Bishop of Winchester." *Oxford Dictionary of National Biography* (23 September 2004), <https://www.oxforddnb.com>.

Zagorin, Perez. *Ways of Lying: Dissimulation, Persecution, and Conformity in Early Modern Europe*. Cambridge, MA: Harvard University Press, 2009.

Zajtay, Imre. "Le Registre de Várad: Un monument judiciaire du début du XIIIe siècle." *Revue historique de droit français et étranger* 31 (1954): 527–62.

Ziegler, Vickie L. *Trial by Fire and Battle in Medieval German Literature*. Rochester: Camden House, 2004.

Zupitza, Julius, ed. *Ælfrics Grammatik und Glossar*, 2nd ed., with contributions by H. Gneuss. Berlin: Weidmann, 1966.

Index

ANGLO-SAXON STUDIES

Please see the Boydell & Brewer website
for details of earlier titles in the series.

Volume 24: The Dating of *Beowulf*: A Reassessment, *edited by Leonard Neidorf*

Volume 25: The Cruciform Brooch and Anglo-Saxon England, *Toby F. Martin*

Volume 26: Trees in the Religions of Early Medieval England, *Michael D.J. Bintley*

Volume 27: The Peterborough Version of the Anglo-Saxon Chronicle: Rewriting Post-Conquest History, *Malasree Home*

Volume 28: The Anglo-Saxon Chancery: The History, Language and Production of Anglo-Saxon Charters from Alfred to Edgar, *Ben Snook*

Volume 29: Representing Beasts in Early Medieval England and Scandinavia, *edited by Michael D.J. Bintley and Thomas J.T. Williams*

Volume 30: Direct Speech in *Beowulf* and Other Old English Narrative Poems, *Elise Louviot*

Volume 31: Old English Philology: Studies in Honour of R.D. Fulk, *edited by Leonard Neidorf, Rafael J. Pascual and Tom Shippey*

Volume 32: 'Charms', Liturgies, and Secret Rites in Early Medieval England, *Ciaran Arthur*

Volume 33: Old Age in Early Medieval England: A Cultural History, *Thijs Porck*

Volume 34: Priests and their Books in Late Anglo-Saxon England, *Gerald P. Dyson*

Volume 35: Burial, Landscape and Identity in Early Medieval Wessex, *Kate Mees*

Volume 36: The Sword in Early Medieval Northern Europe: Experience, Identity, Representation, *Sue Brunning*

Volume 37: The Chronology and Canon of Ælfric of Eynsham, *Aaron J Kleist*

Printed and bound by CPI Group (UK) Ltd, Croydon, CR0 4YY

15/09/2026

14962417-0005